The Secret History of

VLADIMIR
NABOKOV

The Secret History of
VLADIMIR NABOKOV

ANDREA PITZER

PEGASUS BOOKS
NEW YORK LONDON

THE SECRET HISTORY OF VLADIMIR NABOKOV

Pegasus Books LLC
80 Broad Street, 5th Floor
New York, NY 10004

Interior design by Maria Fernandez

ISBN: 978-1-60598-411-7

10 9 8 7 6 5 4 3 2 1

Printed in the United States of America
Distributed by W. W. Norton & Company, Inc.

To the dead and the dreams

of a lost century

CONTENTS

INTRODUCTION

———❦———

The Neva River flows from east to west, sweeping along a wide channel and into the canals of St. Petersburg, the former Imperial capital of Russia. Rounding a hairpin turn just before Kresty Prison, the current follows a more elegant arc past the Field of Mars and the Winter Palace, then slips toward the walls of the Peter and Paul Fortress, lapping at the far bank as it goes by, less than half a mile north of the childhood home of Vladimir Nabokov.

Now a museum, the house where Nabokov was born sits on reclaimed swampland in the middle of an engineered island at the heart of an engineered city built by slaves and veiled in baroque magnificence. The same could be said of Nabokov's writing.

In 2011, during my fourth year of research for this book, I went to Nabokov's home city to see what I might learn from it. Many buildings have been restored in recent years, and in twenty-first-century St. Petersburg it is impossible to go more than a block or two without being startled by spectacle, from the lights framing the long panorama of Palace Square at night to the rainbow-studded onion domes of the Church of the Savior on Spilled Blood.

I immediately thought it the most beautiful city I had ever seen. And yet St. Petersburg still felt uncomfortably imperial, built on a scale that could only have been accomplished by a dynasty willing to spend lives and treasure without much regard for the cost.

The director of the Nabokov Museum, Tatiana Ponomareva, was kind enough to be my guide during two days of the trip. She took me to the Tauride Palace, where Nabokov's father had served in the First Duma, an experiment in constitutional monarchy that was terminated by the Tsar after just three months. We headed to the former site of Tenishev School, where the teenage Nabokov had been mocked as a foreigner for his lack of interest in Russian politics. She pointed out the park where he had walked in winter with his first love, Lyussya, who was later immortalized in the novel *Mary*. And we strolled by the childhood apartment of Véra Slonim, who, years into exile, met Nabokov in Berlin and became his wife.

During other research trips to other countries, I was reminded of the ways in which the story of Nabokov's life and family intersected again and again with not just political upheaval in his home city but also the collapse of democracy in every nation in which he lived until the age of forty-one. It is one thing to know this intellectually. It is quite another to leave St. Petersburg, to leave Berlin, to leave Paris, and to imagine Vladimir Nabokov abandoning the most magnificent cities of Europe one after the other, fleeing the instability that followed him like a plague.

I came to Nabokov as a college student and found myself put off by the abuse he heaped on his characters, whom he described as "galley slaves." I didn't mind violence, or sex, or protagonists who were not *nice*—I didn't even need them to reform—but I wanted the events and the people in his books to matter. I wanted some sense from Nabokov that he loved what he had created, and that, on closer inspection, his characters had something to offer beyond their unblinking submission to his stylistic gifts.

Returning to him as an adult, I found the style more persuasive on its own terms. Can anyone who cares about writing fail to marvel at passages such as this one from *Glory*, the story of Martin, a young man bereft of his country and in love with Sonia, who does not love him in return?

> Martin could not restrain himself. He stepped out into the corridor and caught sight of Sonia hopping downstairs in a flamingo-colored frock, a fluffy fan in one hand and something bright encircling her black hair. She had left her door open and the light on. In her room there remained a cloudlet of powder, like the smoke following a shot; a stocking, killed outright, lay under a chair; and the motley innards of the wardrobe had spilled onto the carpet.

Many writers, myself included, would weep with gratitude to have written those four sentences, just half a paragraph in a throw-away scene from one of Nabokov's least famous books. The more Nabokov I read as an adult, the more I began to suspect that what I had longed for at eighteen was in there somewhere, but hiding. Later, when I became consumed with the idea of putting Nabokov's writing into historical context, it turned out that many things were, in fact, hiding inside his novels—more, in fact, than I could have imagined.

Even though I no longer believe him to be perpetually subjecting his characters to horrific events solely for his own amusement, I am not yet one who believes that Nabokov had a gentle soul. But fury and compassion reside together in his writing in ways that, more often than not, have gone unrecognized. He has taken an unprecedented approach to preserving all the grief of his lifetime—the world's and his own—in his novels.

For those who have read his elegant autobiography *Speak, Memory*, it is hardly a secret that Nabokov narrowly escaped Bolshevik Russia, the Holocaust, and Occupied France—or that friends and members of his family suffered terrible political violence and were rendered mute by history. But by losing the particulars of that violence and that history, the ways in which these events made their way into his stories have often also been lost. And a whole layer of meaning in his work has vanished.

This lost, forgotten, and sometimes secret history suggests that behind the art-for-art's-sake façade that Nabokov both cultivated and rejected, he was busy detailing the horrors of his era and attending to the destructive power of the Gulag and the Holocaust in one way or another across four decades of his career.

On a local level, this means that court cases, FBI files, and Nazi propaganda shed light on subtle references in *Lolita*. Red Cross records recall Revolutionary trauma hidden in *Despair*. *New York Times* articles suggest a radically different reading of *Pale Fire*. On a global level, it becomes apparent that Nabokov, who was so reluctant to engage in politics in any public forum, was responding to and weaving in the details of the events that he had witnessed or remembered, as if preserving them before they could be forgotten.

Yet as readers focused on Nabokov's shocking subjects and linguistic pyrotechnics, those details *were* forgotten. This book is an attempt to retrieve them.

What if *Lolita* is the story of global anti-Semitism as much as it is Humbert Humbert's molestation of a twelve-year-old girl? What if *Pale Fire* is a love letter to the dead of the Russian Gulag? What if forty years of Nabokov's writing carries an elegy for those who resisted the prisons and camps that devastated his world?

Nabokov presents different faces to different people, and so this book seeks to draw out one particular story. It is not an attempt to replicate the prodigious feats of the biographers of Vladimir and Véra Nabokov, which could hardly be surpassed. It is not a study of butterflies, or an account of Nabokov's views on the afterlife—though both topics were undeniably important to him. This is a story as much about the world around the writer as the writer himself, and a look at how epic events and family history made their way, unseen, into extraordinary literature.

This book covers a lot of territory, from biography to history and criticism. After the first chapter, Nabokov's life unfolds from birth to death. In the beginning, the story of Nabokov's youth is almost eclipsed by the whirlwind events of the new century. As race hatred and concentration camps begin to swamp Europe, they wind their way closer and closer to his world—and his work. The relevance of many events recounted in the early chapters only becomes apparent once Nabokov begins to write in English, fusing the past and everything that has been lost with spectacular invention, creating terrifying fairy tales out of magic and dust.

Not all those he loves escape, and so it hardly comes as a surprise that Nabokov makes use of that history. Personal and political tragedies intertwine as he crafts his greatest novels.

If this history is relevant, it shows Nabokov reinventing the reader's role in literature, creating books with brilliant narratives which have whole *other* stories folded inside them. This interior Nabokov is more vulnerable to the past than he publicly led the world to believe, yet has no interest in comforting us. His hidden stories have something profound to teach us about being human and our very way of interacting with art.

Much of the story of Nabokov's life unspools here in a series of juxtapositions with his contemporaries. Ivan Bunin reigned over the Russian literary emigration until Nabokov replaced him and refused to write about Russia on anyone's terms but his own. Nabokov's cousin Nicholas also went from Russia and Western Europe to America, and likewise faced a life crisis in 1937, but made very different choices in its wake. Walter Duranty, whose reporting from Russia on the fledgling Soviet state deeply influenced the opinions of educated Americans for more than two decades, laid the foundation for a kind of blindness about the U.S.S.R. that drove Nabokov to despair. Critic Edmund Wilson, who was devoted to literature but had a very different way of interpreting it—and indeed of understanding history itself—forced Nabokov to define himself explicitly.

Among Nabokov's other contemporaries were filmmakers and writers who, for reasons honorable or selfish, put their gifts wholly at the service of politics. And capping the beginning and end of these comparisons is Alexander Solzhenitsyn, that other Russian exile whose books horrified and unnerved twentieth-century readers, a man with whom Vladimir Nabokov has more in common than has ever been imagined.

My first full day in St. Petersburg in 2011, I was accompanied by Fedor, the son of a professor at St. Petersburg State University. He took me to see the major sites, and at the top of my wish list were prisons.

We met at Vladimir Nabokov's house and began to work our way up the Neva, heading first to the Peter and Paul Fortress, where so many writers and revolutionaries had been incarcerated. A Nabokov had once been its commander. Standing in a pitch-black cell, Fedor dug in his pocket for a lighter and talked about history. He was young enough not to remember life in the Soviet Union.

We walked back out into the sunlight and made our way farther along the river. My guidebook also listed a penal museum at Kresty Prison, where Nabokov's father had been sentenced to solitary confinement in 1908 under Tsar Nicholas II.

Fedor seemed uncertain about going at first—he had never heard of a museum there—but agreed to take me anyway. As we talked on the way, I realized he was trying to explain that Kresty was still a prison, an operational prison, and, as such, was someplace that most people would rather not go.

He was still game, however, so we kept walking until we came to Kresty's red brick perimeter walls and buildings. When Nabokov's father had served his sentence, the facility's innovative design was celebrated for its modern approach to incarceration; but by 2010 its buildings looked like factories or tenements in the heart of any mid-size American city, with some ornate brick flourishes added. It is today the largest functioning prison in Europe.

We had trouble finding a main door, but in time we stumbled on an unlocked entrance to a side building. The door opened onto a stairwell that made up in graffiti what it lacked in plaster. We went up. After one or two floors, a smell of cooking food drifted by. The building was strangely silent. We were hardly in danger, but I was struck by the feeling that we had wandered into someplace we were not supposed to be—that we were trespassing.

Back outside, a handful of people stood at a door across the way near a sign listing hours—a grown man and a child among them, looking as if they were waiting to pay a visit, but not to a museum. I had realized that there were prisoners inside the facility, but seeing friends or family waiting to go in somehow crashed the present into the past. We decided to leave.

The museum stayed hidden that day, and I did not go back to Kresty. In a place so bound up with history, the cityscape preserves enough of the past; it is its own museum.

My last day in Russia, I walked a little over twelve miles, trying in vain to check off all the places I could not bear to leave without seeing. I especially wanted to visit a pink-and-white candy-cane-striped church located next to one of the first concentration camp sites in St. Petersburg. The bloody history of the city does not exist in opposition to its monumental beauty; they sit side by side, part and parcel of the same thing.[1]

That afternoon, caught in the rain again, this time with blistered feet, it occurred to me that, intentionally or not, Nabokov had used the architectural presence of his home city as a model for a unique kind of literature—a place where a walk to a museum could transport you to a jailer's doorstep.[2] The exquisite form and baroque inventions appear in direct proportion to the history they have to hide.

CHAPTER ONE

Waiting for Solzhenitsyn

‒‒‒‒⬦‒‒‒‒

1

On October 6, 1974, Russian novelist Vladimir Nabokov and his wife Véra sat in a private dining room of the Montreux Palace Hotel in Switzerland, waiting for Alexander Solzhenitsyn to join them for lunch. The two men had never met.

By then the Nabokovs had been living in the opulent Palace Hotel, tucked along the eastern shore of Lake Geneva, for thirteen years. During those years, literary pilgrims had traveled to Montreux in hopes of an audience with the master. When they were lucky enough to meet with him, Nabokov had fielded their questions and returned biting, playful answers. They had sipped coffee, tea, or grappa at lunchtime with one of the most celebrated wordsmiths in the world, and plumbed his cryptic statements for meaning. Pursuing him as he pursued butterflies, they had climbed the Alpine slopes that vaulted up behind the hotel.

The seventy-five-year-old Nabokov saw himself as Russian and American, yet lived in rented rooms in neither country, continuing to work on new books and translations at an exhausting pace that *Lolita*'s breakthrough more than a decade before had rendered financially unnecessary. He had grown accustomed to being courted, and to delighting his guests. But a visit from Solzhenitsyn was something different.

The morning of October 6 revealed itself early on as a rainy day, but in truth, the weather on the drive south from Zurich may not have mattered to Solzhenitsyn. Only eight months earlier, Solzhenitsyn had been sitting in a cell at Moscow's Lefortovo Prison, charged with treason against the Soviet Union. The deportation that followed his arrest had been bitter, but there were, he knew, more permanent penalties than exile.

Solzhenitsyn had dreamed of face-to-face confrontation with Soviet leaders, believing that pressure at the right moment by the right person might topple the whole system of repression, or at least begin its destruction. Instead, expulsion had delivered him into Frankfurt, Germany, and an uncharted life. And so he was not in prison, not shouting his defiance to the Politburo or meeting privately with Soviet leader Leonid Brezhnev. After a spring and summer spent making his way in the new world, he instead found himself cruising the Swiss countryside with his wife Natalia, circling Lake Geneva, traveling Montreux's elegant Grand Rue on his way to see one of the most celebrated authors in the world—a man he himself had nominated for the Nobel Prize just two years earlier. Yet Solzhenitsyn was nervous.

At that moment, it would have been hard to find two bigger literary superstars than the man who had written *The Gulag Archipelago* and the author of *Lolita*. They were both Russian, but the nineteen years between their births had destined them to grow up in separate universes. Nabokov had come of age in the last days of the Tsar and Empire, ceding Russia to the Bolsheviks, sailing away under machine-gun fire before the infant Solzhenitsyn had learned to walk. Solzhenitsyn had grown up in the Soviet state, spending years inside its concentration camps and prisons before emerging from behind the Iron Curtain on a mission to reveal a reign of terror and end it forever.

Physically, the men were as dissimilar as their histories. With Nabokov, molasses candy and modern dentures had created a plump, mild professor from a gaunt émigré, while Solzhenitsyn's scarred forehead, wild hair, and prophet's beard marked him as a more volatile presence. Their writing voices, too, stood distinct one from the other, Nabokov's exquisite language and baroque experiments contrasting with Solzhenitsyn's open fury and direct appeals to emotion.

Even their most famous books seem opposite in nature. *The Gulag Archipelago* chronicles the entire history of the Soviet concentration camp system, bluntly cataloguing the abuse of power on an epic scale, while Nabokov's *Lolita* maps a more individual horror: the willful savaging of one human being by another. A microscopically detailed account of a middle-aged man's sexual obsession with a young girl, *Lolita* has been variously described as "funny," "the only convincing love story of our century," and "the filthiest book I have ever read." Humbert Humbert's tale of the two-year molestation of his stepdaughter describes their relationship, her escape with another man, and Humbert's revenge on his romantic rival in merciless, vivid language. The narrator's frankness about his desire for and relations with a child destined the book to pass through scandal on its way to immortality.[1]

Lolita had started her long reign over the American bestseller lists in 1958, by which point Nabokov had been garnering critical attention on both sides of the Atlantic for decades. But it was his nymphet novel—and the risqué film Stanley Kubrick made from it— that launched him into notoriety, then celebrity. Banned in Australia, Buenos Aires, and at the Cincinnati Public Library, Nabokov's novel had managed to sell more copies in its first three weeks in America than any book since *Gone with the Wind*.

And just as Solzhenitsyn mapped a uniquely Soviet geography in *The Gulag Archipelago*, Nabokov laid out the landscape of postwar America in *Lolita*. It was an entirely different archipelago—one of roadside motels, sanatoriums, hotel conferences, pop psychology, immigrant drifters, a Kansas barber, a one-armed veteran, Safeways and drugstores, sanctimonious book clubs, and an unnerving religiosity. It was a glorious, expansive, intolerant, and amnesiac backdrop, one that revealed just as much as Solzhenitsyn's opus about the country in which it was set, a stage perfectly suited for a story of betrayal and corruption.

After *Lolita*'s phenomenal launch, Nabokov had sold the film and paperback rights for six figures each. Traveling to Hollywood, he rubbed shoulders with John Wayne, whom he did not recognize, and Marilyn Monroe, whom he did. He left his career as an American college professor, becoming the subject of *New Yorker* cartoons and late-night television comedy. On overseas trips, he was accosted by the press and written up in a half-dozen languages across the continent.[2]

His morals were called into question ("utterly corrupt," raged one *New York Times* critic), but over time his detractors tended to be mocked as puritans and killjoys. The sexually swinging era that followed *Lolita*'s creation was not of Nabokov's making, but its mores helped influence the perception of the book in subsequent years. By the time Solzhenitsyn arrived in Germany, *Lolita* had become part of a stable of stories about older men with an itch for underage, promiscuous partners. Webster's, Nabokov's favorite dictionary, would eventually add Lolita's name to its pages, offering up the off-kilter definition of "a precociously seductive girl."[3]

The book's linguistic richness and power vaulted it into an existence in which it took on meanings independent of its creator. In vain would Nabokov describe how his nymphet was one of the most innocent and pure among the gallery of slaves he had created as characters; to no avail would Véra remind reporters of how a captive *Lolita* cried herself to sleep each night.[4]

Setting aside those who thought *Lolita* a tease and her author an arted-up dirty-books writer, Nabokov had many admirers among the literary set. But it was a peculiar fan club. Despite their cool reverence for *Lolita*, her most famous fans were prone to calling her author cruel. Bestselling novelist Joyce Carol Oates checked Nabokov for having "the most amazing capacity for loathing" and "a genius for dehumanizing"—and this from someone who *liked* the book.[5]

Oates's 1973 comment was not even the first shot across the bow. Many others, before and after, took up the same cry, from John Updike, who acknowledged the difficulty of distinguishing the callousness of Nabokov's characters from their author's "zest for describing deformity and pain," to Martin Amis, who would be even more direct decades later: "*Lolita* is a cruel book about cruelty." Whether they were meant to praise or damn, such comments had a long history. By the time Oates's article on *Lolita* appeared, Nabokov's fellow writers had been describing his work as inhuman or dehumanizing for forty years.[6]

2

After the celebrity of *Lolita*, Nabokov moved to Europe but continued to spark the American imagination. He followed up with *Pale Fire*, an academic satire starring Charles Kinbote, yet another tormented pedophile, along with a dead poet named John Shade. It was hailed by Mary McCarthy in the pages of *The New Republic* as "one of the very great works of art of this century." Profiled in *LIFE* and *Esquire* ("The Man Who Scandalized the World"), Nabokov had become so popular that his fifteenth novel, *Ada*, a convoluted narrative smorgasbord of brother–sister incest, won him the cover of *Time* magazine—a portrait of the writer as an enigma. Before it was even published, one Hollywood mogul after another flew to Switzerland to be permitted a few hours with the manuscript.

As time went on, the world came more and more to Nabokov, and he went less and less into the world. Despite occasional thoughts of moving elsewhere, he ended up settling with Véra into a protected existence in Montreux. He welcomed visitors for what he called interviews, giving written answers to questions submitted in advance, and trying to restrain the untamed journalists who preferred to use words he had actually spoken aloud.

When he could, he worked to script his television appearances just as completely, hiding note cards among the potted plants and tea cups of a studio set. Collecting his interviews with *The New York Times*, the BBC, and other organizations, he revised them to be more to his liking and published the Nabokov-approved versions in a separate book. He was a man in almost perfect control of his public persona, and the persona he created was that of the reserved, jolly genius who was both a master and a devotee of his art.

His genius may have been beyond judgment at that point, but Nabokov was himself more than willing to judge. He had a lifetime habit of mocking other authors, calling T. S. Eliot "a fraud and a fake" and despising the moral lectures of Dostoyevsky (whose characters were "sinning their way to Jesus"), Faulkner (filled with "skeletonized triteness" and "biblical rumblings"), and Pasternak ("melodramatic and vilely written"). He likewise dismissed Hemingway, Henry James, Balzac, Ezra Pound, Stendhal, D. H. Lawrence, Thomas Mann, André Gide, André Malraux, Jean-Paul Sartre, and women novelists as a group. While he sometimes disapproved of the phrase, Nabokov had become an avatar of art for art's sake: a playful experimenter for whom the stylistic needs of a story trumped all moral consideration.[7]

He ranked pride between kindness and fearlessness on his list of the highest human virtues, and he wielded that pride like a surgeon's knife in literary exchanges and mocking repartee that, in his younger days, had earned him at least one bloody nose. More often, however, Nabokov was gracious when met on his own terms. And since *Lolita*'s success, he had more and more often been able to impose those terms.[8]

In the heyday of political activism, he was inclined to abstain. He had never made a secret of his loathing for the Soviet system, which came up even more frequently than his disdain for Freud (which came up often). But he never voted, he never put a yard sign out for a candidate, he never signed a petition. He did, however, coyly send a congratulatory telegram to President Lyndon Johnson in 1965, praising his "admirable work." Were the accolades for sending troops to Vietnam to fight the Communist menace, or for the Civil Rights Act of 1964? Most likely it was both. And he equally coyly avoided criticizing Joseph McCarthy's tactics by saying they could not, at any rate, be compared to Stalin's. It was his habit not to run for office, endorse candidates, or otherwise enter the political fray. He had settled, in fact, in an entirely neutral country, which was itself occasionally criticized as mercenary and uncaring—one which had, at the time of Nabokov's arrival, not fought in a war for a hundred and forty-six years.[9]

His suite of rooms on the sixth floor of the Palace Hotel were more professorial than palatial. He had an ancient, battered lectern on loan from the hotel, which the staff said had once been used by Flaubert—a writer Nabokov *did* admire. The unabridged Webster's dictionary lay open as he worked, with his shorts and casual shoes and books and butterfly nets bundled into a private corner of a hotel, the temporary shelter turned permanent, his long residence there serving as conclusive evidence of his own exile.

Exile had been a theme in Nabokov's life since childhood. He had left Russia with his family in the aftermath of the Revolution. He later escaped Hitler's Berlin and Occupied France, though people he loved had not. He had gone hungry with much of Europe during the war, but knew better than to call that suffering. He had not been broken by history; instead, he had in many ways defied it. His Jewish wife and son, a boy who had entered the world in the crucible of Nazi Germany, were still alive. And as if simply living through two wars and a Revolution were not enough, he had also somehow managed to reinvent himself in another language, astounding the world with playfulness, unreliable narrators, and the narrow ledge between coherence and coincidence. He had become both an artist and a

symbol of an artist. By writing exactly the kind of books he wanted
to, he had reached an iconic level of celebrity, the kind recognized
by the pre-teen girl who knocked at his door one Halloween dressed
as *Lolita*.

3

Solzhenitsyn possessed another kind of fame—the kind reserved
for David fighting Goliath: the fame of the crusader. His 1962 novel
about the stark reality of a Soviet labor camp, *One Day in the Life
of Ivan Denisovich*, had shocked the West and received praise from
unexpected sources—including Soviet Premier Nikita Khrushchev,
who had used the book to underline the abuse of power under Joseph
Stalin: "So long as we work we can and must clear up many points
and tell the truth. . . . This we must do so that such things never
happen again."[10]

Just two years after championing Solzhenitsyn's novel, however,
Khrushchev had been forced out of power, replaced by others less
interested in addressing the crimes of the past. The Party reversed
itself and began to censor and confiscate Solzhenitsyn's writing. His
hidden archive was raided. He began to be slandered in meetings. In
a plot worthy of Nabokov, a fake double showed up to impersonate
Solzhenitsyn, drinking and harassing women in public until the
author's friends caught the impostor and turned him over to authorities, who released him.

As long as Solzhenitsyn insisted on writing about Russian history—which was the only thing he wanted to do—it was inevitable
that official trouble would follow. In 1968, his works were banned.
The Union of Soviet Writers, which had welcomed and praised him
when Khrushchev had done the same, became nervous. What should
they do about this unpredictable, difficult man? Nobel Prize-winning
Soviet writer Mikhail Sholokhov, who had always been a harsh critic
of his fellow novelist, advocated not just banning Solzhenitsyn's
work but keeping him from writing altogether. And indeed, a year
later, Solzhenitsyn was expelled from the Union of Soviet Writers.

Expulsion made it impossible for him to publish in the Soviet Union or to hire anyone to help him with his work. He had no legal occupation, reducing him to a state of existence beyond precarious in the U.S.S.R. He was ripe for arrest.[11]

In protest, Solzhenitsyn wrote open letters for Russian and foreign distribution. He met with friends and supporters, seeking their aid. He directed the smuggling of microfilms of his manuscripts to the West, where they would be ready to publish if he could not publish at home.

The world's response was massive. Arthur Miller, John Updike, Jean-Paul Sartre, Muriel Spark, Graham Greene, and Kurt Vonnegut spoke out with hundreds of other writers for Solzhenitsyn, condemning the decision of the Writers' Union. The outcry drew attention to his plight and his work.

The following year, Solzhenitsyn was awarded the Nobel Prize for Literature. Public letters had been written to the Swedish Academy by prior winners on his behalf. A poll of literary critics that year had Jorge Luis Borges and Solzhenitsyn as the clear leaders among possible contenders, with Vladimir Nabokov receiving only two votes. By selecting Solzhenitsyn, the awards committee publicly announced its recognition of "the ethical force of literature," and its choice was understood immediately to have many political consequences (which likely helped a rumor persist for years that the CIA had prepared Solzhenitsyn's materials for submission).[12]

After the announcement, Solzhenitsyn cabled Stockholm with his thanks, confirming that he would attend the award ceremony that December. But the Soviet Union quickly denounced the award as "deplorable," and weeks later Solzhenitsyn announced he would not ask for permission to leave the country after all. He feared that if he left, he would never be allowed to return, and would find himself forced into exile.[13]

The secretary of the Nobel committee, mindful of the absent Solzhenitsyn's safety, read only the words of the Soviet newspaper *Pravda* at the awards ceremony, quoting its 1962 review of *One Day in the Life of Ivan Denisovich*: "Why is it that our heart contracts with pain as we read this remarkable story at the same time as we feel our spirit soar? The explanation lies in its profound humanity, in the quality of mankind even in the hour of degradation."[14]

The speech Solzhenitsyn had planned to give that night explained that throughout history, debates had raged over the artist's obligation either to live for himself or to serve society. "For me," he said, "there is no dilemma." Baldly refuting the idea of art for art's sake, he titled his lecture "Art—for Man's Sake." In it, he described how "in the midst of exhausting prison camp relocations, marching in a column of prisoners in the gloom of bitterly cold evenings, with strings of camp lights glimmering through the darkness, we would often feel rising in our breast what we would have wanted to shout out to the whole world—if only the whole world could have heard us."[15]

The Nobel drama over Solzhenitsyn offered only a hint of what was to come. By 1974, Solzhenitsyn had long nursed a great scheme to call authorities to account for the dead of the camps, the prisoners broken by a police state, and the ongoing crippled society that was their legacy. But after the winning of the Nobel Prize, his scheme was thrown off-balance. Had the award raised his profile enough that he might be allowed to write again? Could political pressure from the world guarantee his status to take on history unfettered? He had long ago finished *The Gulag Archipelago*, but held back from publishing it, perhaps cautious about making a move which he knew would completely change the game. Here was a book that could not be "lightened" or tailored to sneak its way through open channels. Its very premise—a four-decade summary of government injustice—was a condemnation of the Soviet state. Once released, the genie would not be contained. So Solzhenitsyn waited for the right moment.

But the KGB had no reason to wait, and agents discovered the hiding place of the manuscript by interrogating his typist, a woman in her sixties named Elizaveta Voronyanskaya, for five days and nights. Released under house arrest and unable to warn Solzhenitsyn, she died two weeks later. But another copy of Solzhenitsyn's manuscript had already been smuggled out of the country, and three months after her death, *The Gulag Archipelago* was published in Paris.

KGB agents eventually came for Solzhenitsyn, too. News of his arrest made it to network television in the U.S. that night in a four-minute segment on the CBS Evening News. A harrowing twenty-four-hour period followed, where it was not clear exactly what would happen. In his cell at Lefortovo Prison he played out potential confrontations and conversations in his mind again and again before being hauled out, bundled onto a plane, and deported.[16]

At a moment in history with no shortage of dramatic events—Watergate had exploded, there was talk of impeachment, and ransom negotiations were underway for a kidnapped heiress named Patty Hearst—Solzhenitsyn's arrival in Frankfurt on Valentine's Day dominated the news. Journalists gleefully noted that no Soviet citizen had been forcibly expelled since Leon Trotsky in 1929.[17]

The New York Times alone ran dozens of articles about the latest Russian deportee in the first week of his post-Soviet life, poking into everything from his conversations with his wife to a gift of flowers he received. His attire was dissected, and speculation in the press about his every action was rampant, leading to outraged harangues from the new exile, who was accustomed to an entirely different kind of harassment from the press back home.

Solzhenitsyn's presence in Germany rattled the careful choreography of détente. In light of the media attention, Bonn felt a chill in its relations with Russia and was glad to see Solzhenitsyn off its soil. Others welcomed him more defiantly: Swedish premier Olof Palme—still a dozen years ahead of the anonymous assassin's bullet that would end his life—condemned Soviet treatment of Solzhenitsyn as a "frightening example of brutality and persecution." The same day, U.S. Secretary of State Henry Kissinger, trying to maintain a delicate balance in U.S.–Soviet relations, hastened to make clear that

Solzhenitsyn would be welcome in the U.S., but America in no way condemned Soviet domestic policy.[18]

In the weeks that followed, Soviet representatives tried to discredit Solzhenitsyn with formal charges of treason and salacious poetry mocking him. Later they would produce forged records suggesting that he had been an informer in the camps. He countered by calling out by name a list of the people in the Soviet Union who had helped him, or whose safety he feared for: a young assistant, people institutionalized in Soviet psychiatric hospitals, and others expelled from literary institutes because of their association with him. He established a fund to help Russian political prisoners and their families, into which he funneled money from sales of his books.[19]

Solzhenitsyn's presence in the West on the heels of the publication of his latest book combined to generate a global shock wave, as the world came to understand the meaning of the word *gulag*. When the American translation finally came out that summer, its stories about mind-numbing forced labor, torture, executions, and a deliberate dehumanization of prisoners on a scale too vast to comprehend stunned the world. With a singular ability to deliver testimony, the book piled on decade after decade of horror with a righteous fury. George Kennan, the de facto architect of U.S. Cold War policy, immediately recognized its importance, calling it "the most powerful single indictment of a political regime ever to be levied in modern times." Its global impact led the Italian Communist Party to open dissent with the Soviet Union, boosted anti-Communist conservatives in America, and triggered a public firestorm in French politics.[20]

The subject of Solzhenitsyn's latest book had come as a surprise to no one. Advance rumors about the project—as well as its mysterious title—had floated into Europe and America years ahead of the work itself. But no one other than its author could have predicted its explosiveness.

Many of the facts he had to offer were not new—by the 1970s the West had been hearing about Soviet camps in shouts or whispers for fifty years. It had been widely assumed that during the worst years of the Purges, millions of Soviet citizens had been imprisoned and a staggering number of them executed. But Solzhenitsyn's account made the numbers human, revealing the suffering scattered across a country that had gone about its business while engineers, Orthodox priests, children, Old Bolshevik stalwarts, common criminals, toadies, accused Trotskyites, Ukrainians, Poles, physicists, thieves, delusional Emperors, embezzlers, spouses of the convicted, members of the intelligentsia, and writers like Solzhenitsyn himself lived out the drama of incarceration in a massive Underworld. He offered an extensive education in the geography of terror—the Lubyanka Prison perched dead-center in the heart of Moscow, the notorious Arctic camps of Vorkuta and Kolyma, and the network of trains, trucks, and boats that transferred people across the thousands of miles of facilities, punishments playing out in secret research *sharashkas*, brutal logging camps, and the mines that tried to extract clay, coal, and gold from unforgiving landscapes. Combining first-hand stories from hundreds of voices with his own years spent as a prisoner, Solzhenitsyn captured the system's elephantine vastness and its existence as a parallel society in a way that surpassed the reach and authority of every other account.[21]

Solzhenitsyn not only resembled a prophet, he acted the part, with a spiritual anxiety that weighed on his political crusade. Each city he visited, crowds gathered to see him at the dock or on the tarmac. A street in a northern suburb of Paris was named after him. Photographers stalked him in Germany, through Denmark, Norway, and Switzerland as he searched for a permanent home. Prime ministers and presidents around the world weighed in on his exile. Walter Cronkite interviewed him for his own CBS News special. He had become the conscience of the world.

4

Both Nabokov's and Solzhenitsyn's versions of fame reflected, in part, their life stories. In 1919, Nabokov had fled Russia by ship on the eve of his twentieth birthday, leaving behind what he called "the happiest childhood imaginable." That fantasy childhood had unfolded in luxury, with devoted parents, a stable of fifty servants, multiple tutors, and visits to the French Riviera. His father had been at court under Nicholas II. His grandfather had been Minister of Justice under Tsars Alexander II and III. According to a cousin, the family name came from a fourteenth-century Tatar prince. Even Nabokov's pets had a spectacular pedigree, with one family dog descended from Chekhov's dachshund.

Nabokov had been born to greatness, and he embraced it. Possessing a profound awareness of his own gifts, he named himself without apparent irony alongside Shakespeare and Pushkin in a trinity of his favorite writers. Yet he had also seen all the external signs of grace evaporate overnight—loved ones lost, an estate confiscated, his entire community turned into refugees, wandering through host countries subject to ridicule and resentment. Nabokov's confidence in his art was electrified by the knowledge that everything except his imagination could be taken away.[22]

If Nabokov's life had descended from Eden into harsh reality, Solzhenitsyn's childhood had spared him the disappointment of the fall. In the words of biographer Michael Scammell, "The Solzhenitsyn family was not special enough to have kept track of its ancestry." The boy Alexander never knew his father, who died after a hunting injury six months before his birth. He had grown up in a hut without running water, surviving the famine of the 1930s with one set of clothes for years at a time. He mucked out stalls for the Russian Army and rose to first lieutenant on the battlefield during the war.[23]

But he then encountered a tribulation that would savage every aspect of his life. Arrested on the thinnest of pretexts—jokes about Stalin—he was convicted and sentenced to eight years in the Gulag. Already a writer, he never stopped composing as he moved from camp to camp, even when there was no place to record his words except in his memory. But he knew he would tell the story of it all one day: Russia, her people, and their anguish.

Before *One Day in the Life of Ivan Denisovich* had been taken up as a cudgel for reform and de-Stalinization in 1962, he had published a lone article in a regional paper criticizing the Soviet postal system. His first book had circled the globe and catapulted him into comparisons with Tolstoy, Dostoyevsky, and Chekhov. Solzhenitsyn had come to believe that his subsequent works might trigger even more change. He spent the next decade writing thinly veiled accounts drawing on Russian history. Even Solzhenitsyn's ostensible fiction revealed the past, which had not been forgotten but could not be discussed without adopting the mask of invention.[24]

Out of their distinct experiences, Nabokov and Solzhenitsyn came to very different ways of being in the world. Both worked relentlessly, but Nabokov lived comfortably in a luxury hotel, while Solzhenitsyn longed for a remote and rustic cabin. If pride was a cardinal virtue for Nabokov, Solzhenitsyn feared it. "Pride grows in the human heart," he wrote, "like lard on a pig."[25]

Yet their differences somehow led Nabokov and Solzhenitsyn to similar understandings of Russian history, loathing Communism in equal measure. Solzhenitsyn's writing narrated his slow disillusionment first with Stalin, then with Lenin, eventually showing the roots of the Gulag stretching back to torture and mass murder in the first years after the Revolution. Attentive readers had been aware of Uncle Joe's dark side for some time, but Solzhenitsyn made the case that terror and excess predated Stalin, originating instead under Lenin at the dawn of the Soviet state.

Nabokov also despised Lenin, but had seen first-hand the esteem in which he was held by segments of the European and American literary establishment. Edmund Wilson, once Nabokov's best friend in America, had penned a book-length tribute to revolution that culminated in Lenin's 1917 return to Russia. From almost their first meeting, Wilson had written frankly of his hope to one day change Nabokov's mind about Lenin. So perhaps it is not shocking that as Solzhenitsyn proceeded to savage the Soviet regime from its inception, Nabokov reveled in the vindication, noting with glee Solzhenitsyn's success at "annihilating the smugness of old Leninists."[26]

But Nabokov had reservations about the newest Russian exile. Before Solzhenitsyn's expulsion, Nabokov had been sure that the former prisoner was somehow serving KGB ends. How else could his work appear in Russia and make its way to the West, while Solzhenitsyn himself remained free? Nabokov also disparaged Solzhenitsyn's literary abilities, calling him an inferior writer in an interview for *The New York Times* and labeling his work "juicy journalese" in personal notes. Véra thought even less of Solzhenitsyn as a writer, calling his work "third-rate" and noting to a friend that he wrote like a shoemaker.[27]

After Solzhenitsyn had been awarded the Nobel Prize, Nabokov spent summer evenings reading his novel *August 1914* to Véra on the small balcony of their Montreux Palace suite. *The New York Times Magazine* reported their "cackles of laughter" over Solzhenitsyn's "manly prose" and amusement that the former inmate refused to leave Russia to receive the Nobel for fear he would not be allowed to return. Who in his right mind would *want* to return to Soviet Russia? In a letter written days after the piece ran, Véra took exception to the word *cackle* and underlined her admiration for Solzhenitsyn's bravery but admitted that the Nabokovs did not think much of Solzhenitsyn's talent as a writer.[28]

Solzhenitsyn, on the other hand, deeply admired Nabokov's style. Nobelists were encouraged to nominate candidates for consideration in future years, and in 1972 Solzhenitsyn, still in the Soviet Union, sent a note to the Academy to recommend Nabokov, whose works were banned in Russia, for the Prize. He wrote separately to Nabokov and forwarded a copy of the recommendation.

Whether due to suspicions about Solzhenitsyn or out of fear of harming a dissident, Nabokov never responded to that letter. But on Solzhenitsyn's first day as an exile, Nabokov did not hesitate to write a note welcoming the chronicler of the Gulag to the free world. Endorsing Solzhenitsyn's crusade, Nabokov wrote that "ever since the vile times of Lenin, I have not ceased to mock the philistinism of Sovietized Russia and to thunder against the very kind of vicious cruelty of which you write."[29]

Solzhenitsyn, for all that he admired Nabokov's talent, was less than convinced. He seems not to have agreed with Nabokov's claim to unrelenting thunder against the Soviet state. In the first volume of *The Gulag Archipelago*—which Nabokov would read that summer—Solzhenitsyn had included the account of a Russian officer who wondered why Nabokov and other émigré authors ignored the "blood flowing from Russia's living wounds," suggesting that they "wrote as if there had been no Revolution in Russia, or as if it were too complex for them to explain."

In addition to its utter failure to address Revolutionary trauma, *Lolita* was also not Solzhenitsyn's idea of literature. Where Nabokov experimented and provoked, shocking and baffling his readers, Solzhenitsyn dreamed of writing a *War and Peace* for twentieth-century Russia. He was, he admitted, a traditionalist at heart.[30]

In novels he wrote in Russian and then in English, Nabokov had accosted readers with pedophiles' sexual pursuits and the gleeful malice of murderers, not to mention the grotesque comedy of a child tortured and killed by mistake. He celebrated the power of human imagination by creating worlds that relentlessly kicked his characters in the teeth: Lolita, molested by Humbert Humbert day after day; *Pale Fire*'s poet John Shade shot dead within moments of expressing his faith in the universe. He himself claimed in his autobiography to be more interested as a writer in thematic elegance than the life or death of a character—even when that character was a real person in his autobiography.[31]

While Solzhenitsyn also agonized over language, trying to create a writing voice that was innovative yet rooted in tradition, he felt a patriotic obligation to point directly to the brutality of the Soviet enterprise from start to finish. Going so far as to disparage those who had voluntarily left Russia—even to flee persecution—he noted repeatedly that he had had no choice in his expulsion. He believed that the artist's responsibility lay in staying to defend the ideals of his native land.

Solzhenitsyn longed for Nabokov's "genius" to address the same issues, telling an interviewer that the Russian émigré could have placed his "colossal, I repeat colossal, talent at the service of his homeland," and "could have written marvellously about our Revolution. But he didn't do it."[32]

What Solzhenitsyn—and the world—didn't realize was that Nabokov had spent decades burying some of history's darkest moments within the framework of his fiction. Global history predating his most famous books had driven and shaped his work, and Nabokov had found a way to integrate the past into his exacting literary vision. But the events he memorialized had fallen so completely out of public memory that they went unnoticed. Widely regarded as only literary experiments or parodies, his writing had become so closely identified with his artistic stance that readers missed the horrific history that haunted even his most famous novels. By the time Solzhenitsyn drove into Montreux to pay his respects to the literary giant, Nabokov had been making enigmatic hints to readers about this history for decades, to no avail.

So perhaps it is no surprise that by 1974, Nabokov was eager to welcome his fellow writer to the West and to freedom, extending an open invitation to visit. Solzhenitsyn responded with an unusual literary humility, telling Nabokov that fate had delivered them both to Switzerland so that they could finally meet.

Yet that fall, when the Solzhenitsyns wrote to say they would come to the Palace Hotel on October 6, they received no reply. Trying repeatedly to reach the Nabokovs by phone and post, the Solzhenitsyns heard nothing.

Despite the silence, they took a chance and headed to Montreux. Their destination, a seven-story Belle Époque building in a cosmopolitan town of music festivals, was home to celebrated actors and writers. When Nabokov moved in, the staff had put him at ease, making him comfortable enough to keep him as a guest for the rest of his life. But the fifty-five-year-old Solzhenitsyn, newly exiled, hounded by the press and rattled by an alien culture, was an outsider looking in. Was he expected? Was he welcome? Pulling up to the hotel driveway, Solzhenitsyn wondered.

A stone's throw away, Vladimir and Véra Nabokov sat waiting in the hotel's Salon de Musique, which had been reserved for the event. A clock face somewhere registered the hour; it was not yet noon. Through the trio of French windows, each one three times as tall as a man of average height—and Nabokov was a little taller than average—the sky could be seen. Overcast as it was, daylight still poured in, forming three reflecting pools on the zigzag parquet. A half-moon swag of drapery hung from a bar above each window, mirroring the crystal swag of the beaded chandelier. An octet of gilt letters, all *M* for "Montreux," hovered like angels of aristocracy near the corners of the ceiling, nestled among laurel wreaths, monsters, and winged maidens carrying garlands.

A table for four was ready. The Palace was a luxury hotel, its restaurant surely capable of providing Solzhenitsyn one of the finest meals of his life. As the hosts waited for their guests, Véra was probably wearing, as was her habit, something simple against her white halo of hair and blue eyes. Nabokov might have dressed for the occasion, too, at least a little more formally than the long shorts and knee socks in which he typically climbed hillsides hunting for butterflies (and still out-hiked reporters half his age).

What did Nabokov imagine the two writers would talk about— one whose Russian existence was born with the Revolution, and the other whose died with it? If asked, Nabokov could have detailed his defiance, in life and in fiction: the invitation to return as a guest of the state, an invitation refused despite his longing to see his homeland; the friends he had cut off or rebuked for their perceived sympathies with Soviet rule; the conversations about the Vietnam War that upset some friends but which would have found a sympathetic listener in Solzhenitsyn.

A visit with the newly minted exile was a chance to meet his distorted Soviet double, someone who had attained his own measure of celebrity, someone who understood the corruption of the Soviet state from Lenin's first Terrors and had rejected the romance of the Revolution. Solzhenitsyn had managed to expose the system publicly, to chronicle its crimes, and he had survived to tell the story.

But for half a century—for all of Solzhenitsyn's life—Nabokov had lived that defiance from across the border. While Solzhenitsyn could imagine returning, *longed* to return, Nabokov's Russia had been obliterated; his Russia could only exist in his books and the hidden corners of his heart. In 1962 he had explained, "All the Russia I need is always with me: literature, language, and my own Russian childhood. I will never return. I will never surrender."[33]

Solzhenitsyn believed that in order to survive, Nabokov had turned his back on Russia and the human suffering he had seen. But the Nabokov who sat waiting for Solzhenitsyn had done things in his stories that had never been noticed. He had crafted an exquisite chronicle of his own, in which his modernist pyrotechnics and linguistic acrobatics cloaked a devotion to the very mission Solzhenitsyn had taken on.

Inside the stories that earned him the label *cruel*, Nabokov had folded other narratives that had gone undetected, documenting intolerance and atrocity. The names, dates, and places he had woven into his poetry, plays, and fiction decade after decade created his own private map, revealing the most profound losses of his life and the forgotten traumas of his age. As the story of his family became the story of not just St. Petersburg or Russia but twentieth-century Europe and America, Nabokov had bound together the beauty and the horror of all of it inside his art. A ledger recording the forgotten and dead had been exquisitely preserved in Nabokov's stories for more than thirty years—even in *Lolita*. And readers had missed almost all of it.

The lost history inside the stories had been sitting there for so long—including Russian tragedy that Solzhenitsyn himself had referenced. Had he seen through Nabokov's mask to the denunciation of injustice and the tenderness in the work, a tenderness not always apparent in the public face of the man? Did he know the story of Nabokov's life beyond the obvious theme of flight and exile? What would they say to each other? One floor above the street where Solzhenitsyn approached in his car, Nabokov sat and waited.

Chapter Two

Childhood

---◇◇◇---

1

Vladimir Vladimirovich Nabokov entered the world during the last spring of a dying century on April 22, 1899, in St. Petersburg, Russia. The date was not yet notable for also being the birthday of Vladimir Ilyich Ulyanov, a twenty-nine-year-old radical exiled to Siberia and three years away from immortality as Lenin.

Nabokov's mother had already given birth to one stillborn child, and her second pregnancy had no doubt worried her—Elena Ivanovna was a sensitive woman given to fretting. But if the care she had in reserve to lavish on her newborn could make the difference, he would be among the most fortunate souls on the planet.[1]

Along with love, money and culture were also in plentiful supply. The house at 47 Bolshaya Morskaya had been Elena's dowry, and Nabokov's father, Vladimir Dmitrievich, came from a family that had been in the service of the Tsar for decades. A legal scholar with a taste for opera and literature, V. D. Nabokov not only had a magnificent library, he had a librarian to go with it. A passion for luxury, a fascination with butterflies, and a rebellious streak characterized the father, who from the beginning "idolized" his first-born son.[2]

As always in the world, the moment held harbingers of hope and despair. History has little regard for clean breaks, and so the best and worst of the passing century found no barrier to entering the new. In Russia, Tsar Nicholas II was in his fifth year of rule over the largest contiguous nation in the world. His work toward the Hague Convention of 1899, which created a court to settle international disputes and sought to eliminate aerial bombing, would soon garner him a nomination for the first Nobel Peace Prize. The conference would be remembered as one of Nicholas's few shining moments.

In Paris a French Jew named Alfred Dreyfus, who had been framed as a German spy and imprisoned years before in disease-ridden isolation on Devil's Island, was brought back to the land of the living to stand trial again. New evidence was presented that spring, revealing the anti-Semitism responsible for his conviction. But evidence and public outrage would not be enough to defeat it, and he would once again be found guilty before being granted an extraordinary pardon.

In Cuba, a group of "re-concentration camps" established by the Spanish military had just been shut down amid outcry over the horrible conditions—conditions that helped earn their creator the nickname "the Butcher." Despite the reports of widespread suffering, however, the concept had already caught on. As Nabokov crawled and walked and ran into the new century, concentration camps would be introduced in colonial territories by one Western nation after another: the U.S. in the Philippines, the British in South Africa, and the Germans in South-West Africa.[3]

In time, Vladimir Nabokov would have good reason to ponder Lenin, tsars, virulent anti-Semitism, and concentration camps. But opening his eyes on the second floor of an elegant pink granite house, the newborn child arriving auspiciously at daybreak, would, at most, find himself the first live child of Elena Nabokov. And if he could not yet appreciate that fact, he would still benefit tremendously from it.

During the child's first weeks he was taken to a nearby church, where he was baptized and nearly christened Victor by mistake. If the Russian Orthodox archpriest followed the full traditional rite, the newly named Vladimir was immersed naked in a tub of holy water before losing four locks of hair (in the shape of a cross) and being anointed with oil over his entire body to help him slip from the grasp of evil forever. In the life he was to lead, he would need all the assistance he could get.[4]

The Nabokov home sat on the western half of Bolshaya Morskaya, an elegant street just around the corner from St. Isaac's Cathedral. Commissioned by a Russian Tsar, designed by a French architect, the largest Orthodox cathedral in the city also contained Greek, Byzantine, and Russian elements. St. Isaac's had an eclectic style that, given the magic required to escape, might have successfully emigrated to Paris, Berlin, or beyond.

St. Isaac's was, however, firmly rooted in St. Petersburg, the capital city founded by Peter the Great two centuries before. And like so many buildings in the old city, whose beauty was shot through by a network of canals, St. Isaac's foundations had been laid on reclaimed swampland. Because the terrain lacked the stability to support the weight of granite pillars and pediments, a forest of wooden timbers had to be driven into the ground as a base before construction began. That reclamation came at a price: tens of thousands of serfs died in the initial effort to create a modern European capital, and Peter's unhappy wife had cursed it to become a "city built on bones," a landscape of crumbling families.[5]

The cathedral had risen in sight of the Neva River and just a half-mile southwest from the Peter and Paul Fortress. The first building Peter had constructed in the city, the fortress was meant at first to ensure the security of the then-frontier town, but had quickly become the site of a political prison. In 1718 Peter's own son paid a price for trying to flee the country, becoming one of the prison's first occupants. Tortured on orders from his father, he died there at the age of twenty-eight.[6]

The fortress secured Peter's capital, and the city that Peter raised had in turn lifted up the Nabokov family. More than a hundred years later, one of Nabokov's great-great-uncles was appointed commander of the prison. During his tenure, he loaned books to the imprisoned Fyodor Dostoyevsky, then charged with plotting revolution and reading banned literature.[7]

2

At the time of Nabokov's birth, his family's affairs had been bound up with Russian Imperial politics for centuries, but from the beginning he belonged to both Russia and the world. His earliest memories were of the web of cotton cords padding his crib at home and a fleeting image of rain on a roof during a trip to his uncle's chateau in southern France. He had a wet nurse who complained that he never slept. He had a daily bath. He was not spanked. At a time when his Russian literacy extended no further than the words for *cocoa* and *Mama*, he was already reading and writing in English. His British governess, Miss Norcott, fell in love with another woman. His Russian tutor, Ordyntsev, fell in love with his mother. He reorganized the cushions of the family sofa to create a dark tunnel behind it for adventuring.

When he was small, his mother read him tales of knights and damsels, and stories of the button-eyed blackface Golliwogg doll. Later, he himself read Dickens and Daudet, *Punch* and H. G. Wells. He was exquisitely well-read, even as a child. Sherlock Holmes, Conrad, and Kipling all caught his fancy for a time.

Vladimir grew up alongside Sergei, a brother born less than a year after him, an almost-twin and companion in early childhood. As has been the lot of so many younger siblings since the dawn of family life, less time and attention were bestowed on the second-born. Each subsequent child—Olga in 1903, Elena in 1906, and Kirill in 1911—would be provided for magnificently. But unlike their oldest brother, they would learn to live more or less in the arms of governesses.[8]

Standing closest to the dazzling Vladimir, Sergei was, often as not, cast into shadow. The brothers had little in common. Vladimir inherited his father's fondness for boxing and butterfly hunting; Sergei, a love of opera. Vladimir was charismatic and extroverted, while Sergei possessed a severe stutter and no physical grace. The boys nonetheless had to serve as playmates for one another, and under Vladimir's leadership, they eluded their guardians more than once. At the ages of four and five, they managed to lose their governess on a visit to Germany, boarding a steamboat and traveling down the Rhine from Wiesbaden. Two years later, to escape the equally chafing rule of their French tutor, they fled the family's country estate on foot in their parents' absence, striking out with Turka, the family's Great Dane. Vladimir led the way as they tramped through the snow to the main road. When Sergei became tired and cold, he was assigned to ride the dog. Heading out into the moonlit night, with Sergei occasionally falling off Turka, they were miles from home before they were retrieved.

Vladimir and Sergei shared a nursery for the first decade of their lives, sleeping on either side of a Japanned screen. Both boys were permitted to browse their father's massive library. Physically slight but athletically confident, Vladimir liked to lap his brother at the roller rink, or to sneak up on him as he practiced piano, vulnerable to attack. Sergei acquired a fondness for Napoleon, and slept cradling a little bronze bust of the foreign emperor. Unlike many grade school stutterers, his affliction stuck with him, and his poor vision required the additional indignity of spectacles. The boys were never friends. Frequently subject to Vladimir's teasing as well as his brilliance, Sergei played the moon to his brother's bright sun.[9]

3

Vladimir remained his parents' favorite, but he was also a sickly child, afflicted by quinsy, scarlet fever, and pneumonia in turn. In the winter when he was ill, his mother Elena had a driver take her in a sled to the busy international shops on Nevsky Prospect, where she bought her invalid a new present each day. It was a life of crimson crystal eggs for Easter, and his mother's tiaras and necklaces from a wall safe to play with before bed.

The Nabokovs' wealth came from Elena's side of the family—her millionaire father had been born into a mining family. He had loved the theater and devoted himself to philanthropic projects, but was also given to legendary rages in which he intimidated his daughter and terrorized his son. He had died when Nabokov was a toddler, leaving behind the St. Petersburg house and a country estate at Vyra, forty-five miles south of the city.[10]

When in the country, Elena Nabokov painted watercolor landscapes and picked mushrooms. In town, she stayed out until three in the morning playing poker. She was emotional and expressive with her children; but with those outside the immediate family, she could be guarded and slow to friendship. She remained a nervous, brittle woman all her life. As a Lent-and-Easter-Sunday churchgoer, she leaned toward signs and portents: furtive knocks and apparitions populated her personal belief system in such a way that she was spiritual without being religious. Seeing letters and numbers in color, just as her son Vladimir did, she believed in second sight.[11]

She was also her son's formative instructor in matters of deception, the first practitioner to model what would become the defining feature of his literary style. He would pay tribute to her cunning later in life, recounting two incidents from childhood in his autobiography.

In the first, Nabokov describes his mother's anxiety over a longtime servant. Like most women of her class, Elena Nabokov did not work. She also had little interest in running the household, leaving the task to her childhood nurse, a woman in her seventies who had been born a serf. Slipping into dementia, the former nurse hoarded scraps and jealously guarded the family food, parceling it out reluctantly even to the Nabokovs themselves.

Unwilling to humiliate the woman by relieving her of her duties, Nabokov's mother encouraged the former nurse in a convoluted fantasy that she ruled over the pantry, when in fact, she controlled only a "moldy and remote little kingdom" maintained to reinforce her delusion. Everyone else knew what was happening and mocked the nurse behind her back—she herself had suspicions about the arrangement from time to time. But the pity Nabokov's mother felt kept her from ever divulging the truth. He would remember his mother's guile for decades, and would mention the former nurse in *Speak, Memory*, along with an even more intricate ploy.[12]

By the time Nabokov was four, his paternal grandfather, Dmitri Nikolaevich Nabokov, had begun to lose his mind. The former Minister to the Tsar put rocks in his mouth. He pounded the floor with his cane for attention. He swore. He confused his attendant for nobility and the Queen of Belgium for a troublemaker. He became convinced that he was only safe in his apartment at Nice, on the French Riviera. The presence of Nabokov's mother there soothed him, but his condition worsened, and doctors recommended moving him to a northern climate.

During one insensible spell, the old man was brought to live in St. Petersburg, where Elena Nabokov recreated his room in Nice. Someone gathered furnishings recalling his old apartment, and some of his possessions were brought in by special messenger. Mediterranean flowers were obtained for his room.

It was not just a question of making him comfortable—Elena Nabokov fostered the illusion that he had never moved at all. She had the side of the house that was visible from his window painted Riviera white. He lived out his few remaining days under the happy delusion that he was safe in Nice and nowhere near a Russia that had just embarked on a catastrophic conflict with Japan.[13]

That same winter, Nabokov watched General Kuropatkin, a friend of the family, begin to demonstrate a trick with matches on the living room sofa, only to be interrupted by the call to war. Four years later, Vladimir would watch the boys' Ukrainian tutor make a coin disappear right before their eyes. A pre-teen Nabokov would sit through yet another tutor's magic lantern slides—glass plates in which large stories were reduced to a handful of images, and tiny moments became epic. But for all the inversion, sleight of hand, and trickery Nabokov would hoard and deploy in his writing across his lifetime, it was his mother who first blended reality and illusion, veiling hard truths in fantasy, and offering comforting lies with a deception born from power and pity.

4

The young Nabokov was so shielded by his parents from the violence of history that to review the political traumas that surrounded his family from his birth is also to note their absence from his daily life, to register that he somehow lived his first decades as a bystander to a cultural maelstrom.

This simultaneous immersion in and distance from social upheaval would eventually find a mirror in his writing. Like his family, Nabokov's characters would be shaped by history, though their invented pasts would often be less lordly than his own. The grandfather dying in St. Petersburg but imagining himself on the Riviera had once owned 390 human beings. At the height of his influence he had been Minister of Justice under Tsars Alexander II and III—the first a reform-minded ruler who freed the serfs and established independent courts, and the second a regressive one who began to roll back the liberties bestowed by his predecessor.

As a result of that political career, Nabokov's father, Vladimir Dmitrievich Nabokov, had been born at Tsarskoe Selo, the Tsar's country estate. He had grown up in St. Petersburg in the political beehive of the Winter Palace. As a child, V. D. Nabokov had lived through assassination of Alexander II and the anti-Semitic pogroms that had convulsed the country in its wake. He had witnessed his own father's struggle to preserve at least some of Russia's reforms.[14]

Surrounded by political turmoil, Nabokov's father had chosen to make a life in it. Establishing himself early on as a liberal, V. D. Nabokov had been a student protester facing arrest, choosing to stay with his fellow detainees rather than take advantage of his father's influence. He had grown up to become a legal scholar with a strong sense of justice.[15]

His democratic inclinations, however, stopped short of material possessions: he had lived among finery from birth and loved elegant things. He owned two automobiles—a Benz sedan and a black limousine—and a wardrobe that attracted more attention than his wife's. His house was filled with soap and books imported from England, while his mind was filled with dreams of a British parliamentary system that he hoped to import as well. His fastidiousness was severe, his intelligence was fierce, and he had dedicated himself to promoting civil rights for everyone.[16]

Nabokov's father would be the formative influence on him from childhood until death. And when Vladimir, nicknamed Volodya, was about to turn four—still a small boy delighting in riding sleeper cars to the Riviera and finding bits of colored glass on the beach—V. D. Nabokov made a choice that would define his legacy.

In 1903 at Kishinev, in the far southwest corner of the Russian Empire, a local newspaper printed stories about the centuries-old slur of blood libel—Jews murdering Christians to collect blood for religious rites. The paper called for Christians "inspired by the love of Christ" and affection for the Tsar to band together to "massacre these vile Jews." Sparked to action on Easter weekend, a mob went on a rampage. And once the pogrom erupted, it ran unimpeded. The destruction continued for almost three days. By the time it was over, 49 Jews had been killed outright, with hundreds injured, businesses broken into, and more than a thousand people homeless.[17]

At a time when it was forbidden for members of the Russian court to take a public stand on any matter without Imperial approval, Nabokov's father wrote about the massacre directly and without permission. In "The Blood Bath of Kishinev," he attacked the madness of anti-Semitism, noting the damage it did not only to the Jews who were its victims but also to a society crippled by blind hatred. He condemned the government for tacitly permitting the pogrom and the police for not stopping it.

Anti-Semitism was woven deeply into the national culture, and Russia's Jews were blamed for nearly every revolutionary tendency and economic disenfranchisement in the country.[18] Gentiles who sympathized with their plight were portrayed as treasonous by reactionary groups. Elena Nabokov kept a collection of political cartoons that attacked her husband for his political stances, including one image in which Nabokov recalled his father "handing over Saint Russia on a plate to World Jewry."[19]

Pogroms had taken place intermittently for centuries, but widespread use of the telegraph made it possible for news of the carnage at Kishinev to travel in hours rather than days. Russian brutality instantly made headlines around the globe. Community organizations and newspapers from Warsaw to London and Texas condemned the assaults. They were a matter of such international outrage that Chinese immigrants in New York banded together to raise money for the victims of Kishinev.[20]

Less attention was paid in that moment to another series of articles that would profoundly affect the lives of millions in subsequent decades. A newspaper in Nabokov's hometown circulated what it trumpeted as the discovery of the records of a secret plan of Jews to take over the world. The fictional material had been lifted from unrelated sources written across centuries, imported into Germany and Prussia, and stitched together into its final form in all probability by the Tsar's secret police. The plan appeared first in stories printed by the same publisher whose newspaper had called for the pogrom in Kishinev. *The Protocols of the Elders of Zion*, complete forgeries, began to make their way across Russia, where they played to existing prejudice and fears.[21]

As anti-Semitism wore new masks, denouncing bigotry in every form became a key facet of V. D. Nabokov's politics, one that his son would embrace with equal fervor as an adult. Nabokov's father particularly despised the government strategy of encouraging prejudice by manipulating uneducated peasants. Yet it was not just government-fostered anti-Semitism that moved him to protest the tsarist regime. He argued vehemently against the death penalty, and, despite his belief that homosexuality was abnormal, he criticized Imperial laws against sodomy.

Nabokov's father had been active in the St. Petersburg congress that demanded a constitution, a legislative body, and permanent civil rights. And he was far from alone—liberal and socialist ideals had been actively pursued during the nineteenth century by whole communities of Russian writers and thinkers, from anarchist pacifists like Leo Tolstoy to radicals more inclined toward violence.

In the face of such activism, repressive laws and calls to patriotism in the midst of the war with Japan did not have the desired effect. Momentum gained from civil rights granted in the nineteenth century could not be indefinitely stalled in the twentieth. As the old year gave way to 1905, strikes erupted across St. Petersburg. Protesters who went to the Winter Palace that January to deliver a petition to the Tsar asking for reforms found cavalry units charging them with swords drawn. When the crowd refused to disperse, the shooting began.

Demonstrators who ran from live bullets were hunted down. People threw themselves off low bridges onto the ice beneath. Looters were corralled breaking windows and taking fruit from the elegant shops on Nevsky Prospect. And just around the corner from the home of five-year-old Vladimir Nabokov, children searching for refuge who had climbed trees in front of St. Isaac's Cathedral were picked off by soldiers.[22]

Members of the Committee of Journalists and Poets—including V. D. Nabokov's friend Joseph Hessen—were thrown into the Peter and Paul Fortress. Newspapers were closed. It was forbidden to gather in public places. City residents were frightened and outraged at the conduct of the troops, who, they noted, apparently found shooting unarmed civilians easier than fighting Japanese sailors.[23]

Nabokov's father immediately condemned the massacre and proposed compensation for the families of the dead. Days later he was stripped of his court title. Suddenly V. D. Nabokov's liberalism was no longer a tolerable eccentricity in a brilliant legal scholar. Even his family judged him: V. D. Nabokov's mother bemoaned her son's susceptibility to "dark forces" that she predicted would doom his career and fortune.[24]

The strikes continued across the year, gathering millions of workers and paralyzing transportation. Military mutinies flared up and were fiercely extinguished. The ranks of the dead swelled from hundreds to thousands. When the Tsar finally acceded to political pressure and allowed the formation of a parliamentary-style Duma with limited powers, the Constitutional Democratic ("Kadet") Party emerged, with V. D. Nabokov elected to membership on its Central Committee. Nabokov's father, descended from men and women who had served the Tsars, was openly advocating sweeping changes to the autocratic system that had ruled Russia for centuries.

5

That winter, Vladimir and Sergei Nabokov started taking French lessons from a hypersensitive Swiss tutor, Mademoiselle Cécile Miauton. If V. D. Nabokov had hoped to insulate his children from the turbulence of government, he could not have done much better than to hire Mademoiselle. She was uninterested in Russian and Russia, and she faced life in a foreign land with exaggerated fortitude and chronic despair. She lived inside a world of literary escapism from daily insults in which the past was a beautifully constructed illusion to which the present could always be compared and found wanting. Nabokov would later devote a whole chapter of *Speak, Memory* to her foibles and melodrama.

Soon after Mademoiselle's arrival, a seven-year-old Volodya found a parallel refuge—not yet in the past, but in the natural world. He became obsessed with butterflies. He learned to chase the rare swallowtails and common pearl-bordered fritillaries at Vyra, and also how to dispatch them with ether, insert a pin through the thorax, and spread their veined wings for display and classification. Specimens accumulated in direct proportion to the instability that kept the children from returning to St. Petersburg.

That same season, elections for the first Duma were held. Revolutionary parties officially boycotted them, allowing the Kadets, in coalition with a peasant labor party, to dominate. An eloquent speech from V. D. Nabokov against the death penalty led to the unanimous passage of a measure outlawing it. Steps were proposed to relieve famine conditions, which had swept the countryside after crop failures during the war. The Kadets led the preparation of a petition demanding the power to select ministers, the surrender of some estates for redistribution, and the release of political prisoners—including those sentenced as terrorists. The deputies believed they had the upper hand—when Nicholas II gave his speech before the Duma, V. D. Nabokov was reported to have been seen "lounging in the front row with his hands in his pockets and openly smirking."[25]

The Duma learned, however, that its demands would not even be considered. They passed a resolution of no confidence in the government. The Tsar's ministers, they insisted, must be answerable to them. The Tsar begged to differ, and dissolved the Duma.

The following day, V. D. Nabokov and nearly two hundred other deputies decamped to Vyborg, across the Finnish border. They signed an appeal calling on the Russian people to refuse to serve in the military or to pay taxes, understanding that a government with a crippled budget and no army would be unable to govern.[26]

It was an act of shocking defiance, born of frustration, yet the Vyborg signers' dramatic stand did nothing but injury to their own cause. Returning to Russia, they lost their political rights. New elections would be held, but the signers, including Nabokov's father, were barred from running for office.

Violence exploded at both ends of the political spectrum. A leading Kadet found himself denounced in an anti-Semitic political cartoon. He had converted to Christianity long ago, but in the eyes of the reactionaries he remained part of the Jewish conspiracy bent on destroying Russia. He was murdered that July. For his troubles, V. D. Nabokov learned that his name was next on the list of the group's targets for assassination. His friends convinced him of the wisdom of traveling abroad.[27]

Strategic violence was also stepped up on the Left. The Socialist Revolutionary Party spawned a terrorist offshoot focused on mass casualties. Holdups and burglaries, along with attacks on landowners and small businesses, became commonplace. The Bolsheviks, too, embraced similar economic opportunities. With an aggressive approach to tactics and organization, Vladimir Lenin had by 1905 become one of a triumvirate of Bolshevik fundraisers. Lenin supervised bank robberies, deployed Bolshevik agents in sham marriages to swindle heiresses, and brought in professional criminals experienced in gunrunning. Among his lieutenants in these efforts was Joseph Stalin.[28]

As parties scrambled to gather funds and followers, elections for a second Duma were held early in 1907. Banned from political life, Nabokov's father could not appear as a candidate; but, writing in the pages of the Kadet Party newspaper, he continued to press for liberalization, staking out a middle path between reactionary extremism and revolution.

Lenin, too, remained outside contention for a Duma seat—he would not put himself in jeopardy by returning to Russia. Denouncing calls for moderation, he issued a pamphlet insulting V. D. Nabokov and his allies by name, declaring war on the Kadets and condemning their peasant allies. He threatened the Socialist Revolutionaries, who were also considering an alliance with the Kadets. He wrote of the "dirty business" that would lead anyone, after the sacrifices of Bloody Sunday, to help elect V. D. Nabokov's party to the Duma. Lenin acknowledged his cause might be betrayed by his partners in revolution, but he claimed to understand exactly what he was up against. And, he noted, "He who laughs last laughs best."[29]

Lenin's pamphlet was seized, and many copies of it destroyed, but history was already tilting his way. The Kadets lost ground in the elections, and the makeup of the Second Duma became far more radical than the first. After four months, the Tsar dissolved it, too.

The defiant members of the First Duma had likewise not been forgotten by Nicholas II. Former deputies who had signed the Vyborg Manifesto, including Nabokov's father, were put on trial later that year and convicted of advocating the overthrow of the government. V. D. Nabokov was sentenced to three months in solitary confinement.[30]

After a failed appeal, he headed just a few minutes up the Neva River from his home to serve his time in Kresty Prison. While there, he wrote reassuring notes on toilet paper to his wife Elena, produced several legal articles, and studied Italian before tackling Dante. It was hardly the worst of prison conditions—he brought his collapsible bathtub along with him. But downplaying every aspect of incarceration, he was keen to demonstrate that his sentence was merely an inconvenience.[31]

By the time of V. D. Nabokov's incarceration, a shared passion for butterflies marked his close relations with his son. He had already given his first-born a treasured catch from his own childhood; in return, Vladimir sent a butterfly to his father in prison.[32]

When Nabokov's father was released, he rode to see his children in the country, making his way from the railroad station to a welcome party in the neighboring village on his way home. V. D. Nabokov's mother had forbidden residents of her own land from celebrating his release from jail, but the local schoolteacher near Vyra had planned festivities, with decorations of red bunting, blue cornflowers, and pine boughs.[33]

In a twelve-month period, V. D. Nabokov had been denounced by Vladimir Lenin and convicted by the courts his father had supervised as Minister of Justice. His own mother had disavowed his politics. As he headed toward his country house, the carriage rolled past the river and the trees and the church and the mausoleum, the new schoolhouse and the old cabins. Volodya waited in the village to welcome his father home.

By the time of V. D. Nabokov's return, the boy was infatuated with books and butterflies, he adored his parents, and no one but the very old had ever died. He had already escaped political upheaval once, and the concepts that would become recurring themes in his work—flight, revolution, political tyranny, anti-Semitism, and imprisonment—had crept into the margins of his life before his tenth birthday.

6

The constants of Nabokov's early years were his tender exchanges with his parents and the compulsory companionship of Sergei and his governesses. As he grew older, however, other characters moved center stage.

Elena Nabokov's brother, Uncle Ruka, adored the young Volodya and made much of him. Nabokov remembered for decades the attention paid to him by his uncle, who took him on his knee and, with special names and sweet words, fondled him. *Fondle* is Nabokov's word, and his account of their interactions was so nuanced as to leave events entirely unclear, while still striking an insistent note of unease.[34]

With five languages and pride in his cryptography, Uncle Ruka had a career in some type of diplomacy. He wore opera capes and furs, rode to hounds, and composed romantic music. He survived at least one airplane crash. Though it was Sergei who learned his uncle's best composition by heart, Ruka was drawn to Vladimir.

Nabokov's father was willing to leave his son with Ruka, at least in the company of others; yet he was short with his brother-in-law and would rebuke him (as he would later rebuke Nabokov) for rudeness to servants. He watched disapprovingly when Ruka turned melodramatic, lying down on the floor in the middle of dinner and claiming an incurable heart ailment.

V. D. Nabokov did not lie down on the floor in the middle of dinner. Nabokov's father was a liberal, but he was also a man with a traditional sense of honor. He had criticized in print the archaic custom of dueling; but when a newspaper story suggested he had married his wife to obtain her fortune, he demanded that the editor of the paper distance himself from the story with a retraction or be called out to fight.[35]

If a gallery of role models existed, V. D. Nabokov represented the heroic father, a Russian man motivated by honor and duty to serve his country. Uncle Ruka appeared to be something else—melancholy, homosexual, with artistic inclinations. As odd as his uncle was, Nabokov would long be troubled by the condescension Ruka endured even from those who liked him. As if in response, Nabokov would later build character after unsettling character who is mocked and misunderstood but who has his own secret life in tow.[36]

In addition to an object lesson in empathy—or at least pity— Nabokov's family would also provide him with his closest child-hood friend, Baron Yuri Rausch von Traubenberg. The son of V. D. Nabokov's sister, Yuri was a year and a half older at an age when these things mattered, and he made for a much more adventurous playmate than the younger Sergei.

Above all, Nabokov admired his cousin's preternatural fearless-ness. Yuri was as enamored with guns as the prepubescent Nabokov was with butterflies. When they were together, the older boy's inter-ests dominated; they read and re-enacted Western novels, shooting at each other in an ascending calculus of weaponry, from toy pistols to dart guns and air guns, eventually progressing to nerve-rattling feats with a real revolver. Not long after their last, lethal toy was confiscated, Yuri would be old enough to begin training for real war.

Nabokov did not see Yuri often, and so occupied himself with his own interests. He wept over butterflies he failed to catch. He aban-doned playmates less exciting than Yuri for his own solitary pursuits. But not all his time was spent playing; governesses overlapped and were followed by tutors, in whose company Nabokov studied at home until the age of twelve.

The tutors, he later noted, exposed him to almost every kind of Russian character at one point or another, as if his father had designed a roster of the cultural and religious cross-currents of the Empire. The village schoolmaster, an anti-war revolutionary who taught him at Vyra, was succeeded by the son of an Orthodox carpenter. A Ukrainian mathematician was followed by a Latvian, who was replaced in turn by a Catholic Pole and a Lutheran of Jewish descent.

This panoply of diversity was not admired by everyone in the household. Nabokov's aunts were prone to carrying on in the same vein as his grandmother, discussing the Jewish origins of the boys' latest tutor, Filip Zelenski, and visibly unnerving their guest when Nabokov's parents were not around. If Nabokov was then too young to understand the ramifications of the cultural and political divides within the walls of his own home, Zelenski became the first outsider the young Nabokov allied himself with as a human being, the first person he realized needed protection, the first person he would, even as a child, want to defend.[37]

Yet protectiveness toward Zelenski did not prevent the development of the adversarial relations Nabokov seemed to enjoy creating with every tutor—and some family members. Relatives, for better or worse, were not dispensable—but in the case of the tutors, he tracked the speed at which he could wear them out and drive them away.

As his tutors' primacy gave way to institutional education, however, Volodya may have waxed nostalgic for the liberty of their care. In 1911, his parents enrolled him at the Tenishev School, known for its progressive spirit and democratic makeup. Future literary giant Osip Mandelstam also hailed from Tenishev, though Nabokov would later remember it as a typical school, distinguished mainly by its lack of discrimination in accepting students of different classes, races, and beliefs.[38]

Nabokov was a brilliant student and, although thin, a confident athlete. School nonetheless opened up a new, discouraging universe. For the first time, he was forced into ongoing proximity with people unrelated to him by blood or friendship. He did not want to use the filthy hand towels in the bathroom, and his first overnight school field trip—a three-day excursion to Finland—was a singularly unpleasant experience. Not only did he feel that the teachers found his interest in butterflies eccentric, Nabokov later recalled it as the first time he had gone twenty-four hours without a bath.[39]

Vladimir Nabokov was vaguely dissatisfied with Tenishev, and he sensed that his teachers were likewise unhappy with him. Tenishev was devoted to producing active, educated citizens of a future Russian democracy; and as the first-born son of V. D. Nabokov, Nabokov felt himself hectored on this point by his instructors—even those who were normally kind. Nabokov helped edit the school's literary journal, but why would he not join a debating society? Why would the son of V. D. Nabokov not walk the last blocks to school, instead of rubbing the other students' noses in the chauffeur he commanded? Vladimir felt that even his position as goalkeeper in Tenishev soccer games was suspect, seen as a desire not to run and mingle with normal boys.[40]

If Vladimir perplexed his Tenishev teachers, Sergei, who seemed to trail adolescent drama in his wake, unsettled them more profoundly. Vladimir may already have been aware of the nature of these dramas; but if not, he soon would be: snooping in his brother's diary as a teenager, he found passages that clarified Sergei's homosexuality. Startled by what he had found, Vladimir gave the diary to his tutor, who gave it to the Nabokovs; and so one brother outed the other to their parents. Sergei would have several distressing romances with boys at Tenishev before being transferred to another school.[41]

Vladimir stayed on, still feeling pressured to conform to the Tenishev way. The anxiety, however, may have been more his than theirs—his schoolmaster described him in records as morally decent, modest, and respected by all. But in Nabokov's young mind, being the son of V. D. Nabokov might have been enough to create its own unreachable standards.[42]

Nabokov continued to resist engagement in any activities promoting social change or democracy. He did not attend meetings, historical groups, or political discussions—any of the things that might make him a leader, or at least a productive member, of a hazily imagined (but still somehow substantial, real, and perhaps just around the corner) democratic Russia. Despite the marvelous example provided by his father, he was not a joiner.

At that moment in time, joining was thought to be the only hope for Russia. The sweep of history was away from kings and emperors, and it was understood that something different would emerge within years rather than centuries. But how to get from Tsarist Russia in 1911 to some post-Imperial state had become a burning question. The change that had once seemed almost in the grasp of the politically active opposition had retreated as they approached it.

Meanwhile, Nabokov did not know how to explain to his teachers his growing awareness that shaping his ideas in concert with others not only went against the free spirit of his own curiosity, but that engagement had real risks. His father's meetings, held so often in the security of his own home, did not just offer the rhetoric of point and counterpoint. Meeting nights, Nabokov would hear the pencil sharpener grinding in anticipation of the note-taking; he would see the coats and overshoes shed by their visitors. The meeting could have been any one of his father's interests, from criminology to philanthropy, except, of course, that one kind of meeting was actually completely different from the others—not that a child could tell the difference. Some meetings could lead to arrest and prison. Some activities could lead servants to betray their masters—as the Nabokovs were eventually betrayed by their servant Ustin, who would in time escort the Bolsheviks to the Nabokovs' wall safe filled with jewels. The price of political involvement was that a spy for the Tsar's secret police could be discovered hiding in the private closets and back rooms of one's childhood home, hoping to eavesdrop on anti-government plots that could lead to arrests, begging on his knees for the librarian to keep silent when she found him. The price of engagement was that enemies might be anywhere. Even home was not secure, and those ostensibly charged with protection were the ones just waiting to denounce.[43]

As Nabokov attended his classes at Tenishev and started down a long road of resisting political activism, other Russians got involved, but did so cautiously. Banned parties continued to meet furtively, producing vast archives of pamphlets and newspapers. Socialist parties had been forced underground; major unions had been outlawed. The Socialist Revolutionaries' terrorist wing collapsed. Lenin and the Bolsheviks continued to squabble with Leon Trotsky's Mensheviks, holding competing party conferences and jockeying for control of Marxism in the East. Russia settled into an ongoing state of suppressed instability.[44]

Six years on from what had seemed like a Revolution, joining together had only accomplished so much. The Kadets' idealism began to falter amid the polarization of extremes, in which there appeared to be no room for politics like V. D. Nabokov's. The Kadets continued to modify their platform in an attempt to expand support, but their effort to develop a broader coalition left them hamstrung. Their support of women's suffrage riled the Tatar Muslims; their frank defense of Jews and other minorities alienated many on the right.[45]

Yet when the accusation of blood libel reared its head again, V. D. Nabokov would not give ground on anti-Semitism. The brutal murder of a thirteen-year-old boy in southwestern Russia led to the arrest of Mendel Beilis, a thirty-seven-year-old Jewish man. Beilis sat in jail for more than two years before being brought to trial, accused of ritually murdering a Christian boy to use his blood for religious purposes. Nabokov's father reported on the case, sending telegrams from Kiev to St. Petersburg to update his accounts of the proceedings. His reporting on the dubious arguments and evidence of the trial was picked up by the *Manchester Guardian* and *The New York Times*, and drew a fine from the government.[46]

The disgust with anti-Semitism that would later make its way into Vladimir Nabokov's work had its seeds in his father's own writing on the issue. V. D. Nabokov described the wonder of finding a nearly illiterate jury in an educated city (the pool would later turn out to have been rigged far in advance), of the simultaneous accusations against Beilis and indictment of an entire religion, of the legal violations of the trial, these "ravings . . . from anti-Semitic literature of the lowest kind," cloaked in the guise of scientific authority and admitted as evidence. Indicating the deterioration of justice in Russia, he wrote that staging the Beilis trial even a decade earlier "would have been impossible."[47]

Workers struck and took up fund drives in Beilis's support. But prosecutors played on the fear and prejudice of the jurors. A priest was brought in to describe Jewish practices, which he claimed required Christian blood for such a wide variety of purposes that a correspondent for the *Times of London* wondered mockingly how Jews had managed to find enough Christians to go around. American George Kennan (whose nephew of the same name would one day hail Solzhenitsyn's arrival in the West) observed the Duma seriously debating the existence of a Jewish sect that ritually murdered Christians for religious purposes. The arguments were ominous; one deputy warned that if Russian liberals made it impossible for a Jew who murdered a Christian child to be tried, there would be no Jews left to save, because they would all be slaughtered by mobs.[48]

Outside Russia, Western public reaction formed a tidal wave of revulsion. But from certain corners, a more qualified disapproval appeared. One trial chronicler would later note that in between the groups clearly supporting Beilis's prosecution and those who anguished over a Russia trapped in the Middle Ages lay a third, slippery faction. To that faction belonged many normally reasonable people, who warned Russia's Jews against pursuing "their vendetta with Russia"—at a time when all the vengeance seemed to be running the other way. Advising against public protests, *The Oxford and Cambridge Review* suggested that while Judaism as a whole, even Orthodox Judaism, should not be held liable for the crimes laid at Beilis's feet, it was entirely possible that some Jewish sect somewhere *might* be committing ritual murder.[49]

Despite the unwillingness of some observers to condemn prosecutors, the mythical horror story that they had fabricated was so ludicrous it could not be kept aloft. Many of the best lawyers in the country joined Beilis's defense team, and they discredited lie after lie. After approximately two hours of deliberation, a jury of Russian Christians rendered a verdict of not guilty and freed Beilis.[50]

In 1903, Russia had shocked the world with the pogroms unleashed in Kishinev, followed by a disastrous war that strained patriotism and national unity. A decade later, as teachers prompted the teenage Nabokov to engage politically for the future of his country, the spiral of history wound its way full circle. The Beilis trial revisited the slur of blood libel, and one year later, the same incompetent government found itself again facing the threat of war.

The challenges of this new war would again eclipse the abilities of the Tsar. This time, however, Nicholas would have company: much of the known world would descend into madness with Russia. In the wake of the Beilis trial, one Russian newspaper commentator identified Jews as "an exclusively criminal species," which led him to pray, "May Russia be saved from Jewish equality even more than from fire, sword, or open invasion by enemies."[51] As it turned out, he would have his wish, and its fulfillment would mark the beginning of the end of Nabokov's childhood.

CHAPTER THREE

War

1

In the summer of 1914, the world went to war, and Vladimir Nabokov became a poet. He had already been composing verse for years, but in the season of the assassination of Archduke Franz Ferdinand, a fever took hold of him that never left. The metamorphosis would be linked later in his mind with a pavilion that sat over a small bridge on the family's summer estate, its jewel-colored glass with some panes shattered and "Down with Austria!" graffiti providing a premonition of everything that would follow.[1]

In truth, however, the fifteen-year-old Nabokov was cocooned enough from the currents of history that he was spared much of the reality of the First World War. The six years that elapsed between the births of Wilfred Owen, the British martyr poet of the war, and Vladimir Nabokov set a generation gap between their respective fates. In a few short years, Nabokov would turn his literary attention to those whose lives had been shattered by conflict, but he would never become a war writer.

Instead, he wrote Romantic poetry, caught up for the first time in creation and inspiration that threatened to slip away but could sometimes be recovered. He would remember fashioning and refashioning his first *real* poem in his mind, waiting until it was polished and ready before reciting it to his mother, who, as he hoped (and expected), wept at the performance.

Cousin Yuri visited that June, and reported that he had, at sixteen, taken up with a married countess and a general's wife. The following summer, Nabokov found his own romance in the countryside with Lyussya Shulgin, a fifteen-year-old Petrograd girl staying for the summer at a dacha in the village. They met alone in the pavilion with the panes of colored glass, and Nabokov spent August 1915 in a state of rapture, escaping for trysts, eating the fruit his mother had a servant leave out for his late-night returns. His mother copied the love poems he recited to her into a special album but, perhaps fearing to break his illusion or hers, asked no other questions. His father, more practical or more suspicious, subjected his teenage son to pesky interrogations aimed at preventing premature fatherhood.[2]

While the composition of romantic verse and the passion of first love occupied Nabokov, Europe had exploded. As country after country entered the war, V. D. Nabokov was mobilized with an infantry regiment. Elena Nabokov organized a private hospital for soldiers, where she volunteered, but she found the services she offered bitterly insufficient for the needs of the wounded veterans she encountered. Furthermore, she felt that her efforts failed in the breach: her kindnesses could not bridge the deep-rooted subservience of the injured peasants she had hoped to help.[3]

At the start of hostilities Russia had initially responded with the kind of patriotism Nicholas II had been dreaming of for decades. St. Petersburg was renamed Petrograd, in order to seem less German. V. D. Nabokov suspended his political activities in light of the conflict.

Across Europe, paranoia set in. The British Parliament discussed completely impossible numbers of German spy networks and saboteurs. The Germans feared that fellow countrymen deported by Russia were engaged in espionage against their homeland. Across the continent, these suspicions provided the impetus to import concentration camps from far-flung colonies into Europe itself. Facilities were constructed from London to Petrograd and built even more widely abroad, from Canada to Australia.

Hundreds of thousands of innocent civilians—both men and women—were labeled as "enemy aliens" and subject to arrest and internment. A year into the war, Britain had locked up more than 32,000 German, Hungarian, and Austrian civilians of military age. German facilities housed more than 100,000 French, British, and Russian prisoners. And in Russia, more than 300,000 civilians from Germany and other Central Power nations were placed into camps by 1917. Civilians were also held in prisons or concentration camps in France, the United States, Austria, Hungary, Romania, Egypt, Togoland, the Cameroons, Singapore, India, Palestine, the Habsburg lands, Bulgaria, Siam, Brazil, Panama, Haiti, Hong Kong, Australia, New Zealand, and elsewhere. From the handful of camps that had existed in Cuba before Nabokov's birth, concentration camps had expanded to circle the globe.[4]

The initial strategy for these camps was that detainees would be arrested, then investigated, with the clearly innocent being freed. And occasional waves of releases did happen, but continuous or widespread exonerations did not take place as planned. Many cross-border families had no idea where their relations were and so could not contact them. In some countries, civilian prisoners—many of whom were loyal to the countries that had imprisoned them—languished near starvation for years.[5]

When it came to selecting internees, being of military age and a subject or citizen of an enemy country were the most common determinants, but criteria for arrest could be arbitrary and inconsistent. If, instead of a German mother and a Russian father, V. D. Nabokov had been born to a Russian mother and German father, he himself might have been a candidate for a concentration camp.[6]

The camps of the Great War provided a stepping-stone to darker incarnations that would directly impact the Nabokov family, yet the concept of prison camp itself was not new to Russia. The country had a long history of punitive measures against political activists, and Siberian exile and hard labor had been regular tools of Imperial justice for centuries. But the phenomenon of the concentration camp—in which people were arrested and imprisoned for years without trial, without rights of correspondence, and often without judicial review of any kind, simply on the basis that they *might* represent a threat—was new.[7]

Absorbed in his first love and protected from the war by his parents, Nabokov nonetheless noticed the arrival of Russia's first concentration camps. He would later make use of one in a novel, but even then, his attention to history would largely be in vain. His narrator's past would remain an enigma to readers because less than two decades after their creation, the camps from the First World War would be as good as forgotten.

2

Nabokov's affair with Lyussya survived the bitter winter of 1915–16 in Petrograd, sustained by furtive meetings in which the lovers had little privacy. He continued composing poetry in tribute to their passion, and in the spring she cheered him on at a soccer match. The following summer, romance returned when they met again in the more idyllic, more permissive countryside.

Nabokov immortalized his first love by publishing a collection of his own poems about her. Printed in the second year of the war, the book was a fearless stab at establishing an identity in the world. It was also a vanity project. Many teenagers might have fantasized about becoming the next Alexander Pushkin, but few had the wherewithal to pay a publisher to further the dream.

At Tenishev, such presumption may have seemed less than democratic. In what can only have been a nightmare for even the most self-assured child, Nabokov's literature professor, Vladimir Hippius (a poet himself), obtained a copy of the book and brought it in to mock the most intimate lines out loud in front of Vladimir and his classmates. Nabokov would later recall the book being savaged in the minor press. In case the reviews had not provided a clear response to V. D. Nabokov, his friend Joseph Hessen expressed his dismay over the book. Hippius's cousin, a poet of some distinction, told Nabokov's father that Vladimir would under no circumstances make it as a writer.[8]

During that summer at Vyra, Nabokov saw not only Lyussya but also Yuri, who took leave from officer training school to spend a week with his cousin. The teenagers improvised a game with a rope swing in the garden. Each taking turns standing on a board that, at its lowest point, passed just barely above where the other one lay on the ground, they learned not to move as the swing moved at greater speeds from higher distances, despite every indication of disaster.[9]

They went for their usual stroll in the village. On a lark this time, the young men exchanged clothes before setting out, Yuri wearing white flannels and a striped tie, and Vladimir buttoned into his cousin's military uniform, with its dark pants, gray jacket, and white leather belt. They went to the village and came back, then traded clothes again, the boy poet and boy soldier, protected offspring of one of the most cosmopolitan cultures in the world, each seeking his own inimitable destiny and dreaming of different kinds of glory.

3

As the war entered its third year, Uncle Ruka died in Paris. With him went his declarations of heart trouble (which proved to be prescient), as well as his foppish canes, his stutter, his high-heeled shoes, his father's legendary cruelty to him, and his attention to his nephew Vladimir. The young Nabokov inherited Ruka's two-thousand-acre country house at Rozhdestveno, along with a fortune that made him a millionaire. The inheritance had long been planned, with other properties from Elena's side of the family slated for Sergei and Olga, but V. D. Nabokov was less than pleased about his brash son's new, independent wealth.[10]

In clear contravention of the rules of romance, by the time Nabokov got the money, he had lost the girl. The end of summer had already begun to seal a distance between Nabokov and Lyussya. He would not remember their final encounter that season at Vyra, but it seems likely that they were dogged by their different, irreconcilable futures. Lyussya had promised her mother she would look for a job that fall; Vladimir returned to Tenishev. The marriage he had promised, which she seemed to have believed in far less than he did, never materialized. He would move on to a series of affairs, from one-night stands to more earnest associations, the two sometimes overlapping.[11]

In the meantime, life for many Russians was on a downward trajectory as steep as Nabokov's enchanted ascent. Fielding the biggest army in the war, with more than twelve million soldiers mobilized, Russia paid a proportionate price. In all, the war would take nearly two million Russian lives, a total only Germany would surpass. With such staggering losses, the reflexive patriotism from the war's early months had faded.

By the end of 1916, political discontent was still fragmented but rising dramatically. As the New Year rolled in, strikes erupted continuously. In mid-February, female textile workers in Petrograd protested war shortages and called for increased bread rations. Munitions factory workers reprised the role they had played in 1905 and joined the demonstrations. When the police failed to re-establish order, guards regiments were called out, to no avail. Soldiers who initially followed orders to fire on demonstrators began to mutiny.

Protesters took over Nevsky Prospect. A dozen years after Trotsky had been arrested as leader of the St. Petersburg Soviet, the Mensheviks resurrected the banned organization and began to advocate for a republic.[12]

If the war had been happening somewhere off-stage for Vladimir Nabokov, the Revolution would take place at closer range. Children had been shot from the trees in front of St. Isaac's in 1905, but by

March 1917, grown men had taken their place, and they were ready to shed more blood on St. Isaac's Square for the prize that had been lost a dozen years before.

Nabokov's neighborhood—which included the cathedral, the War Office, the Admiralty Building, and the Military Hotel—was the last holdout against revolutionary forces. Besieged officials sent frenzied dispatches to the front, seeking some kind of military support greater than the last regiments still loyal to the Tsar packed around St. Issac's.

No help, however, was forthcoming. Gun battles raged on Bolshaya Morskaya. Russian officers were herded in front of St. Isaac's Cathedral and executed, and a red flag was hung from the pole outside the Admiralty. In the street shootings and violence that erupted and subsided in that year of Revolution, Nabokov sat suspended over Morskaya Street, looking from his mother's bay window at two soldiers trying to bear away a man on a stretcher at a run while they kept an interloper from stealing the dead man's boots. Russia was in her third year of war, but he would remember it as the first corpse he had seen.[13]

In time that war, along with its food shortages and repressions, triggered what had been avoided more than a decade before. As Petrograd rose in revolt, the Tsar was away, but it became clear that his reign was over. Nicholas II, Emperor and Autocrat of All the Russias, abdicated in favor of his son, then reversed himself to turn the throne over to his brother, the Grand Duke Mikhail.[14]

But Mikhail refused the Imperial crown. V. D. Nabokov, whose legal brilliance was undisputed, helped to draft an abdication letter vesting power in a provisional body until elections could be held. On March 16, 1917, more than two centuries of Romanov rule ended.

The Petrograd Soviet began issuing orders, while opposition parties set about negotiating a Provisional Government. In the immediate aftermath of the Revolution, Joseph Stalin came back to Petrograd from Arctic exile—his seventh. Taking over *Pravda*, he offered conditional support to Russia's transitional leadership.[15]

In Zurich, Lenin had heard news of the Revolution and at first refused to believe it was true. He had spent almost no time in Russia since the end of his Siberian exile, but hoped to return immediately. Sending telegrams ahead, he insisted that no accommodation be made by revolutionaries—under no circumstances should they support any decision to continue the war.

But the war, in that moment, possessed an undeniable reality that blocked Lenin's ambition. To get back to Russia, he would have to cross territory in which he would be an enemy alien, subject to arrest and detention in a concentration camp. His brief taste of internment in 1914 did not make him anxious to revisit it. He proposed to make himself part of a prisoner exchange, in which the Provisional Government would request safe passage for him and release German nationals held in Russia in exchange. Yet V. D. Nabokov's friend, Minister of Foreign Affairs Paul Milyukov, refused to call for Lenin's return.[16]

Lenin reached out through other channels and found that the Germans (no doubt imagining the effect that Lenin would have on the collapsing Empire) would be delighted to guarantee him and other political émigrés safe passage. So Lenin, who would otherwise have been put in a camp on German territory, was permitted to pass through undisturbed, reading newspapers to catch up on all he had missed. The Provisional Government, with V. D. Nabokov as its executive secretary, was sure that he would be discredited as a German agent, and made no move to bar his return.[17]

As his train pulled into Petrograd's Finland Station, Lenin was met on the platform by thousands of cheering revolutionaries. He was furious with his own party. He was first greeted by an honor guard of sailors, who expected congratulations. Instead, he told them they had been duped. Heading along the platform through the station to the street, he gave the cold shoulder to a fellow socialist who pleaded for cooperation. Leaving the station, he climbed on top of an armored car and announced to the crowd that the first thing to do was to cut off all support for the Provisional Government.

After more than a decade in opposing camps, Lenin and V. D. Nabokov were no closer to agreement. But the Tsars had been consigned to history, and the future of Russia lay completely open.

4

As the clouds of Russia's post-Revolutionary destiny began to gather in Petrograd, Leon Trotsky was delayed in North America. At the moment the Romanovs abdicated, he was in New York City working as a journalist. Trotsky immediately made plans to return home, booking passage on a ship that left New York Harbor less than two weeks later.

The ship pulled out on schedule but was stopped at Nova Scotia, Canada, where Trotsky, his wife, and his sons were arrested. Trotsky and other male revolutionaries were taken from the ship to nearby Amherst, where they were put into a concentration camp run by a British colonel, a veteran of the Boer War. "So much for British democracy," Trotsky wrote.[18]

He found himself sleeping behind barbed wire in an old barracks of a foundry alongside more than eight hundred captured German sailors and a group of civilians held as enemy aliens. He protested his internment bitterly. What charges were there against him? He was a civilian and *not* an enemy alien; he had committed no crime. He attempted to send telegrams to the Provisional Government through the Russian consul at Montreal; he wrote to the British Prime Minister—to no avail. Russian foreign minister Paul Milyukov initially requested his release, but then thought better of it, and two days later rescinded the request.[19]

Word leaked of Trotsky's detention, and international calls were made for his release. News of the arrest became public in Petrograd, where the British ambassador proclaimed Trotsky a paid agent of Germany. The Provisional Government was faced with a dilemma: knowing as they did that Trotsky had already denounced the fragile government and would seek to destroy it, should they call for his release and meet the demands of their more radical allies?

War raged on, and the Provisional Government was planning for Russia to stay in the fight. Trotsky would certainly try to undermine that plan, and would present a formidable threat. But public pressure for his release was too strong. A month after he had left New York Harbor, Trotsky was freed. By May he was back in Petrograd.

He would take the time in his first days back to write a pamphlet about his weeks inside a *kontslager* (*Konzentrationslager*, concentration camp) and like Vladimir Nabokov, would not forget the camps of the First World War. Trotsky, however, would make use of his recollections much sooner, and in an infinitely more direct manner.[20]

Crisis after crisis followed. The Provisional Government did not have a strong base of support from rank-and-file soldiers, but nonetheless recommitted to war. Many Russians, however, had dreamed of not just freedom from the Tsar but freedom from combat; the government lost supporters by supporting an inherently unpopular conflict.

Stalemates followed, making it impossible to govern. The Kadets, including V. D. Nabokov, left the government in a dramatic July resignation. A Bolshevik uprising followed immediately and was put down at the last minute only by the arrival of a cavalry unit loyal to the Provisional Government. There was talk of arresting Lenin. Trotsky *was* arrested and taken to Kresty Prison, which had housed V. D. Nabokov years before. But a deliberate choice was made, as Nabokov's father phrased it, not "to eliminate Lenin and Co."[21]

Instead, the uprising resulted in concessions to socialists and the installation of a new prime minister, Alexander Kerensky. Short-haired, shortsighted, and quick to passion, Kerensky was caught between dramatic public posturing and halting efforts to forge a faith in the government that might ensure its survival until the elections that fall.

From the beginning, Nabokov's father had little hope that the Provisional Government could succeed—and as small as it started out, that hope continued to diminish. The government was assailed on a daily basis by those who saw it as incompetent and sinister, or simply viewed its search for stability as a naïve investment in the status quo.

The outlook for democracy in Russia had turned so grim that fall that V. D. Nabokov wavered in his lifelong fight against capital punishment, supporting the imposition of the death penalty in an army he felt had been infected by revolutionary agitators. That September, he found himself listening in amazement to stories of a furious argument erupting among leaders over whether the old Imperial eagle buttons on formal chamber attire should be banned. The Tsars had failed Russia; now the Provisional Government was failing her, too. National elections were delayed again but scheduled for November.[22]

Vladimir Nabokov turned eighteen that year at the center of an empire in the process of imploding. Amid the destruction, Russia's future was taking shape, and a new kind of concentration camp was just a year away.

Yet Nabokov's world still intersected only tangentially with the political upheaval around him. His refusal to engage, he would later recall, led to his being denounced as a foreigner by his Tenishev teachers and classmates. Otherwise, his life was taken up with mundane events. In May, he was operated on for appendicitis in Petrograd; in the summer, he went, as usual, away to Vyra. Day after day, he wrote new poems. He returned to Petrograd with a school friend; he wrote tributes to a new love, a sophisticated older Jewish girl whom he had met in Finland.[23]

If those more politically minded than the young Nabokov were holding their collective breath to see what the elections would bring, history and the Bolsheviks would not wait that long. Faith in the Provisional Government continued to decline, and the first week of November, Bolshevik forces captured strategic points in the city and launched another attempt to seize power. The following morning, Kerensky—who had pledged to have loyal forces that could put down just such an uprising—was revealed to have no support at all.

V. D. Nabokov went to the Winter Palace to see what the government would do in response. On discovering that they would do nothing, he left. Minutes later, Bolshevik forces streamed in, sealed the Palace, and dissolved the Council, taking its members to the Peter and Paul Fortress. There was, in that moment, no grand battle for control of the city or Russia. No defiant stands were made in the name of the government or its leader. Alexander Kerensky was seen in an open car and said to be fleeing south out of Petrograd. The Bolsheviks had seized power.

Nabokov's father remained in place as the head of the electoral commission, refusing to acknowledge Bolshevik rule and investing whatever hope he had left in the will of the voters. The elections, for which so many people had hoped for so long, could not be so easily crushed.

Looting and commandeering of property across Russia continued. While Nabokov wrote at night, he heard machine-gun fire in the streets. One afternoon during the unrest, armed street fighters charged through the ground-floor window of the library into the Nabokov family home, believing that Vladimir, who was assaulting only his father's punching bag, had been taking potshots at them. A servant dissuaded them from seeking retribution for the ghost insult, and for the first time in his life, Nabokov eluded imminent danger.[24]

Nabokov finished school, taking his exams weeks early. The family had planned for Vladimir and Sergei to enroll in English universities, but not for several months. In the meantime, the boys could not stay in Petrograd and avoid the consequences of the Revolution forever. It was understood that a call would soon go out for Red Army conscripts, and those who were unwilling to serve would find themselves unable to refuse.[25]

Ten days before the election, Vladimir Nabokov and his brother Sergei stood at a Petrograd train station before their father, who made the sign of the cross over each of them and explained that he might never see them again. They left the city on a southbound train that night. Soldiers who had abandoned their posts at the front rode the top of the train, slept in the corridors, and tried to force their way into the boys' locked first-class compartment. Men on the roof relieved themselves down the ventilator shafts of the car, while other soldiers eventually broke in, only to find Sergei giving a dramatic rendition of a patient in the throes of deadly typhus—a deception that served to protect both Nabokov brothers.[26]

The free elections took place as scheduled at the end of November, and thirty-three million voters made their voices heard. It took weeks for the final results to be tallied, but when the numbers came in, the Socialist Revolutionaries had clearly dominated, with their chief rivals, the Bolsheviks, garnering just a quarter of the vote. V. D. Nabokov's party, the Kadets, had lost all but a tiny percentage of support. The results were a rebuke to Bolshevik rule, but the Bolsheviks argued that the election results were meaningless, because all power should go to the revolutionary councils—the soviets—which were, they claimed, the real representatives of the people's will.

The week after the elections, V. D. Nabokov was arrested, along with the other members of the electoral commission. But after five days in jail and repeated attempts to intimidate them, the commissioners were all inexplicably released. V. D. Nabokov realized that staying in the capital would merely return him to prison. His wife and three youngest children had already followed Vladimir and Sergei to the Crimea. The time had come for him to leave Petrograd, too.[27]

The Constituent Assembly, the result of Russia's first national elections, would soon convene for the first time. Though the Kadet Party had been outlawed, there was still the possibility that the entire election would not be in vain. The people, by and large, had rejected both the party of Nabokov's father and the party of Lenin. They had chosen the Socialist Revolutionaries and vested them with the authority to govern. At that point, it was still possible to imagine that elected delegates would somehow find a way to move forward into a post-Imperial Russia.

But on January 18, 1918, the first day the Constituent Assembly convened, the Bolsheviks demanded to be recognized as the majority.

The Assembly refused. The Bolsheviks and a bloc of Socialist Revolutionaries who had allied themselves with the Bolsheviks walked
out. The next day, the entrance to the Tauride Palace was locked,
and the Assembly was not permitted to meet. It was a quiet coda
for Russian democracy.[28]

5

In the far southwestern corner of the former Empire, Kadets and
monarchists lived a half-hidden existence. Tsar Nicholas's mother,
the Dowager Empress, camped out near Yalta discreetly with several
members of her court.

The Crimea was nominally under revolutionary control, and
troops with Bolshevik sympathies were emphasizing how far they
would go to defend the new order against opponents. Tying the
hands and feet of suspected enemies, they took their captives out
on barges and threw them into the Black Sea.[29]

Arriving in this outpost of Imperial Russia, Vladimir and Sergei
found a different world. Nabokov had been at ease on the Riviera,
in St. Petersburg, and among the fields and forests of Vyra, but
now found himself in an alien environment, disoriented by braying
donkeys, Muslim calls to prayer, almond and oleander trees, and
mountains plunging down to the sea. A plaintive letter from Lyussya
made its way south to further establish his exile.

Soon after Vladimir and Sergei's trip south, their mother followed
with Olga, Elena, and six-year-old Kirill—and then came their father
in December. The family settled in for the winter five miles outside
the resort city of Yalta, in a guest house on an estate that Tolstoy had
visited years before. V. D. Nabokov, very much a person of interest
to the Bolsheviks, kept his name but hid his identity, lying low and
pretending to be a lung specialist named Dr. Nabokov.[30]

By June some bodies from the Bolshevik executions had washed
up on shore—but not all of them. The Germans had invaded the
Crimea that spring, and when Kaiser Wilhelm's divers swept the
harbor, reports emerged that the upright corpses of those who had

drowned had been found, still trapped underwater. Nabokov vividly imagined them sunk to the bottom of the sea floor, bones beginning to show through, their arms stretched to the sky, mute but gathered together and seeming to converse. He wrote a poem about the bodies that July, in which he felt himself drawn into that underwater world, floating among the dead of Yalta, who vowed to forget nothing.[31]

The violence of the world had entered Nabokov's writing. During his Crimean stay, he would also make use of seraphim and guardian angels in his work; but in exile from his home city, he could no longer ignore the changes convulsing Russia. He would continue to generate poems reflecting the brutality around him. In response to Russian poet Alexander Blok's revolutionary tribute "The Twelve," which ends with Jesus Christ leading a mob of Bolshevik revolutionaries in Petrograd, Nabokov wrote "The Two," an account of an educated young man and his wife who find themselves brutalized by a mob of twelve peasants and forced to flee into a blizzard, where they die.[32]

The Tsar, his wife, and his children were executed at Yekaterinburg that July. Having definitively eliminated one potential rival, the Bolsheviks nevertheless faced several additional threats. Other Socialists protested Bolshevik dictatorship. A global workers' revolution (anticipated by Lenin to arrive immediately in Europe) failed to materialize. The smooth path to a fully Revolutionary Russia that Lenin had envisioned was just as elusive. An anti-Bolshevik White Army began to rise in the east and the south.

As V. D. Nabokov started working on a memoir of the short-lived Russian Provisional Government, Vladimir and Sergei spent time with new friends at a neighboring villa, adopting an expatriate lifestyle in the far reaches of their homeland. For companions, they had White Army officers on the cusp of battle, along with a famous artist, a ballet *danseur*, and several young women. Generous amounts of local wine conspired to lull the boys into suspended days of beach parties and bonfires. Nabokov wrote poem after poem, imagining a heart true to his memories of Lyussya even as he exploited his opportunities for local romance with guilt and gusto. And somewhere not far enough away, the Allied fight with the Kaiser was picked up, turned inside out, and transformed into a Russian civil war.

It was a war with more than two sides. Shifting allegiances of former Imperial troops, liberals, monarchists, Socialist Revolutionaries of all stripes, and independent Cossack regiments would combine with sporadic deliveries of Allied munitions to take a toll on civilian populations. Anti-Semitic laws had historically constrained most Jews to the Pale of Settlement in the regions of the Ukraine, Lithuania, and Poland. Even though these restrictions had been abolished by the Provisional Government, the front lines of the civil war crossed and recrossed territory that was home to a disproportionately Jewish population.

By this point, Judaism had come so thoroughly to represent the Revolution in the minds of many Russians and Europeans—even those not inclined toward bigotry—it would have been difficult to protect local Jewish communities, which were highly visible and omnipresent. But at least some of those creating propaganda for the Volunteer Army seem to have been largely untroubled by such concerns. Posters depicting the Jewish Trotsky as a hook-nosed subhuman monster supervising the executions of true Russians appeared in the company of White Army slogans like "Strike at the Jews and save Russia!" White Army forces committed hundreds of pogroms during the Russian Civil War.[33] British Minister of Munitions Winston Churchill, warned of the atrocities by Prime Minister Lloyd George, repeatedly told his ostensible allies that their failure to control the anti-Semitic massacres would result in a cutoff of weapons and support.[34]

Ukrainian separatists were similarly brutal. Under the drive for independence led by Simon Petliura, tens of thousands of Jews were massacred. Even the Red Army allies of the Bolsheviks, who publicly embraced Jews and denounced the brutality of White forces, committed more than a hundred pogroms. In the end, despite some innovative efforts at collaborative government and Jewish militias formed for self-defense, an estimated fifty to one hundred thousand Jews were slaughtered in the Ukraine during the Civil War.[35]

The virulence of the identification of Revolution with Jewry in that time and place was such that it found reflection even in the writings of V. D. Nabokov. As he prepared a highly critical but fair account of Kerensky and other actors in the Provisional Government, a strange note sounds again and again in his story. "Jewish-looking young men" bar the doors to the Duma building after the Revolution. For no apparent reason, he notes that there were so many Jews on Russia's Council of Elders in 1917 that it could "have been called the Sanhedrin." Jews are singled out for their secretive or "servile" behavior—writing documents behind V. D. Nabokov's back or hiding a Jewish identity behind a more elegant adopted name. In another aside, V. D. Nabokov describes the "impudent Jewish face" belonging to "the repulsive figure" of a Bolshevik revolutionary.[36]

V. D. Nabokov had Jewish men among his closest friends. He had risked his career defying official anti-Semitism, and had dedicated himself to covering the injustice of the Beilis trial. But the climate of Russian anti-Semitism was such that even he could not entirely refrain from saddling Jews with ugly clichés, on some level holding his enemies responsible, not just as Bolsheviks but as Jews, for the bitter reality of the Revolution.[37]

One of Nabokov's closest companions at Tenishev School, Samuil Rosov, was Jewish. Rosov would later recall his friend's indifference to race and creed. In 1919, however, the general sense of opposition between those seen as true Russians and Jews had infected every level of the debate about the Revolution. The young Nabokov would soon find himself affiliated with a wave of Russian émigrés which was seen—often correctly so—as hateful and bigoted.

6

While pogroms flared in the Ukraine, a new kind of cruelty simultaneously took root in Russia. Trotsky's 1917 internment in a concentration camp had left him with a "burning hatred of the English," but his loathing did not keep him from adopting their measures. In his third month commanding Red Army forces, Trotsky called for a contingent of problematic prisoners of war to be put in a concentration camp.[38]

Those prisoners were the sort of people who had been put in camps by England, Germany, and Russia since 1914. But just days later, Trotsky wrote a memo in which he theorized that the bourgeoisie, too, might be placed in similar concentration camps, doing "menial work (cleaning barracks, camps, streets, digging trenches, etc.)." The kinds of projects recommended were similar to those that prisoners in Canadian camps had been required to do—tasks that the Central Powers and Allies alike had demanded of their civilian and military prisoners. Trotsky himself elsewhere recalled his stint in Amherst "sweeping floors, peeling potatoes, washing crockery, and cleaning the common lavatory."[39]

Lenin likewise turned his attention to concentration camps as a revolutionary tool later that summer. In a telegram sent to the site of an anti-Bolshevik uprising, he called for mass terror against his opponents and for suspect individuals to be "locked up in a concentration camp outside town."[40]

After Russia's exit from the war, many prisoners of war and enemy aliens were in the process of being released. The concentration camp facilities, with their communal living, their extrajudicial status, and their history of forced labor, were handed over to the new secret police, the Cheka, which had been actively assigned the task of sowing terror across the country.[41]

Brutal measures were already under way but had proved insufficient to quell the unrest. Lenin unleashed the first of several waves of strategically applied Red Terror that fall. Widespread executions and detentions in concentration camps, known as "special camps," quickly took on a key role.

When camps had been in the colonies of imperial powers, the native populations of those outposts had been the target populations. When camps had come to the heart of Europe, with few exceptions, foreign civilians and prisoners of war served as inmates. Now, Russia had opened a new chapter in concentration camp history—the government in power's own citizens had become the target population that had to be preemptively incarcerated.[42]

As an adult, Nabokov would refer to the "regime of bloodshed, concentration camps, and hostages" that followed on the heels of the Bolshevik takeover. He would consistently lay responsibility for the first post-Revolutionary camps at the feet of Lenin, and in one form or another they would haunt his writing for the next five decades.[43]

7

In the small window of time before the Civil War consumed Russia, and before the Bolsheviks repurposed Russia's system of wartime camps, Vladimir Nabokov took to the hills above the Black Sea to catch butterflies. As he walked between the bushes looking for prize specimens, a Bolshevik sentry suspected that his purported hunt for beauty masked some political purpose—surely he was signaling the British with his net. But the skinny boy, all head and legs, managed to extricate himself and his butterfly net from military arrest, avoiding the fate of the dead of Yalta.[44]

With an occasional turn from affairs of the heart toward the history unfolding all around him, Nabokov's verse began to find publication in local newspapers. But as dark as news across the country had become, life still offered some shelter from the worst events underway. With plenty of romance and endless diversions, Nabokov had time to make his stage debut in the lively regional the-ater.[45] He imagined himself in spiritual communion with Alexander Pushkin, who had also been exiled to the Crimea a century before. Nabokov sent letters to Lyussya, not knowing she had already left Petrograd. She wrote him, wondering why he did not write back. As letters slowly made their way to him, he toyed with joining the White Army in order to head inland to where she was now living, somewhere in the Ukraine.

V. D. Nabokov described the corner of the Crimea they had come to occupy as godforsaken, but conditions could have been worse. In the fall of 1919, the family moved into a former Tsarist villa closer to town, so that the younger children could attend school and Nabokov could make use of the libraries at the house and in Yalta.[46]

German occupation, or the threat of it, kept the Red Army out of Yalta and extended Vladimir Nabokov's innocence one more year. But once the First World War ended in November 1918, Germany withdrew, and a Regional Government was formed, with Nabokov's father holding a political portfolio once again, as Minister of Justice. The state survived a few months before the tensions of foreign intervention, a dispirited army, and an unsustainable fledgling democracy replayed the collapse of the Provisional Government on a smaller scale.[47]

The terrain had all the beauty and trappings of the Arabian Nights for Nabokov, but the romance was stretched so thin over the yawning abyss of the future that at times it became transparent. His family was running out of ways to protect him; the violence of the world and the search to escape it would soon become a theme in Nabokov's life and a dominant feature of his work.

The theaters and cafes of Crimean Russia became the shelters of ever-dwindling White Army power. A surging Red Army soon began to dislodge the refugees from their tentative hold on even this foreign piece of home and to disperse them across the globe, from China and Europe to America.

The less fortunate would never leave. Near the end of winter, Nabokov's cousin Yuri Traubenberg rode ahead of a cavalry charge into a nest of Bolshevik machine gunners in northern Crimea, ending his short life. The war had finally managed to lay a finger on the nineteen-year-old Nabokov. He served as a pallbearer for his closest friend, who was laid to rest in the alien terrain of Yalta.[48]

Nabokov's hedging on whether to enlist finally outlasted White Army control over the Crimea. White forces still had a series of improbable victories and dramatic defeats to go before they would be completely crushed, but the children born in the forge of that winter—Alexander Solzhenitsyn among them—would grow up with no memories of life under the Tsar or the Russian Empire.

The situation disintegrated quickly, and all the Nabokovs crossed westward to Sebastopol in a car winding up and down mountainsides, with Sergei throwing up on one side of the car, Elena on the other. After two days in the port city, they managed to board a vessel with other ministers of the regional government, only to be kicked off due to (incorrect) suspicions about misappropriated government funds. By the time the family set sail aboard a cargo ship named *Nadezhda* ("*Hope*"), the Bolsheviks had already retaken the harbor. But they escaped together: V. D. and Elena Nabokov, Vladimir and Sergei, Olga, Elena, Kirill, and their servant and companion Evgenia Hofeld, who had run the household since 1914.[49]

They possessed little more than a handful of valuables grabbed by a chambermaid from a dresser as the family fled Petrograd. The jewels that had been the playthings of the infant Volodya had so far been hidden in a bottle of talcum powder and buried in the ground. They now lay tucked into the small pigskin valise that had been part of Elena's honeymoon trousseau.

As the *Nadezhda* pulled out into the Black Sea, Bolshevik machine-gun fire crossing its wake, Nabokov sat down to a game of chess with his father. He had already seen first-hand the disappointments that roared up from the gap between an ideal and its execution, and the choices between bad and worse that so often accompanied political action. But the future was not yet set.

Just days before his twentieth birthday, Nabokov surrendered his homeland to the sorrows that had come into the century with him: the fury of Lenin, the blight of the concentration camps, the rabid anti-Semitism that could lay waste to a whole universe. But these things—and the memory of the dead—had only begun to shape his world.

CHAPTER FOUR
Exile

⎯⎯∞⎯⎯

1

A short trip across the Black Sea was all it took to turn Vladimir Nabokov into an exile. While almost any kind of voyage was preferable to the reception the Bolsheviks were offering in Sebastopol, the passengers on the *Nadezhda* were left with only the things they had carried aboard, including food and water. In an instant, beds and mattresses became luxuries. Nabokov made use of a bench, while his thirteen-year-old sister Elena camped on a door taken off its hinges. They slept in lice-ridden quarters and ate dog biscuits. Nabokov took turns with his father using a collapsible rubber bathtub like the one that had accompanied V. D. Nabokov to prison eleven years before. Sergei, even more fastidious, had a second tub to himself, and won a bet that he could bathe using a single glass of water.[1]

Constantinople was already swamped with refugees and had no use for more Russians. After waiting two days for permission to land, the passengers on the *Nadezhda* were refused entry. The boat sailed on to Athens. Detained shipboard in quarantine with all the passengers for two more days at the Port of Piraeus, Nabokov finally stepped onto a foreign shore on his twentieth birthday.[2]

The family regrouped in Athens, where Nabokov found time for three romances in as many weeks. Then it was on to Marseilles, where they caught a train north to Paris. The city did not block their entry on arrival, but, as in Constantinople, Nabokov suddenly found himself a member of an undesirable class. He had been preceded in emigration by any number of anti-Bolshevik Russians, many of whom had fled their homeland a year or more earlier. The earlier arrivals had not made a particularly good impression on their hosts, who had begun to fear that the Russians might not leave any time soon.

Nabokov's new status was underlined for him when he went to the Cartier boutique on Rue de la Paix with family servant Evgenia Hofeld. He had intended to sell his mother's jewelry to raise cash for the family to live on. But by May 1919 Russian refugees were a suspect class, and Cartier's staff called the police. It may have been the magnificence of Elena Nabokov's pearls in combination with her son's "unbelievable" attire which were to blame, but fortunately Nabokov and Hofeld managed to persuade the staff to release them before officers arrived.[3] The pearls would eventually finance the first half of Nabokov's college career.

Crossing the Channel to England, V. D. Nabokov began to consider how to counter Lenin's and Trotsky's successes—and how best to persuade the English to expand Allied intervention in Russia. He wrote an essay on the pogroms of southern Russia, claiming, perhaps wishfully, that they were occurring despite the Volunteer Army's best efforts. The rest of his argument was designed to refute the very equation of Bolshevism with Jewry that had crept *sub rosa* into the fringes of his memoir. Acknowledging the number of Jewish leaders in the Bolshevik movement, he absolutely rejected the idea that the Bolsheviks were representative of all Jews and called on the Russian Jewish majority to join the fight for Russian democracy.[4]

Partnering with fellow Kadet Paul Milyukov in London, V. D. Nabokov also began to work on the English-language journal *New*

Russia. More jewels were sold to pay rent, and Nabokov's parents settled in London.[5]

That fall, Nabokov entered Trinity College, Cambridge, showing administrators the transcript of Samuil Rosov, his former Tenishev classmate, in order to avoid taking qualifying exams. Sergei started at Oxford, but quickly became unhappy there and after just one semester joined his brother at Cambridge. Nabokov began by studying natural sciences, and Sergei French literature; but as Sergei moved from Oxford to Cambridge, Nabokov, who identified more and more strongly as a writer, changed to literature, too.[6]

The brothers' years at Cambridge meant more time together and more cordial relations. They often played tennis. Nabokov was the more gifted athlete, but left-handed Sergei, despite his weak serve and nonexistent backhand, had a relentless ability to return the ball. A friend from those years contrasted the two young men, describing Vladimir as a charmer with a hint "of malice at the back of his voice" and Sergei as a towheaded dandy with a curl over his eye, attending the Diaghilev *Ballets Russes* premieres "wearing a flowing black theater cape and carrying a pommeled cane."[7]

Nabokov boxed and played goalkeeper for the Trinity men's soccer team, which brought him into the orbit of British students. But his chosen topics for poetry were still women and Russia. His main companions were aristocratic Russians, too, including not just Sergei, but a count, an exiled prince, and roommate Mikhail Kalashnikov.[8]

Nabokov's letters to his mother were filled with mentions of family, home, and politics—but he also found time for misbehavior. He was threatened with fines on campus for walking on the grass. He got into fistfights with those who disparaged Russian speakers. In the kind of antics undertaken by students for centuries, he broke two of his landlady's chairs, he neglected to pay his tailor, and he smeared food on the walls.[9]

If Nabokov still delighted in playing the child, he was also finding that one by one, the indulgences of childhood were being scraped away. He and his Russian friends did not see eye to eye with progressive British students. While Nabokov was at Cambridge, H. G. Wells—whom V. D. Nabokov had hosted at his home in 1914—visited Lenin and praised Bolshevik ideals before the Petrograd Soviet. Wells's son George, who had made the trip too, got into a dormitory dispute with Nabokov in which each son defended his father's views. Their disagreement escalated into a shouting match, with Nabokov condemning all socialists, and Kalashnikov chiming in with "Kill the Yids!"[10]

In a letter to his mother, Nabokov found his roommate's comment amusing and regrettable, but the argument cannot be counted as a shining moment for any of the participants. Kalashnikov handily confirmed at least one stereotype Wells likely had about White Russian émigrés, which was fair enough, as Nabokov's roommate was not known as a rigorous thinker. During their two years together, Kalashnikov threatened to burn Nabokov's books and expounded on the mysteries of the anti-Semitic *Protocols of the Elders of Zion*.[11]

Anti-Semitism, Nabokov quickly learned, was not limited to Russia; Kalashnikov's vicious conflation of Jews and Bolsheviks found a reflection in more elegant generalizations by others. In *The Jews*, written during Nabokov's years at Cambridge, the Anglo-French writer Hilaire Belloc—a former member of Parliament and one of the leading historians of his day—tried to tackle what he termed "the Jewish problem." His ideas reveal the state of British thought in that era on the rising global tide of anti-Semitism.

Explaining the causes and effects of the 1917 "Jewish revolution," Belloc explained that during the prior decade, the Boer War in South Africa had been "provoked and promoted by Jewish interests." Over time, he believed "a monopoly of Jewish international news agents" developed, as well as a Jewish presence in "the governing institutions of Western Europe" at a rate of fifty to one hundred times any proportional representation.[12] Belloc concluded that the Jews were in part to blame for the animosity they faced, because they acted superior to others, behaved in deceptive and secretive ways, and refused to acknowledge the evidence of Jewish conspiracy marshaled against them.

Such arguments were mixed in with more measured thinking but rank among the best that the nation received at the time from an ostensibly careful thinker who was by and large sympathetic to the plight of the Jews. Similar ideas would become less subtle and more consequential in the coming years.

But for the twenty-year-old Vladimir Nabokov at Cambridge, if a choice had to be made between Bolshevik sympathizers and Kalashnikov's kind, he was sticking with the Russians. Nabokov headed back to Berlin that June with Sergei and Kalashnikov, and over the summer began dating Kalashnikov's cousin Svetlana.

Like Lyussya before her, Svetlana received her romantic due in poems, but the love for which Nabokov pined most was much farther away. Nostalgia for his own Russian geography overwhelmed him. If he had been called a foreigner in St. Petersburg, he was painfully Russian in London. He clung to Russian things. He found a copy of Dahl's Russian dictionary and did exercises in it, so as not to lose his native language. He wrote his mother longing letters about the details of Vyra, as if the act of remembering might itself create some road for return, though he had begun to suspect that that road might not exist. He wrote poem after poem, expressing fidelity by "composing verse in a tongue nobody understood about a remote country nobody knew."[13]

2

One year into their exile, Nabokov's parents moved to Germany. The new home was far from their oldest sons, who still had two years to go at Cambridge, but postwar Berlin was a much more affordable city and ideal for re-entering the world of publishing. V. D. Nabokov planned to collaborate on the founding of a new newspaper. Moving quickly into a cultural leadership role in the community of Russian exiles in Berlin that autumn, V. D. Nabokov helped to launch *Rul* (*The Rudder*), which soon became Berlin's largest Russian-language daily.

Events in Russia led Nabokov in a new direction, inspiring him to tackle fiction. In January 1921, *Rul* published a story from him, in which fairy-tale woodland spirits of Russian legend collide with the new Bolshevik reality of fields of beheaded, rotting corpses and bodies floating downstream.[14] All the enchanted fairies of Russia, one sprite laments, have been turned into exiles. The story is thin, and not long, but it makes plain the fact that from the first days of his career as a prose writer, Nabokov combined myth and fantasy with modern political horror.

By the time "The Wood-Sprite" appeared in print, most White Army remnants had retreated across the Black Sea. Hundreds of thousands had been killed in combat. Even more had died from disease—the toll from typhus alone ran into the millions. The war would continue to play out in skirmishes and uprisings, but by 1921, military conflict no longer topped the list of Russia's troubles.

Other tragedies were waiting in the wings. Three years of scorched-earth tactics, combined with crop failures, led to starvation through the breadbasket of the country. By 1921, full-blown famine had spread across whole sections of Russia, adding to the death toll.

Revolutionary Russian writer Maxim Gorky put out an international plea for assistance on behalf of the Bolsheviks. The situation became so dire that the Bolsheviks created an All-Russian Committee for Aid to the Hungry. The International Red Cross suddenly found itself back in the region, not to visit the concentration camps as they had during the war (the Russian camps were now closed to them), but to try to arrange relief. Global efforts followed, with Nabokov's mother raising money for those starving to death in a homeland to which her family could not return.[15]

Full-page appeals for money in British newspapers led to an outpouring of funds and a massive commitment from Herbert Hoover's American Relief Administration. Even with the influx of foreign aid, the disaster eventually brought slow death to at least five million people.[16]

Nabokov moved through his student years never far from news of the violence unfolding in his country but surrounded by socialists who considered the new Russian state just and admired it. His attempts to persuade his peers otherwise were ignored or ineffective. After committing one of his father's articles to memory for a debate on Bolshevism during his first year at Cambridge, Nabokov found himself incapable of offering any points or rebuttal on his own and was easily defeated.[17] He could parrot his father's ideas, but in print and in person, he had not yet found the words to reflect events in his native land.

It was 1922, and the world tilted on the verge of modernity. International leaders met to de-escalate a buildup of dreadnoughts that threatened to reignite an arms race. The head of the Indian National Congress, Mohandas Gandhi, went to jail for sedition over his nonviolent struggle for Indian independence. The film industry was in its infancy, with *Nanook of the North* appearing as the first narrative documentary. England was not yet ready to publish the frank sexual content of James Joyce's *Ulysses*, but pieces of it had seen the light of day in a small American review, and that February Sylvia Beach in Paris would take a chance on the book, making it the first title to be published by Shakespeare and Company.

Germany faced widespread unrest. In the wake of the Russian Revolution, the nation had gone through its own revolution and civil conflict, a fight that left more than 1,200 dead and Berlin a very uneasy place.[18] The establishment of the Weimar Republic led to a democracy, but the First World War had ended on bitter terms for Germany, fostering economic ruin and discontent across the political spectrum and fueling interest in a young speaker named Adolf Hitler.

Hitler was already publicly labeling Bolsheviks as corrupt Jewish seducers threatening Germany. In 1922, however, the Nazis were merely a fringe group; it was, instead, the specter of assassination that haunted Europe. Targeted killings—by Socialist Revolutionaries, the Irish Republican Army, right-wing German reactionaries, or left-wing anarchists—remained a popular political tool. Ultra-right extremists in Germany used machine guns and a hand grenade to kill Jewish politician and industrialist Walter Rathenau that summer, triggering more political violence and ushering in massive economic instability.

Spies were everywhere. Frank Foley, British Passport Control officer by day, was Berlin station chief of the British intelligence organization MI6 by night. Willi Lehmann, tasked with counterespionage for the Berlin police force, would turn into a paid informer for the Soviet secret police. A Russian intelligence memo from the era refers to Berlin as the Soviet "central office for espionage abroad," listing among its priorities the infiltration of the many anti-Bolshevik organizations that populated the city, the recruitment of formerly Tsarist officers, and luring émigrés back east.[19] If the danger often felt veiled or vague, intermittent murders underlined the stakes of political gamesmanship.

Newspapers and propaganda were likewise omnipresent, and it was not always easy to tell the difference. Every organization, every cause, and every party, it seemed, had its own newspaper, running the political gamut from soft promotion of ideology to strident calls to anarchy.

From his new post as an editor in Paris, fellow Kadet Paul Milyukov openly bickered with Nabokov's father over the best strategy to wrest Russia from Bolshevik hands. The dispute between the men continued for months, becoming more contentious.[20] Their differences lay in their interpretations of history, with Milyukov backing the Socialist Revolutionaries and some Marxism, and Nabokov's father still unconvinced of the merits of revolution.

Yet possible alliances with outside parties or governments were sometimes all the exiles, powerless and removed as they were, had to dream of. In truth, for all they could effect change in that moment, their debates over the future of Russia might as well have taken place on another planet.

The community of exiles in which Nabokov's family lived was just as spiritually distant—and physically distinct—from its Berlin setting. Wilmersdorf, the neighborhood around the City Zoo, served as the social center for Russian émigrés, the place where they rented rooms from formerly well-to-do military families. But for the most part, the Russians kept to themselves and had no interest in assimilating. Their real interest was in leaving as soon as possible. The exiles in Berlin built an island of Russian anti-Bolshevik resistance, but had no front on which to resist. And so they fretted over next steps and waited for some new cataclysm to destroy them or call them home. With each year, the likelihood of return would grow smaller and smaller, but who could blame them for expecting the known universe to reverse itself before their eyes? It had already happened once.

3

During his last year at Cambridge, Vladimir Nabokov continued to accumulate police attention and university rebukes for his social activities (smashing streetlights, setting off rockets), provoking lectures from his tutor about time better spent in the library. On a bet, Nabokov had also begun a French translation for his father, who likewise had to goad him to get results. He nonetheless managed to win a prize for his performance on the first set of exams required for his undergraduate degree.[21]

V. D. Nabokov hounded his son to keep him accountable, but cherished his company. Their spirited conversations ranged from writerly humor to chess, tennis, and boxing. V. D. Nabokov also promoted his son's artistic emergence, continuing to publish Vladimir's fiction and poetry in *Rul* and commissioning work from him for Slovo, the new Russian-language publishing house he helped to establish in Berlin.

When Nabokov returned to Germany in 1922 for his month-long Easter break, father and son had just finished preparing the next set of Nabokov's poems for publication under the pseudonym Vladimir Sirin. A half-human bird of paradise dangerous to mortals, the sirin was a creature of Russian legends that serenaded saints and gods. Nabokov imagined it as a firebird that embodied the soul of Russian art.[22]

On the last Thursday in March, V. D. Nabokov got home from *Rul* in time to have dinner with his son. The two men sparred playfully afterward, as Nabokov showed his father a boxing technique. Changing for bed, they called to each other from their separate rooms, then came together to try to recall the details of an elusive scene in the opera *Boris Godunov*. They discussed Sergei and the "abnormal inclinations" of his homosexuality.[23] Nabokov's father cleaned a pair of shoes, then helped to press his son's pants. Heading to bed, V. D. Nabokov slipped some newspapers to his son through the slit between two barely open doors. Later, Nabokov would recall the strange sensation of not seeing his father's face or even his hands in that moment.

The next evening, V. D. Nabokov went out to a meeting at Berlin's Philharmonic Hall for a speech by Paul Milyukov. After nearly a year of public disputes, they had still not reconciled. An overture in that morning's paper made by Nabokov's father announced Milyukov's speech and called for the remembrance of the shared goals that had bound them together in the past. But there was no response.

Speaking to more than 1,500 people seated in the elegant symphony hall, Milyukov described the role America could play in Russian liberation. After an hour, he called a brief break. As he headed toward the exit, confusion erupted.

A man sitting in the front row stood up, pulled out a revolver, and fired shots toward the retreating Milyukov. A man in the crowd shouted, "For the Tsar's family and Russia." Milyukov threw himself to the ground or was pushed down. V. D. Nabokov raced toward the gunman to grab his arm. Nabokov's father and a friend pinned the gunman. As the friend went to check on Milyukov, V. D. Nabokov continued to hold the assailant.

A second man stepped onstage amid the chaos and shot Nabokov's father three times. He hit V. D. Nabokov twice in the spine and once with a bullet that pierced his left lung and his heart. In all, twelve shots were fired, killing or injuring eight people. "Curiously," one paper mistakenly reported, "all were struck in the knees or ankles."[24] The body of the unconscious V. D. Nabokov was carried into a nearby room.

Five plainclothes police officers present in the auditorium tried to arrest the first gunman. But they ended up fighting with the crowd, who were convinced they were part of the assassination plot and refused to turn him over. The plainclothesmen called in uniformed policemen to whom the Russians finally surrendered the captive.[25]

Both assailants were arrested, but only by luck. The crowd had been so intent on apprehending the first shooter that the second had almost escaped, edging toward the exit until someone in the crowd noticed him. The first shooter, who had been caught by the journalists, launched into a vitriolic harangue against Jews.[26] Beaten bloody by the crowd as he was led across the hall, he was nearly lynched.

A car was sent immediately to fetch family members, but before the twenty-two-year-old Nabokov and his mother could arrive, the police surgeon announced that V. D. Nabokov was dead.

The Berlin Police Murder Commission interrogated the two assailants in the hall and, determining that it was a premeditated assassination, called in the political police. The prisoners, Peter Shabelski-Bork and Sergei Taboritski, turned out to be Tsarist cavalry officers. The gunmen had been living in poverty and working as interpreters at a publishing house in Munich. They had traveled to Berlin with few possessions, including a photograph of the late Russian Empress, and had taken up residence in a modest hotel.[27]

Shabelski-Bork, undersized and wild-eyed, blamed Milyukov for all Russia's troubles and admitted to stalking him for years. Without Milyukov, he believed the Tsar would surely have concluded a separate peace with Germany and forestalled the Revolution.[28]

The day after the assassination, the Congress of Constitutional Monarchists met in Berlin. It opened with a speech in honor of V. D. Nabokov, after which the audience rose to pay tribute to the fallen Kadet. The murder was condemned and a resolution offering condolences to Nabokov's mother passed, at which point, the police—perhaps not recognizing the distinctions between reactionary assassins and democratically inclined mourners—showed up and arrested thirty Russians as suspects. Attendees were taken in for questioning but quickly released.[29]

On March 30 a memorial service attended by hundreds took place in the chapel of the former Russian Embassy in Berlin's Unter den Linden. The church could not hold everyone, and an overflow crowd formed in the embassy courtyard. Twenty-two-year-old Vladimir Nabokov was there with his mother, Sergei, and the rest of the children. Also in attendance were the German Minister of Foreign Affairs, ambassadors, professors, doctors, journalists, as well as members of the Russian Red Cross, the German Red Cross, and the aid organization for Russian refugees that V. D. Nabokov had chaired and whose latest financial report was published in *Rul* the morning after his death.[30]

A final service was held on April Fool's Day at the St. Constantine and Helena Russian Orthodox Church on the outskirts of the city. Inside the narrow stone building with its three onion domes lofting their three lighter crosses skyward, pale flowers crowded the open casket in which V. D. Nabokov lay, his face turned sharp and strange, its boyish plumpness surrendered in death.

Nabokov looked on his father for the last time. Mixed with the tragedy was a terrible irony: three years after outrunning arrest and certain execution by the Bolsheviks, Vladimir Dmitrievich Nabokov had been shot dead in another country by an assassin intent on killing someone else.

A large photo of V. D. Nabokov, the flower of St. Petersburg culture, ran on the front page in the April 5 edition of *Rul* and was sent out around the globe to more than thirty countries.[31] Condolences poured in from Berlin, Paris, and Prague, calling Nabokov's father "a bright paladin of freedom." The Union of Russian Jews held a special meeting to pay tribute to the loss of V. D. Nabokov and to request permission to send a delegation to the funeral.

Nabokov's father was eulogized in sanctuaries and in print by what seems like half the Russian community living in Berlin, from Russian literary titan Ivan Bunin to former ambassadors and German cabinet ministers. Anton Chekhov's widow sent condolences.

On the day of his murder, V. D. Nabokov had extended the hand of friendship to Paul Milyukov. After his death, Milyukov had remained with the body all night. The next day, in mourning, Milyukov described V. D. Nabokov in generous terms. The murderers, he wrote, acting on deluded nationalism, had "killed a Russian patriot, who is eternally above their tiny horizon."[32]

The murder of V. D. Nabokov ended his dispute with Milyukov. And in the way that history has of making vital questions moot, their fight over the Socialist Revolutionary Party would also be sidelined. Milyukov did not yet know that Vladimir Lenin had just declared a new wave of terror, designed in part to crush any internal support for the Socialist Revolutionaries and "Milyukovites."[33]

Rumors circulated in European and American newspapers that the Socialist Revolutionaries who had been rounded up would all be executed in secret. But just days before V. D. Nabokov's death, under pressure to make international gestures of goodwill, the Politburo had surprised the world by announcing that the Bolsheviks would put their political enemies on trial in sessions open to the public. Those proceedings would rattle Russian exiles around the globe, holding the gaze of the entire world. And the fate of the defendants would linger in Nabokov's mind for forty years.

4

The trial of the Socialist Revolutionaries opened in Moscow on June 8. The proceedings took place in the converted ballroom of the Noble Assembly, the Great Hall of Columns where Pushkin had fallen in love a century before, a place Nabokov would reference decades later in his commentary on the masterpiece *Eugene Onegin*. Towering pillars and crystal chandeliers stood as reminders of a lost world, one that was receding into the past at an accelerating rate. A table hoisted onto a red-carpeted stage sat facing hundreds of chairs, and above the table hung a red banner with gold letters stating that the people's court would safeguard the people's revolution.[34]

The trial had ongoing coverage by wire services and European correspondents, with all the information filtered and summarized in the pages of the Russian émigré papers in Berlin. Soldiers stood at the door of the courtroom, granting admission to more than a thousand ticketholders who had been selected in advance. Some of the most famous socialists in the world had come to Moscow to represent the accused.[35]

The outcome of the trial had already been arranged with these socialists. In exchange for a united front that set aside the animosity the Bolsheviks had generated among revolutionaries in Europe, the twelve key defendants would have the right to choose their own attorneys and would not be given the death penalty.

But Russian delegates in Germany who had negotiated those terms had not cleared them with Lenin, who publicly rebuked the representatives in the pages of *Pravda*. The international panic triggered by Lenin's displeasure quieted when European attorneys were permitted to come to the aid of the accused as promised.

On the opening day of the trial, one of the defendants rose to deny the legitimacy of the court. After hours of arguing, which one reporter suggested threatened to re-enact the entire Russian Revolution, the charges were finally read.[36] The members of the tribunal announced that while they could not be impartial, bias would not create a problem as long as their partiality "was in the interests of the revolution." Defendants and defense attorneys alike were given leeway to criticize the current government, but they were not allowed to call witnesses. The tribunal refused to grant them the right even to introduce evidence into the court record.

Realizing, only a week in, that their presence was meaningless, the foreign attorneys announced that they would no longer allow their involvement to support the charade of a fair trial. They withdrew from the proceedings and did not show up the next day.[37]

An orchestrated mob made its way to the courtroom, where eight demonstrators spoke in favor of execution. It seemed for a moment that the defendants might be killed then and there. When the remaining defense attorney complained that allowing insults and harangues in the hall would prejudice the court against their clients, the tribunal declared that the "workers did not go through any law school and do not know the laws of etiquette." Presiding judge Georgy Pyatakov again dismissed the idea that impartiality was the goal. A defense attorney who chided the court for its bias was jailed for his trouble. Newspaper headlines around the world began to announce that the death penalty was inevitable.

The Socialist Revolutionaries had already lost their European attorneys; now they had lost their Russian counsel. But they remained defiant. They had come of age fighting and going to prison under the Tsar. If it was true that many had taken part in the Provisional Government or fought Bolshevik rule, they had also been steadfast radicals for years and were not easily intimidated.

They had led hunger strikes; some among them had killed. Defendant Abram Gotz had already been sentenced to death once by a Tsarist court in 1907, launching a commuted sentence of exile in Siberia that had ended only with the Revolution. Yet this trial held one key distinction from the other, earlier proceedings: it was a trial by fellow revolutionaries.

The writer Maxim Gorky appealed in print to Soviet leaders, begging them to take the message to Trotsky, writing, "If the trial of the Socialists-Revolutionists [sic] results in murder it will be preconceived contemptible murder.... I have pointed out repeatedly the crime and stupidity of rooting out the intelligentsia in our illiterate and uncultured country."[38]

During the last days of deliberations, in a clear bid to have an excuse to offer clemency, the defendants were presented with the opportunity to plead with the court a final time, to save their lives if they would repudiate their party. Not one of the twelve asked for mercy.

Were the Russian people torn by the events taking place in their midst? Not if *New York Times* reporter Walter Duranty's accounts of the 1922 trial are to be believed. The citizens of Moscow, Duranty wrote, were tired of politics and interested only in getting on with their lives. In his coverage of the trial from Moscow, well on his way to being the elder statesman of Western journalists in Moscow, Duranty suggested that while groups could be ginned up to riot in support of the death penalty, in truth, no one cared what happened to the defendants one way or the other: "Once the peasants followed the Social Revolutionary banner because the Socialist Revolutionaries promised them land. Now that they have it from the Bolsheviki they desire to enjoy its fruits in peace and prosperity. If the Soviets give them that, they may shoot a thousand revolutionary leaders, for all the peasants care."[39]

Yet perhaps Duranty missed something, as even the tribunal seemed conflicted in its last moments. On its way out to consider the verdict, the judges paused to ask once more if the prisoners' intentions toward the government might change if they were freed. The defendants, again, did not budge.

And so in a dramatic sentencing session, twelve of the thirty-four public defendants were given the death penalty. The sentence was sent to the Soviet for final review. Trotsky and Stalin pushed for signed oaths from the prisoners swearing to cease resistance against the government and to dissociate themselves from the party. If they signed, the defendants would receive reduced sentences—and if they did not, execution would follow.

Others pressed for commuting the executions to permanent exile. A compromise emerged: the death penalty would be left in place, but the executions would be "postponed." The prisoners would become permanent hostages. In the event of any action by the Socialist Revolutionary Party against the Soviet, the prisoners' death sentences would immediately be carried out: "Let there be one attempt to burn a factory or one attempt at murder—and the Socialists-Revolutionists [sic] will be punished."[40]

On August 10, 1922, the assistant commander of the Lubyanka Prison in Moscow misled the defendants, telling them that their verdict had been confirmed, and they would be killed. They waited ten hours to be taken for execution. That night, the head of the prison came to explain their new status as hostages. Soon after, they were turned over to the secret police. And then they disappeared.[41]

The Bolshevik seizure of power in 1917 split revolutionary from revolutionary, creating a rift that made it hard to imagine how global revolution could progress in the coming years. Alexander Blok's poem "The Twelve," already parodied by Nabokov, found another response in a book called "The Twelve Who Are To Die," printed in Berlin and distributed in Europe and America that fall. It detailed the background for and events of the trial, and condemned the Bolsheviks for planning the murder of their revolutionary brethren.[42]

Those who had supported the Russian revolutionaries in their long march to power balked at the idea of killing of fellow radicals. Denunciations rang out in the U.S. and Europe, with socialist groups from more than a dozen countries making public protests. Former head of the Provisional Government Alexander Kerensky volunteered to exchange himself for the defendants. H. G. Wells, who had previously supported the Bolsheviks in principle, now joined a declaration to the Soviet government calling on it to "abandon, in the name of humanity and universal reconciliation, what will otherwise be regarded by mankind as an act of vengeance." Albert Einstein, then in Germany, also protested the verdict.

Back in Berlin, *Rul*, too, continued to report on the trial. The day the verdict was announced, thousands marched in the streets of Prague. The suspended sentence was called nothing but "a slow torturous death." *Rul* reported that the Russian defense attorneys for the twelve had also been convicted by the tribunal and sent to concentration camps.[43]

The Socialist Revolutionaries stayed hidden from view, with no announcement as to their location. Hundreds more intellectuals were arrested, exiled, or sentenced. Days later, a wire story explained that, given the recent escapes from the concentration camps at the port city of Archangel, some of the convicted intellectuals and Socialist Revolutionaries would be shipped north of the Russian mainland to Arctic islands more likely to hold them securely. The prisoners, it was reported across Europe, would be exiled to Nova Zembla, a place so desolate and inhospitable that even the Tsar had never sent prisoners there.

The trial of the Socialist Revolutionaries and the humiliating defeat of the White Army together ended the notion that Bolshevik rule might collapse at any moment—and with it the fantasy that Russian democracy was just around the corner. Three months later, on December 30, 1922, the Bolsheviks convened the All-Union Congress of Soviets at the Bolshoi Theater in Moscow. Delegates from the Russian, Ukrainian, Transcaucasian, and Byelorussian Soviet Socialist Republics came together to create a revolutionary state and sign the treaty marking the official formation of the Soviet Union.

Vladimir Nabokov's bitter Berlin spring gave way to a fall and winter that redeemed nothing. The year Nabokov lost his father was the year he lost his country.

Chapter Five

Aftermath

—⚬⚬⚬—

1

V. D. Nabokov's murder devastated his family's world. After just three weeks in which to mourn, Nabokov returned to Cambridge to finish his degree. Sergei stayed in Berlin during his final term to care for their bereft mother, going back to Cambridge only for exams.[1]

In his anguish, Nabokov immediately sought solace in words. For the pages of *Rul*, he crafted "Easter," a poem commemorating the loss of his father. Its narrator, immersed in grief, sees new life emerging everywhere in spring. Death—so incongruous in the natural world during a season of birth—cannot be denied. But if spring's beauty and rebirth is not just "bedazzling lies," he writes, perhaps it carries some promise of resurrection in nature and in the very poem the author is writing, where love and memory bring the dead to life.[2]

"Easter" sings with hope, but in the real world, Nabokov was staggered by the loss of his father. During his last weeks in England, Vladimir wrote in despair to his mother saying, "At times it's all so oppressive I could go out of my mind—but I have to hide. There are things and feelings no one will ever find out."[3]

By the middle of 1922, Vladimir Nabokov had returned to Berlin a young man with a university degree living in a city he would come to loathe, the oldest son of a widow with little and diminishing prospects of regaining his home or wealth. At the moment of his entry into adulthood, his future still floated in the ether. His mother was one of thousands of educated aristocrats thrown back on whatever could be conjured from thin air. Yet she was still responsible for three of her children; that summer Nabokov's sister Olga was nineteen, Elena was sixteen, and Kirill turned eleven.

Grieving for his father and not yet knowing how the family would manage, Nabokov picked an unsettled time to propose to his current girlfriend, seventeen-year-old Svetlana Siewert. The girl's family was not opposed to the engagement but was worried enough about the charismatic Vladimir to make the marriage conditional on the acquisition of a steady job. While there may have been some whiff of propriety behind the demand, the Siewerts were not alone in their concerns. Russian girls in emigration who supported their parents and husbands had become a stereotype among exiles, furthering the popular judgment offered by one observer that "if [Russian] men, on the average, had been as good as the women, Bolshevism would never have succeeded."[4]

Newspapers in Europe and America were filled with tales of down-at-heel Russian aristocrats. At a New York City hotel, a count who had taken the post of head waiter was struck by a patron after he accidentally spilled wine on a customer. The count calmly removed his jacket and laid it over a chair with a striking delicacy before bloodying the customer, who required the assistance of several policemen in fighting off his opponent. After witnessing such elegance in responding to the insult as a matter of honor, the other patrons took up a collection to pay his fine and send him to Paris, where he hoped to find more suitable work.[5]

Countless just-so stories proliferated from China to New York. An actress who had lost her own servants and theater in Russia was dancing in a Broadway café and down to one meal a day. Princesses were seen working in Riga as typists. Some of the well-born, like Nabokov's family, had escaped with at least a few of their treasures. Many others, believing they would return in short order, had not. Their abandoned necklaces and tiaras stoked the fever for hidden jewels that raged in Russia during the first years of Bolshevik rule.[6]

The riches-to-rags stories of Russia's ruined aristocracy thrilled reporters, who did not have so far to fall and could appreciate the humbling of the mighty. But the vague *Schadenfreude* of the humorous stories was offset by other accounts of the refugees' plight. Headlines such as "Dying Refugees Crawl into Brest-Litovsk" had also become commonplace.[7] Scattered to London, Paris, Prague, Warsaw, Harbin, Stockholm, Berlin, and beyond, many were now in their third or fourth year of exile and simply had no money left and no way of earning any.

By this time, the shattered remnants of the White Army were holed up in a barracks in Constantinople, dependent on the Red Cross for insubstantial daily rations of tea, soup, and sometimes bread. A leaky loft housed tubercular patients, including row after row of families in stagnant quarters divided only by hanging rugs and blankets. More than one outsider suggested that the White Russians were a dead class in flight from a dead society, imagining their resurrection and return while the rest of the world understood that they were doomed to exile and starvation. And if they did not have the means for survival, one reporter noted, they at least had mastered the "unusually difficult art of dying with a slow grace."[8]

Small wonder that Svetlana's parents were keeping an eye on the ability of their daughter's fiancé to find a job. And whether Nabokov felt desire to win his girl's hand, distaste at appearing the indolent aristocrat, or pressure to provide for his family, when the time came to go to work, Vladimir Vladimirovich complied.

Joining his brother Sergei at positions arranged for them at a German bank, he showed up for his first day of work in a sweater. Reinforcing the stereotype of the shiftless Russian aristocrat, he managed to hold the job for three hours. Sergei, attire unknown, stayed the course for a week.[9]

Nabokov did not care for Germany's Teutonic face or commercial character. But in 1922 it was a mercifully cheap place for a writer without employment, or for one who had assembled just enough freelance tutoring and coaching to hold a day job at bay. Sessions teaching children and adults everything from English to boxing allowed Nabokov to get by.

What Nabokov *did* do enthusiastically was write, and years of prior effort came to fruition all at once. Beginning late in 1922, he saw four books published under his Sirin pseudonym in as many months, including a Russian translation of *Alice in Wonderland*.[10] Following on the tentative start he had made during his Cambridge years, he also began to write short fiction in earnest, turning out fifteen stories in 1923 and 1924.

"Russian Spoken Here," one of the first, was written not long after the trial of the Socialist Revolutionaries. The son of a White Russian émigré in Berlin punches out a Soviet visitor in the middle of his father's tobacco shop. They determine from the contents of his pockets that the visitor is with the GPU, the successors to the Cheka secret police who had imprisoned the father years before. Father and son hold a sham trial in which the defendant is given the nominal last word. The two debate what sentence to impose—and whether to execute the man for the sins of all the secret police. They reject the death penalty and prepare a cell for their prisoner, whom they hide from the world. The kidnapped man is supplied with food, books, and daily walks, but is informed that he will be kept in a locked bathroom as a permanent hostage until the Bolsheviks fall from power. When they entrust their secret to the narrator of the story, they explain that if the father dies before the end of the Bolshevik era, the son will inherit the captive. This prisoner, the shopkeeper explains, has become a family jewel.

If the least sophisticated kind of storytelling deals in wish fulfillment, the young Nabokov laid bare a fantasy, using fiction to wield power over the GPU from a thousand miles away. A son with fast fists and the father he loves—a father who, like V. D. Nabokov, was once captured by the Bolsheviks but survived—collaborate on redemptive justice, providing a service to their homeland. Six months later, they remain happy and decidedly more humane than their Soviet counterparts. No complications ensue; no moral dilemmas exist. In the last line, the father wonders how long they will hold their prisoner. The question would outlive its author.

Far from being able to feed a hidden GPU officer himself, Nabokov could not even support his mother. Dubious of his prospects, Svetlana's parents ended the engagement. The sudden separation from his fiancée released a torrent of grief-stricken poetry but did not long keep Nabokov from other women. Before leaving for a summer job picking cherries and peaches in the orchards of southern France, Nabokov managed romances with at least two women, both Jewish, and met a third at a costume ball.[11] This last prospect, an elegant Russian with fair hair wearing a wolf's-head mask, quoted his poetry back to him but didn't reveal her face, even as he followed her out of the ballroom.

Her name, he would discover, was Véra. And in France, just weeks later, he would write a poem, speculating on whether she might be the "awaited one." Learning her last name, he realized that he already knew her father, Evsei Slonim, whom he had called on as a potential publisher. A law-school graduate, Slonim had lost permission to practice law in Russia after the occupation had been closed to Jews. He had moved on to forestry, and found great success as a businessman. But having surrendered his land with his country, he was now in Berlin trying to build a career yet again. Véra was the second of his three multilingual daughters. She often sat in the office that Vladimir had visited, yet somehow they had never run into each other.[12]

Véra was on Nabokov's mind that summer, but thoughts of her did not keep him from mailing an aching missive to Svetlana. And it did not in the least dam up the continuing stream of poetry, fiction, and now plays, which he drafted in the room on the farm where he stayed up at night to write. One drama, *The Pole*, fictionalized the final hours of delirium and death faced by Captain Robert Scott's 1910 polar expedition.[13] Another script deviated from reality even further in telling of a determined executioner going after his escaped prey years after the French Revolution.

On his return to Germany that fall, Nabokov also dipped his pen into a universe more familiar to his fellow Russians—one populated with angels and Biblical themes. To that universe belongs *Agasfer*, his retelling of the story of the Wandering Jew.

The story was well known to any religious or literate European of the day. In the Christian legend, a Jewish cobbler chided Jesus on his way to the cross. Because of his cruelty, he was condemned to travel the earth learning repentance and love until Christ's return. Pushkin, Shelley, Wordsworth, Goethe, and Hans Christian Andersen, among a host of others, had already done their own versions of the tale before Nabokov's birth. Even before their efforts, the story had become perhaps the most common way for Christians to explore the global predicament of the Jewish people—the idea being that they had sinned against God by being responsible for the death of Christ, were guilty of rejecting him, or both. As a result, the entire race was said to be doomed to suffer and roam the face of the earth.[14]

While the degree to which the story was used to justify religious violence had waxed and waned, after more than seven centuries as a religious parable and two centuries as a literary trope, the theme had not lost its popularity. It had even moved to the stage in 1906. But the definitive script was Ernest Temple Thurston's *The Wandering Jew*, which was produced in theaters across England—and even on Broadway, where it starred Tyrone Power—during Nabokov's Cambridge years.[15]

By 1923, Thurston's play had already been adapted into a feature film. In it, the man who becomes the Wandering Jew does, in fact, curse Christ on the way to the cross, believing Jesus has filled his dying wife's head with a fantasy of a cure. He forbids her to follow Christ's injunction and spits on the Messiah. After Christ condemns him to wander the earth, the man's beloved dies.

More than a thousand years later, he becomes obsessed with another woman, whom he pursues across the globe in order to possess her, against her will if necessary. During his centuries on earth, he proceeds to take on different identities (a knight, a merchant of jewels). Witnessing the hatred and trauma of the world, he finally reforms and recognizes his sin, becoming holier than the people who, century after century, continue to condemn him—including, at last, the priests of the Inquisition.

The year *The Wandering Jew* debuted as a movie, Nabokov sat down with a collaborator to work on his own version. *Agasfer* opens as an extended monologue meant to accompany a "staged symphony." Echoing the template of Thurston's play, Nabokov gave the Wandering Jew many key roles across history. In Nabokov's case, however, the identities were sometimes real historical figures: in the prologue, the Wandering Jew reveals that he exploded in Judas, who betrayed Christ, and later appeared again as the sexual swashbuckler Lord Byron, accused of incest and homosexuality. Several other eras are mentioned, from Greece and Medici-era Florence to the Inquisition. The Jew's most recent incarnation was Jean-Paul Marat, a hero of the French Revolution who was also much beloved by the Soviets. In Nabokov's verses, the Wandering Jew declares that he is learning how to love and that one day his love will fill the heavens, but in the world as it is, he sells the sky for sin.[16]

The identities Nabokov chose for *Agasfer* were rooted in betrayal, murder, sexual perversion, and anarchy. Though clearly an attempt at something more expansive, Nabokov's portrayal of the Wandering Jew as a sick but remorseful merchant of corruption fell short, particularly when trotted out as the frame for a love story.

His approach incorporated a softer version of stereotypes about Jews that were part of a rising trend of political thought in Germany, where extremists were already drawing similar conclusions, minus Nabokov's romanticism. Yet perhaps even vaguely human stereotypes were becoming passé by then; *Agasfer* was performed only once.

This early effort for the stage disappeared with little trace, leaving only the prologue for posterity, but it would influence Nabokov's writing in profound ways for much of his life. A half-century later he would denounce his fledgling attempt at the story, declaring the work *horrible* and swearing that if he found an existing copy, he would destroy it himself.[17]

2

Vladimir's romance with the twenty-one-year-old Véra Slonim blossomed. By the time Nabokov returned to Berlin that August, the pair had seen their work (his inventions and her translations) published simultaneously in *Rul*, and had already begun to know each other through their literary output.[18]

What more did Nabokov have to learn? Véra Evseevna Slonim had been born in 1902 in St. Petersburg. Growing up in much the same environment as Nabokov, she had her share of governesses, as well as math lessons and language instruction that led her to speak not only Russian, but also German, French, and English. Her father had given all three of his daughters—Lena, Véra, and Sonia—an education befitting an aristocratic family; but as a Jewish man facing vast occupational and residential restrictions under Nicholas II, he had leaped many more hurdles than the Nabokovs in order to do so.

When the time had come to flee Russia after the Revolution, the three Slonim girls had traveled separately from their father, who left ahead of them to avoid arrest. Lena was twenty years old, Véra was seventeen, and Sonia just ten. Heading south by train, they had ridden through territory where Ukrainian troops were rampaging and pogroms were legion. The train had been filled with Ukrainian separatists, who were likewise fleeing the Bolsheviks but had little affection for Jews. Sleeping on the floor that night, Véra had been awakened by a confrontation between another passenger—a Jew—and a separatist threatening to throw him from the train. Véra had spoken in the passenger's defense, and the Ukrainian backed down. But more than simply backing down, he and his friends had become enthusiastic escorts for the Slonim girls, warning them not to get off in Kiev, where battle was imminent, delivering a message to their father, and keeping them safe in a region rife with anti-Semitism.[19]

Véra was a regal blue-eyed blonde who looked every inch the indomitable spirit she was. If her childhood had been similar to Nabokov's, her response to Russia's political turmoil had been more proactive. At the start of the Revolution, she had considered herself a socialist. While Nabokov fantasized about revenge, Véra had apparently plotted hers. Classes with a marksman in Berlin had left her a crack shot, and it was known that she carried a pistol in her purse. She told more than one person of her involvement in an anti-Bolshevik assassination plot in the early 1920s—one said to have targeted Trotsky, or perhaps the Soviet ambassador.[20]

Véra, like her father, was proud of her Jewish identity. Fiercely intelligent, she turned out to be more than capable of quoting Sirin's poetry to him from memory. Before long, she began transcribing his work and quickly became his staunchest defender.

Their romance had all the makings of a happy ending; but that fall, hyperinflation savaged Germany, hitting the already-destitute émigré community especially hard. The Beer Hall Putsch, a failed Nazi coup put down the same season, did little to promote German stability. Sliding from being the least expensive refugee hub to a financial catastrophe, Berlin's cost of living suddenly broke the backs of its many publishing houses and cast bankrupt Russians to the wind, scattering them once more.

By Christmas, Nabokov's mother could no longer survive in Germany. Elena Nabokov left with her younger daughter for Czechoslovakia, where a government pension was offered to her and other prominent refugees. Olga followed, and, soon after, Nabokov escorted Evgenia Hofeld, a maid, and his brother Kirill as they relocated to Prague.[21]

Nabokov intended to return alone to Berlin once everyone was settled. Véra was not the only attraction that made Germany seem more congenial for the moment; the Prague apartment was cold, squalid, and bug-infested. Back in Berlin, Nabokov wrote to his mother soon after her move, describing how in two months, or "as soon as possible I shall have you come here."[22]

Material circumstances were hard enough, but Elena Nabokov was less battered by them than by the loss of her husband, playing down her financial deprivation as a comfort. In Russia, she explained, she sometimes had woken up anxious about which among her fifty hats to choose on any given day, while the benefit of having only one reduced the choice to simply whether to wear it or not.[23]

However bad things were in Germany or Prague, it was understood that those still in Russia had it worse. Typhus had become so widespread that letters leaving the country were thought to have infected postal workers in Estonia. All Russian mail was stopped and left untouched by German postal employees, who demanded disinfection measures. Berlin newspapers carried stories of mass starvation, of wolves, dogs, and cats all eaten, of towns where two thirds of the residents were dead, of people buried naked because their clothes were desperately needed by the living, of others buried in shallow graves and dug up by dogs, of dogs and wolves hunted by humans until there was nothing left to eat.[24]

While the remaining Nabokovs were not yet starving, they were also not together. Nabokov stayed in Berlin, and Sergei went to Paris, even farther from their mother and younger siblings in Czechoslovakia. Both brothers made ends meet by giving English and Russian lessons.[25]

Nabokov earned enough money to visit his mother that summer, but if she had any hope of being invited to return to Berlin with him, she was disappointed. What was likely the biggest announcement of that trip was of a very different order: he was engaged to Véra. Elena still dreamed of visiting her husband's grave, but by this point, Nabokov supporting even himself had become a dubious proposition. After another visit to Prague, he found his coat had been confiscated by his landlady, who suspected he might run out on his rent tab.[26]

Vowing to make more money to bring his mother back, Nabokov imagined taking on more students, or even doing manual labor breaking rocks.[27] But the possibility of a traditional job, such as his brief stint in banking, had disappeared with the rest of the German economy. Even if one might have been found, a conventional career, which started out as an already improbable fate for Vladimir Nabokov, had become almost unimaginable.

And still he wrote. In 1924 he began a novel with the title *Happiness*. The cost of living continued to rise, forcing him to load up on clients. Offering boxing, tennis, French, and English several days a week, he careered across the city from student to student, staying up late at night to write. He could not bring his mother to Berlin, but he managed to earn enough to send money to her each month.

Nabokov failed to finish *Happiness*, which was aborted for the time being. But he produced short stories at a steady clip, and thought about how they might be turned into movies. He collaborated on comedy sketches for the Bluebird Theater; he worked as an extra in Berlin film productions. And in the town hall of Berlin on April 15, 1925, he married the twenty-three-year-old Véra Slonim.[28]

Marriage provided a more auspicious start to his efforts as a novelist. Yet as he began to work on the first novel he would actually complete, *Mary (Mashenka)*, it was Nabokov's childhood love Lyussya who gave him a road back to Russia through his writing. With *Mary*, he folded his past and his present into a love song for his native land.

In a very recognizable grim Berlin filled with Russian refugees, the protagonist, Ganin, is a former White Army soldier injured in the Crimea and now living in Germany. The sad minor characters of the Russian emigration surround him—among them a dying poet trying desperately to get to Paris, a young woman surviving by working in a German office, and two giggling male ballet dancers.

Ganin discovers that his childhood love, Mary, whom he has not seen in years, is married to his neighbor in the same Berlin pension. She has been trapped in the Soviet Union but will soon come to join her husband in Germany. Ganin is caught up in his recollections of their time together, their meeting in a gazebo on the family estate, and the jewel-colored panes of glass there. He recalls the sorrow at the end of summer when they parted, and their frustrating reunion in St. Petersburg, with no place to meet alone.

The night before Mary's return, Ganin encourages her husband to get thoroughly drunk and leaves the man passed out with an alarm clock set for the wrong hour. He abandons his old apartment for good, planning to meet Mary at the train station himself.

Nabokov had marshaled more than enough coincidences to put a bow on his tale. But just before meeting Mary, his young protagonist takes flight, realizing that he has his love and his memory of her in his heart, and these memories suffice and transcend all the short-comings of reality. Implicit in the book's end is that Mary, who has lived the drudgery—and horror—of daily life under the Bolsheviks, will stand waiting at the train station utterly alone, met by no one. The narrator, who cherishes the memory of her, imagines that he needs from her only what he already possesses, and apparently owes her nothing. She no longer exists for him except as a figment of his past, where she remains vibrant and untouchable.

Like Ganin, Nabokov would come to be defined by his departures. Having already left Russia to the Bolsheviks and his mother in Prague, his writing now acknowledged the punishing gap between longing and reality. Nabokov was still working to seduce readers with the tenderness or nostalgia that had characterized his early poetry, but he had begun to resist the temptations of sentiment. If *Mary* showed Nabokov looking to the East wondering if everything that had been lost might be recovered, he was suggesting it could happen, but only through art and memory—never in life.

Nabokov described his main character as "not a very likeable person" but was delighted he had been able to slip five love letters Lyussya had written to him into the book.[29] Folding the details of his life into the story in such a way that no one but Lyussya and himself (and perhaps Véra) would recognize them, he wrote a letter sharing the secret with his mother.

His self-absorbed protagonist had served as the fulcrum for magic. By tucking Lyussya's words in with his own inventions, Nabokov did in fact immortalize a sliver of that time, their love, and their lost country forever.

3

In his second published novel, *King, Queen, Knave*, Nabokov crafted a more overtly unpleasant group of characters. The callow, self-absorbed Franz arrives center stage in Berlin and proceeds to have an affair with his aunt and take part in a plot to kill his uncle. The novel marks Nabokov's first use of principally German characters and contains only a shadow of the tenderness shown in *Mary*—offering a faint, oblique indictment of Germany that would become more pronounced over time.

The uncle, a flawed, failed dreamer, offers financial backing to an inventor who is crafting more and more realistic mobile mannequins. Discovering how to rattle his audience, Nabokov, like the inventor, was learning to make readers engage with increasingly more lifelike creatures, some of them corrupt and repellent.

Outside of fiction, however, Nabokov could summon more gallant human responses. In 1927 the wife of a Romanian violinist committed suicide, seeking relief from her husband's abuse. The violinist evaded German legal penalties, but news of his violence spread. Hearing the story, Nabokov and a friend went to a restaurant to find the musician, and drew straws for the privilege of taking the first swing at him. Nabokov won, and chaos ensued. At some point after the whole orchestra joined in, Nabokov, his co-conspirator, and the violinist were briefly taken to the police station.[30] Nabokov had accommodated himself to creating fictional cads, but in dealing with real-life cruelty he retained his father's longing for justice.

He remained bitterly homesick for Russia. "The University Poem," written between his two first novels, is a long account by a Russian exile attending college in England. It is a litany of absences and departures: a spring that is not like the Russian spring, the smell of a bird cherry tree that becomes painful to recall; a girl ripe for spinsterhood who now expects to be abandoned each year by departing students; the Russian narrator who tells himself that return to his homeland will one day be possible, but who may not himself believe it.

A more literal return was, of course, already available to Nabokov. The U.S.S.R. regularly tried to lure cultural figures back, leaning heavily on the exiles' nostalgia for their homeland and the fact that the collapse of the Soviet government hoped for by so many had failed to transpire. Major émigrés had already heeded the call. The "fairly talented" (in Nabokov's words) poet Boris Pasternak, novelist Aleksey Tolstoy (a distant relation of Leo Tolstoy), and Andrei Bely (whose novel *Petersburg* Nabokov believed one of the best books of the twentieth century) had all gone home, or at least to live in closer proximity to its ghost.[31] Maxim Gorky, who had been living in Europe during the 1920s, made a triumphant return in 1928 to his homeland in time for a massive public celebration of his sixtieth birthday. He would return for good in 1933.

But a literal return to the Soviet Union was not what Nabokov wanted. His fiction—dark enough to begin with—took on a bleaker edge. Nineteen twenty-nine found him creating his first novel with a protagonist tortured by madness. *The Defense* tells the story of Luzhin, a Russian chess grandmaster who succumbs to despair, eventually becoming trapped inside a game that is both chess and life, a game he cannot finish. The narrative mimics events surrounding the death of a chess master whom Nabokov had known who, like Luzhin, had abandoned a championship match, later jumping to his death from a bathroom window in Berlin.[32]

A few chapters into the book, Luzhin's father, a writer of books for boys, plans to create a melodramatic tale of his son's rise to celebrity as a prodigy. But contemplating his structure, he agonizes over the degree to which the war and the Revolution hover in the background of his story. Like Nabokov, the young Luzhin had not been directly involved in Russia's upheaval. Unlike Nabokov, he had been turned over to a Svengali who managed his career in Europe. Still, the intrusion of history on the father's tale—his own memories of starvation, arrest, and exile; the story he does not want to tell—frustrates his attempt to clear the way for a simple, sentimental narrative.

Nabokov already knew by this point that such a story, one stripped of history, was not the kind of art he wanted to make. His first two novels had reflected the Russian past and 1920s Berlin in a traditional way—history and geography provide a backdrop which informs the plots and helps to sketch the characters. But by *The Defense*, Nabokov had begun to think strategically about the intersection of world events and the creation of art, and a more innovative relationship between the two.

The protagonist of Nabokov's first novel, *Mary*, was a wounded soldier, but with *The Defense*, Nabokov began to move his characters onto the periphery of history's epic violence, showing how even bystander status cannot protect them from madness or keep them from being hobbled by the past. As a child, Luzhin fears being overtaken by the glass-rattling explosions of the cannon at St. Petersburg's Peter and Paul Fortress. By 1917, the threat has become real, as he stares at windows in fear that shooting will break out.

It remains a mystery exactly what Luzhin has seen in the interval between those two moments—his exterior life during wartime is glossed over in a single paragraph that covers more than a decade. This kind of literary ellipsis would become a mainstay of Nabokov's style. *The Defense*, in fact, would set the pattern for many Nabokov novels that followed. Never again would he write a book without destabilizing a main character's past or fate and turning the story into a puzzle.

Despite a handful of critics who assailed Nabokov's dark worldview, the stylistic achievements of *The Defense* astonished the literary community and sealed Nabokov's reputation as the leading author of the emigration. Ivan Bunin himself acknowledged that Nabokov had "snatched a gun and done away with the whole older generation, myself included." Russian writer Nina Berberova later recalled the amazement of reading the first chapters of the novel in Paris and her sudden belief that everything the exiles had lost would live on in Nabokov's work—his literary legacy would redeem their very existence.[33]

4

Nabokov heard the applause from Berberova and Bunin in France, where there were richer possibilities for émigré authors. And with the support of Véra, the breadwinner of the family, he built enough of a literary reputation that Paris came to court him in the form of Ilya Fondaminsky. An editor with the Socialist Revolutionary émigré journal *Contemporary Annals*, Fondaminsky was a patron saint of Russian émigré literature, known for paying good money to the best authors he could find. *Contemporary Annals* had published Nabokov's fiction before, but Fondaminsky was hoping for more. To Nabokov's delight, Fondaminsky agreed to buy his next project—soon to be called *Glory*—unfinished as it was, without conditions, intending to serialize it.[34] It was Fondaminsky's first extravagant acknowledgement of Nabokov's genius, but it would not be the last.

Months later, Nabokov finished drafting *Glory* (originally *Podvig* in Russian), the story of Martin, a young man who, like Nabokov, fled Russia in 1919, lost his father at a young age, and played goalkeeper for Trinity College at Cambridge. The young protagonist exists in a suspended netherworld, where émigré Russians are waiting for history to resolve, even as they are slowly left behind.

Martin finds himself irritated by his maudlin Swiss uncle, who wonders if Russia needs a dictator to put things right. The uncle dramatically bemoans the execution of Martin's former tutor by the Bolsheviks, only to be told that she is alive and well and living in Finland. At Cambridge, Martin meets a professor who fetishizes his own narrative about Russia in a different way, waxing nostalgic over it as others do Rome or Babylon—as an ancient, dead culture. Alienated by these men's treatment of Russia as completely lost,

Martin longs to engage it as a living force himself but lacks the creative gifts to do so.[35]

Person after person in *Glory* (originally *Podvig* in Russian) fails to acknowledge the specificity of experience and human individuality. Even a Socialist Revolutionary, whose heroic border-crossing and espionage Martin admires, speaks of the devastation of Russia and its famines and executions; but at the end of an entire evening spent in Martin's company mistakes him for someone else.

Martin develops a romantic attachment to Sonia, a Russian girl who has a "half-witted" cousin, Irina. As a normal teenager fleeing Russia after the Revolution, Irina was molested and witnessed deserting soldiers or peasants shoving her father through the window of a moving train. The traumas of the trip and a severe typhus infection took away her ability to speak, leaving her, as one character notes, a "living symbol" of all that has happened. Irina's survival and damaged state reflect the brutalization of Russia and Martin's own muteness—his inability to transcend or express the events that have overtaken him. He hides briefly behind a Swiss passport, and on one trip pretends to *be* Swiss, in an attempt to relieve himself of his historical burden.

With Sonia, who flirts with him for a time, Martin invents the fantastic country of Zoorland. They discuss the strange habits of residents in their imaginary land, riffing on its rules and customs in an absurdist take on the Soviet Union. The untalented and unlucky Martin fails to win Sonia's love, and is likewise disappointed when he finds his only real stab at creation—the magical world of Zoorland—has been turned into a novella by a romantic rival to whom Sonia has described it in detail.

Inspired by the Socialist Revolutionaries he knows, Martin eventually sets out to sneak back into the Soviet Union alone for twenty-four hours, though he suspects his exploit will end badly. One of the anti-Bolshevik activists in the novel is said to have escaped the Soviet Union wrapped in a shroud; Martin, too, plays at death in his attempt to live.

Unlike the professionals, he does not go in the service of any larger cause. No actual mission or agenda burdens his trip with exterior meaning. He is a pure spy, an unaffiliated intruder, harming no one, entering a world clandestinely with no possibility of political repercussions against anyone but himself. He understands the risks—he has already imagined his execution. Like Nabokov himself, Martin tries to use longing to create an artistic experience from historical exigencies, refusing to serve or engage on anyone's terms but his own. The end of the book takes place among his friends and family after he has disappeared, leaving Martin's fate unknown forever.[36]

5

In *Mary*, Nabokov had nodded toward an absent love living through "years of horror" in the Soviet Union. In *The Defense*, he had mentioned penal servitude, torture, and hard labor camps, but without specifics. In *Glory*, he has Martin briefly imagine himself escaping from labor camps, but only in passing. Concentration camps had started to cast a pall over Nabokov's novels, just as they were continuing to expand into his century, but they had only begun to shadow his own life.

In the beginning Nabokov no doubt found it easier to write from the point of view of émigrés who had, like him, escaped the worst of Russia's fate. But his initial silence may have been due in part to how few specifics were known early on about the camps. There were trials, of course—and not just of the Socialist Revolutionaries, but also priests and intellectuals. After the trials came the rumors of people being sent north and east en masse, but for a time, much of what followed was touched with mystery.

Some facts, however, were known. By 1923, Russian exiles in the West understood that *katorga*, the hard labor in exile first established under the Tsars, had a new face and a new home. The heart of the Soviet penal system had moved onto the Solovetsky Islands—to a monastery familiarly known as Solovki.

Perched northeast of the Russian mainland, Solovki had been established five hundred years before as an outpost of the Russian Orthodox Church. As early as the sixteenth century, the first religious prisoner had been sent there by the Tsar. Others had followed, with the monastery of Solovki becoming a jail for the Empire's religious dissidents.[37]

The Bolshevik takeover, however, quickly changed Solovki's identity. Initially, post-Revolutionary Russian concentration camps had been run on an *ad hoc* basis, but in June of 1923, more than a hundred inmates were sent to the islands, followed by additional waves of prisoners. That fall, Solovetsky monastery grounds were officially turned over to the secret police. In November of the same year, Lenin named Solovki a "northern camp of special significance."[38]

Lenin died just months later; but for Nabokov, Solovki would become a symbol of the country's suffering and shorthand for Bolshevik cruelty under Lenin. Newspaper readers in Europe and even America soon learned its name, as reports of suicide and executions on Solovki trickled out, offering little hope to those whose family members had been sent there. By 1926, it was internationally known as "the most feared prison in Soviet Russia."[39]

The struggle for succession after Lenin's death was eventually won by Joseph Stalin, but those hoping the camps would play a diminished role under his rule were disappointed. The number of prisoners held at Solovki increased exponentially, and Western newspapers carried a Soviet announcement detailing the inauguration of airline service between the port city of Kem and Solovki, to speed up incarceration and free prisoner transport from seasonal restrictions of ice and winter.[40]

Meanwhile, conditions on Solovki deteriorated. Whispers of bizarre abuse in the camps made their way into print outside Russia. The Soviet use of a "mosquito torture," in which inmates were stripped naked and left to the mercies of swarms of biting insects, was noted in English-language newspapers for the first time.[41]

Prisoners soon emerged to tell their own tales of torture and starvation. Some inmates served out their sentences or were released because of their shattered health, returning to the mainland. Others managed to escape into exile, and got their stories published in newspapers across Europe and America. The first full-length accounts from former prisoners appeared in the mid-1920s; by 1931 several more had arrived.

Former political prisoners at Solovki recounted torture and executions. Non-political prisoners reported harvesting lumber in grueling conditions. Testimony from a member of a lumber crew detailed how those who failed to complete a daily quota by evening would be beaten by guards and kept working far into the night. Forced laborers resorted to chopping off their own hands, feet, or fingers in a search for relief from the endless work. Conditions in the camps entered the public debate on Capitol Hill in the U.S. and the British Parliament, resulting in an international boycott of some Soviet exports, including lumber.[42]

Solovki horror stories and testimony continued to spread internationally, spurring an internal investigation. But the outrage did not shake Soviet faith in the rehabilitative possibilities of concentration camps. Solovki-style camps soon became the template for incarcerating and rehabilitating political opponents. A 1929 Politburo resolution called for the creation of a network of camps to build on the Solovki model, using prison labor to develop the nation's natural resources.[43]

In the beginning the word GULag was merely an acronym for *Glavnoe Upravlenie Lagerei*, meaning "Main Administration of Camps." Convicts might unlearn their opposition to the Bolsheviks; and in the meantime, their work would help to build the Soviet state.

6

With a burgeoning prison culture back home, few economic prospects in Europe, and nowhere to turn, some émigrés immolated themselves via suicide, alcohol, or the oblivion of cocaine.[44] In

Germany, Nazi Party brownshirts skirmished with Communists in street fights that echoed a clash of extremes that émigrés had lived through more than a decade before. More Russians left Berlin for Paris or America. Others trudged on. And some chose Luzhin's end.

For those who remained, a less lethal escape was available through cinema, which blossomed in Germany through the 1920s and 1930s. Filmmakers came from around the world to work in Berlin in the postwar years. Germany, like Nabokov, had begun to produce harrowing stories of madmen and monsters, from *The Cabinet of Dr. Caligari* to *Nosferatu*. But the Nabokovs, who went to the movies regularly, had a wide range of films from which to choose. French, British, and American movies made the rounds, including comedy from the Marx Brothers and Buster Keaton—two of Nabokov's favorites.[45]

Like her husband, Véra had played an extra in Berlin productions. More than acting, however, Nabokov had an interest in developing scenarios—screenwriting promised more money than poetry or fiction could provide. And at one point Hollywood beckoned—a Russian-American director took an interest in Nabokov's "The Potato Elf," a story about a dwarf who falls in love. There was talk of bringing Nabokov to California, but as he sent additional material along, interest declined.[46]

Véra's younger sister Sonia was also serious about a cinematic vocation, and spent two years training at a Berlin drama school in hopes of becoming an actress. Nabokov, in contrast, seems to have approached acting more recreationally—he once found himself chosen as an extra simply because the evening clothes he showed up in fit that day's scene.[47]

Perhaps he enjoyed the creative hubbub, watching the dirty work of making art. Or maybe there was some satisfaction in the de facto deception inherent in all film. Cartier staff had called the police on Nabokov in Paris when his attire had made him seem something he was not; why not use his dinner jacket to create the illusion of an identity that no longer existed?

Along with big-budget German projects and smaller émigré productions, Berlin was also home to a large group of Communist filmmakers. In the early 1920s, German Marxist Clara Zetkin had called for a new kind of Revolutionary art, saying, "The cinema must reflect social reality, instead of the lies and fairy tales with which the bourgeois cinema enchants and deceives the working man." As an artistic statement, it was the loose antithesis of Nabokov, who had begun to rework fairy tales and fashion new worlds from the husks of history, making enchantment and deception the very basis of his art. But talented filmmakers responded to Zetkin's appeal and began to produce movies that focused on the harsh realities of poverty and oppression.[48]

Sergei Eisenstein in Russia had already created powerful narratives about the Revolution with movies like *Strike* and *Battleship Potemkin*. His breathtaking work straddled the line between art and propaganda, and profoundly influenced his Communist counterparts in Berlin.[49] By 1928 German documentarians such as Carl Junghans were already unveiling montage-style films in tribute to Lenin and the Revolution.

Lenin's death had not increased Nabokov's appreciation for the Communists, and, if such a thing were possible, Véra held them in even lower esteem. And so it seems unlikely to have garnered the approval of either Nabokov when Véra's gregarious sister Sonia became involved with Junghans, a freewheeling Communist filmmaker more than a decade her senior.[50] Others knew the fashion-forward Sonia as Junghans's girlfriend, and the affair was public as early as 1930—likely a particular embarrassment for Véra in the small world of Russian emigration.

And in the way that so much of Nabokov's life seeped into his art, his next book told the story of a self-absorbed and mercenary young woman who dreams of being an actress and the older married German whose marriage and life she destroys. The cinematically structured *Camera Obscura* marked Nabokov's first book about a sexually charged younger woman and a reprehensible older man helpless in the face of his obsession.

7

Véra's sister Sonia, however, was not destined to stay in Berlin much longer. In 1931, she left not just Junghans but also her job at a perfume company and Germany itself, heading for Paris to make a new start.[51]

A year later, Nabokov followed, on a different mission. He planned to do a public reading, and hoped to find out if his reputation had grown enough for Paris to support him as a writer. Staying first with his cousin Nicholas, who had become a composer for the ballet, Nabokov went every day to the house of Ilya Fondaminsky, where he saw all the living literary and political figures of the emigration. In mid-November, Nabokov moved from Nicholas's rooms to stay with the Fondaminskys, where his hosts enjoyed his brilliance and tolerated his smoking.

Preparing for Nabokov's Parisian debut, an unofficial committee came together to dress him on the night of his reading. Wearing a shirt and tuxedo borrowed from a former Tenishev classmate, armbands improvised by Fondaminsky's wife, and suspenders borrowed from a Socialist Revolutionary (whose pants threatened to fall down all evening), Nabokov was simultaneously himself and a product of the Russian emigration.[52] He read several poems, a short story, and two chapters from the forthcoming novel *Despair*. Staged and promoted by Fondaminsky, the program took place in front of a sold-out audience, which responded enthusiastically.

Paris also provided Nabokov a chance to see his brother. Sergei had converted to Roman Catholicism in 1926—the city, apparently, was still worth a Mass.[53] But whatever piety he had acquired had not curbed his sense of style. Partnered with his ever-present bow tie, the dramatic cane and cape of his university years found their match in the full makeup in which Sergei was said to attend services. Still living in the difficult circumstances that afflicted Russian émigrés everywhere, he had nonetheless conquered the cultural ramparts of the city. With his cousin Nicholas, he had entered the social circles of some of Paris's most prominent artists, including Ballets Russes founder Sergei Diaghilev, novelist and rising filmmaker Jean Cocteau, Edith Sitwell, and Gertrude Stein. Sergei had also become involved with an Austrian heir named Hermann Thieme.

The brothers' reunion went badly. Despite possessing gifts of his own, Sergei was achieving nothing on the scale of his brother Vladimir, the newly crowned literary king of the Parisian émigrés. There was their childhood history to navigate, and Nabokov was still unsettled by Sergei's homosexuality, by then a public part of his identity. Sergei's stutter also made conversation tricky—the more urgent and important the words, the less able he was to get them out quickly.[54]

Sergei longed for a more meaningful connection to his brother. He made another overture during Vladimir's Paris visit, saying that he wanted to address the distance between them. They met for lunch at a restaurant, and Sergei brought the handsome and charismatic Hermann along.[55]

Vladimir and Sergei's conversation that day hinted at the possibility of bridging the gulf that had separated them since childhood. But Nabokov was still who he was: writing to Véra after the meeting, he had been surprised that Sergei's "husband" was so congenial and "not at all the pederast type." And he acknowledged being uncomfortable during the conversation, the more so when a friend of Sergei's came over to talk.[56]

After five weeks in Paris, Nabokov continued on to Belgium, where he pulled off another successful reading. From a literary standpoint, Nabokov's trip was a roaring success. He wrote to Véra, convinced that they should move to France at the beginning of the New Year.

By December, Nabokov had returned to Berlin. In elections held during his absence, the Nazi Party had won a third or more of the German vote for the second time that year. Communist paramilitary groups were banned—it was not hard to see that the Party itself would be the next to go. Communist filmmaker Carl Junghans, already abandoned by Véra's sister Sonia, divorced his wife and fled to Moscow.[57]

8

Moving from a pension into the Berlin apartment of Véra's cousin in 1932, Nabokov plumbed a very different emigration in his next novel.

Drafted in less than three months, *Despair* would deliver yet another madman for a central character, this one as lethal as the chess master Luzhin had been harmless. This time, however, Nabokov would turn the story over to his delusional narrator and let him portray that madness from the inside.[58]

Despair is recounted by Hermann, a chocolatier living in Berlin at the beginning of the 1930s. On a trip to Prague, Hermann meets a tramp named Felix and is taken with their mirror resemblance. Over time, Hermann develops the idea of faking his own death by killing Felix. Dressing Felix as himself, Hermann believes he can murder his double and disappear to start a new life, his secret safe forever. He imagines his execution as a work of art, and hatches a convoluted plan that he seems to pull off. But after he commits murder, Hermann realizes that he has left a crucial piece of evidence behind—and, more disastrous for him, no one else seems to see any resemblance between him and Felix. Hermann flees to France, but is quickly identified as the killer.

A tale from a madman with a twist that redefines the story—the same narrative arc was nearly a prerequisite in German films of the 1920s. Nabokov also overtly nods to, and mocks, Dostoyevksy's fascination with doubles. But unlike Dostoyevksy's books, there was no remorse for the crime and no apparent lesson to draw from it. Some reviewers—Jean-Paul Sartre among them—would later find the novel second-rate.[59]

But no one pursued the history Nabokov had scattered throughout *Despair*. Dates, places, and facts dropped at odd intervals can be gathered to reveal what happened to the narrator before the beginning of the novel—before he envisioned that murder might allow him to start over. Hermann, we learn, had a German father and Russian mother, which made him German by law. As a teenager, he had begun to study in Russia at St. Petersburg University. When the Great War broke out in 1914, he was interned as a German subject and sent to a concentration camp in the southern reaches of Russia.

He ended up living outside the city of Astrakhan, where reading was the only thing that helped him survive: two books every three days or so, a thousand eighteen books in all, across more than four years. Later, during the action of the novel—far from Russia and on his way to murder his imaginary double—Hermann has delusions that he is still in that camp, watching a man in an embroidered skullcap and a barefoot peasant girl outside his window, as dust scatters in the wind.[60]

Concentration camps in the real world had been a global phenomenon during the First World War, but the plight of those interned near Astrakhan had been particularly hard. Civilians there were held in bitter conditions without money, and they could not find paying work or get food at all. By 1915, news from Russia relayed that not only the prisoners' comfort but also their lives were at stake. They were starving to death.[61]

The fact that Hermann's confinement in Astrakhan stretches through the middle of 1919 reveals just as much. Russia had left the war in March of the prior year, but like the fictional Hermann, many real-world internees were trapped by the Civil War and could not escape. In the spring of 1919, a month before the Nabokovs fled Russia, Astrakhan fell into the hands of Bolshevik forces. Secret police units were sent en masse to the region to sow terror and force compliance. The people killed there were mostly starving Socialist Revolutionaries; they had been striking to restore reduced bread rations. Some were shot in the streets, while others were loaded with the bourgeoisie onto barges floated out into the Volga River. Like the dead of the Yalta pier who had haunted Nabokov the year before, their hands and feet were bound; some had stones tied to their feet. Across three days, dead or alive, resigned or pleading, thousands of people were sent to their own mute eternity at the bottom of the river.[62]

Knowing that civilians were interned in starvation conditions for years by the Tsar and then liberated by the Bolsheviks amid mass murder lends a different frame to Hermann's faith in Communism and his willingness to kill. Nabokov's first truly loathsome narrator, a murderer without even the recklessness of passion, on examination turns out to have spent nearly five years in a concentration camp.[63] He is undeniably a villain, but to condemn him without acknowledging the devastating events that he lived through is to miss half the story.

Reports of millions held in prison and labor camps inside the Soviet Union had spread worldwide by 1931. And yet Nabokov chose not to write about the Soviet camps, but to look back in history and make use of a camp founded under the Tsar before the Revolution. Perhaps he wanted to thumb his nose at Russian émigré readers, many of whom were already romanticizing the bygone days of Empire.[64] Perhaps he was not quite ready to tackle more recent history. In either case, he was just getting started.

CHAPTER SIX

Descent

---∞∞∞---

1

By the time Nabokov slipped a camp from the Great War into *Despair*, the Soviet penal system had mushroomed into a network of rehabilitative perversity, an economic engine of modernization with brutal methods and unrealizable goals. Corrective labor camps had been implemented nationwide, spreading across Russia's vastness from the Finnish border eastward almost to Alaska. Using prisoners to harvest lumber and cultivate land had been a tradition dating back centuries under the Tsars, and even to the Roman era. But when it came to strategic use of prison labor, Stalin's Five-Year Plans surpassed the Tsar's greatest ambitions.

The first major work project using the labor of camp prisoners to build Soviet infrastructure was the construction of a canal linking the White and Baltic Seas. From 1931 to 1933, for twenty months, political prisoners were brought in—many from Solovki. They were put to work in the swamps and marshes of the Russian northwest with only crude tools—axes, saws, hammers, and improvised wheelbarrows jokingly referred to as "Fords."[1]

An estimated 25,000 prisoners died building the White Sea Canal in just the first winter of the project, under conditions of disease and torture that recreated the experience at Solovki. Corpses that season were so ubiquitous that some were never carted away from where they had frozen to death, and their bones still lay in the open the following summer.[2]

Those who had not actually visited the canal worksite found it easy to sing the praises of the enterprise. *The New York Times*'s Walter Duranty noted that the new Soviet effort was longer than the Panama and Suez Canals and likely to surpass both in importance to the shipping industry. After prison amnesties were awarded upon the timely completion of the project, Duranty announced in a front-page story that "Soviet power can be merciful as well as merciless." He was sure the U.S.S.R. had turned a corner, with police reforms in place and a bumper crop on the way.[3]

Duranty, who had covered the trial of the Socialist Revolution-aries a decade before, won the Pulitzer Prize in 1932 for his posts from Russia on the first Five-Year Plan. The award helped establish him as Russia's interpreter in the West.[4]

Not everyone, however, was so sanguine about Duranty's reporting. The notion of the Soviet state as merciful seemed rich to journalists with other sources. Duranty's regular stories about the bumper crops of 1933 also began to be contradicted by coverage of starvation in the south. Two things became apparent: not only was there a famine of historic proportions under way, but the catas-trophe was due in large part to deliberate decisions by government officials. Millions were dying preventable deaths while Duranty labeled stories of famine "bunk" and responded viciously to journal-ists who questioned his reporting.[5]

Duranty was not the only one touting progress in the Soviet state. Maxim Gorky, who had challenged Lenin over the fate of the Socialist Revolutionaries, took on a very different role with the White Sea Canal project, spearheading a tribute to it. He was joined in the effort by a number of writers and artists, some of whom had likewise returned to Russia. Aleksey Tolstoy, who had once traveled with V. D. Nabokov to England and was celebrated in the Nabokov family apartment in Berlin, joined with many other contemporary writers in surveying the gem of Stalin's progress. Viktor Shklovsky, who had captured the anguish of Russian exiles in Berlin's Zoo district, made his own trip to the canal site, participating in the project in an attempt to secure the release of his brother. The group's propaganda volume, *The Stalin White Sea-Baltic Canal,* put its literary skills at the service of not just the state but a fabrication, one that did not acknowledge the price paid by the dead for a waterway so shoddy and shallow that it was incapable of serving most of the vessels that it had been designed to accommodate.[6]

But Gorky's service to the U.S.S.R. assured his place for the moment as its literary don. He had become the person to whom parents or grandparents wrote, submitting copies of their offspring's literary efforts in the hopes that their children might grow up to become state-sanctioned authors. One such letter sent during the construction of the White Sea Canal was mailed by the aunt and uncle of the teenage Alexander Solzhenitsyn, who had begun to write. The couple included their nephew's travelogue of a trip with the Young Pioneers. A response from one of Gorky's secretaries assured Solzhenitsyn's relatives that the boy surely had what it took to be a Soviet author.[7]

An eye toward writers who would carry the torch for Communism in the coming years led not just to the encouragement of rising Soviet youth but also to another round of attempts to bring prominent exiles home. And so in the first weeks of the White Sea Canal project, Soviet novelist Alexander Tarasov-Rodionov traveled to a Berlin bookstore frequented by Vladimir Nabokov and left a note for him.

Nabokov met Tarasov-Rodionov at a café, where the latter expounded on life in modern Russia and invited Nabokov to return. Tarasov-Rodionov had built his reputation on a novel called *Chocolate,* a romantic treatment of martyrdom in a revolutionary dictatorship in which innocence is irrelevant. Nabokov broached the question of artistic freedom, a condition completely impossible for Tarasov-Rodionov to guarantee. At some point, the Soviet visitor grew alarmed, fearing he had been set up. Nabokov seems never to have considered the offer seriously. He let his characters dream helplessly of Russia, but he would not go to the Soviet Union.[8]

2

As if the spiral of history were winding its way around to repeat Nabokov's last years in Russia, Germany edged closer and closer to civil war. Laws banning Nazi paramilitary groups passed and were repealed; street violence escalated. German Communists, losing political ground, took up their own extreme tactics. Strikes, beatings, and crossfire dominated news stories in and outside Germany, with one Anglo-German expatriate mourning his country's emergence as a "sinister and dangerous character" that had eclipsed even Russia on the world stage.[9]

Political compromise led to Hitler's installation as Chancellor in January 1933 and Nazi control over German police forces. With the Reichstag fire in February and new elections in March, support for the Nazi party skyrocketed. Legislation passed later that month effectively sealed Hitler's role as dictator.

The Nazis had left little doubt what their priorities would be, and they did not wait to begin delivering on them. Two days before Hitler secured power over Germany, Heinrich Himmler announced in a press release the creation of a concentration camp at Dachau. The camp, it was explained, could accommodate five thousand people and was built to house "all Communists" as well as Social Democrats "who endanger state security." Within months, Dachau had become a byword for brutality in Europe and America, and "an ogre" haunting stories and lullabies in Germany.[10]

As the Nazis moved to establish other labor camps and prisons to hold their left-wing political opponents, newspaper accounts were quick to label some of the more distant sites as "'Siberias' of the

German revolution." Augsburg police arrested leading members of the Social Democratic Party, even as they admitted that there were no charges against them. Radicals were, officials explained, being taken into "preventive custody."[11]

With measures underway to eliminate armed political opposition, Nazis turned their attention toward other targets. Jews became subject to home invasions, forced resignations, random beatings, and assault without recourse. Dead bodies recovered on the outskirts of cities were listed by the police as unidentified suicides.[12]

On her way home from work that May, Véra Nabokov witnessed just one of the bonfires held nationwide to burn works by Jewish and other "decadent" authors. Books destroyed that evening in Berlin included the writing of Karl Marx, Bertolt Brecht, Thomas and Heinrich Mann, and the archives of Magnus Hirschfeld, a Jewish advocate for decriminalizing homosexuality—to whose journals V. D. Nabokov had once contributed an article on the subject.[13]

Closure of gay and lesbian social clubs and cultural organizations had already begun, and Hirschfeld, in America at the time of the inferno, never returned to Germany. At the bonfire, seeing the early signs of what was to come—the singing crowd, the celebratory dancing, and the delight in hatred—Véra moved on.[14]

Nabokov, too, had an early introduction to life under the Nazis, finding the *Sportpalast* where he and George Hessen went to watch boxing matches decked out in Nazi banners and ringed with flags. It was the same arena in which Hitler would make his most important speeches, where the crowds would salute and shout "Heil!" for the movie cameras that captured history while Joseph Goebbels egged them on.

After one fight night at the *Sportpalast*, Nabokov, Hessen (who was Jewish), and another friend rode the tram home next to a Nazi couple. Hessen would later claim that during the ride, Nabokov had toyed with the woman's hat, intentionally rattling him and delighting in his anxiety. Nabokov denied being the responsible member of their party, but it is tempting to give credence to Hessen's account. At a time when political radicals were already being sent to concentration camps, and the Red Cross was reporting on the brutality there, Hessen also remembered Nabokov prank-calling him to ask when their Communist cell would meet.[15] Nabokov's sense of humor included a dash of heartlessness, because the danger was real.

Nazi anti-Semitism mirrored sentiment among the more reactionary Russian exiles. When Ivan Bunin received the Nobel Prize for Literature in 1933, the first literary Nobel ever awarded to a Russian, a banquet was held in his honor that December by the Union of Russian Writers. Bunin was living in a run-down house in southern France at the time, but serendipitously was in Berlin for the festivities. Before the banquet, a Russian businessman and publisher announced that his staff had decided that Joseph Hessen and Nabokov—the "kike and the half-kike"—should not speak at the dinner.[16] Nabokov and Hessen disregarded the threat and presented anyway.

In an anti-Semitic dig only slightly more subtle, émigrés critical of Sirin's writing suggested that all of the work Nabokov had been doing with the Jewish editors at *Contemporary Annals* had ruined him: "Educated among monkeys, he has become one himself." And in the wake of his marriage to Véra, it was not just strangers who assigned a Jewish identity to Nabokov. Criticism among his acquaintances about becoming "completely Jewified" after his marriage to Véra had enough momentum to roll on for decades.[17]

Nabokov, for his part, wore his philosemitism proudly. He made a point of entering Jewish-owned businesses with a friend the day after the Nazis first imposed a boycott on them, despite the fact that coming to the attention of the regime was a more and more unpleasant prospect.[18]

Early on, Hitler made a pretense of asking his followers to refrain from street violence, but the half-hearted messages were at odds with official actions. The Nazis had based their campaign on a repudiation of fifteen years of German shame since the loss of the war, but as a *New York Times* editorial noted, one might more

appropriately have to return to the Dark Ages—or Tsarist Russia—
to find a comparable complicity in generating race hatred on the
part of a government.[19]

3

As the rising tide of stories about prison, exile, forced labor, camps,
and executions in both Russia and Germany found their way into
newspapers, Nabokov contemplated his next novel. *The Gift* would
become a book within a book: the fictional story of a Russian émigré
in Berlin who reveals his genius by writing a biography of another
writer, revolutionary Nikolai Chernyshevsky. A real-world hero of
the political left for almost a century, Chernyshevsky had inspired
generation after generation—not only Lenin but also the Socialist
Revolutionaries who were publishing so much of Nabokov's work
in Paris.[20]

Spending more than a year researching Chernyshevsky's life,
Nabokov planned to tuck a nonfiction biography into a single chapter
at the heart of his novel. From *Despair*'s nod to real-world concentration camps during the Great War, Nabokov moved on to tackle one
of the most legendary incarcerations in Russian history.

The broad facts of Chernyshevsky's life were already well-known
to Nabokov's readers. Arrested for political activity under Tsar Alexander II, Chernyshevsky had been sent to the Peter and Paul Fortress
in 1862, where he wrote *What Is To Be Done?*—a novel that served
as the template for revolutionary idealism right up to the Revolution itself. After more than a year of imprisonment and a cruel mock
execution, Chernyshevsky had spent the rest of his life working in
mines on the Chinese border more than four thousand miles from
St. Petersburg, then living in exile in Siberia and Astrakhan.

Rather than simply relaying the familiar story, however, Nabokov
collected details that had been forgotten by most readers. He traced
the improbable path of the manuscript for Chernyshevsky's famous
novel, which was smuggled out of the Peter and Paul Fortress by a
doctor but slid off a sleigh into the snow, only to be found by a clerk

(who did not hear Nabokov's small voice crying from the future to destroy it).[21]

Nabokov extracted Chernyshevsky's humanity from the legend—his freckles, his nearsightedness, his failed attempts to follow *What Is To Be Done?* with anything memorable—treating his subject not as a revolutionary juggernaut but as an accident of history, someone "half-crushed by years of penal servitude," living out his last decades an old man "unable to reproach himself for a single carnal thought." Parodying Chernyshevsky's account of a fictional revolutionary who slept on a bed of nails to prepare for the rigors of arrest and imprisonment, Nabokov focused on the frailty and foibles of a real human being, arrested and imprisoned. Fighting despair and helplessness, Chernyshevsky writes to his wife about the wonderful stories he is making up. And his guards relay that at night, their prisoner "sometimes sings, sometimes dances, and sometimes weeps and sobs."[22]

A strange hybrid of ridicule and tenderness, *The Gift* represented another Nabokov story in which a character who has taken arms up against no one is crushed by banishment and imprisonment. As the threat of the modern camps loomed larger in the world, Nabokov ventured farther back in history, exploring their roots and historical foundations.

4

Despite his immersion in the past, pressing matters demanded Nabokov's attention in the present. A visit by Joseph Hessen to Prague that February revealed that Elena Nabokov was seriously ill.[23] Nabokov agonized over what to do—it was not just his mother he had to consider. Evgenia Hofeld was in Prague as well, along with both his sisters, now married. Olga had a toddler son, Rostislav—the first grandchild of V. D. Nabokov.

More than a decade after Nabokov had promised to bring his mother to Berlin, he was further from that prospect than ever. If he and Véra left Germany, which they had begun to realize was inevitable, it would add even more distance. The prior summer, he had looked into teaching at a Swiss university, which would have solved several problems at once, but no offer was forthcoming.[24]

Yet—even with his mother's illness, the intensifying Nazi nightmare, and the lack of money, of which there was sometimes more and sometimes less but never enough, the spring was a joyful one. If fate's most generous gesture had been introducing Nabokov to Véra, it now offered a close runner-up. Into a world of hardship and multiplying hatreds came a gift: on May 10, 1934, in one of Berlin's private clinics, a healthy son was born.[25] Nabokov walked home from the maternity clinic at five A.M. down a street half in sunlight, half in shadow, past windowshop portraits of Hitler and Hindenburg framed with flowers, measuring his newfound love against all the mortal threats arrayed against it.

In a deception that may have owed as much to privation as to skill, Véra had concealed her pregnancy from start to finish, surprising friends so greatly with the news of the birth that the announcement may have been taken for a prank.[26] The couple wrote their friends and family in Paris, London, and Prague with news of the birth of their son Dmitri.

For all the delight his parents took in his arrival, Dmitri's timing was not propitious. Jews were being forced out of public life in Germany; a Russian Jew was doubly suspect. And as a Semitic foreigner with a tendency to speak her mind, Véra's associations might not have helped. She had once served as a translator at the home of Albert Einstein, whose pacifism and statements against the Nazis led to the revocation of his citizenship and a raid on his home in search of a hidden cache of weapons—a cache the authorities were sorely disappointed not to find. Reich propaganda cast Véra's former client as the reviled face of Semitism, with his abstract, difficult theories used as examples of the idiocies of "liberalistic" German university education.[27]

Even Hitler's allies had reason to be nervous. During late June and early July 1934, potential rivals were rounded up during the Night of the Long Knives and arrested or executed. More than eighty people were killed in the summer purge.

Véra kept up with the German papers, but news of the executions—which sailed around the world—might actually have escaped Nabokov's notice. In the midst of *The Gift*, he had been struck by inspiration. Shifting gears to draft an entire novel in a two-week frenzy, he wrote through three days of arrests and assassinations that would seal Nazi power for more than a decade.

The result of that inspiration was *Invitation to a Beheading*, the story of Cincinnatus, sentenced to death for the crime of "gnostical turpitude" in a dislocated universe. Unfolding in the window between Cincinnatus's sentencing and his execution, the book takes place in a fortress in which he is the first prisoner—a facility as changeable, incomplete, and improvised as a stage set. Cincinnatus's individualism is set against the machinations of the prison staff, who conspire against him; his wife and family, from whom he feels alienated by his singular fate; and a strangely promiscuous little girl with a red and blue ball.

In a Kafkaesque punishment for corrupt thinking (an antecedent to George Orwell's thoughtcrime), Cincinnatus remains perpetually uncertain of when he will be executed. Wondering if he might find a way to avoid his fate, he is told by a fellow prisoner that "only in fairy tales do people escape from prison."[28]

The prison has a circus atmosphere—the same prisoner flips onto his hands and performs a trick upside down. His identity will soon be inverted, too, for he is actually Cincinnatus's future executioner. Cincinnatus spends his remaining days in a revolving, unstable unreality, but just prior to his beheading realizes that it is possible to step out of the story, that his mind has the power to free him. Just as he is executed, he climbs down from the scaffold amid the outraged cries of his jailers, whose theater he is disrupting, and the universe begins to unravel.

Invitation to a Beheading, like *Despair* and *The Gift*, marked Nabokov's third novel in a row with a key character imprisoned not for his deeds but his thoughts, his words, or his identity. The imprisoned characters' stories ranged from pure history to pure invention, but refracting the madness of the police state, Nabokov was in the throes of a new theme, and he would spend many more years devoted to it.

5

Berlin in the 1930s hardly required a dystopian fairy tale—the monstrous comedy of a police state unfolded daily. But by writing his own version, Nabokov could shape the story to his own ends, retaining some kind of control over his circumstances, even if it were only imaginary.

The money from Nabokov's books and stories was still insufficient, and work for Véra had become more complicated. She had taken Americans on guided tours of the city. She had been employed at the French Embassy in Berlin for a time, and had done translation to pay medical debts from her father's final illness. And, as always, she was typing and revising Nabokov's work for him. In the meantime, the family had expanded, and parental obligations pressed at her from one side, while restrictions under the Nazis hemmed her in on the other.

The authorities were willing to overlook those restrictions for a time. Needing a stenographer, the Nazis invited her to take shorthand at an International wool congress held in Berlin, where she ended up transcribing the speeches of four ministers. After she made a point of explaining that she was Jewish, they claimed to be surprised she would think they cared.[29]

They did, of course, care deeply. Such work would become rarer, and Véra's safety was less and less certain. The Nabokovs knew they would have to leave at some point—but where precisely they could go remained an unanswered question. Véra was wary of France, where, despite the experience of her sister Sonia, Russian emigrants faced challenges in getting identity papers and work permits. Where could they survive?

Nabokov headed to Brussels again. Doing three readings in quick succession, he saw his brother Kirill before heading on to France. In

Paris he could no longer beg a room from his cousin Nicholas, who had already moved to America with his own wife and young son. Instead, he stayed again with Fondaminsky and ended up having dinner with Ivan Bunin, who both admired and disliked his literary usurper. Nabokov was resentful of having been collared for the meal, writing to his wife of the miserable evening he had.

Trying to bond over stereotypically Russian food, Bunin succeeded only in irritating Nabokov. The Nobel laureate waxed profane and wanted to discuss the end of history—which at that point surely must have seemed as if it had already come—but Nabokov refused to engage. As they left their table, Bunin said, "You will die in dreadful pain and complete isolation."[30]

The night of February 8, Nabokov read again in Paris to enormous acclaim. Heading back to Brussels without a visa, he used a trick passed on by the Socialist Revolutionaries of *Contemporary Annals*—who had themselves made a number of furtive crossings—to switch trains underground and reenter Belgian territory on the sly.[31]

From there Nabokov made his way back to Berlin, whose Nuremberg Laws must have made Paris seem like a haven. Jews could not hold office or vote. Sex between Jews and Germanic "Aryans" was illegal. Jews were also forbidden from entering state hospitals, parks, libraries, and beaches. They could not be journalists or doctors. Jewish professors had been removed from University faculties.[32]

And in the background, always playing out or threatening to, were spasms of violence. Just weeks after Nabokov returned from France, they took on a more orchestrated feel. Hitler began to build up military forces in the Rhineland along the French border, and introduced a two-year draft. It became obvious that he was planning for war.

Censorship was so widespread, however, that it was difficult for those living in Europe and America to know exactly what was happening inside Germany. Terrifying anecdotes of killings and abuse emerged, but outside Germany many accounts were suspected of being hyperbole or written off as propaganda by pro-German Westerners.

6

Faced with dismal (if accurate) publicity, the German government began to foster a gentler international image, suggesting to reporters that the nascent concentration-camp system was being shuttered, and that policies against Jews had been eased. Nazi rhetoric cooled, and signs barring Jews from restaurants and other public places were removed.

It was, however, only a charade, put on with targeted coyness in the run up to the 1936 Summer Olympics. During the Weimar era, Germany had won the bid to host both the Winter and Summer Games. But with reports of political opponents in concentration camps and the increasing persecution of Jews appearing again and again in Western newspapers, Hitler feared Germany would lose its right to host, and thus a chance to show the triumphant face of the Third Reich.

A movement had already arisen urging the United States to boycott the Olympics in response to recent events. But Avery Brundage, the head of the United States National Olympic Committee, argued in favor of participation, publicly announcing his opinion that there should be a wall between sports and politics. Privately to friends, he blamed the boycott movement on Jewish special interest groups.[33]

In the end, Hitler not only hosted both Winter and Summer Olympics, but saw to it that they were commemorated by his favorite cinematographers. Leni Riefenstahl, who had created propaganda to rival Eisenstein's with her 1934 movie *Triumph of the Will*, was invited to film the Summer games, using dramatic visuals that glorified the Nazi aesthetic and found endless beauty in physical power.

There was no question of whose overall agenda Riefenstahl would serve or which cause had her allegiance. But it was another matter entirely when it came to the director chosen for the Winter Olympics earlier in the year: Carl Junghans, Sonia Slonim's old boyfriend.

Despite his Communist roots, filmmaker Carl Junghans had made his way from the Soviet Union back to Berlin. On his return to Germany, Junghans had denounced the Soviets and, a little over a year later, started making propaganda for the Nazis. He directed the Germans' 1936 Winter Olympics documentary and, later that year, assisted Riefenstahl in filming the Summer Olympics.[34]

When the Olympics ended in mid-August, any German pretense at easing up on Reich opponents disappeared. Over the summer the *SS-Totenkopfverbände*, the Death's Head division of the SS, had quietly gained official designation as concentration-camp guards and administrators. By November, news stories began appearing in the U.S. and Europe describing the creation of labor camps in northwestern Germany. Six thousand prisoners were sent to reclaim 250,000 acres of marshland in land "deadly to every living being." The Nazis claimed that the laborers were not political prisoners but common criminals; newspapers of the time noted that recent legislation had made it impossible to tell the difference. As on Russia's White Sea Canal, the work done in the swampland by the prisoners was to be undertaken not using current engineering techniques, but through medieval methods, with spades used to dig drainage ditches and canals. Similar work, it was explained, was being done in camps across Germany.[35]

The inmates were housed in spare barracks without bars on the windows. Their food rations were said to be higher than in standard prisons, because of the workload, and prisoners interviewed in the camps (presumably in front of guards) told reporters that they were happier in labor camps than they would be in prisons.

The first articles on these camps portray a veneer of austere wholesomeness undergirded by vague unease. Escapes were rare, reporters were told, because of the deadly swamp conditions that lay between prisoners and the Dutch border. The barbed-wire fences surrounding the camps, "dotted with watchtowers that are equipped with searchlights and machine-guns," no doubt also deterred escape. Visually, the labor camps reminded one reporter distinctly of the camps from the Great War.[36]

By 1936, the Germans had three decades of their own camp history to draw on, from the murderous forced-labor camps of Southwest Africa to internment camps from the war—not to mention the more recent experiments at Dachau and Oranienburg. Nonetheless, for a little while longer Germany would remain a relative beginner in the machinery of atrocity.[37]

7

By the early 1930s, in contrast to the increasing tone of dread in coverage of Nazi Germany, news stories on the Soviet Union ran curiously hot and cold. Horror stories continued to leak out, but tales of Russian economic miracles and a resolute march into the future still abounded in the popular press.

Nabokov had no faith in the new society that was being built on the ruins of the Russian Empire. He had already parodied Soviet dreams of progress in his writing, from a commissar teaching sociology to Leningrad schoolchildren in *The Defense*, to the new world Hermann imagines in *Despair*, in which one worker falls dead at his machine only to be replaced by his double.

But in the wake of the stock market crash of 1929 and the start of the Great Depression, faith in capitalism had declined precipitously, and many Americans were hoping that Communism might offer an alternative.[38] Stories crept westward of the new industrial centers springing up throughout Russia—mining at Vorkuta in the Arctic, oil extraction on Nova Zembla, and gold at Magadan in the Kolyma region. Vladimir Nabokov might refuse to set foot in the Soviet Union, but bevies of American intellectuals, students, and reporters were willing to make their way east in his stead, eager to see the Soviet experiment in progress.

During the summer of 1935, American literary critic Edmund Wilson went on a Guggenheim fellowship to Russia, a place he had dreamed might hold answers he had not seen in his reporting on the unraveling of capitalism in the United States. Walter Duranty was known for welcoming visitors from the West to his Moscow rooms, and after special efforts to get his visa, including an appeal for Gorky's assistance, Wilson visited Duranty and then stayed at his apartment while the latter went on vacation.[39]

Some who traveled to Moscow with less of an agenda ended up profoundly disappointed. After his own visit to the U.S.S.R., seeing the sadness and surveillance of a police state, writer E. E. Cummings lost his sympathy for the fledgling state.[40] But Wilson, like Duranty, seemed to note the hardships, anxiety, and even despondency of the population without being ready to shift his essential outlook as a consequence. Wilson, who understood the failures of American capitalism, still seemed to find aspects of Communist society enthralling.

Ignorant of the extent of the suffering around him, Wilson attended a Red Army banquet and theater performances. In Leningrad—formerly St. Petersburg—he passed, unknowing, near Nabokov's old home, visiting St. Isaac's Cathedral and then the Peter and Paul Fortress.[41]

Wilson understood on some level that conditions were repressive; when he met with critic D. S. Mirsky, he confided that the country felt like a prison. In other places, however, Wilson's Soviet diary caught the spirit of Duranty himself. He wrote of finding himself sitting in Moscow at the "moral top of the world where the light never really goes out." On his return to the U.S., Wilson played down the authoritarian feel of the Soviet Union and puffed up the romance of the historic moment.[42]

Wilson should have known better. By the time of his visit, new repression had already begun to bare its teeth. Stalin lieutenant Sergei Kirov had been assassinated on December 1, 1934, and his death had served as the pretext to launch a new wave of trials and executions. While Kirov's body lay in state—in the same room where the trial of the Socialist Revolutionaries had taken place—sixty-six people had been rounded up, tried by troika tribunals resurrected from a dozen years before, and immediately executed.

From the first days of the purges in Russia, émigrés drew parallels between Stalin's handiwork and the Night of the Long Knives in Germany. Even before Wilson had left the U.S. on his way to visit Russia, novelist John Dos Passos had suggested to him that the Soviet response was out of control. Wilson had countered that such brutality was a legacy inherited from the Imperial era and might fade over time.[43]

But in the days and weeks that followed, additional trials and dozens more executions were reported. Those who had calmly accepted the admiring characterizations of Stalin along with Duranty's genial aphorism that "you can't make an omelette without breaking eggs" began to wonder how far the Russian leader would go to eliminate dissent. Official Soviet accounts framed those executed as operatives in a massive conspiracy, saying the "chief instigator and ringleader of this gang of assassins and spies was Judas Trotsky." But interviewed in New York at the Soviet Consulate in 1934, a Soviet official reassured reporters that no new reign of terror would begin, because "there is no one left to purge."[44]

New candidates were found. In the months and years that followed, the killings continued, swelling the ranks of the dead. Stalin tried to consolidate his authority, resurrecting the national affection for the Tsars and forming a cult around himself that borrowed from their legacies, using the burgeoning Great Purge as an indiscriminate cudgel. In 1937 and 1938, the two deadliest years, more than 670,000 people would be executed and as many imprisoned, all sacrificed to the nightmare travesty of a workers' paradise.

The dead are not nameless. Maxim Gorky's life ended in 1936 under mysterious circumstances. Secret police official Gleb Bokii, whose name graced the steamer that carried so many thousands to their doom on Solovki, was shot in November 1937 in the basement of the Lubyanka Prison in Moscow. Alexander Tarasov-Rodionov, the Soviet novelist who met with Nabokov in Berlin to entice him back to Russia, was arrested in 1937 and died in a camp soon after. Osip Mandelstam, who had preceded Nabokov as a student at Tenishev School, mocked Stalin in a biting poem that led to his end in a transit camp in 1938. Arrested after one too many visits from Westerners,

Russian historian D. S. Mirsky—alternately ridiculed and lionized by Nabokov—would die in the Gulag in 1939.

And fate finally also caught up with those Socialist Revolutionaries whose executions had been halted in 1922—and whose show trial under Lenin provided the precedent for the tribunals of the current purges. Abram Gotz, the key defendant in that trial, was shot in 1937.

Gotz outlived some of those responsible for his conviction. Lev Kamenev, to whom credit must be given for the notion of making the Socialist Revolutionaries permanent hostages, was executed in 1936. Judge Georgy Pyatakov, chief of the tribunal that sentenced them, was convicted of somehow flying to Oslo to confer with Trotsky and the Nazis; he was put to death in January 1937. Nikolai Bukharin, who had led the mob rioting against the Socialist Revolutionaries, was executed the following March. And that July, Nikolai Krylenko, the lead prosecutor so many years before, was given twenty minutes for his own trial before being found guilty and shot on the spot.[45]

8

Soon after the end of the 1936 Summer Olympics, Germany signed a pact with Italy, then just a few weeks later allied itself with Japan. International opinion shifted from talking about whether there would be war to predicting when it would start.

The Nabokovs had debated leaving for France since at least 1930, with the reasons for staying or going pivoting on the very thing that Svetlana Siewert's family had found unsettling about the young Vladimir: the uncertainty of a dependable income. In Germany, Véra had been a magnet for employment, with her skills in technical translation and her several languages. Nabokov had become Dmitri's de facto babysitter during Véra's work hours, delighting in the young son whom both parents loved to indulge.

When Dmitri was less than a year old, Véra had managed to land a position with a manufacturing firm, taking care of their foreign correspondence. Within months, however, the Nazis had banned both the Jewish owners and Jewish employees from the firm, and the coveted paycheck vanished. Her work permit soon disappeared, too, the staggering loss offset only by a chance windfall from the estate settlement of one of Nabokov's German ancestors.[46]

They had been hesitant to leave reliable money for the fantasy dream of Paris, where, as émigrés, they would be denied legal employment. But by the end of 1936, their situation was dire. The Nazis placed more stringent restrictions on Jews and some foreigners. Sergei Taboritski, one of the assassins of Nabokov's father, was named Hitler's undersecretary of émigré affairs, with the expectation that he would ferret out Russian Jews. That September, the department began a census of all resident Russians.[47] Life in Berlin had turned from unpleasant and bitter to ominous.

Nabokov headed west for another series of literary readings and meetings, in an attempt to find a writing or teaching position that would allow his family to leave Germany forever. Perhaps Paris, which he had twice wowed that decade, would offer something they could not imagine. Or perhaps England or America would open some hidden door.

On January 18, 1937, Nabokov boarded a train to Belgium with everything still unsettled. Véra and Dmitri stayed behind with her cousin Anna Feigin in Berlin. Exchanging a torrent of letters with her husband, Véra evolved a vague plan to reunite that spring—perhaps in Belgium, or France, or England, or at his mother's lodgings in Prague. Whatever escape route they could conjure, it was nearly time to outrun history again.

CHAPTER SEVEN
Purgatory

———⊗⊗⊗———

1

From London and Paris, Nabokov wrote to Véra in Nazi Germany every day.He found that he had achieved a measure of fame abroad, but it was not yet clear if his celebrity was of an occupationally useful kind. At his readings, Nabokov drew crowds filled with familiar faces: Ivan Bunin, critic Mark Aldanov, and Nabokov's Parisian champion Vladislav Khodasevich, all of whom acknowledged Sirin's brilliance in one way or another.[1]

Other faces were less familiar but not altogether unknown. A mother-daughter pair he had had tea with the year before reappeared, this time with a dinner invitation for him and Fondaminsky. Nabokov had clearly understood during the earlier trip that the mother was playing matchmaker, but knowing did not keep him from joining them.

The daughter, Irina Guadanini, was a former St. Petersburg resident, six years younger than Nabokov and, in the words of Aldanov, a heartbreaker. As with so many White Russian émigrés, Irina belonged to a topsy-turvy social class—one that could contain her dual identities as a poodle trimmer and aspiring poet. Her family, like Nabokov's, had been part of the educated set that had given its children over to Kadet ideals but found death or exile its only post-Revolutionary rewards.

Irina was a divorcée with a reputation. Like Véra, she was beautiful and sophisticated and could speak multiple languages. Like Véra, she adored Sirin's poetry. Unlike Véra, she was not at risk of arrest or assault. She was not trapped in a country gone mad. She had no young son whose fate hung on his father's ability to transform words into money. Nabokov stopped in to see Irina three times in the week after his reading. They went to movies, they went to cafés, they became lovers.[2]

From Berlin, Véra wrote reminding Nabokov that he had promised his mother they would bring Dmitri to Prague; more than three years after his birth, Elena Nabokov had yet to lay eyes on her newest grandson. But Nabokov refused to head east. He pleaded with Véra to meet him in southern France. He did not want, he wrote, to be trapped in Czechoslovakia. Véra balked at his alternate plans, becoming contrary at every turn.

She mentioned the rumors she had heard about Irina. He mocked the comments as gossip. He gave Véra a second name that had also been circulated with his, as if widening the rumor pool would render it more shallow and inaccurate. He threatened to waste money— money he reminded her they did not have—on a trip to Berlin to see her. It is not clear who was paying for the movies and meals with Irina.[3]

Nabokov could not resist describing the happiness of his marriage, even to his lover. But he did not change course. And that February, he developed a painful case of psoriasis, a skin condition that typically includes itching, dandruff, and scaly skin.[4] It requires a certain confidence to conduct an illicit romance with any of those symptoms, but along with his disease and his bleak prospects, his infatuation for Irina tormented him for months. He was failing his wife, he was failing his son. At a private reading in Fondaminsky's apartment, Irina sat next to him as he spoke about the deteriorating conditions in Germany. Perhaps it came as a relief to be adored by someone whose tragedy resided more safely in the past, who was not trapped in history's maw—someone to whom he owed nothing.

He now inhabited the split worlds that he had begun to write about in his fiction. On one level, his work was celebrated everywhere he went, and he continued his glad-handing socialization, trying to ingratiate himself in conversation at literary soirées and on the reading circuit. Substituting at the last minute for another novelist, he ended up addressing a tiny crowd that included former prime minister of the Russian Provisional Government Alexander Kerensky, a Hungarian soccer team, and James Joyce.[5]

On another plane, a harsher reality lurked. Moving on to England, he gave Russian readings to raise money for the trip. Despite the help of friends, he could find no university position in England. His lack of involvement in émigré politics and religious observance alienated members of the anti-Bolshevik and Orthodox communities.[6] Though his talent could not be denied, it could make enemies as easily as it won friends, and his caustic wit did not always endear him to others.

While his travels did not deliver economic salvation, they were not entirely in vain. He helped to finalize preparations for the English-language version of *Despair*. He visited Cambridge and saw his old tutor. Readings were more popular than he had expected, and, as a result, he went back to France with some extra money.

But the trip did not unfold seamlessly. To compound the anxieties of looming war, Véra and Dmitri's predicament in Germany, a rampaging skin disease, and his half-hidden life with a mistress, Nabokov also had passport difficulties. He was not a citizen of the Soviet Union; he was not a citizen of Germany. He was technically stateless. Émigrés had only disreputable green Nansen refugee passports to vouch for their former status as Russian citizens. These passports had been issued to Russian exiles in the wake of the Revolution, as well as to the hundreds of thousands of dis-placed Armenians who faced slaughter or forced relocation by the Turkish government after 1915. Most Nansens had to be renewed annually, and though they did not automatically confer the right to work or anything beyond temporary residency, refugees could be deported without them.

So Nabokov found himself in Paris with an expired Nansen, whose renewal might require his return to Germany, which he wanted to avoid at all costs. A French official who had lost Nabokov's applica-tion for new documentation joked about throwing the old passport out the window. The Nabokov who had meted out justice with his fists in a café brawl years earlier could also manage his rage. Being stateless not only meant losing a homeland; his status put him at the mercy of every petty bureaucrat.

2

Nabokov was indiscreet about his involvement with Irina, and the émigré community in Paris knew well enough what he was up to. In April, Véra had a direct answer to the suspicions her husband had tried to dismiss—a four-page letter anonymously outlining Guadanini's entire relationship with Nabokov. Seeing her husband's affair laid out on paper and knowing that he had lied to her week after week could not have made life in Berlin less miserable. But she had to focus on the immediate task of escaping from Germany with Dmitri.

In the midst of her preparations for departure, Véra received a visit from John Shakhovskoy, Nicholas Nabokov's brother-in-law. He noted that the Nabokovs seemed to be leaving the country. When she mentioned the dangers confronting Jews as inspiration for relocation, she would later recall that Shakhovskoy, an Orthodox priest, suggested that perhaps they should stay and suffer.[7]

Such calls to embrace suffering would find traction elsewhere in Nabokov's circle, but the Véra Nabokov who had flirted with political assassination years before was no longer inclined to be a martyr to history, or to surrender her son to its crueler whims. With violence on the rise in Berlin and her husband's adultery in France, she stopped delaying. She wrote Nabokov, saying that she would go to Paris immediately. So as not to burden Ilya Fondaminsky, she and Dmitri could stay with her sister Sonia. It was as good as decided.

Véra could not have expected such an arrangement to be pleasant. While Sonia had been in Paris for several years and would know the ropes better than either Nabokov, neither Véra nor Vladimir adored her sister. Sonia had an overdeveloped sense of her own worth and could be just as stubborn as Véra.

It was a bitter truth that none of the Slonim girls' marriage choices looked particularly wise at that moment. Nabokov had no job, no prospects, and was in another country with another woman. Lena's husband, a Russian prince, had made the newspapers even before their marriage with a history of jail time for writing bad checks. She would soon leave him. Sonia's 1932 marriage to Max Berlstein, an Austrian Jew, had fallen apart after just eight months and was about to end in divorce. In the meantime, she was living in a hotel and seemed to have plenty of companions.[8] Other than the fact that Sonia had not renounced her Jewish identity—Lena had converted to Catholicism, much to Véra's dismay—it was hard to imagine an aspect of her sister's life that Véra Nabokov might actually endorse. The plan to stay with Sonia seems to indicate Véra's desperation in the moment.

But at the prospect of his wife and his mistress in the same city, Nabokov balked. They continued to write letters about where they would meet in the short run and live in the long run, their exchanges becoming tense. Véra asked again about Irina, wondering why he did not turn his biting sarcasm on her, as he did everyone else in his daily reportage from Paris.

Véra finally bolted Germany with Dmitri, leaving for Prague the first week of May. Nabokov obtained the necessary papers and made his way to meet her two weeks later, avoiding Germany by traveling through Switzerland and Austria. The reunion was complicated. Véra was unhappy and afflicted with rheumatism. Nabokov's mother was in decline. He kept writing Irina, and gave her a clandestine postal address at which to write him back.

After a little more than a month in Czechoslovakia, the family left for France. Nabokov's mother stayed behind with Evgenia Hofeld, his sisters Elena and Olga, their husbands, and the six-year-old Rostislav. When Nabokov left Prague this time, it did not need to be said that his mother would never go back to Berlin.

The three Nabokovs made their way to Paris, where Vladimir lodged again with Fondaminsky, and Véra took Dmitri to stay with a friend of the family. Early in July they headed south to Cannes, where the affair exploded. Nabokov confessed everything and promised to stop writing Irina. Véra later claimed that she told her husband if he were in love with Irina, he should leave. They appear to have argued bitterly over his infidelity.[9] Despite his promise, Nabokov continued to write to his lover, who took a train to Cannes and ran up to him on the beach.

The agony of the situation no doubt felt singular enough, though the storyline was repeating elsewhere. Across the Atlantic, Nabokov's cousin, the composer Nicholas Nabokov, played out a similar drama: the charming artist with a lost country and a wandering eye, his wife, his son, and his mistress. It was a plot so trite, it would have needed some ghastly addition (murder, madness, a winged creature) to be a plausible storyline in Nabokov's literary universe. But Nicholas's wife Nathalie—who, like Véra, knew well enough what her husband had been up to—had enough that summer. She filed for divorce, leaving Nicholas to the attentions of the students for whom he had traded his marriage. Nicholas had a nervous breakdown, committing himself to a psychiatric hospital.[10] The mental illness that was on its way to being a dominant feature of Nabokov's fiction had found its way into his family.

Unwilling to leave Véra, unable to forget Irina, Vladimir Nabokov also struggled to stay sane. Working through the worst point in his life after his father's murder—this crisis, unlike the prior one, completely of his own making—he ended his affair and returned to writing *The Gift*.[11]

The first installment of the novel, in which a young Russian poet searches for his place in 1920s Berlin, had already appeared in Fondaminsky's magazine. In subsequent chapters, the writer Fyodor contemplates writing a biography of his lost father, who disappeared in Siberia in 1919. But he finds himself daunted by the monumental story of his father's life.

After several false starts, he finally meets Zina, a beautiful half-Jewish émigré who admires his work. Realizing that what he wants to write is the life story of Russian revolutionary Nikolai Chernyshevsky, Fyodor throws himself into an innovative biography—the biography that Nabokov had researched and composed years earlier.

Having taken on the saint of Russia's revolutionary movement, Fyodor finds himself castigated when the biography comes out. In Nabokov's world—our world—Chernyshevsky had faced mock execution, followed by hard labor and exile. But in the fictional world of *The Gift*, Chernyshevsky had been subjected not to mock execution but the real thing. Fyodor has added more than two decades onto his cramped and miserable life.

What Fyodor invents as fiction in the novel is historical truth in our world. He imagines what Nabokov knows: the rest of Chernyshevsky's life has much to offer readers who are willing to see him as a human being subjected to political oppression rather than an idealized political symbol.

Through Fyodor's experiences, Nabokov recreated the small world of the emigration and its critics. And in a gesture of charity to the Russian émigré community, despite the widespread condemnation of Fyodor in the novel, his talent does not go unnoticed. But even those who denounce Fyodor can no longer touch him—he has Zina, and he has delivered on his gift.

Chapter Two of *The Gift* was nearly due by the time the Nabokovs got to Cannes that July, but Nabokov was not finished revising it.

He improvised, and instead sent Chapter Four—the biography of Chernyshevsky—north to Paris.[12]

A colleague of Fondaminsky's received the chapter and refused to publish the novel out of sequence. First he demanded Chapter Two. Then he read the chapter Nabokov *had* sent and responded in horror. Not only would they not run the chapters out of order, the magazine would not run the biography of Chernyshevsky at all.[13]

What was Nabokov thinking? For the editors of *Contemporary Annals*, Chernyshevsky was a martyr whose life had been stolen, a legend who had given everything for his ideals and his country. He had fought for the emancipation of the serfs, helped promote many of the most gifted writers in Russian history, and faced arrest, mock execution, labor camps, and exile for his ideals. Nabokov, it would have been glaringly apparent to the editors, had been born with great talent and privilege and, unlike Chernyshevsky, in the face of the brutality afflicting his homeland, had risked nothing for his country, refusing to take a political stand or even to engage in any literary movement beyond socializing in writers' groups that located themselves farther and farther from the tempestuous politics of the day. While the facts from his life of Chernyshevsky were scrupulously accurate, Nabokov's attention to the revolutionary's failings, the author's unforgiving checklist of a hero's pettiness and pathetic aspects, smacked of mockery.

Nabokov had insulted his most reliable benefactor at a time when he had few sources of income. But he wrote saying he would not bend. If Chapter Four were refused, he would not allow any more of *The Gift* to be published in the pages of *Contemporary Annals*. He was grieved by the decision; he had admired the journal for its independence and the range of political viewpoints and literary styles it had published. But he would not change a word; he would not cut a line.[14]

Two weeks passed without surrender on either side. Nabokov's stance was doomed; he could not afford his pride. Whether Véra or his own better judgment made the point clear to him, Nabokov capitulated in the end, mailing off Chapter Two. He had no job, he had lost his mistress, and he had savaged his marriage; now his masterpiece would be hollowed out by censorship. The overdue chapter arrived at the last possible moment to meet the printer's deadline.[15]

3

While Nabokov rehashed nineteenth-century Russian history with his editors, twentieth-century Russia continued to writhe under Stalin's purges. Foreign correspondents reporting what they could uncover about the trials got a surprising amount of accurate information directly from Soviet publications, which trumpeted each new set of tribunals as victories for the people—up to and including the purge of the Press Bureau itself. One *New York Times* reporter summarized the groups of people who had been eliminated in the prior year, starting with heroes of the 1917 Revolution and continuing through the generals of the Red Army, the leaders of the NKVD secret police, top staff of the Ministry of Foreign Affairs, Communist party leaders around the country, officials of the Young Communist League, agricultural managers, and thousands of railway administrators. The purges had become so widespread, the story claimed, that officials had to settle for cooks and nurses when hunting for new saboteurs. A wire report from October 1937 announced that the head keeper at the Moscow Zoo had been tried for connections to spies, playing loud music at the park, and for feeding badgers sausage stuffed with strychnine.[16]

Prosecutors argued that in a complicated effort to sabotage the Revolution, doctors had injected their patients with syphilis, and people on the street had conspired with foreign assassins, spies, and snipers. Those who had seemed to be Communists to the core had been secretly working for decades to destroy Soviet Russia from the inside.

Outsiders became confused. Stalin's purges were so extensive that their legitimacy broke the back of credulity on a daily basis.

But why would the accused confess publicly, as they had at trials of some of the most senior Soviet officials? Left-wing sympathizers and those who looked to Russia as a potential ally against the growing German threat hoped fervently that some truth existed that could excuse the burgeoning atrocities.

Émigrés had a clearer idea than most of what was happening in Moscow, in part because not everyone who was arrested was shot or sent to the camps for life. Accused foreigners were sometimes released without being sentenced or after serving short terms. As they managed to leave the U.S.S.R., proof of trumped-up charges leaked out, along with more details on interrogations, confessions, and executions.[17]

While Nabokov remained outside political activism, several in his circle did not. Alexander Kerensky in Paris continued to issue statements as a spokesman for anti-Soviet Russians. Responding to growing concerns about Russian stability and German aggression in 1938, Kerensky hit the lecture circuit in America. Sporting a tall crew cut and a gold-rimmed monocle, he talked about the essential sameness of the Soviet and Nazi dictatorships. Kerensky suggested that the way of the future was not a choice between fascism and communism, but a rededication to democracy. He predicted (as he had for more than a decade) that democracy would return to Russia. Asked for a specific date, Kerensky demurred that he was no prophet but offered that the Russian people might taste freedom in as little as four months or as long as four years. That November, Kerensky would also come out forcefully against Father Coughlin, a Catholic priest and radio personality in the U.S. who blamed the Russian Revolution on a conspiracy of Jewish activists and bankers.[18]

Inside Russia, people knew both more and less than exiled Russians abroad. Critical analysis of conspiracies fabricated by Stalin and his secret police did not find its way into the Soviet press. But signs of the scope—and the absurdity—of the purges were everywhere. An official given honors in the afternoon could be arrested the same night. Not wanting to affiliate too closely with those targeted by the purges, Soviet citizens learned not to ask about friends or colleagues who had disappeared.[19]

In the southern Russian city of Rostov-on-Don, even the nineteen-year-old Alexander Solzhenitsyn and his compatriots—ardent Soviets all—knew enough to see through the show trials, laying the blame for the problems of the state at the feet of Joseph Stalin. If only the Revolution had followed the trail blazed by Lenin, the argument went, Russia's suffering would never have been so enormous. It was an argument that could be made only quietly, among trusted friends.[20]

Like the true believers inside Russia at the close of the 1930s, leftists in Europe and America who had cheered Soviet progress or been sympathetic to the Communist Party found themselves confronted with evidence of a system gone haywire. Edmund Wilson's *Travels in Two Democracies*, based on his Russian trip, appeared in 1936. Its critical details did not endear him to the Soviet Union—and they embarrassed Walter Duranty—but Party officials should, perhaps, have been grateful. Wilson included unflattering observations but censored his realization that the U.S.S.R. had become a totalitarian state.

A polarity emerged which seemed to offer Europe only Communist Russia or Nazi Germany as a political model (although for a time, Mussolini had his own shadow contingent). In June 1936, France feinted left and elected Léon Blum, its first socialist, and first Jewish, president.

Nabokov had moved to France in the midst of Blum's one-year tenure, which included battles over bitterly contested workers' rights. French conservatives played to racial and political anxieties with the slogan "Better Hitler Than Blum." Though Blum had been born in Paris, one National Assembly member suggested he was not really a Frenchman but "a subtle Talmudist." In turn, Trotsky, in Mexico after being expelled by Stalin, condemned Blum for not being revolutionary *enough*. Blum was, Trotsky claimed in a statement echoed by others, the Kerensky of France.[21]

By the time Nabokov said a final good-bye to his mistress on the French Riviera, Léon Blum had resigned under economic and political pressure. Writers on the left throughout Europe had finally begun to openly denounce the Soviet system. André Gide detailed Soviet human-rights abuses in 1936 with *Return from the U.S.S.R.* A year after his statement that the Soviet Union represented the moral top of the world, Edmund Wilson, too, acknowledged that Soviet justice was a sham. He joined a group of writers with Communist sympathies who labeled Stalin a liar and a villain.[22]

John Dos Passos and E. E. Cummings may have rethought their sympathies after visiting the Soviet state, but never having offered a kind word about Soviet rule, Vladimir Nabokov had nothing to recant. In two decades of exile he had not given an inch on the question of Bolshevik legitimacy, and he had never subordinated his writing to any political party. He admired his father's ideals; but unlike V. D. Nabokov, he stood apart from the fray.

During his trip in England at the beginning of 1937, he had visited his alma mater to have lunch with an old Cambridge classmate, who in his student days had supported the Bolsheviks. Nabokov braced himself for the rationalization he knew would follow: the surgical attempt to separate Stalin from Lenin, the willingness to mourn the victims of the current purges, without any acknowledgment, as Nabokov would later put it, of "the groans coming from the Solovki forced labor camp or the Lubyanka dungeon" under Lenin.[23]

If, arbitrarily, the world of writers were reduced to just two camps—those who dreamed of reinventing literature and those devoted to reforming society—Nabokov would not have hesitated to choose the former. But in *The Gift*, he managed to sidestep the choice. Pulling off a spectacular literary invention, he also addressed the roots of Russian revolutionary history, pointing to the fruit of that legacy in the twentieth century—the very reason for the existence of the émigré community.

He also immortalized the world of Berlin's Russian émigrés, who had largely surrendered that city by the time the book was finished.

The émigrés, however, were offended by his transparent portrait of their world, and by his lionization of the genius protagonist who seemed like a stand-in for Nabokov himself.

Even under a pseudonym, the condemnation of Georgy Adamovich, a critic particularly loathed by Nabokov, was recognizable in *The Gift*. Charged with malicious insult of a fellow writer, Nabokov responded that in creating immortal literature, if it became necessary to "take along for the ride, free of charge" contemporaries who would otherwise be forgotten by history, those he had selected should not complain.[24]

Nabokov was doing for, or *to*, his literary compatriots what his character Fyodor had done to Chernyshevsky. He had immortalized the human eccentricities and the tiny world of the Berlin exiles before their lives could be reduced to sentiment and hagiography. He would not wax nostalgic about them, but neither would he let them vanish into the past.

4

In September 1937, Adolf Hitler and Italian dictator Benito Mussolini paraded their alliance in front of a million people in Berlin. Two months later, an exhibit opened in Munich called "The Eternal Jew." The title, the German name for the Wandering Jew legend, reinforced the idea of the dislocated, immortal Jew, morally and politically depraved, at the helm of a Bolshevik revolutionary tide threatening the world. The exhibit was developed in direct response to a New York exhibition called "The Eternal Road," which recorded the persecution of Jews throughout history.[25]

A book (also called "The Eternal Jew") put out the same year by the Nazi Party showed images of ghetto Jews purportedly carrying out "criminal activities" amid their "bad smells and piles of filth," while employing "the glittering world of perversion as a way of unnerving and enslaving" others. The Nazis had moved from mass propaganda projects extolling the virtues of Aryans to trying to create a groundswell of anti-Semitism solid enough to act on. The exhibition was condemned in newspapers in Europe and America, but was visited by hundreds of thousands of Germans before it began a tour of Germany and Austria.[26]

Details of the exhibit and book's Wandering Jew theme echoed *Agasfer*, Nabokov's own literary treatment of the legend from fourteen years before, but drew the stereotype in a cruder fashion, characterizing the representative Jew as the harbinger of political instability and a sexually perverted merchant of corruption for more than a millennium. But where the twenty-three-year-old Nabokov had held out the possibility of redemption and love for his broken traveler, the Nazis framed the myth to argue that Jews were congenitally defective, beyond salvation, and a threat to the entire world.

Whatever use the young Nabokov had made of cultural stereotypes floating in the ether in the 1920s, many things in his life had changed by the fall of 1937. In *The Gift*, Fyodor notes how Zina, at first irritatingly but then more persuasively, slowly shifted his callousness about anti-Semitism into a deep sensitivity, leading him to regret that he had previously ignored hateful comments from friends and associates.[27] Nabokov had undergone a parallel transformation. He had been married to the proudly Jewish Véra Nabokov more than a decade, and he had a three-year-old son who had been sitting at the center of a public campaign of hate, becoming a potential target of an apparently bottomless reservoir of malice.

By the end of 1937, the Nazis had begun to show that malice in new ways, expanding their network of concentration camps. The 4,800-person facility at Dachau was demolished, and a larger complex erected in its place. In 1937, Buchenwald opened in the forested hills just northwest of Weimar. On the outskirts of Oranienburg, Sachsenhausen concentration camp was receiving prisoners too.[28]

Nabokov, who had already referenced Russian camps and prisons in his stories, began to weave the German nightmare into his work. The specter of violence turns to actual bloodshed in "Cloud, Castle, Lake," a short story written that summer. A Russian man who wins a vacation at a charity ball ends up traveling in the countryside with a group of Germans. Even though his companions turn out to be unpleasant and crude, he believes that the trip holds great promise for him, that something wondrous will be revealed. Though the Germans force him to sing along on their strident songs about tramping along fearlessly through the countryside, the Russian manages to see the world through his own eyes. He finds the transcendent landscape of the story's title and a room with a view of it where he makes plans to stay.

But the Germans refuse to leave him to his own future. They force him back onto the train, where they kick him with their heavy boots and then torture him with a corkscrew and a Soviet-inspired improvised whip. The man survives, but returns to the author of the story, unwilling or unable to continue the narrative. He begs to be released from humanity, and the author lets him go.

Nabokov had written "Cloud, Castle, Lake" in 1937 while he was with Véra and Dmitri at Marienbad, Czechoslovakia. Despite the proximity to Germany—they were just a few miles away—the Nabokovs had been out of harm's way. But how long the rest of Europe would remain safe had become a real question; German anti-Semitism and political upheaval had already crossed the border. Under pressure from Hitler, a March political coup in Vienna ushered in the German annexation of Austria and the creation of as many as 185,000 new refugees, including Sigmund Freud.

Within days, President Franklin Delano Roosevelt called for a world conference on the question of Jewish refugees. That July, representatives of thirty-two nations met in Evian-les-Bains, France, to consider the fate of the Jews. Hitler cannily expressed hope that those who had been expressing "such deep sympathy for these criminals" might finally take action. He was, he said, more than happy to send Germany's Jews to them, on luxury liners if need be.[29]

Some observers, at least, understood how vital the meeting was. On July 4, Independence Day—two days before the Evian conference—*New York Times* correspondent Anne O'Hare McCormick called on Americans and the American delegation to see clearly what was happening. "Can America live with itself," she wrote, "if it lets Germany get away with this policy of extermination, allows the fanaticism of one man to triumph over reason, refuses to take up this gage of battle against barbarism?" She noted that willingness to fight a war was not even required to do the right thing in this case—only a commitment to provide shelter for persecuted people so obviously in need. It was, she argued, "a test of civilization."[30]

As the conference unfolded, civilization would fail that test. America, for a brief time, would fill her annual quota of bringing in more than 25,000 German Jews. But the State Department, which controlled the visa process and worried about incoming anarchists, would soon reduce immigration of German Jews to just a fraction of the number permitted under U.S. law.[31]

At Evian, Swiss representative Heinrich Rothmund explained that Switzerland feared being swamped by Jewish refugees it did not want. Argentina's representative spoke glowingly of the benefits that refugees bring—and then right after the conference, his country passed a new law limiting immigration and giving preference to "assimilable immigrants." While countries tossed the hot potato of sheltering the refugees from one to another, a group of fleeing Austrian Jews languished in the middle of the Danube River, with both Czechoslovakia and Hungary refusing to admit them. Only the Dominican Republic proclaimed its shores open to the refugees.[32]

As Germany pointed out with glee and Machiavellian accuracy, the rest of the world wanted to criticize Germany without having to address its own anxieties over Jewish refugees. Instead of improving the situation, the Evian Conference seemed to worsen it.[33]

This willful hedging of the world's democracies in the face of Third Reich cruelty had consequences in Germany and abroad. Shortly after the Nabokovs returned to Paris after a year in southern France, Herschel Grynszpan, a seventeen-year-old Jew, shot German Embassy staffer Ernst vom Rath in Paris. Within hours, anti-Semitic lectures were advertised in public flyers on the streets of France, accompanying the already-active sticker campaign calling for the

removal of Jews. Germany's official news service immediately suggested that German Jews would be punished in retaliation.[34]

German newspapers trumpeted news of the shooting the next
morning, attributing it to a conspiracy of "International Jewry." Vom
Rath died two days later, and the country exploded in orchestrated
rage against Jews. On November 9 and 10, during what would come
to be called *Kristallnacht*, Germans and Austrians smashed windows,
burned more than two hundred synagogues, and looted thousands
of Jewish businesses. Nearly a hundred Jews were killed outright;
thirty thousand Jewish men were arrested and sent to concentration
camps *en masse.*[35]

Véra had escaped Germany with Dmitri in time, pulling out her
cousin Anna Feigin in their wake. Sonia Slonim had left long ago for
Paris. But Véra's other sister, Lena Massalsky, remained in Germany.

In an official capacity, or perhaps for old times' sake, friends of
Taboritski, V. D. Nabokov's assassin, began sniffing around. Lena
had converted to Catholicism, but it would have been no secret to
Taboritski that she was Jewish. The Nabokovs wrote to friends,
asking for assistance getting her out. But outside help was not forthcoming or had become impossible, and Lena stayed in Germany.[36]

Kristallnacht was witnessed by the world, with foreign correspondents reporting from Berlin and other cities on the death
and destruction, as well as recounting the enthusiasm shown by
some Germans at the humiliation of their Jewish neighbors. The
Nazi government assessed a billion-*Reichsmark* fine (roughly four
hundred million dollars at the time) on German Jews for the damage
done to the nation. And weeks later, Neuengamme, a subcamp of the
Sachsenhausen concentration camp complex, opened for business
on the grounds of an old brick factory near Hamburg.[37]

5

The same month, Nabokov stepped away from the theme of camps,
prisons, and murderous narrators to blaze through his first English-
language novel. The story of two brothers who live their lives at an

emotional remove from each other and their homeland, *The Real Life of Sebastian Knight* takes place in mid-1930s Western Europe. When the celebrated author Sebastian Knight dies at the age of thirty-six, his younger half-brother V. tries to bridge the distance post-mortem by diving into the relics of Sebastian's life and writing a biography. Just as Nabokov was contemplating a move to England or America and trying his hand at a language in which he could build a future as an international writer, the fictional exile Sebastian had surrendered his native Russian for English in an effort to find an audience. Not surprisingly, V. delivers his brother (and his author) from culpability, insisting that Sebastian's love for his lost language and native land was whole, and that Sebastian's writing in English was no betrayal.

Written on luggage laid over a bidet in the bathroom of the Nabokovs' Paris apartment, *The Real Life of Sebastian Knight* also incorporated the flotsam of Nabokov's own relationships. Disconnected in childhood, mysteries to each other even as adults, V. and Sebastian are not entirely separate from Vladimir and Sergei Nabokov. Without fully mirroring himself or Sergei, Nabokov manages to tuck in fragments of each: Sebastian, too, attended Trinity College at Cambridge, where he wore Nabokov's trademark canary yellow sweater. He betrayed his love for a woman who had been his creative muse and partner by having an affair. Sebastian, however, also recalls elements of Sergei: his awkwardness with sports and "feminine coquetry." The book reads almost as if Nabokov wanted not so much to represent himself or Sergei directly in a character, but rather to bridge the distance between them by fusing their worlds.

Their real-life worlds did not merge so smoothly. Sergei spent the 1930s bouncing between Paris and the Austrian castle of his partner, Hermann. It was not uncommon for the brothers to see each other in Paris, and Sergei would sometimes drop by his brother's apartment. But the essential awkwardness between them never vanished. Nabokov still saw his brother as indolent and ineffectual, squandering his talents. For his part, Sergei found Véra difficult and believed that marriage to her had damaged Vladimir. Had Sergei accepted the idea, put forward by some émigrés, that Véra's Jewishness had changed Nabokov or his writing for the worse, or did he simply dislike her? Either way, Sergei reported relief that Véra and Dmitri had had made their way out of Germany, telling his sister Elena that they would have been in dire straits had they not escaped when they did.[38]

At the end of Nabokov's novel about brothers, V. declares that he himself *is* Sebastian Knight, or Sebastian is him, or perhaps they are both a person who remains unknown to either of them. Nabokov's story pivots on the necessity of recovering the past, our terrible inability to do so, and the invention of stories that preserve memory, even memories that we have spun in part ourselves. The narrator somehow succeeds in bridging the chasm inserted by death, fusing with his idea of his brother so completely that he ends up uncertain whose story he is telling.

As with *The Gift*, however, Nabokov had once again preserved political history *sub rosa* for posterity. In Sebastian Knight, a supporting character named Mr. Silbermann meets V. by chance on a train. A dealer in leather goods, he speaks English with a heavy accent ("Dat is not love! Ppah!"). He knows several other languages, and even spoke Russian long ago but has forgotten it. He pointedly asks V. if he is a *traveller*, too, and turns out to be an almost magical sidekick who offers to unearth crucial information on cue for the narrator. Silbermann turns up a few days later with the names and addresses of four women who might be the mystery lover responsible for the destruction of Sebastian's life.

Silbermann's arrival marks *Sebastian Knight*'s turn toward history. With his big nose, past travels, and forgotten languages, like some saintly version of the Wandering Jew, Silbermann's mystic presence redirects the novel to larger matters.[39] Using one of the names provided by Silbermann, V. makes a trip to Berlin, where he meets a young Jewish-Russian woman and her family in Nazi Germany in

1936. The family is in mourning. Her brother-in-law has just died; we are not told why. The narrator realizes immediately that the woman is clearly not Sebastian's cruel paramour; rather, she is unimaginably beautiful, graceful, and generous. From his post-*Kristallnacht* vantage point, Nabokov presents a loving, idealized Jewish family from two years earlier, a portrait clearly defying the real-world German propaganda of the day. The family cannot know, as Nabokov did, what lies ahead, any more than Nabokov in 1938 could imagine everything that would follow *Kristallnacht*. But by putting them in his story, he has immortalized them and denied the Nazis the last word on their lives.

V. never returns to close that loop, so we can only imagine the family's fate. They sit in the novel in plain sight, but, as with *Despair*, Nabokov stitched real-world tragedy into the margins of his tale in such a way that the past becomes an invisible rider on a story ostensibly about something else.

In a scene near the end of the book, graffiti in a phone booth catches the eye of the narrator, providing a quick glimpse into the French political inferno of the day. Someone has posted a slogan for Léon Blum's coalition ("*Vive le front populaire*") and a response is there, too: "Death to the Jews." Written in a white heat in two months after Poland and Austria and Germany had savaged their Jewish communities, *The Real Life of Sebastian Knight* carries in its corners the shadow of expanding persecution.

If Nabokov was casting that shadow, in English, for an English-language audience to see, larger signals of the approaching apocalypse were already being successfully ignored. The British government, which had promised to take in fifty thousand refugee children, stalled on its pledge mid-process. A bill introduced that February in the United States would have allowed twenty thousand refugee children into the country, but an opinion poll revealed that more than sixty percent of Americans were opposed to the measure, and it was defeated in committee without ever receiving a full vote.[40] Soon after, the British, facing the third year of an Arab revolt in Palestine, would limit Jewish immigration to the Middle East as well. With few exceptions, Jews had nowhere to go.

The world continued to watch and not do much. Almost a year to the day after Austria had been subsumed into the Third Reich, the German army entered Prague. Hitler went to Prague Castle, a thousand-year symbol of Czech heritage, and watched his honor guard march in with their heavy boots and helmets, carrying long guns and forming a rectangle of crisp perpendicular rows, facing inward on their jubilant leader. Hitler entered the castle and waved from a third-story window; he stood on the steps of the castle; he announced the Protectorate of Bohemia and Moravia, now under German control. He was just a little over a mile away from the apartment of Nabokov's mother.

The annexation marked an end to the modest pension the Czechs had provided, meaning that Elena Nabokov, now burdened with pleurisy, no longer had any income of her own. Her health continued to decline.

Looking ever more desperately for a job, Nabokov headed to London again. Asking his friend Gleb Struve for a letter of recommendation (along with any other acquaintance he thought might deliver), Nabokov declared that getting a position outside France had become "a life and death question."[41]

Going to London was like crossing into another world. Nabokov stayed again in the home of a former Russian diplomat, where the familiar comforts of childhood—spacious lodgings, a butler, tennis outings, visits to the British Museum, and butterflies—occupied his free time.

He enjoyed these things immensely, but probably did not need Véra to remind him of the urgency of his mission or just what was at stake—though letters prodding him arrived regularly, just in case. Trying to ingratiate himself through an endless round of social engagements, readings, and small talk in an effort to find a position teaching Russian literature did not play to Nabokov's strengths, and he left at the end of the month with few prospects.

The news back in Paris was even worse. Elena Nabokov had died in Prague on May 2. Nabokov did not take a chance on returning to Czechoslovakia, which was now German territory, for the funeral. There was not just Taboritski to worry about; the pro-Nazi Russian newspaper *New Word* in Berlin had called for Nabokov's placement alongside Jewish artists in the "boiling pots" so that a true Russian literature might flourish.[42]

Nabokov's brother Sergei, a less famous target, requested permission from the Gestapo to travel. He made his way to Prague in time for the funeral, but it was a risky move. Sergei was known in Berlin's gay community and had associated with activist Magnus Hirschfeld, whose library had been incinerated six years before.[43] He and his partner, Hermann, had both been straightforward about their relationship with their families. With a past full of capes and canes and makeup, Sergei had never truly been closeted. He had had gay roommates; he had publicly moved in Parisian circles known for their extravagant homosexuality.

When the Nuremberg Laws were put in place, the Nazis had updated the legal code that covered homosexual crimes. In the past, some evidence had been required in order to arrest someone suspected of homosexual activity; under the new measures, gossip, a letter from a gay friend, or even thought or intention could be introduced as evidence.[44]

Since the persecutions of homosexuals in German had first stepped-up five years before, several gay men had been castrated—some against their will, while others were offered a choice between an operation and a longer prison sentence. By the time of Elena Nabokov's funeral, arrests of homosexuals were at their peak, with offenders often sentenced to regular prisons, but also to Dachau and Neuengamme. Foreign homosexuals were not targeted as often, but Sergei's statelessness made him more vulnerable, and his long involvement with Hermann, a once-Austrian and now-German national, heightened the risk for both of them.[45] Yet Sergei went to Prague that May, writing to Vladimir afterward to describe the funeral.

6

Nabokov spent July and August of 1939 with Véra and Dmitri in a pension on the Riviera, which was cheaper than staying in Paris. But a bleak and sudden end to that summer came when war erupted on the first of September, 1939.

The day after the German invasion of Poland, the Nabokovs returned to Paris. On September 3, England and France declared war on Germany. Two weeks later, Russia invaded Poland from the east, effectively splitting the country between German and Russian control. Vladimir and Véra wanted to get out of Europe as quickly as possible. Horrified at the prospect of being drafted into the French army, the forty-year-old Nabokov stepped up his efforts to get visas to America.

Other émigrés, however, felt less pressure to leave. Critic Mark Aldanov intended to stay in Paris; Ivan Bunin had no plans to go. Sonia Slonim was in no rush to depart either. Unlike Véra and Vladimir, she had held French papers for almost a decade, and had found steady employment. As part of her translation career, she had been working on screen treatments for refugee filmmakers in Paris. She also claimed to be working for French intelligence.

In that capacity, she explained to friends, she had been asked to keep an eye on a German refugee who had arrived in Paris not long before, carrying forged papers. The story must have come as a surprise to those who recognized her new companion: the former Communist propagandist turned Nazi filmmaker Carl Junghans.

In addition to his work on the Olympic films, Junghans had done several other pictures for a Nazi-Fascist film collaborative, as well as two tributes to Nazi leadership.[46] But Junghans apparently had a dispute with Goebbels and the Ministry of Propaganda over a film script. He had become so fearful for his safety that he had obtained false papers to escape Germany via Switzerland.

Junghans had picked a good time to leave. He abandoned Nazi propaganda at the very moment that Goebbels began to use movies to redefine the way that people thought about Jews and Judaism. Just as the Nazis had used the "Eternal Jew" exhibition two years before in Munich to counter the influence of an exhibition in New York, Goebbels would remake and recast three British movies from recent years that had offered sympathetic portrayals of Jews. One of the three, a new 1933 version of *The Wandering Jew*, was based on the English play that had been on stage and in movie theaters during Nabokov's years at Cambridge.[47]

Goebbels intended to make his own *Wandering Jew*—in German, *Der Ewige Jude*, portraying a Judaism more in line with the Nazi vision. He would take an obsessive interest in his "documentary" film project for more than two years, writing about it in his diary and discussing it with Hitler. His plan was to use the movie to awaken the public's latent distrust of Jews, understanding that the more alien and disturbing they appeared, the more inhuman the policies that could be applied against them.

"This is Tuesday," the Torah reader announces in the film, speaking in Hebrew to indicate that German officers are forcing him to perform on the wrong day, noting the fraud for posterity.[48] Disturbing footage of kosher slaughter, pictures of Albert Einstein and Charlie Chaplin (both deemed dangerous by the Nazi leadership), as well as fraudulent statistics and ominous narration, round out a film meant to convince Germans once and for all of the perfidy of the Jewish people.

Half the cinematographers for *The Eternal Jew* had previously assisted Carl Junghans on his Olympic documentary.[49] If Junghans had not left Berlin, it is entirely possible that he would have been expected to work on it. Junghans had served the Nazi cause as he had served that of the Soviets. But it was a big step between fetishization of German glory and the demonization of an entire people. Junghans ended up leaving before it became clear whether or not he would be willing to cross that divide.

Junghans's reunion with Sonia Slonim in Paris was brimming with irony: he had managed to ally himself with both the totalitarian regimes that had threatened her family. The road Junghans had chosen ran in direct opposition to the path taken by Nabokov. Both were gifted artists—Junghans's 1929 independent film *Such Is Life* was one of the last great silent movies—but Nabokov refused public engagement in the political realm, while Junghans had repeatedly put his art entirely at the service of extreme ideology.

It is certainly possible that Sonia had been assigned by French intelligence to keep an eye on Junghans, but if so, she seems to have taken on her task happily and at particularly close quarters. Declassified documents, however, do make clear that French intelligence worked very hard to keep track of Junghans. Communists, and even ex-Communists, were not popular in France at the time. As soon as war was declared, the French Communist Party, following the Soviet lead, denounced the French entry into the conflict as imperialist. As a result, the party was outlawed, and forty-four Communist deputies had been sent to prison.

Nazi collaborators, not surprisingly, were also in bad odor in Paris. As a former Communist and former Nazi filmmaker, Junghans was a rare bird indeed. Before the reunion with Sonia, French secret police had been hunting for him, interviewing friends and associates in a desperate effort to find him. By the end of the month, he had begun producing propaganda for the French government.[50]

His cooperation earned his liberty, and, according to him, money. But he was told to stay in Paris. If he tried to leave, he understood that he would be shot. He had a letter he showed to acquaintances everywhere he went, which appeared to be a police document giving him asylum and acknowledging his work for the department. But the French intended to keep him on a short leash.

7

Nabokov had his own collection of letters that he hoped would grant him a broader freedom. One from Bunin drafted by Nabokov himself suggested that Mr. Vladimir Nabokoff was "a novelist of quite exceptional talent" and would make "a teacher . . . of quite exceptional quality at any English or American University." Bunin had elsewhere called Nabokov a "monster" and would refer to him as a "circus clown," but he admitted to a certain affection for circus clowns. And in matters of survival, Bunin was willing to help.[51]

Nabokov was lucky that his dreams of teaching in England had not borne fruit in the lean days of 1939, because the British cancelled all visas upon entry into the war. But via a serendipitous chain of events, a very different hope for deliverance appeared out of nowhere. Through fellow émigré Mark Aldanov—who had written at length on the role of chance in history—Nabokov learned about an opening teaching a summer course in Russian literature at Stanford University in California. Aldanov had been invited to teach himself, but at that time had no plans to leave Europe.

Perhaps Stanford would be interested in Nabokov? Nabokov was certainly interested in Stanford. The thorny path to a visa suddenly became straight and paved, and the still-imaginary future turned its face toward a distant campus more than five thousand miles away in America.

A job offer in America was the first step, but even with a destination, Nabokov faced months of preparation. Exit permits had to be obtained along with American visas, and there were more affidavits to collect from the American side. Alexandra Tolstoy (daughter of the Russian literary titan) shepherded one letter of support from the conductor of the Boston Symphony Orchestra. She even suggested within the community of refugee-aid groups that she could obtain a testimonial for Véra Nabokov's skills as a domestic. With ever-stricter immigration quotas weighing against those who wanted to emigrate, willingness to fulfill demand for cheap domestic work in England and America (or at least to pretend that one would do so) was frequently the fastest, sometimes the only, route for Jews to enter the country.[52]

In the meantime, destitution and war still had to be managed. After pleas written to America the year before, Nabokov had received

ANDREA PITZER

2,500 francs from composer Sergei Rachmaninoff and twenty dollars from the U.S. Russian Literary Fund.[53] By the time war had broken out, he was receiving a thousand francs a month from a friend. He returned to old habits, advertising for students interested in learning English. He collected three pupils, including a businessman and a young harpist named Maria Marinel.

It was not enough. Despite the Nabokovs' efforts to shield him from their poverty, the five-year-old Dmitri felt the need to explain to Marinel that his family was living "a very hard life."[54]

Still Nabokov wrote on and on, embarking that fall on a story spun out from an aside in *The Gift*, in which an unsavory stepfather dreams up a novel about an older man marrying a widow to get at her daughter. The new story's disturbing nature tilted toward the internal thoughts of the man, evoking the agony of his pedophilia.

Nabokov's unnamed main character is a central European jeweler, a traveler in France who fantasizes about young girls. After he marries the invalid mother of the roller-skating object of his obsession, the mother dies. Now a widower, he maneuvers the child into his clutches and promises to take her to the seashore. On the way there, he fails at first to get a room in which to act on his desires, but then claims a vacancy at a second hotel. Because of his suspicious name, the desk clerk calls the police on him, believing he is a wanted man. The police arrive and question him until he manages to convince them he is not the person they are looking for.

Nabokov takes the protagonist, and the reader, right up to the brink of fulfilling his fantasy that night at the hotel. But the stepfather's plan goes awry as the girl wakes up. He flees the room, seeking death, and his desires earn authorial retribution in the form of a large truck barreling down a nighttime street, killing him.

"The Enchanter" carried many of the seeds of what would later become *Lolita*. The novella was read aloud to Fondaminsky and three other friends behind thick curtains in a dim room with the lamp wrapped with the regulation wartime sugarloaf paper to guard against German air raids.[55] Rejected by *Contemporary Annals*,

Nabokov offered the story to at least one other editor before surrendering to the disruptions in publishing brought on by the war.

The start of the war also effectively closed the coffin on the émigré community. The linked webs that had stretched eastward into China and westward through Europe, maintained by the émigré presses in Berlin and Paris, slowly strained and then gave way.

During its last days, Nabokov played an elaborate practical joke on Georgy Adamovich, the critic who had so consistently dismissed his verse. Writing poems under the name Vasily Shishkov, Nabokov managed to get them published in a leading journal. They were praised by Adamovich—who had no idea Nabokov had written them—as heralding the arrival of "a great poet."[56]

A Nabokov short story titled "Vasily Shishkov" appeared months later in the same publication, describing a retiring, gifted poet of the same name who meets with the narrator twice before vanishing. The pseudonymous poems combined with the story—which *was* signed by Nabokov—in such a way to make it apparent that the whole thing had been a ruse engineered to prove that Adamovich was unfairly prejudiced against Nabokov's work.

With characteristic irreverence, Nabokov was delighted with his trap, which had succeeded perfectly in revealing the critic's bias against him. But Mark Aldanov chided Nabokov for his gamesmanship, pointing out that while he had been busy playing pranks, a war was underway.[57]

"Vasily Shishkov" seems to represent Nabokov at his most mean-spirited and superficial. A tremendous amount of work and literary space were given over just to show someone up, and the story's lone trick works only in combination with the pseudonymous poems.

But Aldanov was wrong—even in apparent trifles, Nabokov was attending to the war. Each time the narrator ostensibly holds meetings with his invented poet in the foreground of the story, a group of German Jewish refugees appears in the background, discussing the challenges of French identity papers and expressing anxiety over problems with their passports. Behind the main story, Nabokov had folded in the imminent peril of the refugee Jews.[58]

In the story, the imaginary Shishkov describes his literary technique for the narrator: a deliberate avoidance of boring approaches to "big, burning questions" addressed by everyone in favor of attention to tiny moments unnoticed by most—trivia that carries "embryos of the most obvious monsters."[59] The line was almost a literary mission statement from Nabokov, an explanation of what he had been doing in recent years with the historical concerns, camps, and prisons that haunted his work. But any subtle message in the story was overshadowed by its high-concept prank.

Even before his shaming of Adamovich, Nabokov had intended to say good-bye to the Russian émigré community, with its literary Socialist Revolutionaries, scheming monarchists, and spy networks. Bunin, displaced by Nabokov, was now said to grow furious at the mention of his rival's name, and there were others who would not regret his departure.[60]

Whatever optimism had previously existed for the prospect of political change in the Soviet Union, there was no longer any anticipation among the exiles of a coming Russian democracy. They could not go home, and their shallow roots in Berlin and Paris would be exposed once more.

With the audience for his Russian work cast to the wind again, Nabokov knew he had to try to reinvent himself in English, following the trail he started down with *Sebastian Knight*. But leaving Russian behind was another thing entirely. As soon as it became apparent that Stanford University would be willing to employ Mr. Nabokov for a summer course on Russian literature, he proceeded to keep writing furiously in his native tongue, as if to exorcise the impulse or as if waving a long good-bye. Along with "The Enchanter," he launched himself into a new novel, *Solus Rex*, one more mystical than his other outings.

Of the two surviving chapters which became short stories, the first is a monologue from a Russian émigré addressing his wife, who died pregnant with their child. The émigré wants an answer to the mystery of the universe and his wife's fate. He seeks out a former acquaintance, a man who has become a kind of seer and claims to have solved the riddle of the universe. The mystic—who seems to have become part-madman, part-prophet—had a violent break from the rest of humanity just after hearing that his half-sister had died in a remote and awful country.

By the second story, the émigré himself has gone insane and believes he is the ruler of a fantasy kingdom on the distant northern island of Ultima Thule. A neon sign flashes "Renault" outside his window, anchoring him to France, but he lives only inside the dark world of his imagination, a world filled with arrests, trials, plots, and false confessions. The émigré's efforts to escape his reality just throw him back into a world steeped in the current events of a Russia he fled long ago. The horrors of the concentration camps, show trials, and Solovki—another bleak castle on another sad and distant northern island—hang over the story, as if Nabokov and the narrator could no more escape their lost homeland than the grieving widower can invent a life in which the things he loves are returned to him unbroken.

That spring in Paris hinted at both hope and dread. Nabokov's prior disappearing act had concluded with machine-gun fire chasing his boat. No longer a teenager shielded by his father, he was now responsible for a boy much younger and more vulnerable than he had been when he sailed away from Russia. How would they escape?

A tense visit made by Véra to a préfecture revealed that their passports, submitted in the application for exit permits, were missing. A strategic 200-franc bribe spurred their rediscovery, but they turned up at another Ministry entirely. Despite her fears that they would be arrested for paying off an official, Véra sent Vladimir to pick up both passports and exit permits.[61] The Nabokovs' American visas were finally issued on April 23.

Yet even with a visa, finding a means of departure remained problematic. Fares were prohibitive, and the Nabokovs had no money. But the memory of Nabokov's father and his tireless work on behalf of Russian Jews lived on in the memory of Yakov Frumkin, the head of a Jewish aid association in New York. Frumkin managed to secure the Nabokovs three spaces on a ship scheduled to depart France in late May—and to slash the cost of the tickets. But even at half-fare, the $560 required was a kind of mythic treasure, one completely out of reach of a struggling refugee writer.

More help was solicited from Jewish families, whose giving had been the anchor of so many Nabokov-related causes in the past. A final reading was organized. Other members of the émigré community chipped in until enough was found to cover the fare.[62]

But as the Nabokovs prepared to go, the Germans began to advance in earnest, driving through the Netherlands, Luxembourg, and Belgium before invading France at Sedan. After a three-day battle, devastated Allied forces retreated, and the German army rolled all the way to the English Channel. French propaganda dismissed the German victories, encouraging civilians to stay put ("France has been invaded a hundred times and never beaten"), but tides of refugees streaming in from neighboring countries, and even northern France, triggered an exodus. The "phony war"—in which England and France were technically fighting Germany but not waging visible battles—suddenly became real.[63]

Given German territorial gains, the Nabokovs' original departure site of Le Havre had become unreliable. They were told to embark hundreds of miles southwest on the coast at St. Nazaire. Preparations that had stretched across months dwindled to a series of last-minute arrangements. Nabokov compiled his papers and butterfly collection, dropping them off at the apartment of Ilya Fondaminsky. He went to visit Kerensky, where he also saw Bunin and Zinaida Hippius, the poet who had told his father that Vladimir Nabokov would never, never be a writer. Sergei Nabokov, who was not in Paris at the time, had no idea his brother was already leaving, or that he would be gone before they had a chance to say good-bye.

Just before departure, Dmitri came down with a blistering fever. It was not clear whether or not he could travel, or would be permitted to. After a visit with their doctor, the Nabokovs got sulfa tablets to treat Dmitri's symptoms and boarded their train. By the time they finished the six-hour ride to the harbor in a sleeping car, he had recovered.

The *Champlain* pulled away from the dock on May 19, 1940, leaving a continent behind. Two weeks later, bombs would fall on Paris. The following month, France would surrender and Luftwaffe planes flying over St. Nazaire would kill more than four thousand British soldiers in the midst of evacuating.

But the Nabokovs managed to outrun the havoc of war. On the ship's roster, Nabokov was listed as Russian, Véra as Hebrew, and Dmitri as Russian, distinctions that would have become relevant if they had missed their ship. But they did not miss their ship, and could revel for a moment in the possibilities of what the New World might bring. None of them had seen it before, though surely it would have more to offer than the mossy corner of his mother's property in Russia that her family had once nicknamed America.

What did he imagine? Nabokov could not, of course, know the specifics of his future. But in preparing for it, he left part of his work behind with Fondaminsky. Shipboard, he carried the story of a Central European refugee with a passion for young girls and a tale of a Russian émigré crushed by tragedy, along with a novel of two brothers and the distance between them that is fixed by death.

By the time the passengers on the *Champlain* lost sight of Europe, the first building of the Auschwitz concentration-camp complex had opened a thousand miles away in Poland. Three weeks later, the first trainload of Polish and Jewish prisoners would arrive there. In fleeing the continent that had been his home for the first forty-one years of his life, Nabokov had pulled off another vanishing act just in time. But the past had a geography not so easily dismissed and, for the second time, Nabokov would carry with him the weight of an entire world dissolving into ghosts.

CHAPTER EIGHT

America

——∞∞∞——

1

Aboard the *Champlain*, the crew fired its guns at a whale, mistaking it for an enemy submarine, while Nabokov sailed more than three thousand miles across the Atlantic in a first-class cabin. The elegance of the trip contrasted sharply with the passengers' desperation. Germany and Russia marched deeper into chaos; Paris wobbled at their departure. Arriving on May 26, the ship anchored off Quarantine for a day before sailing into New York Harbor.[1]

The leading novelist of the Russian emigration met with little suspicion and no public acknowledgment, save for a note in New York's Russian-language daily newspaper that "Vladimir Sirin" had come to America. The Nabokovs, along with most of their shipmates, filled out their declarations of intent to become permanent residents of the United States. The decision was likely not complicated for anyone present—the Jewish passengers' home cities read like a map of brutality from the first decades of the century: St. Petersburg, Vienna, Lvov, Krakow, Berlin.[2]

On the forms, Nabokov listed himself as an author and Véra as a housewife. Immigrants also had to answer a standard battery of questions about polygamous tendencies, physical defects, and mental health problems, and were required to assert repeatedly that they were not anarchists and had no intent to overthrow the government. The United States was not at war, but was very much worried about Communists and revolutionaries entering the country.[3]

After they finished with immigration, the Nabokovs' luggage still had to clear customs, but Véra could not find the key to their trunk. Waiting for a locksmith, Nabokov asked where to find a newspaper, and was given *The New York Times* by a porter. With the persuasion of an iron bar, the lock yielded to the locksmith, who promptly relocked it by mistake. When the trunk had finally been opened for good, customs officials remarked on the dead butterflies Nabokov had packed, and began to spar with the boxing gloves they found inside.[4] Vladimir Nabokov was on his way to becoming an American.

Friends and family, however, remained at the mercy of history. The Marinel sisters, who had helped their tutor leave France, were very much on the Nabokovs' minds. Véra's cousin Anna Feigin had not initially planned to leave, but she would soon be headed to Nice with her own thoughts of America. For the time being, Ivan Bunin, Ilya Fondaminsky, and Sergei Nabokov intended to remain in Europe. The Hessens were still there, too, though Mark Aldanov, to whom Nabokov owed his deliverance, was likely already rethinking the wisdom of staying in Paris. Some of them would find a way to escape.

Back in Paris, Véra's sister Sonia had stayed on with Carl Junghans, but the city held out less than a month after Vladimir and Véra's departure. By the time German tanks clanked over the bridges of the Seine and down the silent Champs-Élysées on June 14, Carl and Sonia had left just ahead of the victors. They headed south, making their way to Casablanca, a temporary haven for many fleeing the German advance.[5]

Other refugees would soon set sail under more distressing conditions. In the face of blistering military setbacks, Britain had become obsessed with the threat of invasion and worry over Nazi spies hiding on its territory. Enemy aliens had already been required to register when war had broken out. And just one week before Nabokov's boat sailed from St. Nazaire—Churchill's second full day as Prime Minister—the order was given to arrest all the refugees.[6]

Weeks of dramatic debate followed. Nobel Peace Prize winner Norman Angell denounced the arrests.[7] The majority of enemy aliens were known to be harmless, he noted, and many had already been persecuted by the Nazis. But the invasion of France stoked fears, and arrests continued. Amid a blaze of media coverage, aliens from all walks of life were sent to British concentration camps.

Inmates included the future Nobelist Max Perutz, celebrated Jewish conductor Peter Gellhorn, who had fled the Nazis five years before, and even the son and grandson of Sigmund Freud. By the time Nabokov set foot in America, more than eleven thousand civilians had been interned, including thousands of refugee women, many of whom had been working in England as maids.[8]

A significant percentage of these prisoners were Jewish, but in the midst of paranoia and war, confusion reigned over exactly which prisoners were which. At Huyton near Liverpool, a camp adjutant reviewed the arrival of men he thought were captured German soldiers but who were really civilian refugees. Noting the distinctive clothing of his new charges, he was reported to say, "I never knew so many Jews were Nazis."[9]

With fear of invasion high, the British began to move the prisoners off the continent to places where they could be of no assistance to Germany. And so almost a month to the day after Nabokov departed France, ships left England carrying an ill-matched cargo. Civilian refugees, including some Jews who had once been prisoners in German concentration camps, found themselves berthed in the same quarters as Nazi officers and soldiers, sailing together to North America for internment. Anxiety over a handful of deaths in the crossing and occasional suicide attempts on arrival amplified the prisoners' lingering confusion over their long-term fate. They would soon be scattered across Canada from New Brunswick to Alberta, held in old concentration camps and prisons or housed in new facilities still under construction as they arrived.[10]

Compared to the Canadian welcome the refugees got, the Nabokovs' arrival in America had been a delight. Schedules had gone awry—they were not met by Nathalie Nabokov, the ex-wife of cousin Nicholas, but the family took a taxi to her apartment.[11] They had somewhere to go; they knew people who could give them the names of others who might help them. Gifted with unfettered liberty (so long, apparently, as they did not promote anarchy), Vladimir and Véra made their way into Manhattan with a $100 bill and hope for better prospects.

For all the thrill of arrival on a new continent, Nabokov's routine in the first few weeks must have seemed dispiritingly familiar.[12] Living in a succession of temporary quarters, he once again tried to sell himself and his literary talents—the thing in which he had the most confidence in the world—to a public ignorant of their value.

But at least one visit was not made in search of assistance. Nabokov stopped in at composer Sergei Rachmaninoff's West End Avenue apartment to thank him for the money he had sent to them in France. During the visit, Nabokov announced that he had a teaching job at Stanford, but he may have worn his destitution on his sleeve, as the composer sent him a very out-of-date formal jacket in which Rachmaninoff hoped Nabokov might deliver his lectures. Nabokov could not afford much in the way of pride in the summer of 1940; he nonetheless returned the jacket.[13]

No immediate prospects existed, but the past could still be generous. In karmic recompense for V. D. Nabokov's many years supporting literature and the arts (and his son's own prodigious output), Nabokov received his first small American income from the stateside Russian Literary Fund. After flitting through borrowed rooms, the family managed to sublet quarters briefly from the niece of Countess Panin, whose estate had sheltered the Nabokov family in the Crimea after the Revolution. And the family won a temporary reprieve from their immediate worries with an invitation to spend the summer in Vermont at the country home of Harvard professor and fellow Russian Mikhail Karpovich.[14]

But echoes of their European exile were not limited to financial distress or dependence on others for shelter. The Nabokovs quickly found that anti-Semitism could rear its head in the New World, too, sometimes coming from familiar sources. Shortly after his arrival in New York, Nabokov was praised for his beautiful Russian by an émigré teacher at Columbia University, who then complained of only hearing Russian spoken by "Yids." Another time, when the conversation at an émigré party turned anti-Semitic, Nabokov, who was normally reserved in public and not prone to swearing, cursed and walked out.[15]

2

Their first summer as Americans, Vladimir, Véra, and Dmitri headed north to the country to enjoy butterflies and Russian company in rural New England. And the season of their European escape was replete with gifts.

Nicholas Nabokov, who had made a name for himself in 1930s America with the score for the ballet *Union Pacific*, mentioned his talented cousin to his Massachusetts neighbor Edmund Wilson. Wilson, whose interest in Russian literature had continued to grow in the wake of his trip to the Soviet Union, was then as prominent as any critic in America. He was friends with F. Scott Fitzgerald, who would die that winter, and had written for *Vanity Fair* and *The New Republic*. He had broad connections in magazines and publishing, and was ideally placed to help a newly arrived would-be American writer.

Nicholas had come through for his cousin, but Vladimir, never one to manage mundane details with grace, lost Wilson's phone number.[16] Nabokov sent a note to Wilson instead, and they managed to set a time to meet that October in New York, where the two men hit it off.

From the beginning, they made an odd couple. Nabokov, less prone to emotional displays, carried himself with a gaunt grace only exaggerated by cigarettes and hard times. At just under six feet tall, he weighed in that spring at 124 pounds. Quicker to intimacy, Wilson was a doughy man with little hair, a delicate face, and a sharp gaze. In short order, Wilson began to send commissions for book reviews Nabokov's way and bridged early connections to *The New Yorker* and *The Atlantic*. Through other networking, Nabokov began to write for *The New York Times* and the *Sun*.[17]

While they offered wonderful exposure, these first pieces only made it clear that a freelancer's income would not do to support a family in New York. Nabokov remained desperate for a job, but he was not willing to settle. It was one thing to turn down, as he had, the position of bicycle delivery boy for Scribner's, but quite another to turn down Yale University, which offered him a summer job. The position, however, was not in literature, but as an assistant instructor for language classes, and Nabokov did not think the head instructor's heavily accented Russian was up to snuff.[18]

He had survived inflation in Germany and destitution in France without surrendering his ambition to live a life of letters. In support of that goal, Véra had been willing to work for an engineering firm and take shorthand at meetings in Germany. She was willing to further her husband's career in the States, too. Nabokov would hold out for a literary position in America.

Nabokov's new friendship with Edmund Wilson continued to pay dividends. Wilson—familiarly known as "Bunny"—was delighted to meet an enthusiastic partner for his current obsession with Russian literature. He wrote to others describing Nabokov as a "brilliant fellow" and pondered collaborating with him on a translation and commentary.[19]

Along with lives devoted to literature, the two men had other things in common. Neither knew how to drive; both relied on the women in their lives to ferry them. Both had physical talents that did not match their frames: Nabokov's narrow build did not bar him from boxing or soccer, and Wilson—slight in form but a strong swimmer—once startled a friend by doing a somersault in the middle of the *Vanity Fair* building. But Wilson was a heavy drinker headed toward gout. Having survived two marriages, and well on his way to surviving a third, he had begun a precipitous physical decline.[20]

Nabokov and Wilson were also contrarians at heart. Neither man liked to be tied to groups, though Wilson's life tended to unfold in a series of enthusiasms, an ongoing yearning for political justice akin to a religious impulse. (Hemingway wrote about one of Wilson's books that he wished his friend had just "kept on reporting and not had to save his soul."[21]) Wilson, four years older than Nabokov, was much more likely to flirt with literary schools and political movements; yet he often seemed to adopt a cause as a way to more effectively begin quarreling with it. It was true of his romance with Symbolist poetry. It had also been the case with his drinking partners Fitzgerald and Hemingway. And it was true of Stalin.

Wilson had seen the financial collapse of the United States and, across the 1930s, had become intimately acquainted with the country's moral failings. He had lived through the Great Depression in America and reported on the trial of the Scottsboro boys, a group of young black men repeatedly railroaded by the American justice system. He had traveled to see miners in West Virginia; he had been present when striking union leaders and Communist party members squared off against police officers in Harlan County, Kentucky.[22]

So it was that after more than a decade of bloodshed under Stalin, whose shortcomings he had come to recognize, Wilson remained a little infatuated with the possibilities offered by revolution. He had been cast into despair by the agonies of post-Depression America but had never had to live through the results of the social change he advocated in Russia. In the eyes of Wilson, and many on the American left, Lenin and Trotsky had delivered Russia from the Tsars, setting the country on the path toward an egalitarian society.[23] It was a view Nabokov could not fathom.

Two months after their first meeting, the new friends had dinner with a former student of Nabokov's whose sister Wilson had met in Moscow. Afterward, Wilson forwarded a copy of his latest book to Nabokov. *To the Finland Station* chronicled the history and evolution of revolution, from its seeds in the late seventeenth century all the way up to Lenin, whom Wilson described as "one of the most selfless of great men."[24] The book took six years to finish, and culminated with Lenin's arrival in St. Petersburg in April 1917, ready to lead his country into the future.

Nabokov, who grew up less than two miles from Finland Station and had lived just around the corner or down the street from key events of 1905 and 1917, already had his own opinions on Lenin. He may well have expressed them at their first dinner together, as Wilson had inscribed the book to his new friend "in the hope that this may make him think better of Lenin."[25]

Wilson had stopped his book at a dramatic high point, which made for a strong narrative arc. It also allowed him to avoid addressing the first wave of Terror, or the second, or the decades that followed. Wilson himself knew before he had finished it that the book was flawed and out of date, noting in a letter to a friend that he was finishing up his Finland Station project just as the Soviets were about to invade Finland.[26]

Despite Wilson's use of overwhelmingly sympathetic sources, *Finland Station* reveals a surprising amount about Lenin, from how he was sent back to Russia in 1917 to his Jekyll-and-Hyde comment that those who crafted beautiful art made "you want to say stupid nice things," when it was better to "hit them on the head, without any mercy, though our ideal is not to use force against anyone."[27]

Wilson somehow took the latter statement as a testimony to Lenin's appreciation of the arts but devotion to more practical matters. His notion of helping Nabokov to understand Lenin, however, was more hard-headed than his interpretation of Lenin. Wilson must already have built a solid reservoir of gratitude or affection for their friendship to withstand this overture.

In subsequent months, Nabokov filled out his freelancing schedule as he had in Europe, tutoring students in Russian. Volunteering at the Museum of Natural History, he also wrote his first real articles on Lepidoptera and learned to dissect butterfly genitalia. He began to prepare lectures on literature for the Stanford summer position that had finally materialized. He found a welcome audience for his earlier story "Cloud, Castle, Lake" at *The Atlantic*, which he had revised to reflect more recent history. The lyrics for the song the poor protagonist is forced to sing with marching German hikers were transformed into a call for murder and destruction. An *Atlantic* editor wrote to say that they were eager to see more such works of genius from Nabokov. He happily obliged.[28]

While Nabokov made inroads into literary America, Véra settled Dmitri into school and began looking for work with a selectivity that, for a time, rivaled her husband's. An offer of a more-than-full-time job was declined (too many hours), while a portion of the same translation job on a part-time basis was similarly rejected (too little pay). But that winter, she managed to secure a secretarial position with a Free French newspaper, part of France Forever, a stateside campaign allied with Charles de Gaulle funded in part by British intelligence. In an organization committed to denouncing Vichy policies and promoting American entry into the war, Véra had found her place; it was a job she loved.[29]

3

Just as opportunities began to appear for the Nabokovs, Véra's sister Sonia arrived in New York on the S.S. *Guadeloupe*. Sonia had been in Casablanca for several months before getting a translator's visa, showing up in New York in January 1941.

The Slonim sisters had kept in touch—Sonia listed Véra's latest West Eighty-seventh Street address as her destination. Ship records stated that she was thirty-two years old and stood five feet six inches, with blond hair and brown eyes, but the rest of Sonia's public identity lacked the clarity of her physical self. She first appeared in the ship's register and documents under her middle name, as Sophia. Her marital status has been recorded as single, then written over with a D for divorced and her married name "Berlstein" inserted by hand.

The confusion over Sonia's name was easily cleared up, but others thought she had more to hide. As the *Guadeloupe* sailed into New York Harbor, a telegram arrived at the State Department from the ship's last overseas stop. It was addressed to the U.S. Secretary of State, warning him that Sonia Slonim was suspected of being a German spy. The moment Sonia entered the country, her mail was placed under surveillance.[30]

Carl Junghans had secured a visa just a few days after Sonia, but having heard that the Germans were trying to extradite him from Casablanca, he had caught an earlier ship to America. After fleeing Germany under false papers, he had acquired a foreigner's passport in Casablanca. He traveled through Lisbon on the S.S. *Carvalho Araujho*; his record shows him as stateless. Like Sonia, he had blond hair and brown eyes.[31] Unlike Sonia, who intended to become a permanent resident, Junghans had been able to obtain only a six-month work visa.

The United States was still sitting out the war but was worried enough about it to require registration, ethnic identification, and fingerprinting from all non-citizens in America, with hefty prison terms for anyone dabbling in anarchy. Holding facilities for immigrants viewed as high-risk had been established; but unlike Canada, the U.S. concentration-camp system from the First World War sat dormant for the time being.

Which was not to say that the FBI, under the direction of J. Edgar Hoover, had been sleeping. Since the beginning of the war, agents had been collecting information and files on aliens deemed suspicious, tracking them to prepare for possible U.S. entry into the war. The U.S. Immigration Service, which had recently been folded into the Department of Justice, was happy to coordinate with law enforcement officials in monitoring incoming refugees and alien visitors who might be of interest. Many were identified and their destinations recorded, in case they needed to be tracked down at a future date.

As a former Communist Nazi filmmaker, Junghans was intriguing to many people. He did not even make it off Ellis Island. Instead, he found his first American home in the dorm rooms and common cafeteria with those waiting to be deported: political radicals, criminals, and suspected spies like himself.[32] Sonia arrived three weeks later, but found there was nothing she could do. Junghans's deportation order had been filed; his only chance was to appeal and hope that immigration officials would review his case.

Sonia eventually contacted a refugee professor the couple had known in Berlin for help. Nearly four months into Junghans's detention, he was permitted to leave Ellis Island under a $500 bond, officially free. But the authorities had not forgotten about Carl Junghans.[33]

Sonia taught French and German at the International School of Languages on Madison Avenue and found an apartment just a few blocks away from Vladimir and Véra. The proximity might not have been welcome; it is hard to imagine that either Vladimir or Véra would have been pleased to see Junghans with Sonia in yet another country. But they may have been spared a face-to-face encounter. The Nabokovs finally left for the Stanford summer teaching position in California not long after Junghans's release.

By then, Véra had already left her beloved position at France Forever, but Junghans signed on there in her wake, writing for their information agency and doing scripts for the State Department propaganda station WRUL, which broadcast anti-Nazi, anti-Vichy radio programs into occupied France.[34] It was the fourth country in which he had produced political propaganda.

Junghans had a brief stint on the anti-Nazi lecture circuit, and wrote about the threat of sabotage from German submarines, while privately telling stories of his close association with Hitler and

Goebbels.[35] As a filmmaker, however, there was just one place in America he really wanted to go—Hollywood.

But the Nabokovs would beat Sonia and Carl to the West Coast by several months. In May 1941, nearly a year to the day after his arrival in America—Véra, Vladimir, and Dmitri set out across the United States with one of Nabokov's Russian-language students in her new Pontiac. He had done a series of lectures at Wellesley College that spring and had just learned that they wanted to offer him a one-year post starting that fall, reducing anxiety over mounting bills just in time for their trip west. The family had three weeks in a new car, with stops for reading, walking, and the endless collection of butterflies.

Tennessee, Arkansas, Texas, New Mexico, and Arizona lay open before them—the trip was a coast-to-coast lesson in the topography and sociology of America, one they enjoyed immensely. But whatever dreams they had in the new world, they were still refugees. Asked where he lived by a barber, Dmitri answered that he had no home but lived in "little houses by the road."[36]

4

During his first year in America, Nabokov covered more territory in his adopted homeland than he had ever seen in Russia. And in that California summer, the gap between his current life and the people he had left behind expanded far beyond the physical distance dividing them. He had written months before to the Marinel sisters, still in Paris, of the impossibility of navigating the two realities—one in which he lay in a meadow of flowers in America at "the height of luxury, like some millionaire's coarse dream"; another in which those he loved were still in danger.[37]

A bleaker reality shadowed every good thing that came the Nabokovs' way, and news from Europe only got worse. The world was still in shock from the collapse of Western Europe and the quick humiliation of France, haunted by the nation's surrender at Compiègne, fifty miles outside Paris. The town had previously been the site of

Germany's capitulation at the end of the First World War, but by 1941 Compiègne had become home to a concentration camp.[38]

During his own stay in France, Nabokov had had little love for its bureaucrats and would later lump together the "rat-whiskered consuls and policemen" of France and Germany.[39] He had his own visa nightmares for reference, of course, but that personal, intimate dislike for customs officials preoccupied with the proper papers would soon be borne out by larger events.

Many French policemen turned out to be more than willing to help root out foreigners, particularly foreign Jews, from their communities. After the fall of France, the Vichy government collaborated with the Germans, passing statutes resembling the Nazi Nuremberg Laws that severely restricted the rights of Jews. Officials noted that the French laws were sometimes more restrictive, but Vichy decided in 1941 that where the French law and German law differed, the French law should be used. In truth, whichever law was harsher was often the one that was applied.[40] Had the Nabokovs not escaped France, not only Véra but Dmitri Nabokov, too, would likely have been declared Jewish—as he would not have been under the Nazis—a bureaucratic fine point with high-stakes ramifications.

French anti-Semitic measures began with registrations and censuses and moved on to arrests and detentions. Most Jewish prisoners were held at a newly-inaugurated concentration camp installed in apartment buildings in the Paris suburb of Drancy. A modern low-income housing project in the process of being built when it was commandeered, Drancy was so new that its plumbing and sanitation systems were still incomplete.

Drancy had its true inauguration in the summer of 1941, when French officers collaborating with Nazi occupiers swept through Paris's 11th Arrondissement, arresting foreign Jewish males between the ages of eighteen and fifty, taking another family member when the man in question could not be located. Thousands were loaded onto buses and delivered to Drancy.[41] Eventually, mothers and children followed. It was only the beginning, and among the less fortunate Jews in Paris at the time were Sonia Slonim's ex-husband, Max Berlstein, and Nabokov's literary patron, Ilya Fondaminsky.

5

The Nabokov family arrived in Palo Alto on June 14, ten days before classes were due to start. They moved into a tidy villa just across from the Stanford campus, and Nabokov prepared to teach a group of undergraduates Russian literature and writing.[42]

But news from the war was relentless, and before classes had even begun, Germany invaded the Soviet Union, breaking the nonaggression pact that had divided Poland and other countries between them. The German advance was shocking and brutal. Nabokov, who had few doubts about the appropriateness of Hitler and Stalin as allies, found himself torn by their newfound enmity. Fantasizing an intricate British victory that might somehow pull off a defeat of Hitler, then Stalin, he hoped both dictators might end up in exile with only each other for company, two hundred miles off the coast of Jakarta on desolate Christmas Island.[43]

As the Germans bombed submarine bases, sank tankers, captured the Dnieper Dam, and moved closer to Leningrad, Nabokov spent his Stanford summer in the split reality he did not know how to reconcile, thinking of those trapped by war but also walking the hills above Palo Alto, catching butterflies. He corresponded with Edmund Wilson, whom he was already calling "Bunny," confiding in his new friend the plight of the Russian émigré now that Germany and the Soviet Union were at war. "For almost 25 years," he wrote, "Russians in exile have craved for something—anything—to happen that would destroy the Bolsheviks,—for instance a good bloody war. Now comes this tragic farce."[44]

In the officially neutral America that was worried about the seemingly unstoppable Germans, the public quickly began to root for Stalin. For more than a decade, the Soviet dictator had been referred to in Moscow and the U.S. as Uncle Joe, but for many

Americans the nickname suddenly acquired a sentimental sheen. Even former head of the Provisional Government Alexander Kerensky, now in Manhattan, telegraphed Russia to pledge his support to Stalin, if only the Soviets would seize the opportunity to free prisoners from concentration camps, abolish collectivization, and restore Poland.[45]

He could have included a pony and the crown jewels, for all the difference it would have made. Kerensky received no answer from Stalin, and efforts to reach the Soviet ambassador to America met with similar silence.[46]

Nabokov felt conflicted, but many Soviet Russians felt a simpler patriotism. Traveling to Moscow to sit for graduate exams in the summer of 1941, Alexander Solzhenitsyn arrived just as the invasion began, and found that his tests were cancelled—the nation was going to war. He tried to enlist on the spot but was told to return to Rostov. After the train trip home, his physical examination disqualified him from service for the time being. He was told to wait until he was called up, but he bridled at the delay.[47]

Meanwhile, the German army advanced into Soviet territory at an alarming rate. By the time Nabokov had finished the summer at Stanford and moved back East to start teaching at Wellesley, all Russia's reserve forces had been fully mobilized—and more were needed. Anxious to defend his homeland and to take part in history, Alexander Solzhenitsyn succeeded on his third try. He would be allowed to go to war.

Solzhenitsyn reported for duty with a briefcase in hand and began his military career mucking stables and tending to horses. A greenhorn in equine matters, he was mocked by Cossacks, who lived their lives on horseback, and humiliated by his incompetence at even the basic duties he was given. He slowly learned his assigned tasks and earned a measure of respect, but wrote to his wife in despair about shoveling manure, later claiming that "One cannot become a great Russian writer, living in the Russia of 1941-43, without having been at the front."[48]

Via enthusiasm and trickery—and a crash training course—he managed to get transferred to an artillery unit. Tolstoy himself had been in the artillery during the Crimean War almost a century before, and Solzhenitsyn longed for nothing more than to follow in the footsteps of the master. Tolstoy's experience had provided the basis for writing *War and Peace*, a novel Solzhenitsyn admired and envied. He felt certain that history and military service would combine to make a true Russian writer of him, too.[49]

6

Edmund "Bunny" Wilson had considerably less enthusiasm for the war than Solzhenitsyn, or even Nabokov. In 1940 when *The New Republic* had adopted a position advocating that America join Great Britain in her struggle, Wilson quit in protest and never wrote for the magazine again.[50]

Despite his dramatic resignation, Wilson coordinated with the head of the magazine's editorial board to make sure that Nabokov would continue to get work in his absence. And even after the end of that professional relationship, Wilson and Nabokov continued to write to each other. While Solzhenitsyn dreamed of emulating Tolstoy on the battlefield, Nabokov wrote to Wilson on the finer points of *War and Peace* from a safer vantage point and with less reverence.[51]

Reading Russian literature in the original was Wilson's latest enthusiasm, and he used Nabokov as a sounding board for his literary hypotheses about Russian verse. Nabokov, who had never been shy about his opinions, seemed to admire his effort, writing dismissively but affectionately to Wilson in response. ("I am afraid that the Russians who told you *сволочь* comes from *cheval* are donkeys."[52])

As an influential critic in America, Wilson was accustomed to being a literary king-maker. He had set in stone the reputations of Hemingway and Fitzgerald as top-notch twentieth-century writers; he had made the careers of luminaries both timeless and middling. Wilson fell naturally into his traditional role with Nabokov,

ANDREA PITZER

recommending him for work and offering him advice on how to wade into the cold waters of American publishing. Wilson felt comfortable enough to chide Nabokov repeatedly for his "lamentable weakness for punning," which he maintained was "pretty much excluded from serious journalism."[53]

Connecting Nabokov to a publisher who agreed to acquire *The Real Life of Sebastian Knight*, he weighed in with praise for the book as Nabokov headed to his new position at Wellesley that October. "It has," he wrote, "delighted me and stimulated me more than any new book I have read since I don't know what." In the same letter, Wilson invited the Nabokov family to Thanksgiving at his house in Wellfleet, Massachusetts.[54]

By the time Nabokov went alone to Wellfleet for the holiday, the two friends had exchanged dozens of letters. In person, the voluble, argumentative Wilson, who after three drinks "collapsed like a bag of potatoes," contrasted sharply with Nabokov's mocking reserve.[55] They had developed a rare, close friendship in the year since their first meeting; yet they continued to differ on issues about which both of them felt strongly.

On the question of the war raging in Europe, experience led Wilson and Nabokov to very different positions. Wilson had entered World War I as a private in France and had seen the wounded and dying up close during his months spent in a military hospital. Embracing a pacifism that supported American isolationism, at least in military matters, Wilson was profoundly skeptical of what he would later describe as Jewish-Americans pushing the U.S. to enter the war in an attempt "to save their own people."[56]

While Wilson had made conscious efforts to reject the anti-Semitism his mother had exposed him to in childhood, his position on the war was held by other Americans who were less prone to thinking twice about the issue. That fall, the U.S. Senate convened a special subcommittee to investigate the presence of pro-war propaganda in America's motion-picture industry, expressing particular alarm over the number of foreigners running Hollywood studios. Not blind

178

to their implicit message, President Franklin Delano Roosevelt noted that the Bible, too, had been written almost entirely by foreigners and Jews. U.S. pacifist or isolationist impulses of the day seemed chronically bound up with anti-Semitism.[57]

With his love for his family, his sympathy for Jewish refugees as a group, and his eyewitness perspective on how Nazi policies had evolved from exclusion to extermination, Nabokov felt an acute sensitivity to the casual bigotry of mid-century America, but cheered its entry into the war. Despite his hatred for Stalin, he went so far as to offer conditional, transitory support to his homeland, calling for "Russia, in spite of everything, [to] defeat or rather utterly abolish Germany—so that not a German be left in the world."[58]

Nabokov's comment represented the kind of sweeping demonization of the opposing side that infuriated Wilson, and which he saw as surrendering to the mania for war without regard to its costs. Despite their differences, however, Nabokov sometimes took Wilson's advice to heart. After receiving his friend's corrections to the draft of *Sebastian Knight*, Nabokov wrote Wilson to say, "You are right, quite right about the slips," and incorporated several suggested changes.[59]

For all Nabokov's war sympathy, he was nearly as removed from the war effort as it was possible to get. His writing and occasional lectures at Wellesley were interspersed with time spent at Harvard's Museum of Comparative Zoology. As Europe itself continued to disintegrate into chaos, he brought structure and order to the Museum's European butterfly collection. As if in sympathy, Wilson adopted an ephemeral interest in entomology.[60]

Though they differed in matters of literature, war, and history, the two men admired each other. But even in the early stage of their relationship, Russia was already the sore point between them—and they could not seem to refrain from poking the wound that deepened as their friendship grew. In a letter to a mutual friend Nabokov expressed his affection for Wilson but noted that Russian attachments had a dimension missing in their American counterparts. There were many consolations to the relationship, he wrote, but he did not feel that he could truly unburden himself with Wilson.[61]

Small wonder that Nabokov could not open his heart fully. Russia and Russian literature weighed heavily on him, and he had spent the fall homesick for both. He told Véra that if it were not for her, he would enlist and fight the Germans in Morocco—then he corrected the statement to say that more than fighting Germany, he longed to write a book in Russian. As if there were still some Russian back road on which he could detour from his commitment to write in English, Nabokov submitted "Ultima Thule," a story written in his last year in France, for publication in a new Russian-language journal.[62]

When it came to new material, however, Nabokov soldiered on in English. His first poem in the language of his adopted land would make its way into the pages of *The Atlantic* before the end of the year. But even that poem relays the anguish of perpetual exile ("an endless line of land receding endlessly") and grieves the loss of his native tongue.[63]

Wilson soon dove deep into Russian verse, launching an exploration of meter that Nabokov felt was profoundly wrongheaded. In response, Nabokov created a series of charts and graphics laying out a calculus of Russian poetics via metrics, phonetics, and accents rendered in symbols. These were the weapons of their disagreement, but the heart of the matter can be seen in the degree to which Lenin continued to figure in their early correspondence.

After reading *To the Finland Station*, Nabokov felt compelled to praise his friend's treatment of Marx, but criticized the portrait of Lenin provided by Wilson. Mentioning a heartwarming anecdote in which Lenin once refrained from shooting a beautiful fox, Nabokov speculated it was a "pity that Russia was homely." Nabokov mourned the millions of lives destroyed in the pursuit of a social experiment, saving special disdain for the portrayal of Lenin as jolly—seeming disappointed that Wilson had not seen through the "pail of milk of human kindness" to note the "dead rat at the bottom."[64]

For his part, Wilson had so thoroughly identified with the oppressed in Imperial Russia that he found it hard to believe that Lenin might not have been their deliverer. He appeared to be largely unfamiliar with whole facets of Revolutionary history. First thinking that Nabokov was questioning his nascent Russian skills, Wilson conceded that he might have made some errors. But he heartily protested the criticism of his sources. "I don't believe that Gorky, differing as he did so seriously in matters of opinion from Lenin, could ever have been on such close terms with a man such as you imagine."[65]

Nabokov's affection for or dependence on Wilson was great enough to restrain his response. In a follow up letter, he wrote only that perhaps his own inclination was to portray all of Russia's rulers as "more inhuman and ridiculous than they were." Wilson acknowledged that it must be grating to see an outsider interpret Russian history, understanding just "how peculiarly uncomfortable it is to read books about one's own country by people who have got the subject up but don't really know much about it at first hand."[66]

Yet when it came to Russia, the stakes were too high, and the emotional attachment each man had to his own narrative blocked any real discussion of the issue. Nabokov's political arguments relied on history that was largely unknown in the West. But his lack of admiration for even Soviet ideals and his utter disinterest in questions of class and workers as a group led Wilson to dig in his heels and refuse to acknowledge the facts that Nabokov put on the table. While a ruined aristocrat had romantic potential as literature, Wilson also had a profound dislike for entitled behavior in general, and as difficult as his circumstances had become, Nabokov was never shy about his sense of self.[67]

Given Wilson's eagerness to discuss all things Russian, and the frequency with which disagreements over Russian history and literature cropped up in their earliest letters, it is difficult to imagine Russia *not* coming up during Nabokov's Thanksgiving visit. Neither made a journal record of their holiday or quoted from conversations that transpired there, but a literary relic of the visit—a poem—survives.

"The Refrigerator Awakes" begins with *Crash!* and a noisy icebox straining to do its duty as coils boil volatile chemicals ("dichloridi-somethingmethane"), revealing the gargantuan effort required to keep its cool. But the overheating refrigerator, on the verge of collapse, struggles on. Behind the ham, fruit, and milk, Nabokov weaves in more disturbing imagery of survival and preservation: a torture house, bodies frozen in blue ice for fifty years, "a trembling white heart," and a story that must be told. He mentions the Russian Arctic islands of Nova Zembla and Ernest Shackleton, who went there, and winks at the story of William Barents, an explorer trapped in 1596 for one desperate winter near the islands' northern tip. And he ends with a cycle of references to polar adventurers whose (not always successful) attempts to survive became the stuff of legends.[68]

If Nabokov felt stranded in an alien landscape, burdened with a story that might never be told, or somehow in danger of losing his own cool during his 1941 visit to Wellfleet, the poem was as close as he would ever come to expressing it. Cryptic as it was, Nabokov still worried that he had offended Wilson, writing a week later to say, "I do hope that you do not take my 'Refrigerator' as implying that I spent a bad night at your house. I did not. I really cannot tell you, at least in English, how much I enjoyed my stay."[69]

7

After Thanksgiving, Nabokov returned to Wellesley, where he awaited the publication of *The Real Life of Sebastian Knight* that December. Wilson wrote a glorious blurb for the book, but between Thanksgiving and the book's arrival in mid-December, the American landscape shifted.

Nabokov had escaped the aftermath of the Revolution as a teenager and as an adult had become a veritable Houdini of history, slipping out of Germany before Hitler's march into Poland, and cutting it even closer on his flight from France. But on December 7, 1941, conflict caught up with him in yet another country when hundreds of Japanese planes bombed Pearl Harbor.

The surprise attack marked the Japanese declaration of war against the United States, leading the U.S. to respond in kind on December 8. Three days later, Adolf Hitler took to a podium at the Kroll Opera House before the members of the Reichstag to declare war on America, too, in a speech broadcast and reprinted around the world. "We know, of course," he said, "that the Eternal Jew is behind all this."[70]

Overnight, the country was seized with the kind of paranoia that had led Britain to deport its civilian enemy aliens the year before. The stunned U.S. followed Britain's footsteps in establishing its own concentration camps. In the first days after the bombing of Pearl Harbor and before the U.S. declaration of war on Germany, FBI agents rounded up and interned thousands of Italian, German, and Japanese citizens, often for arbitrary reasons.[71] Initially, prisoners were held in locations both improvised and established, from county jails to immigration centers in New York and California.

On the coasts, the fear of spies and sabotage led to restrictions on handheld cameras and confiscation of shortwave radios. A wave of arrests of Austrian skiers who had married American heiresses drew bemused media attention, and enough people fired employees with "foreign-sounding" names that U.S. Attorney General Francis Biddle made a public declaration against the practice.[72]

An American system of concentration camps—not death camps, but internment facilities—was hastily set up. The most famous casualties of the system were the more than 110,000 Japanese and Japanese-Americans who would eventually be interned for the duration of the war. But early on, when the focus was on catching spies and speed was believed to be critical, a number of Jewish concentration camp survivors and refugees fleeing Germany—particularly those who had a history as political radicals—also found themselves detained alongside Nazi prisoners of war.[73]

Edmund Wilson remained skeptical about the war. He was not quite so conspiracy-minded as to think (as some did) that Pearl Harbor had been a set-up, but he recoiled from American propaganda depicting the Japanese as animals. Nabokov, who had watched Germany's violence against its Jews escalate and had family trapped in German territory, was less eager to listen to reasons for keeping America out of the war. He registered for the draft and started a new novel filled with refractions of Soviet and Nazi totalitarianism.[74]

Pearl Harbor changed neither Wilson's nor Nabokov's opinion of the war or their personal circumstances, but its effects would register elsewhere. Nabokov's cousin Nicholas felt compelled to do something for the war effort outside his chosen field. He held on to his day job as music director at St. Johns College in Annapolis, but soon began doing work as a translator and analyst for the Department of Justice.[75]

When the Japanese struck, Sonia Slonim was in Hollywood working for Max Ophüls, the celebrated director whose scripts she had helped translate in Paris. Ophüls, who was Jewish, had fled Germany in 1933 but managed to establish himself in France as a filmmaker—only to have been forced to flee again. His career was thwarted a third time after Pearl Harbor, when the film industry focused on patriotic films for the American war effort.[76] When Ophüls's career flagged, Slonim found herself out of work.

Carl Junghans had shared Ophüls's Hollywood dream and quickly tapped into his own network of German exiles on the West Coast. He had gotten his foot in the door and started helping with script ideas that fall. But two days after Pearl Harbor, he was picked up by the FBI and held in the Los Angeles County jail on suspicion of being a German spy.[77]

Some inmates were released within weeks, some a year or two later, while others were forced to relocate to assigned camps for the duration of the war. One of Junghans's bunkmates in internment would manage to convince a review board that he was Swiss, not German, thereby securing his freedom. Junghans was not so lucky.

He had by then been named as "a thorough-going Nazi" by a Jewish refugee writing for a small newspaper in New York. The Anti-Defamation League had written a letter bringing his work with Goebbels to the attention of the U.S. Department of Justice. And it turned out that Junghans already had an FBI case file, which provided a good deal of material for review.[78]

Under questioning, Junghans quickly tried to prove himself a valuable asset. He talked of a man with a wooden leg who was somehow responsible for *Kristallnacht*. He spoke of a special spy school in which Nazis trained agents who were blackmailed Jews, or Aryans secretly coached to appear Jewish, before sending them into Allied nations as spies.[79] He talked about clandestine meteorological stations the Germans had established in the Arctic; he offered names of Communist spies. He warned that people who had arrived in America with Swiss passports were particularly likely to be hiding their true identity. He named Charlie Chaplin as a personal reference.

Most of the testimony he gave was invented, conspiracy-minded gibberish, or taken out of recent newspaper reports. But some small statements buried in his testimony appeared to be true, and the FBI wanted his cooperation.

Near the end of January 1942, faced with conflicting information, the hearing board recommended Junghans's release. But someone else in the Justice Department was more skeptical. Instead of release, the Attorney General authorized releasing Junghans under parole and entrusting him to a sponsor who would supervise his liberty. He would have to stay in Los Angeles and check in on a regular basis for the foreseeable future.

In 1942, after several weeks in detention that ended in conditional release from the San Pedro Detention Station, he found himself regarded a pariah in Hollywood and unable to find work with the major studios. Sonia Slonim's prospects were almost as bleak; she returned to New York without him.

Junghans represented just the kind of person Americans might have hoped the government would keep tabs on. But others who were interned and were more deserving of sympathy found little recourse or relief. Open hostility was shown to civilian prisoners.

Wartime propaganda that turned American citizens against Japs and Huns would do collateral damage to the innocent.

8

Overseas, the success of German propaganda demonizing Jews in Germany and Austria encouraged the Nazis to export their efforts to conquered nations. But France, despite her anti-Semitism and an often obliging police force, would not prove quite as enthusiastic in adopting Nazi measures.

Two weeks after the French police first carried out mass arrests of Jews in Paris, the Germans started in earnest to propagandize their defeated neighbor. The German Embassy helped to mount a French version of "The Eternal Jew" exhibition that had made such an impression in Germany. It would draw 200,000 paying visitors. With its careful explanation of racial degeneracy and poisonous depiction of history, the French exhibition also included lectures sponsored by *Paris Soir* and others linking Marxism to Jewry and discussing "the Communist, a Jewish product."[80]

And the Germans did more than talk. In direct and publicly announced retribution for an attack on German officers, ninety-five prisoners were executed in a Western Paris suburb, fifty-one of them Jewish. And in the hopes of fueling French anti-Semitism, Gestapo technicians helped anti-Bolshevik groups detonate bombs at seven Paris synagogues near Yom Kippur. They were surprised when their plan failed to trigger a *Kristallnacht*-style firestorm, as had happened in annexed Austria and occupied Czechoslovakia in 1938. "Although they do not like the Jews," reported one dismayed German propagandist, "the French are displeased when they see [them] massacred and when their places of worship are blown up."[81]

It had become harder and harder for Jews to leave France, but many who had planned to wait out the war now longed to escape. Despite the odds, some of Nabokov's loved ones managed to flee. The Marinel sisters got out through Lisbon—one of the last ports sympathetic to Jews seeking transit—arriving in New York in 1941. Véra's cousin Anna Feigin obtained papers to travel with her brother, and also fled to the U.S. via Lisbon, arriving in Baltimore in mid-1942.[82] The Hessens would run a more circuitous route, making their way from France through Spain, sailing into New Orleans just before Christmas with the help of Yakov Frumkin, who had been the moving force behind delivering the Nabokovs to America.[83]

Others among Nabokov's friends and family fell into the hands of the Nazis. Nabokov's youngest brother Kirill was arrested and questioned, but was eventually released. After the fall of France, Sergei Nabokov and Hermann Thieme made their way east. They began to keep their distance from each other, despite the fact that prosecutions of homosexuals had dropped off precipitously since the beginning of the war.[84]

Whatever distance or discretion they practiced proved to be inadequate—both were soon arrested. Hermann was released to join the German army in Africa. Sergei was charged with homosexual offenses, then jailed for several months before being freed. He began to denounce the Nazis, and somehow still managed to stand as the best man for his second cousin's wedding late that November in Berlin. Before Christmas, he was arrested again. He was eventually assigned to Neuengamme, a concentration camp on the southeastern outskirts of Hamburg, where he arrived in the spring of 1944.[85]

By the time the Hessens sailed west, hundreds of thousands of Jews faced the nightmare of deportation in the opposite direction as part of a formal shift in German policy. After nine years of assaults and the monstrous expansion of concentration camps into Poland, after the targeting of leftists, homosexuals, and Gypsies, the German government had found a way to take intolerable suffering and increase it. Jews as a race, they argued—in a policy now completely freed from the fetters of rhetorical pretense—should be exterminated.

This new policy meant that six camps in Poland had been or soon would be optimized as death factories, with their facilities dedicated to the rapid extinction of millions who were transported over winter snow, over spring mud, over summer fields and fall desolation, to end their lives in unimaginable terror. It meant that Goebbels, as German propaganda minister, would in the summer of 1942 defiantly announce the extermination strategy to the world, pretending that the step was taken in revenge for Allied bombing raids.[86]

The reality of what this would mean, of course, was not fully comprehended in the West at the time—it can hardly be apprehended even in retrospect. After the German policy of Jewish extermination had become explicit, negotiations were held between the French government and Nazi officials in Paris to plan the arrest and deportation of all Jews in France between the ages of sixteen and sixty-five in a project named Spring Wind (*Vent printanier*). French President Pierre Laval balked at turning over Jewish French citizens, but in order to fill quotas, gave the Germans some refugees they had not asked for: the children of foreign Jews. In the days and weeks that followed, scenes of despair and mayhem shocked the world as the French authorities captured and interned more than ten thousand Jewish adults and children.

Laval argued to a group of French diplomats (and perhaps to even himself), that the procedures were aimed at sending back stateless Jews who represented "a dangerous element" in French society. It was a "measure taken out of concern for national health and hygiene." The moral issues involved, however, were clearer to others. Fighting French forces trumpeted stories of three hundred French policemen who were fired for refusing to comply with arrests, and of administrators who were dismissed for being sympathetic to the Jews.[87]

Bused to the *Vélodrome d'hiver*, a racing stadium, families were forced to wait in terrible conditions. The youths, some of whom were not even old enough to identify themselves, wore metal name tags stitched onto their clothing. Their parents were taken to Drancy, while the children remained at the stadium. After several days without food, the children were transported to other camps and then to Drancy, too.[88]

More than sixty thousand Jews had been forcibly relocated eastward from France via Drancy by the middle of 1944.[89] Three locomotives a week loaded with a thousand deportees rolled away from the camp—there were rumors the trains were headed to an extermination center, but there was no way to be sure.

In preparation for their departure, the prisoners' heads were shaved, and they, along with their possessions, were thoroughly searched. They were given a last meal and a final postcard to write to their loved ones. They were not told where they were going. The children, too, would eventually meet the same fate, packed onto trains rolling over the countryside to an unknown destination, sometimes weeks after their parents had traveled the same rail line to the same endpoint.[90]

These stateless Jews were not just German or Polish refugees; they included Russian Jews, adults and children, who would no longer need the Nansen passports that had saved them from nothing. Weeks before George and Joseph Hessen made their circuitous trip south through Spain, Ilya Fondaminsky was taken from Drancy and put on a train. Less than two weeks later, Sonia Slonim's ex-husband Max Berlstein would also be sent east, part of Transport Number 37 from Drancy that September.[91] Both men found themselves where so many of the Jews deported from Paris had ended up. Carried in on the human tidal wave arriving in Auschwitz that fall, they were likely herded into the gas chambers of Birkenau shortly after their arrival, living out the fate that Véra and Dmitri Nabokov had eluded.

9

If the French collaborators, still thinking in terms of forced labor camps, did not grasp or did not want to grasp what they were abetting, though it was happening before their eyes, they were not alone. It was a global failure of imagination, not least in the United States. After it was understood that mass exterminations were underway, a historic eyewitness report was made to Roosevelt by Catholic Polish resistant Jan Karski in September 1943. In order to be able to testify persuasively, Karski had braved entry into the Warsaw ghetto and sneaked *into* the extermination camp at Belzec, Poland—and then survived torture after a brief time in captivity. On behalf of the Polish government in exile, Karski went to England and the U.S. to tell the tale of what he had seen, only to find his story disbelieved by Supreme Court Justice Felix Frankfurter. Karski was shocked by Frankfurter's response, and decades later described the clarification Frankfurter had made to the Polish ambassador to the United States, who was in the room at the time: "I did not say that he was lying, I said that I could not believe him. There is a difference."[92]

Karski's testimony, which he had risked his life to get, made little impact at the highest levels of government. In his absence, Karski was denounced on Nazi radio and, as a result, was dissuaded from returning to the Polish underground. He stayed in America.

Other Catholics joined the fight in occupied Europe. Zinaida Shakhovskoy, who had helped Nabokov with readings in Belgium, aided the French resistance. Véra's sister Lena had begun working with the Jesuits in Berlin, despite having an infant son.[93] She was taken in and twice interrogated by the Gestapo.

Nabokov's literary rival Ivan Bunin, who had already seen rough treatment at the hands of the Gestapo before the war, was living in southern France amid the steep mountains outside the perfume capital of Grasse. During the Occupation, Bunin hid several Jews from the Germans, including pianist Alexander Bakhrakh, who stayed underground with him for nearly the entire war.[94]

In Prague, the twenty-five-year companion of Nabokov's mother, Evgenia Hofeld, found another path to action. Family lore would recall how Hofeld indiscriminately helped Jews in Prague and became known as a Gentile who would sign as an official witness on the identity papers that would certify that the bearer was *not* Jewish.[95]

But on the eastern front, it was a tight squeeze between Hitler and Stalin, with many compelled to choose between fascist and Communist forces. If Nabokov thought Hitler presented the graver danger of the two for the time being, not everyone in his family agreed. Boris Petkevič, the husband of Nabokov's sister Olga, had become deeply involved with anti-Bolshevik forces, in a group apparently supported by the Nazis.[96]

During the war, Nabokov knew little of his friends and families' lives, but he had his own, smaller struggles back home. His contract with Wellesley was not renewed, in part, he feared, for his straight-forwardly anti-Soviet attitude, which had become less fetching now that America was at war and Russia her ally. He had been given a small income from the Museum of Comparative Zoology to continue his work on their butterfly collection, but it was not nearly enough for three Nabokovs to live on, even in small quarters in Cambridge. In desperation, he did a lecture tour with the Institute of International Education, an organization best known for promoting American democracy abroad but whose mission also apparently extended to exposing Americans to foreign intellectuals favoring democratic ideals at home.[97]

Though he still struggled to find a dependable job, Nabokov's literary star had begun to glimmer ever so slightly. New Directions, which had published *Sebastian Knight*, had given him a contract to translate Russian poetry and do a short book on Russian author Nikolai Gogol, which he completed mid-war. With Edmund Wilson's recommendation, he applied for a Guggenheim Fellowship in 1943, becoming the first applicant over the age of forty ever chosen. He even received a new contract to teach Russian at Wellesley the fol-lowing year.[98]

With prodding from Véra, he cut back on time spent with butter-flies to focus on the novel he had begun when the U.S. entered the war. In fits and starts, he continued to build a dystopian parody of a Soviet-German police state, in which a freethinking philosopher (not unlike his earlier character Cincinnatus) is pulled into the prison system of a totalitarian society that is being forced into unthinking conformity. Nowhere close to finished with it, he pulled the first four chapters together and submitted them to a publisher.[99]

The Allies' prospects seemed to be improving as well; they soon turned the tide on the Eastern front in Europe. By the time Nabokov and Edmund Wilson met up with Sonia Slonim in New York in preparation for the locally urgent matter of ten-year-old Dmitri's appendectomy, D-Day was just around the corner.

Following in Véra and Carl Junghans's footsteps, Sonia had joined the war effort by taking her turn at France Forever. She had also, she told several friends, gone unannounced to the office of the French Military attaché in Washington to volunteer her services to the French cause, only to be turned away.[100]

After Normandy, the Allies poured forward, chasing the retreating Germans, and it became clear that the war would soon be over. As U.S. forces liberated Paris and moved across France, the Soviets worked their way back across Poland, Hungary, and Austria from the east, arriving in Prague on May 9. That very day, Soviet forces would go looking for Olga Nabokov's husband, Boris Petkevič, who had chosen the losing side in the war. They would find him long gone to England. But Olga was taken in for questioning.[101] Unlike so many who were interrogated and then sent to the far reaches of the Gulag, she was released after three days.

Over the summer, the Soviets overran the location of the killing center at Belzec that Jan Karski had seen, along with the nearby extermination sites at Sobibor and Treblinka. That July, religious committees confirmed the existence of death camps at Birkenau and Auschwitz, and had seen evidence of more than a million and a half executions.[102]

Writer Arthur Koestler, who years before had plumbed the psyche of true believers in Stalin's purges with *Darkness at Noon*, lamented the disbelief he encountered across three years of speaking to the troops: "They don't believe in concentration camps, they don't believe in the starved children of Greece, in the shot hostages of France, in the mass graves of Poland; they have never heard of Lidice, Treblinka, or Belzec."[103] It soon became apparent that, if anything, the testimony of witnesses like Jan Karski had understated the horrors of what had happened.

Karski's own book, *Story of a Secret State*, had come out at the end of 1944 to tremendous attention in the U.S. He had kept faith with his assignment to testify about what he had seen, but he understood by now that such testimony was not enough to alter history. In his book, a Jewish elder in the Warsaw ghetto says that of course Hitler will be defeated, and Karski's country will rise from its ashes. But the Polish Jews, the elder explains, will by then have ceased to exist. "It is no use telling you all this," he says. "No one in the outside world can possibly understand. You don't understand. Even I don't understand, for my people are dying and I am alive."[104]

10

The dead of the Warsaw ghetto haunted Nabokov that spring. His belief that all Germans should be exterminated—voiced in passing to Wilson years before—had not faded. Writing in 1944 to the chair of the New York Browning Society, Nabokov declined her invitation to speak and responded to material she had enclosed calling for understanding and pity for the suffering of German civilians.

Far from being in need of succor, Nabokov suggested, Germans had already derived quite enough comforts from the bloody belongings stolen from the Jews of Warsaw. Lest she misunderstand, he clarified that at times, castration and improved breeding techniques were insufficient to solve a chronic issue. In his powerlessness, he fantasized turning the final solution on the Germans themselves. Germany, he suggested to Mrs. Hope—and it is not clear whether he meant the country, the culture, or its people—deserved to be chloroformed.[105]

Anti-Semitism within his own émigré community remained equally repellent to him. Not long after his own arrival in America, Nabokov had advised George Hessen on how to get by in the new country: "The only thing you must do is deal with genuine Americans and don't get involved with the local Russian emigration."[106]

Nabokov would pour it all into his writing. In his first short story for *The New Yorker*, originally titled "Double Talk," a Russian émigré explains how he is perpetually mistaken for a bigot with the same name. Decades before, the double had failed to return a copy of *The Protocols of the Wise Men of Zion* to the library, with the narrator receiving the blame. The double's scurrilous activities complicate the narrator's border crossings, while the narrator's provocative writing causes his double to be arrested twice by the Germans.

In wartime Boston, the narrator mistakenly accepts an invitation that was intended for his double, who—it does not surprise readers by this point—belongs to a circle that pities Germany, decrying "the vivid Semitic imagination that controls the American press" and atrocities "invented by the Jews."[107] Seated amid people voicing ideas repellent to him, the narrator is reluctant to speak up in the salon because of his tendency to become inarticulate and stammer under stress. But in the end, he finds his voice and makes a dramatic exit, unfortunately with someone else's coat.

"Double Talk" was written in the wake of the liberation of Auschwitz, which fell into Soviet hands in January 1945. That spring, American troops swept through German territory, taking over hundreds of camps and subcamps along the way, including Buchenwald, which soldiers reached that April. Within days, newspaper stories told of American troops forcing civilians from nearby Weimar to come and see for themselves the crematorium, the dead bodies, the remnants of medical experiments injecting typhus into children, the torture chamber, the gallows, the dead bodies, and the near-dead survivors.[108]

At Auschwitz, Soviet soldiers found that fleeing Germans had destroyed many of the camp warehouses. Nevertheless, more than one million suits and dresses were recovered—clothing that had indeed been intended, as Nabokov had indicated in his letter to Mrs. Hope, to be sent back to German cities as relief supplies.

Deportees from Drancy, however, had been allowed to depart with very little in the way of possessions on their way east. And so when Soviet forces finally got to Poland in January 1945, it is possible that no jacket, no ring, not a recognizable trace of Ilya Fondaminsky or Max Berlstein remained on the grounds of Auschwitz.

Before it was shut down, this largest of the extermination camps had delivered nearly a million Jews and hundreds of thousands of Poles, Gypsies, and Soviet prisoners of war to their deaths. It was not just the graphic revelations of the large camps, but also the sheer numbers that proved overwhelming. Details of genocide began to pour out of Europe. News of the dead—the beloved, the loathed, and the forgotten—radiated like ghost webs to cross and recross the paths of the living. A former student of Nabokov, Mikhail Gorlin, who had himself become a poet, had died at Auschwitz in a mining sub-camp. His wife, another poet, whose writing Nabokov had mocked in a Berlin review, had died too. ("Raissa Blokh," he would later say. "I was horrid to her.") A Jew stopped by the Swiss at the border when she tried to enter, Blokh had been turned over to officials and sent to Drancy.[109]

On her trip east, she wrote a note that she managed to drop from the window of a train.[110] The communication, however, ran only one direction. Too late for affection or apologies, the tenderness, the pettiness, the kind gestures and cruelties alike were frozen in place forever.

Neuengamme sat in the north of Germany, not far from Hamburg. A scouting party arrived the evening of May 2, just hours after the camp had been abandoned by the last members of the SS. Three days later, Allied forces inspected the facilities, escorted by a contingent of former prisoners. The camp, with its train tracks, barracks, morgue, and crematorium, was nearly empty by then.

The British had arrived. The surviving prisoners were freed. But liberation came nearly four months too late to save Sergei Nabokov, who had already been logged into the Neuengamme Book of the Dead.

CHAPTER NINE

After the War

———— ∞∞∞ ————

1

That fall when the war was over, Nabokov dreamed of his brother. Until that dream, Vladimir had imagined Sergei somewhere in hiding with Hermann. But his nightmare delivered up an alternate vision— Sergei alone and suffering in an anonymous concentration camp.[1]

Soon after, Nabokov received two letters from Europe that revealed the truth. Making contact through *The New Yorker*, his other brother Kirill wrote to say that Sergei had died of a stomach ailment at Neuengamme. A separate letter sent by Evgenia Hofeld bearing the same news arrived at almost the same time.[2]

Everyone but Sergei had survived. Hofeld was still in Prague, still taking care of Nabokov's nephew Rostislav. Nabokov's sister Elena had also been spared, as had her husband and son. Nabokov wrote his family back, relaying his joy and relief at hearing they were alive. Kirill, he learned in a brief exchange, was an interpreter for the American army in Berlin. Nabokov was more forthcoming with Elena, taking nearly a thousand words to catch her up on his American life: his lunch of two sandwiches and milk, the details of his own "retreat into entomology," and the weight he had put on that led him to resemble a grossly obese nineteenth-century poet. He mentioned Sergei to Elena ("[p]oor, poor Seryozha"), and told Kirill that he would ask their cousin Nicholas, then in Germany on a mission with U.S. forces, to try to uncover additional information about Sergei's fate.[3]

In a letter to Edmund Wilson later that month, Nabokov mentioned both brothers. Of Sergei, he wrote that his brother had been sent to "one of the worst concentration camps (near Hamburg) and perished there." Nabokov confessed shock at the news that his brother had been arrested as a British sympathizer. Hardly able to imagine an identity for Sergei that included being a political prisoner, Nabokov noted he had been a "harmless, indolent, pathetic person who spent his life vaguely shuttling between the Quartier Latin and a castle in Austria that he shared with a friend."[4]

Just back from an unstable Greece that was about to explode into civil war, Wilson sent his regrets. "Human life," he wrote, "means absolutely nothing in Europe today." Wilson, however, felt a sympathy for Germany that Nabokov did not, and meant the statement to apply to all players in the war. He had been horrified by his homeland's willingness to demolish Dresden and "go the Nazis one better by destroying whole Japanese towns."[5]

Wilson had his own news to share, not tragic but sad enough: he was faced with divorce from his third wife, Mary McCarthy. Nabokov had already heard the rumors about the collapse of their turbulent relationship. McCarthy had briefly been committed to a psychiatric hospital, saying Wilson had beaten her, while Wilson claimed he had done no such thing. Nabokov, who in Europe had competed with friends for the right to punish an abuser, declared himself "'very much' upset" not to have had an initial explanation from Wilson directly.[6]

But in 1945 their mutual affection seemed indestructible. Not only did Nabokov remain friends with Wilson after the divorce, but Véra, too, had developed a fondness for Wilson, adding a personal note to a letter, inviting him to Boston in the midst of his legal turmoil. Vladimir and Véra even moved in with Wilson for a week at his request, to relieve the anxieties of his live-in cook that she would be swept into the divorce proceedings.[7]

Their camaraderie, however, could not erase their ideological differences. Even as the war receded into the past, the friends continued to regard it differently. In light of all the death, Wilson felt the killing had to stop and advocated against condemning Nazi leaders to death.[8]

Hitler's suicide, however, was not recompense enough for Nabokov. Even with the Germans defeated, Nabokov was not inclined toward mercy. A Christmas letter from Dmitri's school asking for clothing to be sent to German children was met with a return missive suggesting that while he was in principle in favor of the ideal of aiding former enemies, it would not be until the needs of desperate "Greek, Czech, French, Belgian, Chinese, Dutch, Norwegian, Russian, [and] Jewish" children had been addressed that he might consider fulfilling the school's request.[9]

Nabokov knew, however, that Soviet troops were already making Germans pay a terrible price for their sins. Newspapers ran stories of refugees streaming westward at Germany's defeat. Editorial writers described scenes in which Soviet forces continued "to strip bare the countries they occupy." Thousands tried to escape Soviet occupation zones, refusing to return home. Some Eastern Europeans were initially given a choice about whether to go back, but others were not. As part of the Allied agreement that emerged from Yalta, Soviet citizens were to be repatriated to Russia whether or not they were willing. Widespread desertion took place among Soviet soldiers stationed in Germany, who filtered out to live on the lam or made their way into camps for displaced persons rather than heading home.[10]

2

As a captain in the Soviet Army, Alexander Solzhenitsyn had traveled through Soviet-occupied territory as the Red Army had advanced. He had crossed paths with liberated Soviet POWs as they marched homeward. Innocent as he still was, he was deeply puzzled by their profound dejection at the prospect of returning to Russia.

More immediately disturbing to him were initial messages sent to soldiers from Stalin encouraging advancing troops to exact revenge on Germany in any form they wished. Their wishes, it turned out, were vicious.[11]

On the headlong dash into Germany, Solzhenitsyn made it as far as Königsberg, over seventy miles west of the border. He witnessed an NKVD tribunal and reprisals in recovered territory, and was also present for at least one execution of collaborators, an event which was promoted as the kick-off to a full-fledged party—one he declined to attend.[12]

Unlike Nabokov, Solzhenitsyn had seen combat; but like his fellow Russian, he had come to see his life's work as writing. Thus it may have been with mixed motives that he managed in 1944 to send a forged army pass and a military disguise with an emissary, bringing his wife, Natalia, to join him at the front. For three weeks, she had occupied herself in the trenches, much as Véra Nabokov had in Cambridge the previous year—making clean drafts of her husband's work and discussing Russian literature with him. Solzhenitsyn hoped his wife might stay indefinitely, but things did not always go smoothly. One point of contention from his perspective was her refusal to stand at attention when he entered the trench.[13]

By that point, Solzhenitsyn was still a true believer in the Revolution, but he had lost all respect for Stalin. He thought little of the military censors and routinely referred to the problems of Soviet life in relation to "the moustachioed one" or in similarly thinly veiled terms to friends also serving in the military.[14] They believed that with enough revolutionary ardor, they might be able to help create a Soviet Union that lived up to its possibilities, helping Russia to recover from Stalin's errors.

This Solzhenitsyn was a very different man than the one who had entered the Army. Despite his early incompetence and anguish, he had managed to learn discipline and leadership. He was pleased by the respect and reputation he had earned.

But on the eve of the push to Berlin—the war was effectively over but yet to be won—Solzhenitsyn was called to the office of his brigadier general. Reporting for what he thought was a special assignment, he found himself in a room with brigade staff and Soviet counterespionage agents. As his revolver was taken away, his cap stripped of its star, and his epaulettes torn from his jacket, he realized he was under arrest.[15]

3

The closest Vladimir Nabokov got to a military campaign in World War II was his attempt to quit smoking. (Véra's biographer records Nabokov's self-mockery: "We shall fight in the hills. We shall never surrender."[16]) Other than the trauma he was willing to do to the reputations of his fellow writers—mostly by this point picking on the famous or the dead—Nabokov confined his violence to literature, or writing letters to organizations that had provoked him. He taught at Wellesley, continued with his Guggenheim funding (now in its second year), caught new specimens, and reorganized Harvard's butterflies. Meanwhile, he treasured his son, worked with Véra, and flirted with women half his age at Wellesley. He had published a half-dozen novels in as many years during his European exile, but he had much less to show for his time in America.

In the end Nabokov, who had lived through two world wars and a revolution, was not called up and never had to serve. Unlike the eastern remnants of his family, he had managed to avoid being pinned between fascism and Communism. He had no medals, and was a hero only, perhaps, to the son and wife with whom he had escaped Europe. For the duration of the war, he had been stateside, writing letters in support of the friends' visas and fretting over the fate of those trying to get to America.

He beat the same drum after the war, encouraging a westward movement away from danger and toward liberty for family members still trapped in the East. Still feeling financial strain, Nabokov was nonetheless more flush than usual with income from Harvard, Wellesley, and the sale of the movie rights to *Camera Obscura*, now titled *Laughter in the Dark*. He continued to send care packages with money and clothing to help Evgenia Hofeld take care of Rostislav, even as he lobbied for them to emigrate.[17]

The postwar landscape evolved quickly. Less than a year after the end of hostilities, Winston Churchill gave a speech in Missouri, announcing that from the Baltic to the Adriatic "an iron curtain has descended across the continent," trapping millions of central Europeans in a sphere in danger of Soviet repression.[18] The Marshall Plan, announced the following year, allocated billions to restore the economies and infrastructure of Europe, with an eye toward strengthening democracy.

Nabokov understood that the Soviets would not treat their new territories of influence any differently than they had their own citizens. As they began to exercise their authority more aggressively in the occupied regions, the free elections that had been promised in Poland were hijacked in January 1947 via fraud and manipulation. A similar process unfolded across two elections in Hungary, with Communists intimidating, arresting, and exiling popular leaders after winning only a minority of the vote. Nabokov continued to think about how to extract his family and wrote a letter of recommendation for Elena, who was trying to get a job with the United Nations.[19]

Nabokov defined himself not just against the Soviets but parts of the émigré community, too. Edmund Wilson had learned that when it came to Russians, Nabokov could be picky. He knew well enough to warn Nabokov when Russian artist Pavel Tchelitchew would be visiting the Wilsons in Wellfleet. A painter who had collaborated with Nicholas Nabokov on a Diaghilev ballet, Tchelitchew had also been Sergei Nabokov's roommate in Paris. Giving Nabokov fair warning of the company he would have if he visited, Wilson added, "I hope this won't keep you away."[20]

Nabokov had not been shy about sharing his thoughts on Russia with Wilson, and he had begun to collect observations and anecdotes about America as well. During his lecture tour through the south, he met W. E. B. Du Bois and learned how the elegant "Negro scholar and organizer" had been welcomed as a Colonel in England because of the *Col.* designation on his passport, signifying "Colored." Less amusing was a filthy man in the Pullman lavatory who reminded Nabokov of the reactionary militias from his childhood, only increasing the resemblance when he started spewing anti-Semitic comments.[21]

If Nabokov had hoped to leave anti-Semitism behind as a European relic, he must have been sorely disappointed, and not just with the encounter in the Pullman coach. Contemplating a trip to New Hampshire in the summer of 1945, he began to decode the foreign language of U.S. property listings. He had learned that "modern comfort" translated into rooms that could offer a toilet but no bathtub. And nastier than exaggerations of amenities, he noticed, were the blatant refusals to serve Jews. He wrote to Wilson, mockingly dismissing places requesting only "Christian clientèle."[22]

New Hampshire would disappoint him in person the following year, when he saw signs barring Jewish patrons. Dmitri and Véra would later tell of one visit to a diner during which Nabokov, infuriated by a similar note on the menu, asked the manager "what would happen if little old bearded Jesus Christ drove up, in an old Ford, with his mother (black scarf, Polish accent)?" Would they serve a young couple who had tied a donkey up outside and come in to eat with their baby boy? The nativity references to the indisputably Jewish holy family momentarily baffled the summertime staff, forcing Nabokov to clarify as he stormed out.[23]

Nabokov had touched on American anti-Semitism in "Double Talk." But in that story, it is principally the immigrants—the German doctor and the White Russian colonel—who are malicious, while their American audience plays the role of enthusiastic dupes. Nabokov's travels, however, revealed home-grown prejudice.

He had learned from his father the obligation to expose bigotry when it took root in a beloved country. And so he was already observing anti-Semitism on a new continent, testing the local strain for variations. It was a genus he knew well, but he had yet to classify the species. Taking events in and biding his time, he would soon find a way to use almost everything he had seen.

4

As the U.S. and U.S.S.R. settled into opposing camps, Nabokov's family members shifted from wartime activities to peace; but for most of them, work remained political in nature. After a stint at the Department of Justice during the war and work as an analyst for the U.S. Strategic Bombing Survey in 1945, Nicholas Nabokov headed to Germany as a negotiations coordinator and cultural advisor. Sonia Slonim had stayed at *La Voix de France* for two years, then remained in New York doing freelance translation for the U.N. But the lack of steady work drove her to look outside the city, so she moved to northern Virginia, where she signed on with the U.S. Army as a cryptographer.[24]

Her relationship with Junghans haunted her. A *pro forma* background check by military intelligence for a security clearance inspired an anonymous letter about her, with a laundry list of allegations. The note offered that she had "worked for several foreign governments AT THE SAME TIME [sic]," that money "talks with her," that she was indiscreet, a showoff, and a "very sleek" blackmailer. In case agents had missed the point of the letter, it further noted that she was of "questionable morality." A six-month internal investigation uncovered the 1941 telegram sent to the secretary of state accusing her of being a German spy. Army Intelligence got the FBI involved in a full-blown loyalty investigation.

The FBI inquiry dragged on for more than a year and, due in part to Slonim's long romance with Junghans, expanded into France and Germany. She had a reputation for being anti-Nazi, but she had been involved with a Nazi propagandist. She was reputed to be

---

anti-Soviet, but Junghans was also believed to have been a Communist. Several of the men she had worked for during the war in New York and Hollywood were themselves being investigated as Communist sympathizers. Her claim to have worked with French intelligence—a claim she did not make to agents, but which was relayed to them by her acquaintances—would only have reinforced the letter accusing her of opportunism. As part of the process, Massachusetts agents looked into the reliability of Vladimir and Véra Nabokov, whom investigators found not at all suspicious.

No concrete evidence of wrongdoing on Sonia's part ever appeared, but her associations were problematic. American anti-Semitism reared its head in her paperwork; particular attention was paid to who was and was not Jewish in the circles she frequented (often mistakenly identifying who was and who wasn't in the process). One informant even insisted—not just incorrectly but nonsensically—that she had changed her original family name from Levin to Slonim, as a way to hide her Jewishness.[25]

There were so many conflicting reports about Sonia, it was impossible to determine her loyalty. In the end, no final decision was made. The process dragged on, and Slonim eventually left her Army post for work at the United Nations in 1949 before the investigation was complete.

Nabokov, too, briefly felt the tug of post-war geopolitics—as well as his own financial precariousness—and made moves toward heading up the programming for the State Department's new Russian radio effort on the Voice of America. Edmund Wilson wrote him a stellar recommendation for the job, and he appeared to pass his background check, only to find out that Nicholas Nabokov, whom he had asked to be one of his references, had acquired the job for himself. Nabokov had Wilson as a reference, but Nicholas had three-time Pulitzer Prize winner Archibald MacLeish, former Ambassador to the Soviet Union George Bohlen, and George Kennan, who had become the influential director of State Department's policy planning staff.[26]

Nicholas beat out Vladimir for the job but, like Sonia Slonim, soon found himself under scrutiny. After eight months, Nicholas applied for a new job that required a new security clearance, only to find that the first years of the Cold War had redefined the meaning of loyalty to America. In the 1948 review of his application, Nicholas's life was dissected to a much more disconcerting degree than Sonia's had been. His psychiatric hospitalizations, his diagnosis as a manic-depressive, his divorces, his enmity with several former friends and co-workers, and his involvement with female students at multiple U.S. colleges were all investigated and appear to have been confirmed. Rumors of drug addiction, venereal disease, admiration for Stalin, membership in the French Communist Party, and efforts to move back to the Soviet Union in the 1930s were unsubstantiated. (Confidential informants notoriously swung for the fences in the wildness of their statements.)

But in the cavalcade of real or imagined offenses, only one matter seems to have truly troubled the FBI: they wanted to know if Nicholas Nabokov was homosexual. They had heard about his association with ballet queen Diaghilev in Paris, and with other friends who were known to be "perverts." Could they establish definitively that he was *not*? As they interviewed co-worker after co-worker, former roommates, employers, and ex-wives, this was the question they came to focus on. They visited Sergei's former roommate Pavel Tchelitchew, to ask him what he knew about Nicholas. From the report, it is impossible to know whether the agent realized that Tchelitchew himself was gay. An informant with experience interviewing more than five hundred applicants suspected of being gay weighed in—the topic seemed to be his expertise—and he believed that Nicholas was, in fact, homosexual.[27]

The Department was torn—Nicholas's services were very much wanted, but the issue of his sexuality could not be resolved with enough clarity. The question was put to Nicholas himself by a State Department employee. Later George Kennan, then in the process of constructing postwar U.S. covert operations overseas, brought it up to Nicholas, too.

Nicholas seemed frightened and annoyed by the relentlessness of the investigators. They had it wrong, Nicholas told Kennan. Of course he knew homosexuals—he had worked in the *ballet* in Paris—but he was not one. Perhaps they had heard stories that confused him with a relative in Paris, Sergei Nabokov, who had also socialized with Diaghilev and Jean Cocteau. It was not he but Sergei who was homosexual. According to Kennan, Nicholas acknowledged that Sergei's sexual activities had certainly brought shame on the Nabokov family name, but that shame should not be laid at Nicholas's feet.[28]

A year into the investigation, Kennan wrote Nicholas with profound regrets, saying that it looked as if the matter could not be cleared up to the investigators' satisfaction. Though Kennan was embarrassed by the government's response, he suggested that it would probably be best to formally withdraw the application—which Nicholas did.[29]

Other postwar transitions would prove less rocky. Princess Lena Slonim Massalsky settled in Sweden, where she found work as a translator.[30] Zinaida Shakhovskoy, Nicholas's former sister-in-law, who had been a longtime supporter of Nabokov's writing, was celebrated for her work with the French resistance. Shakhovskoy went on to cover the Nuremberg Trials and, like Edmund Wilson, traveled to Greece to report on the violence that exploded in the aftermath of the Second World War.[31]

Even Nicholas Nabokov would land on his feet, declaring at the June 1950 Congress for Cultural Freedom in Germany that moving forward, "we must build an organization for war." Academy Award-winning actor and veteran Robert Montgomery, also in attendance, sounded the same drumbeat, arguing that, "No artist who has the right to bear that title can be neutral in the battles of our time."[32]

The call for democratic counterpropaganda against the Soviet cultural onslaught seemed eminently justified when Soviet-occupied North Korea invaded American-occupied South Korea the day before the conference began. Which helped make it even simpler to execute what had been in the planning for some months—the establishment of the Congress for Cultural Freedom as a permanent entity. In short order, Nicholas Nabokov was elected Secretary-General of the newest anti-Communist propaganda effort.[33]

5

With the exception of his lone bid for a job at the Voice of America, Vladimir Nabokov staked a path on a road that would keep him far from the activism in which so many in his life engaged. Politics, albeit in a refracted form, nonetheless managed to dominate the first novel he wrote in America.

Started mid-war and finished a year and a month after the last German forces made their unconditional surrender, *Bend Sinister* tells of the fate of independent philosopher Adam Krug under the tyranny of a ruler nicknamed the Toad. The story takes place in an alternate world—albeit one filled with reflections of Nabokov's own.

The Toad's political philosophy, Ekwilism, promotes a conformist erasure of identity. Krug is prodded to demonstrate that intellectuals are "happy and proud to march with the masses." Presiding over a government in which viciousness vies with dim-wittedness, the Toad wants Krug to support his reign and give it intellectual legitimacy. But the Toad's need to triumph over Krug goes deeper. In passing, we learn that Krug, who has other moral failings, was a classmate of the Toad as a child, and bullied him every day at school for five years. The comic, sadistic, homosexual villain of *Bend Sinister* is in part a product of the childhood cruelty of its hero.[34]

After trying unsuccessfully to cajole and intimidate Krug into joining him, the Toad arrests the philosopher and his young son. Krug is ready to comply to save his son, but officials, who are too incompetent even to brutalize with accuracy, confuse Krug's son with another child and end up killing him by accident.

The horror of the death is too much for the father to bear, leading the narrator to have mercy on Krug and give him the gift of insanity, allowing him to see that he is a character in a story. Hostages are gathered from among Krug's acquaintances and friends, and they explain that they will be shot if Krug does not do the bidding of the Toad. Krug, however, is too mad to understand what is happening. Delusional, he believes he has returned to the apex of his childhood power, when he caught and humiliated his classmate at will. He runs to tackle the Toad and is shot, even as the world seems to reveal itself as illusion. The perspective of the story then pulls away from Krug to give us a view of a narrator very much like Vladimir Nabokov, catching moths in a net by his window at night.

In his earlier novel *Invitation to a Beheading*, Nabokov had weighed in more abstractly and with more hope. Cincinnatus seemed to be executed but simultaneously triumphed over his executioners, whereas the narrator of *Bend Sinister* frankly admits that the immortality he has given to Krug is only "a play on words." Between *Invitation* and *Bend Sinister* lay the Soviet purges and the Holocaust, making faith in art and the power of an individual mind in the face of tyranny that much harder to maintain.

Near the beginning of the book, Krug is forced to shuttle back and forth over a river between two guard stations for lack of correct papers, echoing the experiences of countless refugees. Later, in prison, he hears fellow inmates practicing their English grammar ("My aunt has a visa, Uncle Saul wants to see Uncle Samuel. The child is bold.")[35]—mirroring the Jewish immigrants in the background of "Vasily Shishkov."[36]

Nabokov's foreword directly links the world of *Bend Sinister* with the totalitarian states that he had lived in, those "worlds of tyranny and torture, of Fascists and Bolshevists, of Philistine thinkers and jack-booted baboons." Using snippets of Lenin's speeches and the Soviet constitution, he also nodded to the "gobs of Nazist pseudo-efficiency" he had imported to build his nightmare world.[37]

Bend Sinister winks at Soviet labor camps and nods to Nazi mythologizing run rampant. *Hamlet* is distorted into a play in which the villain becomes that "Judeo-Latin Claudius." Echoing Hitler's complaints, Fortinbras has been subjugated by the machinations of "Shylocks of high finance" but aims to recover the ancestral lands

TOP LEFT: Vladimir Nabokov and his father in 1906, the year V. D. Nabokov was elected to the First Duma. *Photo © the Estate of Vladimir Nabokov, used by permission of The Wylie Agency, LLC.* TOP RIGHT: Vladimir Nabokov's parents, Vladimir and Elena, at Vyra, 1900. *Photo © the Estate of Vladimir Nabokov, used by permission of The Wylie Agency, LLC.* BOTTOM: The house where Vladimir Nabokov was born, 47 Bolshaya Morskaya in St. Petersburg. *Photo courtesy of Andrea Pitzer.*

TOP: Sergei and Vladimir Nabokov at Vyra, 1906. The brothers were born less than a year apart. *Photo © the Estate of Vladimir Nabokov, used by permission of The Wylie Agency, LLC.* LEFT: V. D. Nabokov in uniform. *Photo courtesy of Vladimir Petkevič.*

OPPOSITE TOP: Vladimir, Kirill, Olga, Sergei, and Elena Nabokov in Yalta, 1918, months before the family fled Russia. *Photo © the Estate of Vladimir Nabokov, used by permission of The Wylie Agency, LLC.* OPPOSITE BOTTOM RIGHT: Nabokov's cousin Yuri Rausch von Traubenberg in 1917, two years before his death. *Photo © the Estate of Vladimir Nabokov, used by permission of The Wylie Agency, LLC.* OPPOSITE BOTTOM LEFT: Vladimir Nabokov and his mother, Elena, with her brother, Nabokov's Uncle Ruka, 1907. *Photo © the Estate of Vladimir Nabokov, used by permission of The Wylie Agency, LLC.*

TOP: Vladimir Lenin police photo, 1895.
MIDDLE: Leon Trotsky, police photo, circa
1896. BOTTOM: Joseph Stalin, police photo,
circa 1908.

TOP: Writer Maxim Gorky (second from right) and associates aboard the *Gleb Bokii* on their way to Solovki, June 1929. *Photo courtesy of Tomasz Kizny Gulag collection.* BOTTOM: Camp prisoners work on a section of the narrow-gauge railroad leading to the brickyard, Great Solovetsky Island, 1924-25. *Photo courtesy of Tomasz Kizny Gulag collection.*

TOP: Vladimir, Véra, and Dmitri Nabokov, Berlin, 1935, two years after Hitler's rise to power. *Photo © the Estate of Vladimir Nabokov, used by permission of The Wylie Agency, LLC.* RIGHT: Solzhenitsyn as an artillery captain during World War II. *File/AP Photo.*

LEFT: Nabokov's mother, Elena. Prague, 1931. *Photo courtesy of Vladimir Petkevič.* BOTTOM LEFT: Nabokov's sister Olga with her son Rostislav in Prague near the start of World War II. At right, Evgenia Hofeld, the long-time companion of Nabokov's mother. *Photo courtesy of Vladimir Petkevič.* BOTTOM RIGHT: Boris Petkevič, the husband of Olga Nabokov, whose anti-Soviet activities reportedly gained Nazi support. *Photo courtesy of Vladimir Petkevič.*

U.S. Immigration and visa photos for Véra Nabokov (top left), Vladimir Nabokov (top right), Nicholas Nabokov (center right), Carl Junghans (bottom right), and Sonia Slonim (bottom left), 1934 to 1941.

TOP: The prisoners, hired workers, and indigenous Nenets of the Vaigach Expedition, 1930s. *Photo courtesy of Tomasz Kizny Gulag collection.* BOTTOM: The remains of the Vaigach Expedition today on the southernmost island of the Nova Zemblan archipelago. *Photo by Tomasz Kizny.*

TOP: SS staff at roll call, Neuengamme Concentration Camp. *Photo courtesy of U.S. Holocaust Memorial Museum.* BOTTOM: Prisoners behind the fence, Neuengamme Concentration Camp. *Photo courtesy of U.S. Holocaust Memorial Museum.*

OPPOSITE: Vladimir and Véra Nabokov at a Wellesley sorority house, 1942. *Photo courtesy of the Wellesley College Archives.*

TOP: Vladimir and Véra Nabokov in Paris, 1959. *Photo courtesy of Keystone-France via Getty Images.*
BOTTOM: Dmitri and Vladimir Nabokov, 1959. *Photo courtesy of Keystone via Getty Images.*

OPPOSITE TOP: Mary McCarthy and Edmund Wilson, Wellfleet, Mass.,1942. *Photo courtesy of Sylvia Salmi/Special Collections, Vassar College Libraries.* OPPOSITE BOTTOM RIGHT: Nabokov at Wellesley College, 1942. *Photo by Sarah Collie Smith/courtesy of the Wellesley College Archives.* OPPOSITE BOTTOM LEFT: Alexander Solzhenitsyn, 1946. *File/AP Photo.*

TOP: Kirill and Vladimir Nabokov with their sister Elena, Switzerland, 1959. *Photo © the Estate of Vladimir Nabokov, used by permission of The Wylie Agency, LLC.* LEFT: Nabokov's nephew Rostislav, with wife Milena Svobodova, Prague, 1954. *Photo courtesy of Vladimir Petkevič.* BOTTOM: Vladimir Nabokov with his sister Elena and Véra's sister, Sonia. *Photo © the Estate of Vladimir Nabokov, used by permission of The Wylie Agency, LLC.*

TOP: The Salon de Musique, Montreux Palace Hotel, Switzerland. *Photo courtesy of the Montreux Palace Hotel.* MIDDLE: Alexander Solzhenitsyn in 1973, the year before his deportation to the West. *Photo courtesy of AP Photo.* RIGHT: Edmund Wilson at the *New Yorker*. *Photo by Henri Cartier-Bresson/via Magnum Photos.*

Nabokov in the Montreux Palace Hotel, 1973. *Photo courtesy of Walter Mori/Mondadori Portfolio via Getty Images.*

stolen by Hamlet's father.[38] In Nabokov's rendering, tyranny not only warps worldviews, it can destroy art.

Why does a dictator like the Toad need Krug? Perhaps for the same reason that Lenin and Stalin needed Gorky, for a time at least— as a fig leaf, as someone to bless what was happening or to pretend it was not happening at all. Nabokov's first novel written in America presented the problem of tyranny as a personal question, a moral dilemma to which his hero responds not by joining any opposition but by *resisting* joining the deluded—by refusing to fall in line or speak the lie.[39]

Bend Sinister landed in the midst of an America trying to make sense of the danger presented by the Soviet Union. Richard Watts, writing for *The New Republic*, reviewed its indictment of familiar totalitarian regimes with mixed feelings, noting the self-indulgent literary acrobatics of a single 211-word sentence yet praising the story as "considerably more than the warmed over Arthur Koestler it occasionally seems on the verge of becoming."[40]

The comparison to Koestler reveals how topical the novel appeared in the moment, despite its refracted fantasy setting. Koestler, after being held prisoner under Franco and sentenced to death as a spy during the Spanish Civil War, had shed his revolutionary identity and had become an anti-Communist crusader. As a Hungarian Jew, he had faced an even more desperate flight from Europe than Nabokov. During the war he had been imprisoned as an enemy alien by both the French and the British, sitting in solitary confinement in London even as *Darkness at Noon*, his magnum opus and diatribe against Communist tyranny, was published.[41] Unlike Nabokov's public refusal to submit art to ideology, Koestler had dedicated himself to a literature in the service of human freedom, although which ideology to choose had proved a perpetual challenge.

As a literary-political hybrid, *Bend Sinister* was the first book Nabokov had written that overtly belonged as much in the latter camp as the former. Perhaps for that reason, it was also his most uneven. Nabokov deliberately intended the book to be the "vehement incrimination of a dictatorship" with both Nazi and Communist elements.⁴² But his efforts to blend righteous vehemence, bawdy dialogue, his trademark wit, and ornate language with the murder of a child rendered the book clumsy, particularly in comparison to the power of works similarly addressing the horrors of a totalitarian state. Koestler's latest, Yevgeny Zamyatin's *We* from two decades earlier, and George Orwell's *Nineteen Eighty-Four* all worked better as both indictments and as narratives than *Bend Sinister*. At times it was as if Nabokov was too embarrassed to be forthright, or still struggling with how to fuse politics and art.

In his own life, however, Nabokov clearly felt a sense of urgency about events in the political realm. His stridency expanded along with his sense of crisis, revealing itself in a suspicious streak that sometimes let the political trump the personal.

In the last months of the war, Nabokov had deliberately snubbed Marc Slonim, a former friend (and distant cousin of Véra's) at a party. Nabokov's rude behavior had baffled his hostess, who had apparently expected her guest to be delighted over finding the Jewish critic, with whom he had been on good terms in Paris, alive and well. Nabokov explained the reason for his dismissal later in a letter to Edmund Wilson, writing that Slonim "gets 250 dollars from the Stalinists per month, which is not much, but he is not worth even that."⁴³

While Nabokov had Stalin's number, he was less astute at unearthing spies. Not only was Marc Slonim not an informer, he was anti-Soviet. But the rumors flying around had a real impact on Slonim, who was on the faculty at Sarah Lawrence College. A quarter of the College's professors came under suspicion after relentless attacks by the American Legion. Tremendous pressure was exerted to fire faculty members who had been marked for persecution as potential Communists. Denunciations continued for years against several universities, culminating in hearings conducted by the Jenner Committee on Capitol Hill, where Slonim was eventually forced to testify. Sarah Lawrence resisted public pressure and refused to fire him.⁴⁴

Nabokov, who thought he had Slonim's salary pegged to the dollar, was still in anxiety over his own financial situation. In the postwar period, Nabokov's anti-Soviet stance was no longer an obstacle to employment. He nonetheless wrote to Wilson to voice his "low spirits" at Wellesley's offer of $3,000 for ten hours a week of work.[45] (He did not note it, but it was less per year than Slonim's putative salary from the Soviets.)

Despite his reign over exile literature, despite a body of work comprising a dozen novels and novellas, plays, poems, and criticism, as well as years of service at world-class institutions of higher learning and publication in some of the best magazines in America, he was a man approaching fifty still cobbling together year-to-year contracts. Even an earlier bid to head to Hollywood to be a screenwriter had come to nothing.[46]

Unbeknownst to Nabokov, his chronic problem was about to be solved. Cornell University needed a professor of Russian literature, and search committee chairman Morris Bishop wrote to ask if Nabokov would be interested.[47]

Nabokov had been hoping to get an offer he could use as a stick to bludgeon Wellesley into offering him a permanent position. But Wellesley declined to make a counter-offer. Eight years into his American adventure, Nabokov left his hodgepodge of part-time work to take the first full-time job he had held since his three-hour stint at a Berlin bank twenty-six years before.[48]

6

Like Sarah Lawrence College, Cornell too had been drawn into the debate over professors seen as Soviet sympathizers. Before the war had even ended, when the U.S. was still allied with the U.S.S.R., New York's *World-Telegraph* had run an article titled "Cornell Goes Bolshevist." Professors suspected of affection for post-Revolutionary Russia, a stance that had been lauded during the war, were called on the carpet in due course. University trustees, the Catholic Information Society, and even *Collier's* magazine named names of Cornell

Reds and their allies, polarizing the campus into those who saw themselves as defenders of intellectual thought and those who saw themselves preventing the Communist infiltration of America.[49]

Anti-Communist anxieties played out across the political spectrum—from radical leftists who felt that the Revolution had been hijacked to xenophobic fringe groups, who feared U.N. invasion and vaccination conspiracies. But it was Senator Joseph McCarthy who would become the public face of the anti-Communist movement in America, holding hearings in which he made headlines with accusations about spies infiltrating the U.S. government. McCarthy attacked Communist influence wherever he saw (or imagined) it.

Among his targets were Edmund Wilson's book *The Memoirs of Hecate County*, which he later labeled "pro-Communist pornography." McCarthy was not the first to attack the book as a political danger. In 1947, titillating excerpts from it had been the focus of a hearing in which a congressman had berated librarians at the State Department for choosing *Hecate County* to promote American culture abroad.[50] And even before that, police in New York acted on a complaint from an anti-vice society and seized copies of it in Manhattan. In 1948, the public debates finally took a financial toll on Wilson, when *Hecate County* was declared obscene by the New York Supreme Court and also banned in Boston and Los Angeles.[51]

Despite the documented excesses of the anti-Communist movement—harassment, firings, blacklisting, and the treatment of Wilson—Nabokov was not inclined to publicly criticize McCarthy. Véra, too, when the subject came up, gave no quarter to his opponents, recognizing McCarthy as extremist but refusing to condemn him.[52] After five decades in three countries where Communism had a hand in destabilizing countries that had been around much longer than the U.S., the Nabokovs were already convinced that Bolshevik spies were capable of digging tunnels into the hearts and minds of a naïve America. At a time when the FBI had requested that their field offices generate reports on the presence of Communist agents at major U.S. universities and colleges, Nabokov and Véra stayed quiet on the topic of academic freedom and befriended Ithaca's resident G-man.[53]

Véra was particularly attentive to potential Communist spies, writing a letter to the *Cornell Daily Sun* attacking Owen Lattimore, whom McCarthy had named as the U.S.S.R.'s top agent in America. Lattimore would eventually be hounded out of his consultancies with the State Department and charged with perjury—though the charges would later be dropped.[54]

While there was no basis for describing Lattimore as a Soviet agent, it's not hard to see what might have enraged Véra. In addition to his work on China during the war, he had gone on a mission with the U.S. vice president to the labor camps of Kolyma in Siberia, where both men had admired the pioneering mining projects of the Dalstroy Corporation. Kolyma was home to some the harshest camps of the hundreds that then stretched across the entirety of Soviet territory, and the Dalstroy Corporation, which ran the effort, was nothing more than an arm of the NKVD, a front for Russia's secret police.

Describing Lattimore's trip in *The Unquiet Ghost*, Adam Hochschild notes how guard towers were temporarily dismantled and prisoners were kept in their barracks for three days so the visitors would not see them: "The Soviets worked hard to give the Wallace group the impression that they were visiting a cheerful Russian Klondike full of happy gold miners, and they were wildly successful."

A few years after Lattimore's 1944 trip, books by former prisoners began to be published in English, detailing the horrific conditions at Kolyma—the starvation and sadism, rapes, and harrowing work. The camp's prisoners who had witnessed the visit could not understand how the Americans had been so easily duped.[55]

Against this background of American naïveté, Véra and Vladimir refused to condemn McCarthy. After a childhood amid Tsarist double agents in St. Petersburg, more than a decade in a Berlin teeming with informers, and a postwar landscape in which the Nabokovs' siblings and cousins all seemed to have ties to intelligence work, it seemed more than plausible that not just Washington, D.C., but also the residents of Ithaca, New York, should be on guard against spies and traitors. At Cornell, it was rumored that Véra carried a pistol with her on campus for use in the event of Communist incursion.[56]

7

Nabokov did not find *Hecate County* Communist, but he did find the sex scenes repellent. Faced with the unappealing array of encounters with which Wilson had provided the protagonist, Nabokov wrote, "I should have as soon tried to open a sardine can with my penis."[57]

Wilson by this time counted Nabokov among his closest friends, though the two were as inclined to disagree as much about literature in general as they were each other's writing. By dismissing *Hecate County*, Nabokov had now roundly criticized two of Wilson's books while getting a rave blurb from him for *Sebastian Knight*. It is a rare friendship that can stand such an imbalance.

For his part, Wilson's view of Nabokov's politics seemed to be narrowing, leaving little room for the niche he had once let his friend occupy. The very first weeks of their friendship, Wilson had identified Nabokov as "neither White Russian nor Communist."[58] But as the years progressed, he increasingly seemed to want to shoehorn Nabokov into a reactionary identity that he had not initially assigned to his friend.

Nabokov struggled not to let the shoe fit. In January 1947 Wilson wrote to Nabokov about meeting his Trinity College roommate, Mikhail Kalashnikov, at a Christmas party. Nabokov responded at length, explaining that Wilson had found another "dead fish" from his past, in this case one who was a fascist, anti-Semitic idiot—they had only roomed together one term. Wilson, he added preemptively, should not say anything about it to their friend Nina Chavchavadze, who was somehow under the misapprehension that Nabokov and Kalashnikov had been close. It was, as Nabokov biographer Brian Boyd would later describe it, hardly an accurate characterization of Nabokov's two-year friendship with Kalashnikov.[59]

Along with the refutation of Kalashnikov, Nabokov enclosed a copy of *Bend Sinister*, which was about to be published. Given the opportunity to criticize his friend's writing in kind, Wilson read the book and went into great detail listing his disappointments. Nabokov doing politics left Wilson cold—especially politics in a world abstracted from the precise reality that Nabokov excelled at depicting. Wilson admired Nabokov, but he found that Nabokov taking on the easy work of demonizing a cardboard cut-out dictator was a poor use of his magic.

Reading *The Real Life of Sebastian Knight* years before, Wilson had felt certain Nabokov had constructed some game beneath the story that he was always on the verge of uncovering; but with *Bend Sinister*, he did not seem to make the effort to hunt for it. His assessment was not without insight—deliberately nor not, Nabokov had failed to generate a convincing human villain. But for his part, Wilson had missed the play between the narrator and the reader—the very dance transpiring around the story itself that he had noted in *Sebastian Knight*.

Wilson had focused instead on Nabokov's grotesque burlesque of a totalitarian state. "You aren't good at this kind of subject, which involves questions of politics and social change," he wrote to Nabokov, "because you are totally uninterested in these matters and have never taken the trouble to understand them."[60] Their mutual criticisms drove new cracks into the friendship, but Wilson's remarks were telling. After building a comic story focusing directly on the horrors of a police state, Nabokov would never write an overtly topical novel again.

Across that year, they continued to discuss each other's work, and Nabokov praised Wilson's dissection of Hemingway, Kafka, and Sartre. But they slowly grew increasingly deaf to each other. In a 1948 letter to Wilson that was more devastating than anything in *Bend Sinister*, Nabokov took exception to a comparison of pre-Revolutionary Russian liberals to Confederate loyalists nursing a failed cause after the U.S. Civil War. For Nabokov, the work of his father, the Kadets, and other anti-Bolshevik political parties represented the only chance for democracy and freedom that Russia had ever had. Implying that these men and women were slave-owners willing to destroy the country to salvage their own cultural and economic power was too much.

It was all well and good, Nabokov wrote, that Wilson and his friends had taken note of the murders in Soviet Union in the late 1930s when people who had been cronies of Lenin were put on trial and killed under Stalin. But where had those tender-hearted people been when the whole system had been established under Lenin? They had not heard the moans of those tortured in Solovki or by the secret police in Moscow's Lubyanka Prison in the first Red Terrors. They had not heard them, he suggested, because they were too wedded to their own romantic notions of how the Revolution had happened and what it meant. He did not criticize their misunderstanding of what was happening when they first learned of it, but to be clear, the problem was not a historical nostalgia on the part of Russian exiles; it was a historical nostalgia on the part of the American Left, which could not look back on its youthful infatuation for "St. Lenin" and see it for the sham and the shame that it was.

As for his being part of a retrograde aristocracy feeling sorry for itself, Nabokov pointed to the similarly anti-Bolshevist views that had been held by all sorts of unmourned radicals—including, he noted specifically, the Socialist Revolutionaries and Ilya Fondaminsky. But then again, he could not expect anyone who read Trotsky to get information on Russia to know very much at all.[61]

Nabokov's letter is a precise, careful statement of his political stance, and a devastating indictment of Wilson's lingering affection for the Revolution. The strain of Nabokov's anguish for his country and anger at Wilson is evident, as is his bafflement over everything his normally astute, intelligent friend seems unable to grasp.

For a quarter of a century, newspapers had carried stories of Russian concentration camps, and the camps had become a fixed part of the landscape behind the Iron Curtain. But the reactionary nature of some of those shouting about what *was* known sometimes reduced the camps to a talking point, one trotted out alongside purported fluoridated-water conspiracies and the Communist takeover of elementary schools. A lack of understanding of Russia's past further poisoned any understanding of its present.

Nabokov himself understood better than most that the tragedy of the Holocaust had eclipsed Russia's calamity; he had added his voice to the chorus calling for Stalin to defeat Hitler. But if the circumstances and the details were not the same, the grief and frustration at not being believed or understood—at not even understanding himself—were as profound. His people were dying, were already forgotten, and he was alive.

CHAPTER TEN

Lolita

———⊗⊗⊗———

1

Embarking on the teaching career he had coveted for so long, Vladimir Nabokov gained a financial stability he had not had since 1917. Though he remained acutely aware of financial pressures—Dmitri was now attending an expensive boarding school in New Hampshire—the three-decade specter of the destitute, displaced refugee had been banished.

With Dmitri away, Nabokov's courses were transformed into team productions. Initially Véra served as a combination T.A. and magician's assistant—sitting nearby, handing her husband notecards, writing on the board, running to get missing items, delivering lectures when he was sick, and grading exams. Both prepared exquisitely for classes, with Nabokov fully scripting lectures, including jokes, and delivering them dramatically. One former student described how on one snowy day, Nabokov completely darkened the classroom without explanation. Flipping on one light after another, he announced "This is Pushkin! This is Gogol! This is

Chekhov!" Heading to the back of the room, he released a roller blind to let the sun stream in: "And that is Tolstoy!"[1]

Even before his first lectures at Wellesley, Nabokov had bet on a future filled with teaching, spending his first fall and winter in America creating as many as a hundred lectures. In the intervening years of classes and speeches, he had been able to hone his theory and presentation. By the time he got to Cornell, he had thoroughly organized his approach to discussing writers.

Literature Nabokov-style was an exciting enterprise. Authors could be analyzed, he explained, as storytellers, teachers, or enchanters. The best ones, of course, had elements of all three, and geniuses distinguished themselves especially as enchanters. In case there were any flaws in his audience's reasoning on these matters, Nabokov's students were expected to memorize a hierarchy of writers and the letter grades Nabokov assigned each one. Turgenev rated an A minus, Dostoyevsky a C minus, or perhaps a D plus.[2] The latter had the temerity to imagine that suffering enhanced morality, an argument that left Nabokov cold.

Comparing writing novels to composing diabolical chess problems, Nabokov meant reading literature to be hard work. He claimed that in the best novels "the real clash is not between the characters but between the author and the world." He saw literature as space in which the novelist invents a universe, a planet, a landscape—and the reader struggles to find a path through it. Literature of genius does not settle for repeating traditional truths or parroting lifelike details that come to hand, he argued—it reconfigures them to create things that have never been expressed, in a way that has never before been done. The ideal outcome is to have the exhausted, joyful reader and author meet atop the invented mountain of the novel and embrace, "linked forever if the book lasts forever."[3]

Designing his classes as a detective investigation, Nabokov was a fan of the kind of reading that required a microscope. He relentlessly brought to bear the finer points of biology, history, and politics that could illuminate the tiniest moments in a book. Maps made regular appearances: the sleeping car on the train in *Anna Karenina*, the house from Austen's *Mansfield Park*, and Dublin itself for Joyce's *Ulysses*. For an exam on *Madame Bovary*, he asked students to address Flaubert's use of the word *and*. He announced that anatomical details in Kafka's "The Metamorphosis" showed that Gregor Samsa became not a cockroach but a beetle that had wings and could have flown.[4]

Edmund Wilson was responsible for Nabokov including Austen in his lectures, having taken exception to Nabokov's claim to be "prejudiced, in fact, against all women writers."[5] As bullheaded as they both were, the two men could, and did, make concessions on small points. And despite his dislike for *Bend Sinister*, Wilson continued to offer Nabokov advice on editors and to recommend him to publishers.

Nabokov and Wilson would continue to praise and criticize each other's literary opinions, but they became blunter and more combative on points of disagreement. Nabokov lauded Wilson's discussion of Keats and Pushkin, and noted other remarks in his writing that were brilliant, but he also chided his friend for letting socioeconomic angles rule his stories—"Keep it down, keep it down (the [ideological content]) for God's sake," he wrote, elsewhere telling Wilson "your sociological forays are perfunctory and superficial."[6]

Russian politics continued to be an issue. Interviewed in 1951 by the FBI, Wilson was more than willing to admit to agents that the Revolution had failed. But he was still not yet ready to give up on the romance of the Revolution's beginnings, or to surrender his admiration for Lenin. As Wilson's ex-wife Mary McCarthy would later explain, "It was a mistake for Edmund to like Lenin, but that was the only way he could believe in the Russian Revolution."[7]

Despite everything, Nabokov and Wilson continued down their rocky path with affection. "I don't know what you mean when you say I am not one of your fans," Wilson wrote to Nabokov in May 1950, just before their correspondence erupted in a lively argument over stresses in the word *automobile*.[8]

2

With his immersion in butterfly research and his efforts to find a steady teaching position in the U.S., Nabokov's fiction output had diminished precipitously. Not only did he have just one new novel to show for the eight years between his arrival in America and the beginning of his Cornell years, he had written just a handful of short stories.

But what he *had* written carried traces of its explosive place and time, relentlessly recording the anti-Semitism he had witnessed. A Russian narrator trying to escape France ahead of Hitler's arrival hears his Jewish countrymen speak of "their doomed kinsmen crammed into hellbound trains." "Double Talk" records European-style anti-Semitism making itself at home in America, in what Maxim D. Shrayer would eventually note as perhaps the first fictional representation of Holocaust denial—written before the war was even over.[9]

"Signs and Symbols," published by *The New Yorker* in May 1948, portrays the fate of Jewish Russian refugees in America. A couple frets over their son and debates whether they should remove him from the institution to which he has been committed. The young man was a child when his family escaped Germany, where he had learned to fear even the wallpaper (perhaps not without reason). Soon after, his terrors grew and closed him off from humanity entirely. From the tragedy of the Revolution to the loss of the family's Aunt Rosa, whom the Germans had killed along with "all the people she had worried about," his parents managed to find a way to navigate the grief of the century, but they are unable to inoculate their son against the sense of doom emanating from even clouds and coats. In counterpoint to the relentless anxiety of the story, the couple has chosen a gift for him: ten tiny jars of fruit jellies—quince, apricot, crab apple. As they talk of bringing him home and worry that he will kill himself before they can, the father admires with pleasure the beauty of the jewel-like jars—grape, beech plum—and recites their names.

Nabokov plucked the details of what would stand as his most celebrated short story from the shards his own experience. A vulnerable son is threatened by an apparently malevolent and anti-Semitic universe convulsed by the Holocaust; as a gift his parents buy the same jars of jelly that Vladimir and Véra had shared with friends and babysitters. Nabokov deliberately crafted lush, unforgettable images and dramatic plots to allow his stories to function on a surface level as literature independent of the time and place in which they were set. And that is how many readers, sometimes even careful readers, read them, rarely noticing the other stories waiting underneath, or the supporting role Nabokov gave history in sparking madness and violence in his characters.[10]

"I have never been able to understand," Edmund Wilson wrote to Nabokov in 1948, "how you . . . pretend that it is possible to write about human beings and leave out all account of society and environment. I have come to the conclusion that you simply took over in your youth the *fin de siècle* Art for Art's sake slogan and have never thought it out. I shall soon be sending you a book of mine which may help you to straighten out these problems."[11]

Wilson was a brilliant, prescient reviewer—making his myopia on this point all the more baffling. Anti-Semitism had just led to the death of millions and redefined the capacity for human atrocity, and Nabokov had referenced it persistently in his English-language work, which Wilson read. But Nabokov was so indirect, and Wilson was so focused on other injustices—or on his own way of representing them—that the moral facet of Nabokov's writing was as good as nonexistent.

Anti-Semitism in the work of others preoccupied Nabokov as well. Despite her help in getting his family to America, Nabokov chastised Alexandra Tolstoy for what he read as anti-Semitism in one of her novels. He even began to admire Joyce's *Ulysses* less, feeling its stream of consciousness overdone and Leopold "Bloom's Jewishness too full of clichés."[12]

The year after his arrival at Cornell, Nabokov also reviewed Jean-Paul Sartre's *Nausea* for *The New York Times Book Review*. Clocking at roughly 600 words, the review is a masterpiece of dismemberment. Spending the first section of his critique savaging the translator, whom he compared to a dentist repeatedly pulling the wrong tooth, Nabokov proceeded to skewer Sartre himself, taking particular offense at a passage that imagined a black-browed, ring-wearing Jewish songwriter at work in a Manhattan high-rise.[13]

Nabokov's attention to Jewish matters also found unlikely, even humorous outlets. While at Cornell, he worked on a translation and commentary for *Eugene Onegin*, the nineteenth-century jewel of Russian poetry. At one point in his commentary, he dives into a history of the Wandering Jew legend across four countries in three centuries. Referencing its role as Christian propaganda and detailing *seventeen* different versions of the tale, Nabokov himself points out that "there is no reason to drag in" most of them at all, as they are irrelevant to *Eugene Onegin*. Wandering-Jew entries nonetheless later appear throughout the commentary's Index, where they connect to a playful, inexplicable cross-reference leading to a mention of Jewish *blintzes*.[14]

3

After his arrival at Cornell, Nabokov took to summer road trips again, spending his breaks crossing the country hunting for butterflies. Riding through Montana, Utah, Wyoming, Minnesota, Ontario, Alabama, Arizona, Oregon, New Mexico, Colorado, and on, mile after mile, Vladimir played passenger as Véra drove their black 1946 Oldsmobile into the twilight. Collecting new species just as he had during his first transcontinental trip a decade before, Nabokov found many things to love about America. He had come to claim the country as his own, even as Véra remained more cautious in her interactions with the locals, more inclined to keep her guard up.

Nabokov would capture those expansive vistas and import them wholesale into his next novel. But as he was taking in the American landscape, he turned to the past for *Conclusive Evidence*, his 1951 autobiography. Reaching back to the pre-war years in France and

Germany, and further to his youth in Russia, he constructed a story in chapters that, while arranged in chronological order, sailed individually into their own convoluted chronographies. His "perfect" childhood was all there: his aristocratic background, peasants joyfully throwing his father into the air on their country estate, his mother's jewels taken from a wall safe to serve as his playthings, their dozens of servants, a parade of tutors, his multimillion-dollar inheritance lost in the Revolution, and the summer romance with a bruised French love on the Riviera.

Many of the autobiography's chapters had been written separately for publication in *The New Yorker*—though one, on Nabokov's childhood governess, Mademoiselle Cécile Miauton, was written in France, in French, before Nabokov had even arrived in America.[15] This autobiography-by-installment approach may explain why Mademoiselle got an entire chapter to herself, and so many potentially more important people are pushed into the margins of the book.

But as the chapter on Mademoiselle reveals, the inversion of significant and insignificant things is a key aspect of Nabokov's storytelling. As portrayed by Nabokov across the chapter devoted to her, Mademoiselle is helpless in the face of her young charges' schemes. Her hands have brown spots; she is fat, self-absorbed, self-important, easily offended, and prone to melodrama—an easy mark. But small refinements along the way—the whisper of a failed love affair, a picture of her as a graceful young woman which bears no resemblance to her mature self, her beautiful French—culminate in a reversal during a visit near the end of the chapter in which Nabokov reveals her to be more humane in her treatment of him than he has been to her.

This kind of about-face was becoming Nabokov's special trick. The setup, the long arc of mordant observation or ornate beauty, gets undercut at the last moment by a phrase reframing everything that has just happened, indicting the narrator's callousness and the reader's collaboration with it.[16] After spending pages entertainingly mocking Mademoiselle, Nabokov pays homage to "the radiant deceit" with which she had attempted, at the end, to convince him that he had been kind to her.

Nabokov loved to destabilize his own stories, so that things are not what they seem at first to the characters or the readers—the stories may not even be *about* what they seem to be about. Even the chapter that is entirely given to Mademoiselle ends with an acknowledgement of the staggering loss of his father and the realization that he had learned to recognize suffering only "after the things and beings that I had most loved in the security of my childhood, had been turned to ashes or shot through the heart."[17]

Conclusive Evidence presents illusion as an art by which people treat each other humanely, but the role of deception in survival is also a theme of the book. Nabokov relates how as children, he and his brother Sergei had opened the presents in their Christmas stockings early. After rewrapping the gifts, they opened them again later and pretended to be surprised—but they failed to fool their mother, who had asked them to wait. Such shattered illusions "took on for her the dimensions of a major disaster."[18]

By the time they are teenagers fleeing St. Petersburg on a train, when a real disaster is in motion, their safety depends on their ability to deceive, and they are more skilled than before: Sergei's pretense of typhus keeps the raucous deserting soldiers who break into their compartment at bay.[19] Weeks after the boys' departure and their father's flight south, V. D. Nabokov lives openly in the Crimea under the name Nabokov but pretends to be a doctor.

Deceit is not the only theme of the book, however. Escaping Petrograd disguised as a peasant, a man asks Nabokov's father for a light. He turns out to be the general who had once pulled out matches to do a trick for a four-year-old Vladimir Nabokov on the living room sofa of the house on Bolshaya Morskaya.

Nabokov argues for the recurrent figure of the matches, the thematic linking of elements in a story, as the very basis of art. But in *Conclusive Evidence*, the art that Nabokov creates is built out of lives and moments that elliptically retell the story of Revolutionary

Russia. The reader's full attention reveals the debacle of Russia's 1904 defeat by Japan and the details of other events that set the stage for Russia's loss. V. D. Nabokov's involvement with the early Russian parliament, as well as his arrest and imprisonment, get their due, as does his stand against the pogrom at Kishinev and his coverage of the trial of Mendel Beilis. Nabokov seems well aware that the story of his family is the story of his country.

The autobiography, in fact, includes more references to history than may be initially apparent. An era is ended as Lenin's "regime of bloodshed, concentration camps, and hostages" begins. Nabokov further laments the fate of an early radical village schoolmaster tutor who, he explains, was later executed with "members of the Social-Revolutionary Party."[20] But for all his striking summations and nods toward catastrophe on the outskirts of his story—the pillars of St. Isaac's cathedral that were "polished by slaves" and the "children shot down at random" from trees in front of them in 1905—he was just beginning to make the turn toward the bitterest moments of the history he had left behind.

Despite all the lush details from Nabokov's aristocratic youth, Edmund Wilson declared *Conclusive Evidence* a "wonderful production," though he was baffled by its title. What kind of evidence, he wondered, was Nabokov presenting? Sticking with the odds based on a decade of experience, he wondered if the proof was somehow against the Bolsheviks.[21] Basking in Wilson's praise, admitting it pleased him despite himself, Nabokov did not take umbrage at the question. Small kindnesses were enough to kindle the low-banked fire of their friendship, and their letters would continue on for the next few years in a generous exchange of personal news and ideas, even as they understood each other less and less.

Conclusive Evidence did not, however, endear Nabokov to his fellow émigrés. He gave up roughly three percent of his text to the Russian literary exiles with whom he had spent almost twenty years—and in that three percent, he mocked their obsessions with "soul-saving" and "logrolling" and excoriated their treatment of his friend, fellow writer Vladislav Khodasevich. Stuffed with stories of privilege and a childish love of excess, was this book really written by the genius of their generation, the voice of a Russia that had refused to surrender to the Soviets? Ivan Bunin, stung by a passage about himself, denounced the "Tsar's crown" that perched above Nabokov's name on the cover of the book and the "wild lying" his literary rival had done about him.[22] Nabokov, of course, still had Russian friends, but the émigré community only became more confident that he was already lost to them, that he was somehow no longer truly Russian.

4

Sitting in a jail cell in Moscow, Alexander Solzhenitsyn for the first time had his own reasons to doubt Vladimir Nabokov's commitment to his homeland.

After his arrest at the front, Solzhenitsyn had remained confident that he was a good Soviet citizen, that a mistake had been made. He had held on to his faith in the system despite the obvious incompetence of his captors, who had nearly driven him into an enemy camp, finally turning the map over to Solzhenitsyn as shells exploded around them. Still, Solzhenitsyn remained obedient, from Germany into Poland through the ruins of Brodnica and Białystok, on the platform at Minsk station, all the way back to Russia, leading the inexperienced, confused counterespionage officers (who had never been to Moscow) through the city and onto the glorious metro—riding with the citizen commuters down and up the escalators, the officers lugging suitcases full of booty stolen from the defeated Germans, Solzhenitsyn carrying his own briefcase stuffed with his diaries and writings—delivering himself without question to the doors of Lubyanka Prison, whose four-decade legacy of sorrows haunted Nabokov half a world away.[23]

The Lubyanka had been the headquarters of the secret police since the Revolution, when its five stories of ornate parquet floors, pale green walls, and plush décor had first been claimed by the

Cheka. A series of renovations had made it a more severe place inside and out, but the large clock face mounted on the yellow brick exterior remained, making it clear who administered the days and hours remaining to those who entered. A tired joke declared that it was the tallest building in all Moscow, because from its basement one could see Siberia.

Descending into the corridors and cells of the Soviet penal system, Solzhenitsyn learned about cavity searches, sleep deprivation, and interrogation. He was charged with disseminating propaganda and founding an anti-Soviet organization under the sweeping provisions of Article 58, a magician's bag of counterrevolutionary activity. He agonized over how to protect his wife and friends from arrest. He worried, too, about the briefcase full of papers that had been confiscated from him and was now in the hands of his investigators. The satchel held his treasury of stories and material for future use, but the anecdotes and events from the war he had written down included real names, putting every person he had identified at risk.

After an initial stint in solitary confinement, he was thrown into a cell with other prisoners. An Old Bolshevik, a pro-democracy lawyer, and a stool pigeon began his first formal education about the netherworld in which he had landed.[24]

More cellmates followed. One innocent visionary believed that he was destined to restore the monarchy in 1953 and be hailed as the new Tsar. Equally startling to Solzhenitsyn was a man he called Yuri, who arrived in the cell weeks later. A Soviet officer captured by the Germans, Yuri had spent two years in a Nazi camp, and over time had been turned against the Soviet cause. Now a virulent anti-Communist, he had become a German officer and had returned to the war to fight the Red Army. Solzhenitsyn could not fathom the man's willingness to take up arms against his own country.

In his time abroad, Yuri had traveled Germany and read the work of Russian émigrés in Berlin, including stories by Bunin, Aldanov, and Vladimir Nabokov. The tales Yuri read were a wonder. He had been sure that the free Russian émigrés would write about "the blood flowing from Russia's living wounds," but they had not. Yuri did not have kind words for them: "To what did they devote their unutterably precious freedom? To the female body, to ecstasy, to sunsets, the beauty of noble brows, to anecdotes going back to dusty years. They wrote as if there had been no Revolution in Russia, or as if it were too complex to explain."[25] The most important events of their lifetime had gone unrecorded. They had ignored the suffering of their own people. Nothing they had written would save Russia.

Solzhenitsyn, however, was already thinking of what he himself might do on that score. He had a novel of his own he wanted to write, one whose fragments lay like a bomb in his briefcase sitting in the hands of the investigators. The stories and names he had written down could be used to make a narrative that would consider everything that had gone wrong. But they were just as liable to lead to the arrest and conviction of Solzhenitsyn's acquaintances.

Fortunately for his friends, four months into his interrogation all those notes and papers were thrown into the fire of the Lubyanka furnace, flying away from the highest chimney of the prison as "black butterflies of soot." He would not inadvertently bear witness against those whose stories he had recorded. But the destruction of evidence from his briefcase took with it the raw material of his epic Russian novel.[26]

He dreamed, however, of writing again. He would remember for decades Yuri's indictment of Nabokov and the other émigrés, and would one day use Yuri's words to express his own grief and anger at those who seemed to have abandoned Russia. He did not intend for his work to suffer from their callousness. He would not avoid addressing the Revolution or the Russian people directly. His would be a literature fully dedicated to history. He would tell the story of the Revolution, the millions upon millions of his countrymen and their beautiful, lost cause.

At the conclusion of the investigation, Solzhenitsyn was sentenced to eight years in a labor camp. He would serve those years in their entirety, spending three of them in the relative oasis of a scientific research *sharashka* analyzing acoustics and the human voice. The rest of the time he spent moving timber, digging clay in wet misery, angling for a good bunk, in agonies of desire for a cigarette, casting a homemade spoon out of aluminum and hiding it in his shoe so as not to have to eat soup with his fingers. Working in the smoke-filled inferno of a foundry, he learned to look out for himself as he slowly began to doubt nearly everything he had believed in.[27]

And when written words were not only illegal but too dangerous to contemplate, he began composing entirely in his head. His prodigious feats of recall astounded his fellow prisoners, one of whom noted that Solzhenitsyn had created—and remembered—an epic poem twice as long as *Eugene Onegin*.[28] Memorizing twelve thousand lines using a rosary strung with beads made from clumps of soaked, dried bread, he formed a section of words for each bead, tying together the story of Russia and her people.

5

Any émigrés still hoping Vladimir Nabokov would address Russian history in his next book were profoundly disappointed. The first Nabokov novel of the 1950s would offer a story as un-Russian as anything he had written.[29]

In a letter to Pascal Covici of Viking Press, Nabokov had summed up his current project as dealing "with the problems of a very moral middle-aged gentleman who falls very immorally in love with his stepdaughter, a girl of thirteen."[30] An extraordinary one-sentence summary, Nabokov would build it into much more.

What he had first titled as *The Kingdom by the Sea* would inhabit a very different landscape than Nabokov's earlier look at a child molester. For his new story, Nabokov would invent America itself as seen by a foreigner and explore the notion of timeless love as understood by a pedophile.

He had many sources of inspiration. Since his 1939 story "The Enchanter," Nabokov and Wilson had discussed the memoirs of a Ukrainian man undone by his compulsion for sexual encounters with children. Added to this were newspaper stories of young girls kidnapped, raped, and taken on road trips through America—one of which Nabokov himself would directly reference in his book. A colleague at Stanford had turned out to be obsessed with nymphets. Nabokov rounded out his research with bus rides eavesdropping on pre-pubescents, literary acquisition of various limbs of Dmitri's young friends, and details from textbooks on current theories about the sexual development of girls.[31]

Nabokov did not want the book to be published under his name, knowing that readers (particularly Americans, as Véra noted) would likely interpret the narrator as representing Nabokov himself. Such an assumption would hardly be surprising, given that he had lovingly fostered just such confusion in the two English-language novels he had already written.[32]

The man who had survived "acute nervous exhaustion" from the strain of writing *Bend Sinister* was nearly defeated by the attempt to portray a nymphet and her jailer. During his first year in Ithaca, he was so worried about the challenges and dangers of the novel that he set a blaze going in a galvanized trash can behind the house and had begun to feed his papers into the fire before Véra intervened. He planned to destroy the book multiple times, in each instance relenting and returning to battle with his material. Writing to *The New Yorker*'s Katharine White, he said that he was struggling with the novel amid terrible misgivings. "This great and coily thing," he wrote, "has had no precedent in literature."[33]

Lolita, Nabokov's nymphet novel in its final form, offered up Humbert Humbert, a middle-aged European divorcé sexually obsessed with young girls. In postwar New England, Humbert catches a glimpse of Lolita, a twelve-year-old girl who recalls and then replaces his childhood love, Annabel Leigh. The spark that ignited his obsession with young girls, Leigh had died of typhus in 1923, just four months after a summer spent with the then-teenage Humbert.

Smitten with Lolita, Humbert Humbert moves into her home as a boarder, only to find the girl will be sent away to distant Camp Q for the summer. Humbert marries Charlotte, Lolita's mother, the better to get at the girl, but weeks later Charlotte is hit by a car, bringing Lolita under Humbert's control. Avoiding prying eyes that might eventually guess his secret, Humbert drives his stepdaughter across glorious, oblivious America, staying in the very roadside inns and motor lodges that Nabokov and Véra knew so well from their own cross-country voyages.

While Humbert executes a plan to drug and fondle Lolita at a hotel, she wakes, only to shock him with her forwardness. She spends two years as his sexual captive before escaping with a mysterious pursuer, whom Humbert tracks down and kills. He realizes that he has destroyed Lolita's childhood, and even later, that he loves her as she is, even though she is no longer a nymphet—none of which keeps him from trying to reunite with her and seeking revenge on his rival. Waiting in his cell on trial for murder, he writes a tribute to his love, meant to be published only after her death.

Taking a brief break to send a poem to Burma-Shave for its roadside billboard campaign (they did not use his submission), Nabokov finished *Lolita* in December 1953. Véra wrote to Katharine White, honoring their commitment to give *The New Yorker* a first look at his work, though they realized that she was unlikely to find any part of the novel suitable for publication. Véra requested that White not let anyone else see it, or at least not to let others know who its author was.[34]

Nabokov understood *Lolita* to be the best thing he had written in English; now it was up to America to receive it. But given his detailed descriptions of Humbert's fantasies, and more than one scene in which they were realized, he wondered if his masterpiece would ever make it into print.

6

By the time Nabokov had finished the story of a traumatized girl and her articulate molester, Alexander Solzhenitsyn had served his sentence in the Gulag. He had been operated on for cancer, taken part in a lethal camp strike, and discovered that his wife Natalia had divorced him.[35] A Christianity with roots in his childhood had sprouted again. Concentration camps had taught him more about the Soviet system in eight years than he had managed to absorb in the first twenty-six years of his existence.

In February 1953, he was released into permanent exile. Condemned to live the rest of his life thousands of miles from Moscow, he rode trains with other prisoners, then marched, and, still wearing his battered Army greatcoat, finally caught a lorry into Kok-Terek, a desolate town in Kazakhstan, arriving two days before the death of Joseph Stalin.

On their first night in the village, the new exiles lay down to rest in the yard of the police station. Solzhenitsyn, however, had no plans to sleep. Watching the shadows of horses stabled nearby and listening to the braying of donkeys in the warm air, he could hardly believe his good fortune. He passed the hours walking in wonder all night, free under the stars.[36]

7

As prospective publishers were reading about Humbert Humbert's nighttime visions ("everything soiled, torn, dead"), Nabokov was already well into his next novel. Stepping away from the agony of crafting his tortured nymphet, he plotted a shorter, simpler tale— one that ought to run no risk of offending the censors, one that had already begun unfolding chapter by chapter in *The New Yorker*.

The story of Professor Timofey Pnin introduces a bumbling Russian exile incapable of navigating everyday life. A comic mishap over a discussion of anarchy lands poor Pnin in detention at Ellis Island the moment he arrives in America. English defeats him. Inanimate objects seduce and betray him. His coffee maker explodes; his landlady forbids him access to the washing machine after he puts a pair of shoes in it.

An assistant professor at the fictional Waindell College, Pnin is beset midway through the book by the arrival of the narrator, who undermines Pnin's place at the college. The new professor, one Vladimir Vladimirovich, also happens to be the narrator, a man remarkably like Vladimir Nabokov. The usurper even contradicts earlier accounts of Pnin's life, leaving key scenes in the book permanently in doubt.[37]

Behind Pnin's efforts to transcend the hurdles of everyday existence lurks profound grief. Both his parents died in 1917 from typhus, but he is particularly oppressed by the loss of his first love, Mira Belochkin, a Jewish girl killed at Buchenwald. He talks with an investigator in Washington in an attempt to find out more about her last moments, but there are no answers. Over and over, he forbids himself consideration of her many possible deaths, which spin forever in an irresolvable quantum state: was she infected with tetanus, injected with phenol, set on fire alive, or gassed in a final, false, shower? It is, however, impossible for Pnin not to think of her. He remembers kissing her, and she dies and dies again.[38]

A classic academic satire swirls on *Pnin's* surface level, but underneath Nabokov again nods to the plight of Jews in the Holocaust, and in America. Nabokov creates a Jewish couple who decline attendance at a party once they realize a bigoted professor plans to attend. At Pnin's party, the same unpleasant professor repeats an anti-Semitic story about the absent woman, which Pnin dismisses. The story, Pnin says, is a canard that circulated in Odessa decades before, and even in his youth, it was not funny.

The narrator of *Pnin* directly links Germany to "another torture house"—Russia. And Pnin himself suggests he will one day teach a course titled "On Tyranny," a ledger sheet of terror and cruelty, ranging from Tsar Nicholas the First to imperial horrors in Africa and the massacre of Armenians. "The history of man," Pnin says, "is the history of pain."[39]

For all Nabokov's stated intention of making Timofey Pnin ludicrous, he is a supremely likable main character and triggered exponentially less anxiety than that provoked by Humbert. Yet the book had its own challenges. If Nabokov's nymphet was too unsettling for the pages of *The New Yorker*, Pnin's adventures were sometimes perceived as too slight, or too political. Katharine White accepted several chapters of the novel as standalone pieces, but the magazine rejected Chapter Five, which contained the death of Mira Belochkin—the heart of the book—reportedly because of repeated references to Soviet oppression and torture, references Nabokov refused to remove.[40]

Pnin struggled elsewhere, too. Pascal Covici at Viking paid an early advance on the book, but after long indecision reviewing the final manuscript, refused to publish it without changes. In a friendly letter, Nabokov countered Covici's criticisms, insisting that book was not a series of sketches, and Timofey Pnin was not "a clown."[41]

Unwilling to make the demanded edits, Nabokov returned the advance. He was clearly frustrated at having to explain the novel, but in comparison to the moral posturing over *Lolita*, talking about *Pnin* must have been a relative relief. Still, finding a publisher dragged out several months; *Pnin* took a year and a half from completion to make its way into print.

8

Bringing *Lolita* to America would take much longer. Small wonder that publishers were so hesitant—instead of the quasi-celibate, saintly figure of Timofey Pnin, *Lolita* delivered a monster whose monstrousness is a central aspect of the novel. Publishers could have, perhaps, forgiven Nabokov for creating Humbert Humbert if he had only made everything take place in another room, away from the reader, or if Lolita were only older, or "a boy, or a cow, or a bicycle."[42] But through a strange hybrid of refined language and sophistry, the reader is brought into Humbert's orbit. His complex rationalizations alternate with frankness, and his unsettling euphemisms ("the scepter of my passion," her "brown rose") along with the comedy and dim sympathy he evokes, render the entire process of reading the book disturbing.

If Nabokov was daring Americans to venture out of their comfort zone to tackle the novel, American publishers were not ready to meet that challenge. Viking rejected it in February 1954; Simon & Schuster declined it in March. After Nabokov offered his "timebomb" to James Laughlin, the publisher of *Sebastian Knight*, once more that fall, Laughlin responded that the book was "literature of the highest order" but agonized over the risks involved.[43] Doubleday's Jason Epstein and Roger Straus at Farrar, Straus & Young also politely declined.

Nabokov took standard page-turning genre conventions—detective stories, travelogues, romances—and shot each one point-blank, delivering the most corrupt love affair in American literature. The whodunit is transformed into a who'll-get-it. The traditional travelogue becomes an extended kidnapping. But for all the lofty strains of the violin sonata that Humbert concocts to serenade suspicious readers into complacency, he cannot create romance from rape.[44]

Nabokov had no illusions about what an explosion the novel would make, or the dilemma it would present to readers. If we sympathize with Humbert in any meaningful way, we are monsters. If we read the book as a catalogue of perversity, we are voyeurs. Woven throughout are innumerable comic moments, juxtaposed against the handful of sober scenes in which we see Lolita clearly, as when she delights in trying on new clothes or when she walks down the street talking with a friend about the worst part of death being that you die alone.[45]

With *Pnin*, readers would quickly recognize that Timofey Pnin's drama unfolded over a tapestry of the recent past. Even the humorously mistaken detention of Pnin as an anarchist at Ellis Island knits the war into his story, without ever letting it dominate the action. His memories of Mira Belochkin are suppressed into the margins, forced there not just by the narrator but by Pnin himself, who cannot imagine how he will stay sane unless he distances himself from his past and the suffering of the dead. Epic tragedy—in this case the Russian Revolution and the Holocaust—is made real only in tiny, discrete glimpses.

The past cannot be escaped; the past shapes the present. In *Sebastian Knight*, V. pursues his brother and seeks to close the gap between them before it is too late, indirectly memorializing a beautiful family in Berlin before the lives of all Jews in Berlin will be changed forever. (In Nabokov's life, of course, the book became a double memorial; Sergei died outside the story just as Sebastian did inside it.)

Again and again, Nabokov made use of real-world history that illuminated the lives of his invented characters via events whose repercussions continued to lay out in the very world in which his readers lived. Despite his insistence as a professor that students should not expect to gain historical information from the work of Austen or other brilliant authors, he had pointed out this very history in his own teaching, referencing Austen's nod to the slave plantations of Antigua in *Mansfield Park* and quizzing students about the specific details that anchored a given book in its time and place.[46] In Nabokov's world, history that undergirded the surface story and preserved the past for future discovery was an inextricable part of transcendent literature.

History lurked in *Lolita*, too, shedding light on the most pressing matters of Nabokov's day and going to the heart of the principles that were his father's legacy. But almost all of that history, the moral center of *Lolita*, went unnoticed.

9

American publishers would not touch *Lolita*. Not only had Edmund Wilson's *Hecate County* been banned in New York, but during Nabokov's first year at Cornell, the U.S. Supreme Court had upheld the decision. Publishers were not seeking the losses that would come from printing books only for them to be seized and destroyed.

Nabokov began to realize that he might have to send *Lolita* out into the world under his own name. If it were not pornographic, one editor argued, why would he need to hide—especially when hiding would only advance the argument that it should be banned? Nabokov began to despair, but Edmund Wilson's newest wife Elena felt certain that *Lolita* would find a publisher if Nabokov would look for one in Europe, where houses would not have to contend with censorship and U.S. Supreme Court cases.[47]

Elena Wilson turned out to be prescient. When Nabokov's agent in France met Maurice Girodias of Olympia Press that April, the publisher had just brought out work by Samuel Beckett and Jean Genet. Girodias had shown a willingness to print literature in English that other houses deemed too illicit or pornographic, despite the high quality of the writing. *Lolita* seemed a good fit, and weeks later Girodias made an offer, which Nabokov quickly accepted, despite his family's warnings about the terms of the contract and his new publisher's apparently sympathetic response to Humbert's pedophilia.[48]

Fearing for his job, Nabokov didn't tell Morris Bishop about the book's subject matter until negotiations with Olympia were well underway. Presented with a copy of *Lolita*, Bishop was horrified—he couldn't even finish the novel. Instead, he found himself imagining the scenarios in which outraged parents fretted over their daughters' morals, endowments were withdrawn, and his prize professor removed from his position for loose morals.[49]

Hoping that publication by Olympia would confer a literary sheen on *Lolita* without sullying her name, Nabokov did not yet realize that Girodias had just launched a line of titles including *White Thighs, Rape,* and *The Whip Angels*. His anxiety in the summer before *Lolita*'s arrival in France was nonetheless immense, his letters vibrating with tension. As Girodias planned publicity copy, Nabokov tried to get him to avoid any direct connection to Cornell, and to downplay his status as a university professor. He still hoped to keep his name off the novel, but in the end, he gave in. He underlined that he saw the project as an artistic endeavor. "A *succès de scandale,*" he wrote to Girodias, "would distress me."[50]

Nabokov eventually discovered the salacious company *Lolita* was keeping at Olympia Press. Similarly taken by surprise the same year, fellow Olympia author J. P. Donleavy was so horrified at being included in a pornographer's stable that he vowed revenge on Girodias, powerless as he was to do anything in the moment.[51] Nabokov, however, expressed less outrage at the company he had to keep, believing that Olympia was the only way to get *Lolita* into print.

Yet the novel arrived in France that fall to little fanfare—for some time Nabokov was not even sure if it had been published. In addition, a plan to print excerpts from the book in the *Partisan Review* as a way to pave the road for publication in America fell through over anxieties about obscenity charges.[52] It seemed as if the drama for which Nabokov had braced himself would fail to develop.

10

Edmund Wilson did not incline toward censorship; across the years of his exchanges with Nabokov, he would, in fact, loan or give his friend a copy of more than one Olympia title. But he started to read the manuscript of *Lolita* and found it distasteful: "I like it less than anything else of yours I have read." After loaning it out to Mary McCarthy and his wife Elena, he was quick to add that latter believed it would be an important book.[53]

Nabokov, however, would not be put off so easily by Wilson. Even as he criticized his friend's class-oriented introduction to a new translation of Chekhov, Nabokov wrote that he hoped Wilson would note that *Lolita* "is a highly moral affair." (In typically Nabokovian fashion, months later he would assert to readers that *Lolita* had "no moral in tow.")[54]

Nabokov often revisited and reworked elements of prior stories. He had initially tried an older man/younger girl pairing in his fiction in 1930 when Carl Junghans first dated Véra's sister Sonia in Berlin. A few years later he had tipped his hand to the idea of a novel about a man who fantasizes about his stepdaughter in *The Gift*. He had later realized the story as a full novella with "The Enchanter."

Across time, the age gap became larger and the girls' innocence more pronounced. Despite the interpretations of *Lolita* which suggest she is the agent of Humbert's corruption, Nabokov rarely missed a public opportunity to condemn Humbert for his treatment of Lolita, calling him a "vain and cruel wretch"; Véra was even more protective of Lolita, reminding readers about the girl's nightly tears and expressing admiration for the life she built after escaping from Humbert.[55]

But if Humbert deserves any pity at all, Nabokov leaves one focal point for sympathy: Annabel Leigh, Humbert's first love, who died of typhus in Corfu in 1923 when Humbert was just thirteen. Real history lurks here, too, though Nabokov never explained it.

The sunny, delightful haven that readers likely imagined stood in sharp contrast to the reality of Corfu in 1923. The island was at that moment a hellish place where multiple real-world epidemics were underway when the fictional Annabel Leigh died. Thousands of refugees had taken shelter on Corfu in camps, dislocated by war and the Armenian genocide. Relief agencies opened orphanages for those whose parents had been executed or who had died in transit. Typhus and smallpox raged the entire year in what was then called the greatest humanitarian crisis in history. The suffering was exacerbated when, in retaliation for the assassination of an Italian general, Italy directly bombed the Corfu refugees that fall, sparking fears of another world war.

After her death on Corfu, Annabel Leigh haunted Humbert for twenty-four years, until he "broke her spell" by reincarnating her in Lolita. The loss that triggered Humbert's perversion was rooted in a tragedy the world had forgotten. Like Pnin describing his course on tyranny, recalling the Armenian tragedy and the brutality of European colonial powers in Africa, Humbert was revealing the boundless atrocities of his century—sometimes in ways that reached far beyond Nabokov's lived experience. But that nod to the dead of Corfu was only the beginning of the lost history Nabokov had folded into *Lolita*.[56]

CHAPTER ELEVEN

Fame

——⊶∞⊷——

1

At the end of 1955, Vladimir Nabokov got the best Christmas present of his life. Novelist (and sometime reviewer) Graham Greene acquired a copy of *Lolita* and named it one of the three best books of the year.

Weeks passed before Nabokov found out about Greene's choice, though the fuse lit by his review would trigger explosions on both sides of the Atlantic. Greene's selection, announced in the *Sunday Times* of London, was roundly condemned by *Sunday Express* columnist John Gordon, who denounced the book as "sheer unrestrained pornography."[1] In response, Graham Greene suggested starting a John Gordon Society, which could protect Britons by keeping an eye out for dangerous "books, plays, paintings, sculptures, and ceramics." He went so far as to hold a first meeting of the Society, which garnered even more popular coverage of the controversy, including tentative forays by U.S. critics, many of whom could not yet review *Lolita* but could cover the literary melee.

Not all the doubters were narrow-minded prudes. Even Nabokov's editor at *The New Yorker*, Katharine White, struggled with *Lolita*. Putting Humbert in the company of Othello and Raskolnikov, Nabokov suggested that perhaps there were not many unforgettable fictional characters "we would like our 'teen-age daughters to meet."[2]

Copies began trickling surreptitiously into the U.S., where the novel was twice seized and twice released by customs officials. *The New York Times* mocked the impulse to control access to *Lolita*, comparing the furor surrounding it to the tempest over Joyce's *Ulysses*, which had subsided over time.

With all the attention being generated, U.S. publishers began to scheme to bring *Lolita* home. Hoping to establish the novel as literature, Nabokov wrote an overtly literary postscript for the book, while Doubleday invited a scholar to write an introduction. The *Partisan Review* printed *Lolita*'s first American review in the fall of 1957, in which John Hollander dared to call it "just about the funniest book I remember having read."[3]

Part of the problem was the need to make a distinction between *Lolita* and her publisher. While Maurice Girodias enthusiastically published works of artistic merit, he was less concerned with who viewed what as timeless, alternating meek and charming discussions of literature with frank statements about being a deliberate pornographer.[4]

Publishing houses from all over Europe clamored to print the book in their home countries. Contracts were signed, translations started, but there were complications. One company rushed to highlight all the sexual passages, eliding whole chunks of the novel. More consequentially, *Lolita* was banned in Britain and France, and also shut out of Argentina and Australia.

Nabokov had predicted the future in a letter to Edmund Wilson, in which he feared that *Lolita* would end up "published by some shady firm." In the long run, of course, it was the nature of Nabokov's protagonist more than his publisher that drew the condemnation.

Nonetheless, Nabokov found himself caught up in a French decree banning two dozen books from Olympia Press. Meanwhile, London authorities had already pulled the books from the shelves of the city's libraries. *Lolita* had somehow grown larger than her author, and all Nabokov could do was agonize over the fate of the greatest book he had written, one which would surely determine his legacy as an artist.[5]

2

The question of exactly what Nabokov was trying to do with Humbert intrigued readers from the beginning. Was the book supposed to represent Old Europe debauching young America? Young America corrupting Old Europe? But inasmuch as they considered the question, critics peered at Humbert through the lens of metaphor, rather than attending to events in the world in which he lived.

Addressing Humbert's sins, Nabokov would later compare him to Hermann from *Despair*, drawing some distinctions between the two men. But more unites them than divides them. Both men write stories explaining themselves and the events that led them to kill. Both are cuckolded by their partners—though Lolita's age and tears reveal her as hardly a willing one, despite Humbert's obfuscations. Both have an intimate, extended murder scene with a man they believe to be a shadow double of themselves, a person who has become an obsession. Both men's lives are upended by world wars in which they did not fight. Humbert, like Hermann, is occasionally delusional; he himself describes his battles with insanity and institutionalization during the war, before he met Lolita.

Where their paths seem to diverge, Humbert's background grows murky. Hermann was interned for years as an enemy alien in Russia in World War I, while Humbert fled France during World War II. Yet strange echoes from the war rattle the coherence of Humbert's story.

Lining up Humbert's account of his war years with real-world history suggests that behind the delusional Humbert's account, Nabokov pondered duplicating Hermann's war experience. Arriving in the U.S., Humbert manages at first to make his way without disaster. In the novel, his first institutionalization occurs early in 1942. At that time the U.S. had just entered the war, and the real-world analogs of foreign anarchists like Humbert were being rounded up for detention, facing a very different kind of "institutionalization" in the United States.[6] Humbert's first institutionalization in the novel occurs, in fact, just a month or two after Carl Junghans's internment ended in the real world.

After being institutionalized in the U.S. in the early 1940s, Humbert mentions that he also went on a trip to northern Canada. Humbert's talk of a "hush-hush" trip to Arctic regions involving weather stations and meteorologists mirrors some of the half-real, half-invented Arctic "intelligence" Junghans had passed on to the FBI and had written about in propaganda articles during the war.[7]

Humbert is by no means Junghans, but Junghans makes sense as a partial prototype for Humbert. He was also charming, cosmopolitan, and liked hinting at his (sometimes dubious) links to espionage. Given that Junghans's Berlin romance with Sonia Slonim preceded *Camera Obscura*, Nabokov may have been accustomed to making use of the rich material provided by Junghans's life.

But even ignoring any link to Junghans's tall tales, the details Humbert gives for his trip to northern Canada seem preposterous. He talks of doing "twenty months of cold labor" and "being made to partake in a good deal of menial work" with other unfortunate and troubled people. Accompanying a top-secret expedition to Canada, as Humbert claims was the case, is a strange wartime opportunity for a mad foreigner just released from a mental hospital. But being in Canada in 1943 doing menial labor for twenty months with other displaced people was a typical wartime fate for foreigners who were anarchists.[8]

By 1943, more than twenty-two concentration camps dotted the Canadian landscape. The camps housed anarchists, Communists, Nazi POWs, German sympathizers, and thousands of completely innocent refugees. And by chance or intention, among the most northern of them was Camp Q, the nickname that Humbert invented for Lolita's summer camp.

Camp Q was located in the wilds of Ontario. Open from 1940 to 1946, the camp saw more than 6,700 prisoners delivered to its gates.[9] Jewish civilian refugees, most from Austria and Germany, were forced to bunk in the same quarters with Nazi officers. Some of the refugees had even made their way out of German concentration camps only to find themselves locked up with and threatened by the very people they thought they had escaped.

Dozens of stories about civilians and Nazis alike held in northern Ontario ran in *The New York Times* during the war, along with accounts of civilians interned at other Canadian sites—including one prisoner who had been deputized by President Roosevelt to help rescue Jews from Europe, but who found himself instead arrested by the British.[10]

A story about one of Camp Q's more famous inmates, Ernst Hanfstaengl, ran in *The New Yorker* during the war. "The Talk of the Town" piece mocked the former confidant of Hitler, who, like Junghans, claimed to have had fled Germany in fear for his life after a dispute with Joseph Goebbels. *The New Yorker* noted archly that he appeared to have a lot of free time for reading at his concentration camp, and that his letters from internment requested "a new pair of heavy black Oxfords, size 12D."[11]

Nabokov may well have intended Humbert's months in Canada to replicate Hermann's internment in *Despair*. Nabokov had surely known about Canadian camps housing political radicals since 1917, when the Russian Provisional Government agonized over whether or not to call for Trotsky's release from one of them, with such devastating consequences for Russia.

He had also likely heard of the spirited debate in Britain over the arrests of refugees that had begun to take place during his last days in Europe, stories that continued to run in newspapers after his arrival in America. Had Nabokov sailed for Canada or London instead of New York in May 1940, his family would have remained at liberty, but some of the Jewish passengers with whom he had escaped would have been sent to Allied concentration camps on arrival.

3

Given the publicity surrounding *Lolita* after Graham Greene's review, many American publishing houses expressed interest in providing a home for the novel, but Nabokov's legal obligations to Olympia were a perpetual stumbling block. More than one publisher gave up after Girodias demanded staggering percentages in exchange for American rights to the book. In an attempt to regain control, Nabokov declared his contract with Girodias void two separate times, citing a clause he believed had been broken.[12]

But in the end G. P. Putnam's Sons, which had not been involved in any of the previous discussions or disputes, stepped in after its publisher got a tip from a Copacabana showgirl he had met at a party. The showgirl later ended up in a bottle fight with the publisher at a nightclub in Paris as Girodias looked on, but, miraculously, at some point the paperwork was signed. Girodias would have his money; Minton would get *Lolita*; and Nabokov would gain immortality.[13]

Meanwhile, the Nabokovs were living the last more or less normal year of their lives in America. After two years studying singing at a Boston conservatory, Dmitri had been drafted. He went off to basic training, but returned to Ithaca regularly. Edmund Wilson had also come to visit them at Cornell, taking meals and whiskey with his leg propped up due to gout. Sonia Slonim wrote to Véra about a visit she had made to see Elena in Switzerland. Nabokov in turn wrote to Elena to mourn the recent death of Evgenia Hofeld, and asked how they might best help the family in Prague now that she was gone.[14]

In August 1958 *Lolita* finally made her way from France to America, reversing Humbert Humbert's journey in the novel. Though the original French ban had been lifted in January 1958, a new one was instated in July, boding ill for publication in the more conservative United States.[15]

Vladimir and Véra had by then lived through a nerve-racking, initially inadvertent publicity campaign that rolled on with accelerating momentum—without any guarantee of whether the book would be banned, seized, and destroyed. If the rising tide of notoriety made the novel a target, the Nabokovs could only hope that fame would render it bulletproof.

The United States seemed to have grown tired of McCarthy and the suspicious approach to art that had torpedoed *Hecate County* a decade before. Such stories still tweaked public morality, but perhaps Americans would now be willing to accept the possibility that something more substantial than pornography was lurking in their pages. That summer, the Nabokovs drove their '57 Buick west along the northern U.S. border to Montana, cruising for a few days into Canada and returning via the Black Hills. They made their way back to Ithaca before *Lolita*'s August publication stateside. Understanding that everything was about to change, Vladimir and Véra both began keeping a diary, the better to remember it all.[16]

The Monday that *Lolita* hit stores, reorders soared, finishing up in the thousands before the end of the day. By Friday morning the book was in its third printing.

The furor was now on both sides of the Atlantic. A tourist returning from America found her copy seized by British customs. Officials informed the press that if "the lady does not agree with our decision she is at liberty to appeal." Caught up in a larger discussion over homosexuality and drinking on Sunday, *Lolita* would be debated in the House of Commons, where Nabokov's novel would find opposition from a group that had once rebuked the Prime Minister for a Sunday game of cricket.[17]

There were American detractors as well. In his "Books of the Times" column, *New York Times*' critic Orville Prescott called it "dull, dull, dull" and "repulsive." Alice Dixon Bond of the *Boston Herald* similarly disapproved, writing, "You can emphasize the fact that it is finely written . . . but when you get all through, you have nothing more than plain pornography."[18]

The book met with resistance abroad, and the Newark, New Jersey, Public Library followed suit. The Cincinnati Public Library system similarly refused to allow the book on its shelves, while the subsequent resignation in protest of the ban by library selection committee member Mrs. Campbell Crockett roiled the staff.[19]

For all the outrage, however, seldom had a book been so lauded with blurbs on opening day, praised by a cavalcade of literary giants from Dorothy Parker and Lionel Trilling to William Styron. Whether they were leading or trailing critical opinion, the sales were staggering. Nabokov's newfound Hollywood agent declared that *Lolita* was the fastest-selling novel since *Gone with the Wind*.

But amid the fireworks, a short review from Sylvia Berkman for *The New York Times Book Review* made less noise. Looking at *Nabokov's Dozen*, a collection of short stories also published in 1958, Berkman had a different view of the man with whom she had carpooled to Wellesley a decade earlier—seeing something others had missed. She noted Nabokov's preoccupation with the minute individual "rammed" by impersonal political forces and the "private loss, dislocation, and damaged hope" that trail in the wake of such collisions. What was extraordinary about Nabokov, Berkman wrote, was that he somehow managed to retrieve and record "the simple, single note of agony" from a human being crushed by history.[20]

4

In *Lolita*, Humbert recounts fleeing wartime Europe to design perfume ads for his uncle in New York. Yet even after the war has ended, it haunts his dreams. His sleeping mind drifts to tragic episodes of vivisection. He imagines twenty soldiers lined up in a raping queue. In his nightmares, he sees "the brown wigs of tragic old women who had just been gassed."[21]

Lolita is filled with unforgettable images, but the dead women's wigs may be its most resonant moment. In a book ostensibly about something else entirely, Nabokov blindsides the reader, once again rendering the Holocaust and its death camps vivid. A mid-century refugee, Humbert in the hands of Nabokov cannot exist in isolation from the war.

Those brown wigs surely belong to Orthodox Jewish women, who shave and then cover their heads, but their Jewishness is never mentioned explicitly in the novel. In fact, neither the word "Jew" nor the word "Jewish" appears anywhere in the book, the only novel Nabokov wrote in a thirty-two-year stretch for which that statement is true. This would not be particularly remarkable, except that Humbert and other characters manage to find a spectacular number of ways *not* to use these terms. Eva Rosen, a friend of Lolita's, is described as a "displaced little person from France." Despite the Anglophilic aspirations of her school, she has a Brooklyn accent. Nabokov leaves unsaid that that accent was so recognizably stigmatized as Jewish in mid-century America that Brooklyn Jews who could afford to do so attended elocution lessons (often in vain) in an attempt to hide it. A stranger who wakes in Humbert's hotel room having forgotten who he is likewise speaks in "pure Brooklynese."[22]

Humbert is exquisitely sensitive to the plight of refugees from the war, as well as the blithe American anti-Semitism swirling in its wake. When Lolita's mother wishes for a "trained servant maid, like the German girl the Talbots spoke of," it is, of course, the real-world Jewish refugees who so often could only get into the country by becoming domestics, regardless of their skills or education. When Alexandra Tolstoy was desperately trying to obtain visas for the Nabokovs, service as a maid had been the career for which she thought it possible to secure affidavits for the multilingual Véra.[23]

More tellingly, on Humbert's first visit to The Enchanted Hunters, the hotel where he first rapes Lolita, he notices the hotel manager examining his features and "wrestl[ing] with some dark doubts," then denying him a room. Only with great difficulty does Humbert change the manager's mind. He later tries to make a reservation by mail but is quickly rejected again in a reply addressed to Professor Hamburg.[24]

Humbert also notes that the Enchanted Hunters has "NO DOGS" and "NEAR CHURCHES" stamped on its stationery. "No Dogs" was typically shorthand indicating that Jews and Negroes were also not welcome—although the full phrase "No Dogs, No Coloreds, No Jews" was still used in the United States into and beyond the 1960s.[25] Humbert keenly recalls the dog he had seen in the lobby on his first visit with Lolita, and wonders perhaps if it had been baptized.

In case "No Dogs" proved too subtle, "Near Churches" was a phrase even more directly understood in the era to mean that Jews were not allowed.[26] During the time period that Nabokov worked on *Lolita*—as he looked through listings for summer lodging for butterfly hunting trips with Véra—the same wording appeared in more than a thousand resort ads in *The New York Times* alone.

The words had come into popular use only after more directly discriminatory language had been outlawed. They were so clearly a mark of bigotry that while Nabokov sat in Ithaca working on *Lolita*, the Anti-Defamation League brought an official complaint in the State of New York. A four-month battle raged in New York newspapers, with representatives of Catholic churches claiming that the wording was not intended to be detrimental to Jews and a group of travel agents countering that "the general public understands the 'code' implicit in such expressions . . . and that vacationers need not apply for accommodations if they happen to be Jewish."[27]

The list of oblique nods to American anti-Semitism in *Lolita* is a long one. Lolita's mother suspects that Humbert has "a certain strange strain" in his family and threatens to commit suicide if she ever finds out that he is not a Christian. When Humbert searches desperately in the town of Coalmont for Lolita after she has sent him a letter, he is refused admission to a store by a "wary" employee before he can even say a word. When Humbert finally tracks down Lolita's mystery lover, Clare Quilty, at home, he is told to leave, because it is "a Gentile's house."[28]

Where his initial gestures had been too subtle in the novel, Nabokov would later underline his more opaque Semitic references. Humbert at one point in the novel feels sorry for Lolita's classmate

Irving Flashman. "Poor Irving," Nabokov later told Lolita's annotator. "He is the only Jew among all those Gentiles." When an acquaintance of Humbert's complains about the high numbers of Italian tradesmen in their small town, he adds that at least "we are still spared—." The man's wife, realizing where he is going, cuts him off before he can finish his sentence. But when Nabokov sat down to translate the book into Russian, he was less coy, leaving no doubt whom the townspeople are spared. The speaker clearly begins to say the word "kikes."[29]

A half-dozen people in the novel have their suspicions about Humbert, but it would be more than a decade before one early commentator would name it, mentioning how others in the novel are confused about Humbert's heritage.[30] But there was another explanation, one so strange readers missed it entirely—the possibility that Nabokov intended Humbert Humbert to be Jewish.

5

On their last trip west before Lolita's publication, Vladimir and Véra made an unscheduled stop on the way from Montana to Wyoming's Bighorn Mountains, looking for a cabin to rent for the night. A landlord showed them what was available and wondered where they were from. Expressing relief that they were from upstate New York rather than the city itself, he made a comment about people who "jew" you.

Véra asked what was wrong with Jews, and their host responded that they "always try to knife you, get the better of you." "Well, I am Jewish," Véra replied, "and I have no intention of swindling you." The Nabokovs left precipitously without even asking for their money back.[31]

No amount of notoriety or accolades was a protection from bigotry, and the prejudice to which Nabokov made Humbert Humbert testify in Lolita would continue to play out in the real world long after Nabokov had folded it into his famous, infamous book. Véra wore her identity proudly in the face of it all. Her biographer Stacy Schiff notes that when described as a Russian aristocrat in a New York Post story, Véra wrote the paper to clarify that she was "very proud" of her background, "which actually is Jewish."[32]

Lolita won her author no accolades for his attention to American anti-Semitism. *Lolita*, in fact, won her author no prizes at all—unlike *Pnin*, which became a finalist for the National Book Award. But what *Lolita* lacked in literary awards it would make up in sales, ensuring continuous media attention for the last half of 1958 and most of the following year. The sale of film rights to James Harris and Stanley Kubrick in September 1958 for $150,000 received almost as much attention as the book itself, with people wondering how on earth it would be possible to make a *movie* of *Lolita*.[33]

At that point Nabokov ceased to be a merely a famous author and entered the realm of celebrity. Before winter, the paperback rights sold for $100,000, and Nabokov's little girl was the subject of television skits by Steve Allen, Milton Berle, and Arthur Godfrey. Groucho Marx had by this time already made Lolita's acquaintance but would put off reading her "for six years, till she's eighteen." *Lolita* would go on to become one of the two bestselling novels of 1959.[34]

But massive sales would not sway all critics to support *Lolita*. Not content with having savaged it once, *New York Times* critic Orville Prescott would spit on its success again, noting that it proved only that "a new variety of sexual sensationalism is the surest means to literary fame and prosperity." His fellow critic at the *Times*, Donald Adams, would critique it repeatedly too, in even more personal terms, as "revolting," using a historical quote to suggest that for all his gifts, Nabokov was "utterly corrupt" and "shines and stinks like rotten mackerel in the moonlight."[35]

Against all odds, critics championed another hefty novel by a Russian author that fall, as Boris Pasternak's *Doctor Zhivago* was published in English for the first time. Pasternak's story follows a heroic doctor who lives through the Revolution and both World Wars, trying to find love and meaning in a society that has been stripped of both. It was an arresting production from Pasternak, who started as an inventive poet much admired by Vladimir Nabokov but had chosen a very different path as a writer.

After spending nearly six months in Berlin in the early 1920s when Nabokov was living there, Pasternak had elected to return to the Soviet Union, while his parents had stayed in the West.[36] His style was decidedly un-Soviet, yet Pasternak had somehow remained on good terms with Stalin.

By 1957, however, when *Zhivago* was complete, Stalin was no longer alive. Pasternak had submitted his work to the Soviet Writers' Union for publication, but it was deemed insufficiently Soviet. He managed to smuggle the full manuscript to an Italian publisher, who had it translated. The book received global acclaim, and subsequent editions in language after language appeared. An English-language version popped up just in time to do battle with *Lolita* on the bestseller lists.[37]

Nabokov, however, was not a fan of Pasternak's novel. *Zhivago* was a historical epic critical of the Soviet state and the dull cowardice that cripples lives, but Nabokov found it filled with nostalgia for stereotypes of the Revolution. "Compared to Pasternak," Nabokov told a reporter, "Mr. Steinbeck is a genius."[38]

As Nabokov basked in the acknowledgment that had long been his due, he could not let go of *Zhivago*'s success, talking Wilson's ear off on the phone about the book's shortcomings. Véra believed that the whole project, in fact, was a Communist plot, and that she and her husband had seen through the charade that it had somehow been "smuggled" out of Russia in the first place. People who fell for it were simply "pro-Commie" fools.[39]

The Nabokovs' views might have surprised Soviet authorities, who saw the novel as a massive betrayal. They had worked tirelessly to censor *Zhivago* entirely, in and outside Russia. Pasternak's "nonacceptance of the Socialist Revolution" had become a major embarrassment, but with so much publicity focused on him, it was decided that arresting him would only do more damage.[40]

Nabokov, however, so sure of his own interpretation, would not relent. *Zhivago* was so clumsy and melodramatic, he felt, perhaps it had been written by Pasternak's mistress, Olga Ivinskaya, widely recognized as the inspiration for the novel's heroine.[41]

ANDREA PITZER

Ivinskaya did not, in fact, write the book, but the Soviet authorities, like Nabokov, laid it at her feet. She paid a heavy price for that attribution. While Pasternak worked on *Zhivago*, Ivinskaya served three years in a labor camp for her malign influence on him. After the novel's publication, she would serve another four years.[42]

Though *Zhivago* eventually defeated *Lolita* on the bestseller lists, Nabokov had much to celebrate. Some people condemned him, but others had recognized his novel's greatness. The book was going to be made into a movie. Nabokov's future unfolded before him. What would he do next? He had staggeringly completed *Lolita*, *Pnin*, and the largest project he had ever undertaken, a translation of and commentary on Pushkin's *Eugene Onegin*, all while remaining a professor at Cornell.

The dreaded hordes of fathers calling for the head of Professor Nabokov, author of *Lolita* and teacher of what had long been known as the "Dirty Lit" course, never transpired. Morris Bishop never had to make an impassioned stand for a book that he couldn't even finish. In the midst of all the chaos, Nabokov asked for time off. One Cornell colleague speculated that he would not return, though Véra assured him that Nabokov would not leave.[43]

Given enough money, however, what Nabokov wanted to do was to write. In the end, his earlier anxieties that *Lolita*'s publication might put an end to his job were entirely correct—if not for the reasons he had feared. It soon became apparent he would give up forever classroom hours spent extolling Tolstoy's precision and condemning Dostoyevsky for his sentimental stories of lunatics. So celebrated by then that even the October 1959 announcement of his departure from Cornell made American newspapers, Nabokov began to imagine his possible futures, as free to move and live in the world as he had been for decades in his own imagination.

6

Vladimir and Véra did not have much company on their island of resentment against *Zhivago*. Edmund Wilson called it "a great book" in his review for *The New Yorker*—and in case readers had not heard him the first time, closed by naming the novel "one of the great events in man's literary and moral history."[44]

With insult added to injury, Nabokov mocked Edmund Wilson's review with vehement contrarianism: Wilson had it backward—it was not a bad translation of a good book but a good translation of a bad book. Moreover, Wilson's essay was fat with "symbolico-social criticism and phoney erudition."[45] Furious with his friend, Nabokov told Putnam's never to ask Wilson to endorse any of his books again.

The growing distance from Wilson was as much about *Lolita* as *Zhivago*. Nabokov had insisted to Wilson that his *Lolita* was a deeply moral work, but his friend had dismissed it, had not even finished it, despite Nabokov's entreaties, which were as close, perhaps, as the proud Nabokov would ever come to pleading with Wilson.

If Nabokov had really expected Wilson to revisit his saga of Humbert and *Lolita* with a careful critic's eye and discern something others had missed, he was disappointed. Any subtleties of Humbert's muddled history were lost in a haze of revulsion: "Nasty subjects may make fine books," wrote Wilson, "but I don't feel you have got away with this."[46]

As reader after reader bought the book, Nabokov's Humbert trudged on, writing a literary testament to his personal agony and ecstasy. Lolita suffered his attentions, escaped, and died millions of times across the years in dozens of languages. Folded into the background was Humbert bearing witness to anti-Semitic humiliations of post-war America: Charlotte's lust for a German refugee maid, the motel exclusions, the *kike* slurs, the small-town anxiety about being overrun by Jews. As Lolita crosses the country with her middle-aged captor, Nabokov traces a shadow map with the coordinates of exclusion and bigotry. He had seen it on three continents, and knew where it could lead.

Humbert confesses early in *Lolita* that he comes from a racial mix, with branches of his family tree winding their way through France,

Germany, Switzerland, Austria, and England. With his "Austrian tailor's" fingertips, he ticks off three generations of family occupations on his father's side: wine, jewels, and silk. The choices seem unlikely to be accidental; behind each trade stretches a long history of legal precedents and a people told where to live, kept apart, their prospects restricted by rules.[47] And if the suspicions of the night clerk at The Enchanted Hunters are right, Humbert carries his family's migration to a new level in a new world—America.

If Humbert *is* Jewish, he is a Wandering Jew for the post-Holocaust era. But in a post-Holocaust world, it may not be possible to believe in anything. Humbert notes that some sins are too extraordinary to be forgiven, yet an existence in which they do not require forgiveness seems a travesty.[48]

Nabokov once wrote that Humbert's crimes were enough to damn him to eternity in hell.[49] And a Jewish Humbert would appear to defy Nabokov's monumental sympathy for Jewish suffering—in the wake of the Holocaust, the creation of a pedophile Jew seems monstrous.

Nabokov was toying with something disturbing, but the concept was not born with *Lolita*. The roots of "The Enchanter," that rough draft of *Lolita* written in wartime France, show Nabokov already working on elements he would later polish. His original pedophile, a Central European jeweler and "traveler" in France, also initially has difficulties getting a hotel room and is suspected for the wrong reasons by the desk clerk who finally checks him in.

Nabokov is fond of trumping what we think we know about a character with new information that rattles our expectations. At one point in *Lolita*, Humbert notes that we assume the kind of stability in life that we get in fictional characters. King Lear will never again join his three daughters in a jolly toast. Madame Bovary will never revive from the arsenic she took.[50] But Nabokov is pointing to the fact that Humbert is wrong; he has misjudged a character in the book who has just surprised him. But Nabokov, too, has made a character capable of surprising the reader in a similar way. Nabokov had learned how to tuck history into the seams of his story in such a way that it becomes visible only on a return trip. The lost, recovered history turns the original tale inside out, offering another narrative. And so Humbert first tells us a story about Lolita, and then tells us a story about ourselves.

As a young man in 1923, Nabokov had started off with *Agasfer*, a hackneyed version of the Wandering Jew, a character who was completely corrupt—a revolutionary, perverse, traitor seeking absolution from an unforgivable sin that had launched his grief and exile. Nabokov would utterly reject that early, inherited character, and after having fallen prey in his youth to ugly stereotypes of the tale, he would reverse the stain of the historical legend by transforming the Wandering Jew into a kind of magical sidekick in the form of the beatific, generous Silbermann in *Sebastian Knight* and, to a lesser degree, the equally munificent parents in "Signs and Symbols."

Nabokov had learned to craft characters that were ever more complex, and he had returned again and again to the idea of the Wandering Jew.[51] But after more than a decade of presenting holy Jewish characters to counter the venom of the Third Reich, Nabokov finally heeded his own condemnation of Dostoyevsky's faith in suffering and humiliation as the path to moral transcendence. Suffering and humiliation, he knew, were just as likely to do irreversible damage.[52]

Creating a war refugee fleeing Europe, Nabokov took up the Wandering Jew story in its entirety.[53] Drawing on the myths that had been used as political tools across the centuries, as well as the *Protocols of the Elders of Zion* and hateful Nazi propaganda that further amplified and distorted the stereotype, Nabokov also included elements of the well-meant melodrama of 1920s Broadway that had tried to grapple with the Wandering Jew as a social commentator. Pulling it all together to create Humbert, Nabokov spots the reader almost every cliché of the legend: revolutionary politics, an easy income, cosmopolitan intellectualism, sexual perversion, and a truly monstrous sin—in Nabokov's rendering, not blasphemy against Christ but the relentless, ongoing molestation of a child.

And still Humbert is human—the very thing the Nazi hatemonger Julius Streicher claimed the Jews were not during his Wandering Jew exhibition. What is more, Humbert Humbert can see American anti-Semitic hypocrisy clearly, while those around him (including, no doubt, many of Nabokov's readers of the 1950s and 1960s) remain blind. Just as the Wandering Jew had done with his Inquisitors in the final scenes of the British productions from Nabokov's Cambridge years, a captive Humbert Humbert directly addresses the members of his jury and admits his sin—the entire book is ostensibly his statement to those appointed to judge him. But he, too, has more testimony to give. Documenting their corruption, he denies their right to pass judgment.

In *Lolita*'s afterword, Nabokov names the fictional town of Gray Star, where Lolita dies, "the capital town of the book"—an odd choice, because neither Humbert nor the reader ever goes there.[54] But "Gray Star," which means nothing particular in English, is in German, a language Humbert knows, *grauer star*, the name for a blind spot, a cataract, that blank space in vision caused by disease that keeps someone from seeing what is plainly before him. The degree to which a reader condemns Humbert without attending to his story is the degree to which the reader's incuriosity leads him to be judged in turn, not because Humbert is innocent or pure (he is certainly not), but because Humbert has his own condemnation to offer.

Nabokov adds to the irony of inverting the Wandering Jew story by making the New World as obsessed as the Old—if not as violent—with ferreting out the Jews in its midst. The single-minded vigilance with which Americans try to prevent any Semitic contagion from touching their businesses or communities blinds them to the real tragedy unfolding among them—the immolation of a girl.[55] In drafting *Lolita*, Nabokov considered naming his nymphet Juanita Dark, a play on Joan of Arc (or, as he preferred, *Joaneta Darc*), another legend built from history in which religious piety cloaking moral blindness abets the destruction of an innocent teenager.

As surely as Humbert's sins are his own, and unforgivable, it is also true that he has been broken by history. His suffering has not ennobled him; instead, it has driven him mad, just as historic events had destroyed *Despair's* Hermann decades before, and character after character in Nabokov's novels and short stories in between. After the death of Annabel Leigh, flight from Europe, visions of the Holocaust, and continued bigotry in America after the war, Humbert's delusions and crimes are not only the cause of his persecution in the world; they are, in some measure, the result.[56]

7

Lolita has Gray Star. The cruel narrator of *Pnin* first meets the young Timofey with a speck of coal dust in his eye—a speck that, though removed, seems to block his ability to see Pnin clearly in the decades that follow.[57]

Nabokov would find himself subjected to the same impaired judgments by others. When the complete version of *The Gift*—Nabokov's story of Russian literary exiles and a genius arising in their midst—was finally published in Russian in 1952, it garnered almost no attention from émigrés. But upon *Lolita's* arrival in America six years later, a Russian poet placed an advertisement in a leading émigré paper denouncing writers who were traitors to their native tongue.[58]

It must have seemed at times to Nabokov that he could not win. *The New Yorker* had balked at publishing portions of his work that were openly anti-Soviet. In academic America, he had been seen as a reactionary, with Wellesley friend Isabel Stephens later lamenting that people simply did not understand the degree to which he loathed Stalin and the depth of his passion for Russia.[59]

Many émigrés, however, did not feel or notice that love in the same degree that Stephens observed it. Nabokov had mocked and chastised their community in *The Gift*, even as he preserved their literary universe. In *Conclusive Evidence*, he seemed to ignore them in favor of tsarist nostalgia. And in *Lolita*, he appeared to have lost his moral compass and any link to Russia at all.

Even his dislike of *Zhivago* could be held against him. Gleb Struve—whose father had served with V. D. Nabokov, and whom Nabokov had known since his years at Cambridge—sent a letter to him asking about a rumor that Nabokov had condemned *Doctor Zhivago* as anti-Semitic. "I wish I knew what idiot could have told you that," Nabokov replied, adding that he was surprised that the devout Struve was not put off by the novel's "cheap, churchy-sugary reek."[60]

But the impression in the émigré community that Nabokov had somehow ceded his Russian-ness to Jewish concerns or international celebrity was too deep-rooted to be dispelled by one letter, particularly one that seemed to take offense at Orthodox piety. If he had written the book they wanted, immortalizing their Russia, perhaps they could have forgiven the arrogance, the distance, and the success.

The émigrés, however, had their revenge. Just weeks after *Lolita*'s release, *Zhivago* earned its author the Nobel Prize for Literature. Pasternak was the second Russian ever to win—the first being Ivan Bunin, the only other literary rival Nabokov had ever acknowledged. Pasternak, still in the U.S.S.R., telegraphed his acceptance ("Immensely grateful, touched, proud, astonished, abashed."), and then, pressured by the Soviets, wrote five days later, refusing the prize and declining to attend the award ceremony.[61] The Nobel Committee would hold its ceremony, but Pasternak would not be there. The world could have *Zhivago*, but it could not have Pasternak.

The world, however, could also have Nabokov. With *Lolita* turning into a global sensation, Véra and Vladimir headed west to California for butterfly hunting and negotiations with Stanley Kubrick. The contortions required by censors threatened to undermine the production of any artistically acceptable movie of *Lolita*. As Nabokov weighed possible solutions, Vladimir and Véra left Los Angeles, meeting up with Dmitri in Lake Tahoe before returning to New York. Booking passage on a luxury liner to Europe for the fall, Nabokov exchanged letters with his sister Elena and brother Kirill, making plans to see them in Europe.

As Nabokov began his fifth decade of exile, many émigrés were settled in the belief that Nabokov had turned his back on his country, and they were not shy about saying so. They had accepted the notion that he did not remember, or did not *want* to remember, and that the story of their vanished Russia would never be told by him.

But as they surrendered Nabokov to the world, the past lingered, biding its time. The Soviet leaders, the Socialist Revolutionaries, the Arctic camps, his own shattered family, and all the Russian dead— Nabokov had forgotten nothing.

CHAPTER TWELVE

Pale Fire

———— ∞∞∞ ————

1

Sailing east for seven days, Vladimir and Véra Nabokov reversed their wartime migration and returned to Europe. The Old World, conquered in their absence, anxiously awaited their arrival.

With fame came more obligations. Nabokov still pondered adapting *Lolita* for the screen. *The Real Life of Sebastian Knight*, which had been out of print, got a second life. Dmitri, long graduated from Harvard, had rendered *Invitation to a Beheading* into English. Plans for publishing Nabokov's entire back catalog in England would soon be set. While many communities still banned *Lolita*, translations were negotiated around the world, from Japan to Sweden and Israel. Nabokov's feud with Maurice Girodias of Olympia Press over rights to the novel would continue for years, but the French version published by Gallimard had gone off like a firecracker in Paris that spring.

In the midst of it all, Nabokov wrote his British publisher, protesting the choice of a particular author for a history of Soviet

Russia. Did he not know the man was a Communist? The least they might do, Nabokov noted, would be to let a "real scholar" annotate the "historical myth" the man was sure to create, in order to avoid furthering Soviet propaganda in England.[1]

Articles about Nabokov had already run that year in any number of outlets, including the *Nouvelle Revue Française, Libération, Arts, L'Express, L'Aurore, l'Observateur littéraire*—and all those in just two weeks. One critic argued that *Lolita* did not qualify as erotic but was nonetheless "essentially sadistic." Another suggested that *Lolita* was "in effect, America, her prejudices, her morals, her hypocrisy, her myths, seen by a completely cynical spirit."[2]

Europe, meanwhile, was anxious to see Mr. Nabokov in person. Paris could not get enough of him and his absolutely adult wife. On October 23, Véra and Vladimir made their debut at a celebration in Nabokov's honor thrown by Gallimard. Véra reigned in silk, mink, and pearls. Nabokov, in gray flannel, charmed the crowd, first by hunting for his glasses, then a forgotten pen—the mere mention of which conjured several from the pockets of those in attendance. Two thousand people were present; there was champagne. Véra smiled, reveling in the acknowledgment of her husband, overdue but sweet on arrival. From a distance, Sonia Slonim imagined their triumphant return to Europe as a marvelous ball.[3]

But the discord between Nabokov and Russian émigrés in Europe had not vanished in his absence.[4] At the Paris reception, Nabokov came face-to-face with Zinaida Shakhovskoy, who had been an early believer in his work, helping him repeatedly in the 1930s when he had been desperately poor. He offered a formal hello, as if she were a stranger.

Had Nabokov been overwhelmed by the crowd, or had he snubbed Shakhovskoy deliberately? Several people thought the latter. Véra had accused Shakhovskoy in 1939 of making an anti-Semitic comment, and Nabokov was slow to forgive such slights. But if he felt provoked to rudeness, it was equally likely to have been caused by an incendiary article she had just written under a pseudonym—an article he had seen—savaging his work and claiming everything in his stories was "nightmare and deceit." She lamented the deep wounds of exile that led him to "forget the friends of his darkest days."[5]

Shakhovskoy was the sister of Nathalie Nabokov, and so a former sister-in-law of Nabokov's cousin Nicholas. As such, she was a distant half-relation, but the Nabokovs' interactions with immediate family members could be just as problematic.

Véra's sisters Lena and Sonia had not spoken to each other in decades. Véra still exchanged letters intermittently with her older sister, but they seemed locked in the binary states of outrage or icy recrimination. Véra continued to question Lena's conversion from Judaism, a move that had alienated her profoundly. Lena, unwilling to be scolded, wrote of witnessing death and torture in Berlin and observed how "easy and simple" Véra's life was compared to hers. She furthermore noted that she had heard that Véra was corresponding with a Russian Nazi in England.[6]

Véra denied the charge, but it may have had a whisper of truth. The Nabokovs and Elena had been working to bring Nabokov's nephew Rostislav out of Prague (too late, it would turn out; less than a year after the Gallimard reception, he would be dead). In their efforts to rescue Rostislav, Vladimir or Véra may well have written to Boris Petkevič, Rostislav's Russian father, who had in fact collaborated with the Nazis before escaping to England.[7]

Nabokov's reunion with his sister Elena and brother Kirill in Geneva was considerably less fraught. Elena, a librarian for the United Nations, had kept up a warm exchange of letters with the Nabokovs as a pair, though she chided Vladimir for rarely writing her directly. Kirill, now a travel agent, had not seen his older brother for more than twenty years. What did they talk about? There was no shortage of material. Evgenia Hofeld was gone; Elena's second husband had died the year before. The younger siblings saw fit to correct a few details in their brother's autobiography.[8] They may also have discussed their absent sister Olga, still in Prague behind the Iron Curtain. Nabokov had little contact with her but continued to send money for the care of her son, and he knew that she now had a grandson, also named Vladimir.

We do not know if the conversation turned to the other absent sibling—Sergei. But just as the lost brother haunted *Sebastian Knight* even before Sergei's death, he continued to wind his way through Nabokov's writing long after his life ended at Neuengamme.

At a party early in the decade, Nabokov had announced to dinner companions that he was planning to write a story about a pair of Siamese twins. ("You will not," Véra had declared.[9]) Nabokov nonetheless worked out fragments of the tale of Floyd and Lloyd, two conjoined brothers living on the Black Sea.

The story was meant to be a three-part tragedy, in which the brothers were to maintain their separate identities—even avoid each other—as much as they could, despite the forced intimacy of their condition. In the first section, Floyd dreams of being severed from the twin with whom he has so little communion. When he imagines the aftermath of the separation in nightmares, he is healthy and complete, escaping alone, holding some token object (a crab, a kitten) to his left side where his missing brother should be.[10] But in his dreams, the other brother has not managed to get free—Lloyd staggers along, still somehow hobbled by a twin.

In the remaining parts of Nabokov's triptych, the brothers were to find love and undergo a separation from each other which would result in Lloyd's death. But Nabokov composed only the first part of the story. Having lived through the separation from and death of Sergei in real life, he seems not to have wanted, or not to have been able, to revisit them in fiction. Nabokov never finished his story of the surviving brother and his dead twin. The part he did write, "Scenes from the Life of a Double Monster," was rejected by *The New Yorker* and remained unpublished for eight years, until *Lolita* transformed even his dross into gold.[11]

Nabokov had folded Sergei more overtly into his autobiography years before. *Conclusive Evidence* casts Sergei as "my brother" dozens of times in childhood and in early adolescence, and Nabokov occasionally gave his sibling a reflected primacy. "My brother and I," he wrote, "were born in St. Petersburg, in the capital of Imperial Russia."

Sergei appears again and again, fleeing governesses and enduring tutors with Volodya, escaping Petrograd with him after the Revolution. But as with "Double Monster," Nabokov had not finished the story. Like a Soviet-era photo edited to alter the past, Sergei slowly disappears from *Conclusive Evidence*. *My brother* heads to Cambridge and enrolls at Christ College. *My brother* tags along with Vladimir to see their parents in Berlin late in their college career. And then, nothing. The death that had not been a charade was reduced to a passing reference early in *Conclusive Evidence* ("a brother of mine . . . who is now also dead"), the separation as erased as it could be without being completely denied.

By the time Nabokov had finished his autobiography, he had accomplished what he had not been able to do in fiction—to shape and control the story of the brothers so that the loss of one could be contained. The boys' time together at Cambridge, Sergei's years in Paris, and the events at Neuengamme that had permanently divided them were nowhere to be found in Nabokov's account of his own life. After 1919, it was as if Sergei had vanished.

2

Having conquered Milan and London—which included dinner with Graham Greene—the Nabokovs returned to America in February 1960. They had settled on terms to write a screenplay for *Lolita* and were due in California in mid-March.

Working their way across the country, they stopped in Utah to collect butterflies. Arriving in California, Nabokov spent six months in back-and-forth writing and revising, with Kubrick continually emphasizing the need to cut. Only shards of Nabokov's effort would make it into the final movie; the dismemberment of his work had begun almost as soon as he delivered the script.[12]

And so the crowning moment of the 1960 return to the U.S. happened not in California at all, but back in New York that October in a hotel overlooking Central Park, where Nabokov hit on a clear idea of how to construct his next novel. He had been wrestling with the project for years, and the roots of the story stretched even further back, to the first months of World War II. His aborted 1940 project *Solus Rex*, with its madman who imagines himself a king, had been Nabokov's last Russian-language fiction. He had already borrowed its grieving widower and dystopian framework for *Bend Sinister*, but he was not yet through with the idea of the distant northern kingdom in the earlier work.

In 1957 Nabokov had written to Jason Epstein, his editor at Doubleday, proposing a novel in which a northern king flees to the U.S., creating political headaches for President Kennedy.[13] After being deposed by a coup—whose plotters would have help from nearby Nova Zembla—and then a transatlantic escape, the king was to go on a spiritual quest while an assassin circled the globe, closing in on him.

Doubleday bit, but after just three months of research, Nabokov had put the new novel aside. Two years later, still unsure on how to proceed and wondering if the contractual obligation of the advance were interfering with the story's evolution, he had returned the money and said of the novel, "I am not sure I shall ever write it."[14]

But surrendering the commitment led to a breakthrough. He had spent two full years assembling his 1,300-page treatment of *Eugene Onegin*, caught up in his dizzying, obsessive commentary on Pushkin's verse. A flash of insight led him to imagine a novel in which a whole life was somehow tucked into a commentary on a poem. He fused the story of his ex-king to the afterglow of his *Onegin* project, and once inspiration struck, he was consumed. Nabokov left for France days later, and settling in Nice, began to write a 999-line poem that would serve as the launch pad for his novel. He blazed through it in ten weeks, and headed on to Geneva to spend Easter with Elena.

Leaving Nice with spring underway, Véra and Vladimir went to northern Italy to see Dmitri's opera debut in *La Bohème*. Afterward, they made their way to Stresa, closer to the Swiss border, where Nabokov dove back into work on his poem-novel, which would in time acquire the title *Pale Fire*. Scribbling away on three-by-five-inch index cards, he erased words, revised, and crossed out whole sections. By June the Nabokovs had made their way into Switzerland; by mid-July Nabokov thought himself halfway done with the book; by August 7 they were driving into Montreux.[15]

They got a room away from the shores of Lake Geneva, and started looking for a place where he could settle and finish the novel. Russian actor Peter Ustinov—who had just won an Academy Award for his role in *Spartacus*—recommended over dinner that the Nabokovs join him at the Montreux Palace Hotel. They visited the place and found that the lakeside resort suited them. By the beginning of September, they had signed a contract for rooms at the Palace, and Nabokov prepared to finish his most inventive novel yet.

3

In its completed form, *Pale Fire* would tell the story of two men: John Shade, an American poet who is murdered, and Charles Kinbote, who steals Shade's verse as he lies dying. Shade's magnum opus, the 999-line rhymed poem that Nabokov had written before starting the rest of the book, appears in the novel in its entirety. The rest of the story unfolds through Charles Kinbote's increasingly eccentric commentary on the poem, which establishes him as a narrator who cannot be trusted with facts or young boys.

Along with the two main characters in *Pale Fire*, Nabokov also gave a starring role to a mystery land called Zembla. While the characters inhabit a mundane campus very similar to Nabokov's Cornell, the narrator Kinbote believes he is actually the exiled ruler of the fantasy land of Zembla, a king who has escaped from a guarded prison and made his way to America. Kinbote cares only for what he imagines will be Shade's masterpiece—the story of lost Zembla and its hidden crown jewels, which are so well concealed that Kinbote thinks they will never be found, even though Soviet-style agents have been tearing apart the Zemblan royal castle in search of them.

Kinbote's stories of his homeland include a Communist-style revolution that shattered his happy reign—along with a kitchen-sink hodgepodge of scenes borrowed from real-world literature, history, and even a Marx Brothers movie.[16] Highlights include royal genealogy, murder, and Kinbote's homosexual longings and pedophilia, as well as his prowess at ping-pong. A dramatic account of his escape from Zembla takes up some thirteen pages of the novel and leads him through a tunnel, backstage at a theater, into a racecar, across mountains, and onto a boat before his arrival in Paris.

Despite being a fellow professor at the university where Shade teaches, Kinbote exists in a fantasy world. He hears voices, imagines conspiracies, and his misunderstanding of Shade's poem distorts it into something unrecognizable. Shade's story of love for his wife and the suicide of his daughter are twisted by Kinbote into a chronicle of Zemblan history.

People in the campus town tell stories about Kinbote behind his back and call him a lunatic to his face, though he hardly seems to need their encouragement to gin up paranoia. He reads a confusing note pointing out his halitosis and thinks someone has realized he has hallucinations. Kinbote is the kind of person who wishes Shade would have a heart attack to provide him with an opportunity to comfort his ailing friend.

Shade is the only one who seems to have any sympathy for Kinbote; even Shade's wife avoids Kinbote or shoos him away. Across the course of the book, the ex-king's affairs go awry and his young tenants leave him. The other characters in the book realize Kinbote is ludicrous, and readers easily see how pathetic he is, but he remains oblivious.

Yet, like Pnin, Kinbote is more than a comic figure. Everything readers learn about him seems to have an off-kilter or freakish aspect: his fondness for table tennis, his left-handedness, his star-crossed relations with young men at the college where he teaches, his predilection for even younger boys—a predilection from which, like Humbert with girls, he longs to be delivered. But beneath his self-aggrandizing melodrama, his royal fantasies are laced with grief. He dreams of suicide and absolution from the horror he carries. He writes of the temptation to end his life with a handgun, but manages to keep himself alive long enough to make sure the tale of Zembla is recorded for posterity.[17]

Kinbote's mad take on his dead friend's poem parallels Nabokov's struggle to interpret *Eugene Onegin*. And his despair over exile from a country devastated by revolution directly echoes Nabokov's grief about Russia. Yet the reality of Zembla is more baffling to deconstruct, and Nabokov seems to have wanted it that way. When he was distraught over plans for *Pale Fire*'s pre-release publicity, Véra sent a seven-point list to his publisher on his behalf, directing exactly how the fantasy land should be presented. The Nabokovs particularly balked at labeling Zembla as "non-existent," insisting that "Nobody knows, nobody should know—even Kinbote hardly knows—if Zembla really exists."[18]

What *is* Zembla? Readers found themselves trying to make sense of the place: was it meant to be real in the novel, or only a figment of Kinbote's fierce longing? In one of the first reviews of the book, *New Republic* critic Mary McCarthy noted the existence of "an actual Nova Zembla, a group of islands in the Arctic Ocean, north of Archangel." The link was not a stretch—McCarthy also noted that *Zembla* had been used centuries before by Alexander Pope in reference to the islands as a metaphor for the strange and distant North.[19]

But in the dissection of the book that would obsess readers for the next fifty years, the world did not realize that *Pale Fire*'s mad narrator was not the first king of Zembla. Centuries before Charles Kinbote was a wild spark in Nabokov's eye, a real person had held that title, and he had had a harrowing escape of his own—one that

Nabokov seems to have known about for decades—from a kingdom at once real and imaginary.[20]

4

Of the three voyages that intrepid Dutch sailors made to Nova Zembla at the end of the sixteenth century, the first found luck, the second misfortune, and the third an equal measure of both. All three were piloted by William Barents, who dreamed of finding a Northeast trade route from Europe to China. On the first voyage, the sailors had managed to venture into the great unknown and land near the islands' northern tip. On the second trip, one sailor had been seized unawares and devoured by a polar bear before the fleet was blocked by ice on Zembla's southern end.[21]

And in May 1596, the third time Barents set out from Amsterdam, an initial attempt to find open Polar Sea met only icepack. The sailors looked up into the sky and saw three suns bracketed by a triple rainbow.[22] The optical illusion in the sky was new and strange, but the situation on the water was terrifyingly familiar: more and more ice, and again, polar bears. After nearly a month of disputes over which direction to proceed, the expedition's two ships went their separate ways. As they sailed on, the bears would scale the ice floating near the ship again and again to try to climb aboard, or swim around the boat in search of food.

Following the rocky shore, they rounded the northern tip of Nova Zembla. But ice set in early that season. It soon broke the tiller and the rudder, shattering their smaller boat against the ship. After five days of struggling against the frozen sea, Barents was locked in place.

Amid thunderous booming, ice floes tipped the boat. The ship itself seemed to be coming apart; it was lifted higher and higher out of the water, while even larger icebergs drove in from the sea. After two weeks in fear for the destruction of his ship but holding on to a faint hope of escape, Barents realized that they would have to spend the winter on Nova Zembla.

With a six-month freeze ahead of them, the men knew they needed a cabin. No trees grew on the islands, yet if they were to dismantle their boats entirely, they could never sail home. Searching for driftwood that might suffice, they stumbled onto a gift: whole trees that had been swept from the mainland to Nova Zembla. The trees lay miles away from the ship; the men built sleds to haul them back.

In clear weather, they made progress, but when visibility was poor, they did not venture far, mindful that the bears that could smell the sailors long before the men could see them coming. The ship's carpenter died before a cabin was even begun. A cleft in a hill had to serve for a tomb, as the ground was too hard to dig a grave.

After two weeks of labor, they raised the main beams of a shelter. They continued work on the house for another seven days, and were trailed by the bears as they carried goods from the ship to the crude structure. As if the hungry bears were not enough to manage, a barrel of beer left overnight froze in the arctic air and burst its bottom. For the former, there were noise and bullets; for the latter, there was no harm sustained: it was so cold that the beer had frozen as it ran out of the barrel, and they were able to pick it up and save it. In the house, they set up a clock and a lamp, which they fed with melted polar bear fat.

In the cabin, nominally sheltered from blizzards, they peeked out at a polar moon that rode the sky day and night. A layer of ice more than an inch thick formed on the walls inside the house. Once the two-month polar night set in and their clock froze, they could not tell day from night without tracking the tally of the twelve-hour sandglass they had brought from the ship.

By mid-December, they ran out of kindling, but managed to dig around outside the house for wood they had left there. Christmas came and went, bringing with it foul weather that trapped the men inside and piled snow higher than their house. Their shoes froze solid and became useless, forcing them to wear several pairs of socks under loose clogs they crafted from sheepskins. Running out of wood again, they began burning non-essential possessions. The only way to see outside was to look up the chimney.

Once the weather calmed, they cleaned their filth from the cabin and gathered as much wood as possible. They then recalled that it was January 5th, Twelfth Night, when Dutch tradition held that the world turned upside down and the normal order of life would be reversed.

Celebrating with wine they had left, the men made pancakes and were given some of the captain's biscuit, which they soaked in the wine. Pretending that they were back home, they imagined themselves at a royal feast. Following the holiday tradition, they drew lots. And so it happened that on January 5, 1597, for the hours up until the stroke of midnight—a span remembered for four hundred years even as his name was lost to history—the gunner on William Barents's third expedition drew the winning lot and reigned as the first king of Nova Zembla, an imaginary monarch in a land of ice and death, a ruler over hope and despair, a king of nothing.

5

As Vladimir and Véra Nabokov moved into the Palace Hotel on October 1, 1961, apocalyptic fears rattled the West, and a different kind of history was being made on Nova Zembla.

A series of highly publicized nuclear weapons tests was under way in the Soviet Union, and in the weeks between the Nabokovs signing their contract and moving onto the third floor of the old wing of the hotel, ten explosions had already taken place, with more than a dozen to follow in the next two months.[23]

Competitive series of tests had taken place regularly from 1951 to 1958, in which the Americans and Soviets traded bomb blasts, with an occasional contribution made by the British. But in the fall of 1961 the Soviets began using their tests as a kind of propaganda to intimidate the U.S. and appear to rival its arsenal, which far outstripped the four lonely Soviet intercontinental ballistic missiles then in existence.[24]

Radiation clouds from the test blasts drifted with the wind over neighbors to the west and south, raising fears about the long-term effects of fallout on humans, livestock, and agriculture. Concerns about the tests were raised at the United Nations, where countries' responses tended to fall along the Cold War divide between U.S. allies and the Soviet sphere of influence, with non-member states refraining from taking sides.[25]

If the Swiss government was officially neutral, Switzerland's newest resident was not. Nabokov's guiding principle was to choose "that line of conduct which may be the most displeasing to the Reds and the Russells."[26] The fact that Russian Premier Nikita Khrushchev had launched a thaw and attacked Stalinist myths did nothing to warm Nabokov to him or the Soviet government. Nabokov appears to have been likewise unimpressed by the nuclear drama.

The thermonuclear tests were just one in a series of crises that year. The Berlin Wall had begun to rise in August, and late that October Soviet and U.S. tanks rolled up to the line dividing the city, facing each other for sixteen hours in a standoff that caught the world's attention.[27] Against this backdrop, every few days in September and October a new bomb detonated; sometimes tests were conducted daily.

The earliest Soviet explosions had taken place in eastern Kazakhstan, not far from where Solzhenitsyn had been sent into exile. But in 1958, a year after Nabokov started collecting "bits of straw and fluff" for *Pale Fire*, newspapers announced that the Soviets had inaugurated a new testing ground just north of the Russian mainland.[28] For the entire time that Nabokov had worked on drafting his next novel, the primary Soviet test site had been located on Nova Zembla.

Nabokov, however, had been thinking about Nova Zembla in the context of his new novel even before the nuclear tests began there—he had mentioned it in the pitch letter he sent to Doubleday in 1957. And two years after sending that letter, he had acquired an additional reason to ponder the islands' historic role: he had learned of a personal connection to the place. A cousin had researched family genealogy and sent a letter mentioning their great-grandfather, whom he believed to have taken part in a nineteenth-century expedition that resulted in the naming of the Nabokov River there. Nabokov had written his cousin back, delighted at what felt like the "mystical significance" of the existence of such a river in Nova Zembla.[29]

But during his first weeks in Montreux, Nabokov would have learned that the world was now very much aware of those islands, too. Given the daily news in the last three months of his work on *Pale Fire*, it is hardly surprising to find Nabokov seeding nuclear signs and symbols through the pages of his novel. *Pale Fire* mocks Albert Schweitzer, a peace activist despised by Nabokov, and offers a cutting comment about left-wing professors who fret over "Fall-outs occasioned solely by US-made bombs," as if Russia had not been busy testing her own arsenal. While the poet Shade writes of an "antiatomic chat" on television, Nabokov (or Kinbote, or Shade—it is not clear) ridicules anyone impressed by nuclear stunts, "when any jackass can rig up the stuff." Describing the news during a period in which the real-world U.S.S.R. had played a game of brinksmanship with nuclear tests in Nova Zembla, the novel's poem tells how "Mars glowed," a reference to the Roman god of war.[30]

While Nabokov polished his draft, he was inundated with nuclear news from Nova Zembla. During his daily reading of the *New York Herald Tribune* in Switzerland, he would have seen more than a dozen front-page stories mentioning Nova Zembla. Nova Zembla appeared on maps in newspapers around the globe, with fall-out patterns noted. Debates over safe radiation levels continued. Milk was tested to see if children should still drink it, and at the Twenty-Second Party Congress in Moscow Khrushchev announced plans to detonate a 50-megaton hydrogen bomb. The UN took up the issue, and after long debates, finally passed a resolution imploring the Soviets not to explode the monster device.[31]

Nevertheless, on October 30, the Tsar Bomba, the biggest bomb in history, exploded over Nova Zembla. The casing was too large to even fit in the bomb bay of the airplane assigned to drop it. Pieces of the plane's fuselage had to be cut away to accommodate its cargo, which was suspended underneath, hanging more than halfway out of the plane. When the bomb was released, an enormous parachute trailed behind it, one so large that its assembly was rumored to have triggered shortages in the production of Soviet hosiery.[32]

The blast happened in mid-air, leveling buildings in a seventy-five-mile radius and cracking windows more than five hundred miles away; it was ten times more powerful than the combined total of all the explosives used in World War II. Pregnant women on the other side of the world drank iodine in an effort to stave off birth defects. Front-page stories around the globe announced the blast. Trace levels of radiation crossed the continent to the Nabokovs' suite in Montreux.[33]

Within a week, diplomatic initiatives intensified, and political pressure from the world mounted. And then the frenzied bombing at Nova Zembla stopped. A month later in Montreux, Nabokov mailed his publisher the manuscript for a magical novel about a northern kingdom called Zembla. *Pale Fire* appeared the following spring.

By a quirk of history, the Soviets shifted for a time to another testing ground in southern Russia, and no bombs fell on Nova Zembla in the months before and after *Pale Fire*'s publication. Reminders of real-world tests at Nova Zembla, which might have been obvious in the fall of 1961, sat in the book unnoticed by critics for decades.[34] A straightforward path connecting the Zembla of the novel to the real-world Nova Zembla was lost. And readers puzzling over *Pale Fire* never thought to explore the islands' twentieth-century history, where they would have found that in addition to being a Soviet nuclear test site, Nova Zembla had long been notorious for a very different reason.

6

Five days after the Tsar Bomba set fire to the sky over Nova Zembla, Alexander Solzhenitsyn took a train to Moscow, with a dream of submitting his own short novel for publication. Along with millions of people in and outside Russia, he had listened to the October speeches of the Twenty-Second Party Congress and had been surprised by what he had heard.

It was not, however, Khrushchev's threat to explode a monster bomb that had shaken him. The words that stayed in his mind were those from a speech by Alexander Tvardovsky, editor of *Novy Mir*, the most candid of contemporary Soviet magazines. Tvardovsky declared at the Congress that Soviet literature had praised the victories of the people but had yet to deliver work that also reflected their suffering. Tvardovsky said that he was still waiting for a literature "totally truthful and faithful to life."[35]

Solzhenitsyn had spent almost a decade outside the camps preparing himself for this moment; it was more than long enough to agonize over the possibility of being sent back. No longer even in remote exile, he had built a good life—he was living in Ryazan, a provincial town an afternoon train ride away from Moscow. His wife Natalia had remarried him. His cancer had reappeared, but it had been successfully treated. More miraculously, as part of Khrushchev's thaw he had been rehabilitated by the State.[36]

Many others had been freed or welcomed back by society, but Solzhenitsyn was still aware of those who were not so lucky. He had noticed the spot near Ryazan's railway station where prisoners were still offloaded away from other passengers. He had given a lecture on physics at a local correctional facility, where he found himself thinking of those who would go back to their cells after his talk.[37]

In his life as a free man, he had written several short stories and miniatures. He had tried his hand at a play on personality modification. He had done three revisions of a novel, *The First Circle*, which was based on his years in a scientific research *sharashka*. He had submitted one essay arguing against autobiography to *Literary Gazette*, the official publication of the Union of Soviet Writers—only to see it immediately rejected.[38]

He longed to see his work published, and he had one story about a labor camp that seemed like a good candidate. His readers thought it the best thing he had written; it had made a friend cry. After reading the story, another friend is said to have told Solzhenitsyn that three atom bombs had made their way into the world: "Kennedy has one, Khrushchev has another, and you have the third."[39]

The story that had so moved his friends possessed the ungainly title of *Shch-854*, a reference to the prisoner number of Ivan Denisovich Shukhov. In it, Solzhenitsyn did little more than recount the events in one man's life across a single day in a labor camp. Ivan Denisovich does not suffer the most harrowing events of camp life—torture, rape, or execution—but the depiction of subsistence-level existence and bitter cruelty in which the average prisoner had to find a way to survive was powerful in its restraint. The complicated strategies required to navigate every moment of the day, from reveille to the mess hall, give way to an awareness of the transcendence of Ivan Denisovich, who manages not just to survive but to retain his humanity.

As an unknown writer who had been rehabilitated, Solzhenitsyn could create freely in secrecy. Freely, of course, is hardly the right word. After a fair copy of any given work had been written out, it had to be concealed. Any remaining drafts had to be gathered, and after all the neighbors had gone to sleep, burned one page at a time in the communal kitchen.[40]

If Solzhenitsyn sent out his real work—not just a criticism of something written by someone else, but a story that went to the heart of what he had seen and wanted to say—he knew he would be publicly identified as a writer with an agenda. If the Soviet leaders chose to, they could keep him from writing in the future.

An idea had come to him in 1958 to write a vast account of the Soviet labor camp system, based on what he had seen himself and the experiences of others. If he moved forward with trying to publish his story about a single prisoner, it was entirely possible he would jeopardize the larger project. Unbeknownst to Solzhenitsyn, the camp theme was already percolating among some of the most gifted Russian writers of the day, but it had not yet found officially sanctioned publication.[41] Had Tvardovsky been serious in his speech—were Soviet leaders ready to hear the truth about the suffering of the Russian people?

After consulting with friends again in Moscow, Solzhenitsyn decided his time had come. He was forty-two years old, soon to be forty-three. The wife of a former fellow prisoner would deliver the story of Ivan Denisovich to Tvardovsky at the offices of *Novy Mir*. It was the first piece of fiction he sent out into the world.

7

After *Lolita*, Vladimir Nabokov no longer faced any uncertainty when it came to finding a home for his work. Putnam's was waiting in the wings for *Pale Fire*; within five months his manuscript was proofed and printed.

When the book arrived, Edmund Wilson had no comment on it, but in the pages of *The New Republic* Mary McCarthy called it "one of the very great works of art this century." Others were less enthralled; one critic declared it "the most unreadable novel I've attempted this season."[42] Nabokov's convoluted tale managed to hook on to the bottom of the bestseller lists, despite its opaque structure and baffling mysteries. How can a poem and its commentary be a novel? Who is the narrator? What is Zembla? What is the significance of the crown jewels?

Scholars, fans, and other authors tried to find and dissect hidden codes in the book. Perhaps the poet invented the ex-king—or did the ex-king invent the poet? Readers were encouraged in their speculations and literary autopsies by the novel's author, who coyly proclaimed to the *New York Herald Tribune* that the book was "full of plums that I keep hoping somebody will find."[43]

If Nabokov wanted readers to do the hard work of finding a hidden message in *Pale Fire*, he was not above offering some clues. In the same interview, he told his interviewer that the narrator Charles Kinbote was not actually a king or an ex-king of Zembla, that he was in fact insane. Furthermore, he had committed suicide—at the age of forty-four, if readers trace the chronology—before completing the last entry in the Index, which is *Zembla*.

Perhaps to give additional fodder to interpreters, Nabokov had anchored his fantastic tale in the real world. In addition to nuclear allusions and Cold War references, he had given *The New York Times* a prominent role in *Pale Fire*, spending a page and a half describing articles from the newspaper, some of which mention Zembla.[44] The stories are actual articles taken from July 1959 editions of the newspaper, but as with so much of what Kinbote touches in the novel, the news has been bent and twisted to reflect his mania for his lost country. Kinbote imagines Zemblan children singing songs as part of an international youth exchange, and he inserts Zembla into a story of Khrushchev canceling a visit to Scandinavia.[45]

The *Times* serves as a source for news about Zembla inside *Pale Fire*, but what the real-world *Times* had to offer on the real-world Nova Zembla—if the world had only looked—says more. In 1955, just two years before Nabokov began making his first notes toward his novel, a brief mention of the Arctic islands appeared in a story by an American named John Noble.

Noble had lived through World War II in Germany with his family. When Soviet forces swept in at the end of the war, Noble had been sent to Buchenwald (which was under Russian control) before being deported more than three thousand miles northeast to the labor outpost of Vorkuta. Above the Arctic Circle, he mined coal with thousands of other prisoners, later participating in a prisoner revolt.[46]

Mining coal in the Arctic seems a harsh enough fate, but among Vorkuta inmates it was understood that however bad things got, they could be worse. What they truly feared was the place Noble described as the destination of last resort for the worst offenders: Nova Zembla, the place "from which there is no return."[47] Noble's three-day *Times* account of his experiences in Vorkuta became the book *I Was a Slave in Russia*, a bestseller in America that year.

But the *Times*' accounts of the islands' forgotten history stretch back before Noble's years in the camps. At the beginning of 1942, the Russian army badly needed reinforcements for the war effort, and turned to Polish forces. The *Times* reported on the contentious issues blocking a Soviet-Polish agreement. One question centered on tens of thousands of missing Polish officers (whose bodies would later be found in a mass grave in Katyn Forest); the other related to reports of Polish prisoners being deported to labor camps in horrific conditions on "the barren and desolate island of Nova Zembla."[48]

Yet Nova Zemblan history in the *Times* goes even further back, before the war, winding past stories of plans to build an Arctic resort there in 1934 and sightings of mysterious airplanes on it 1931,[49] all the way back to 1922, where along with a story Walter Duranty had in the paper that day sits an August 28 account explaining that Socialist Revolutionary prisoners would, for the first time, be shipped to Nova Zembla.

In the wake of the trial of the Socialist Revolutionaries, it was noted, the defendants had disappeared. Intellectuals and professors were being arrested, and many of them held in concentration camps at Archangel. But some prisoners, veterans of prison under Tsarist rule, had escaped from the mainland camps. As a result, the remaining prisoners would be "sent to Nova Zembla, two large islands in the Arctic Ocean, where even the former Czars never sent criminals."[50]

The story also ran in the *Times of London*. The news of prisoners sent to certain death had echoed and repeated in Europe and America, appearing two days later in the newspaper with the largest circulation of any Russian-language daily in Germany, a place where Nabokov had published so much of his work—*Rul*, the paper of Nabokov's dead father. Within the camps, inside Russia, and across Europe and America, Nova Zembla had been feared as the cruelest outpost of the camp system, a place of terror for all of Vladimir Nabokov's adult life.

8

Alexander Solzhenitsyn's account of life in a labor camp did not immediately make it onto the desk of Alexander Tvardovsky, *Novy*

Mir's editor in chief. But it astounded the first person who read it, a copy editor at the magazine. Fearing it would be spiked by others or might fall into the wrong hands, she cagily bypassed the usual hierarchy and carried it to Tvardovsky herself.

Taking it home from work that evening, he began reading and stayed up all night, going through it twice. Barely able to contain himself until dawn, he began calling around to discover who had written the treasure that had been delivered to him. He returned to *Novy Mir* offices and broke into a junior editor's desk to find extra copies, which he carried to the house of a friend, calling for vodka and announcing, "A new genius is born!" The only goal he had left in life, he vowed, was to shepherd the story of Ivan Denisovich into print.[51]

Solzhenitsyn was summoned to Moscow for a meeting with the magazine's editorial board, which he attended in deliberately shabby clothes to underline his outsider status. Tvardovsky paid tribute to choice after choice that Solzhenitsyn had made in the story, quoting passages aloud to the group. It was on the level of Dostoyevsky, he said—perhaps better.

Novy Mir signed a contract for what was now being called *One Day in the Life of Ivan Denisovich*. As an advance, the magazine paid Solzhenitsyn one thousand rubles, more than his teaching salary for the entire year.[52]

Though Solzhenitsyn was ecstatic, he understood that the journal having acquired the story was no guarantee that the Party would allow its publication. The steps forward that Khrushchev had pointed to in his October speech had not entirely found support in the Congress. Even though the history Solzhenitsyn referred to in the book had taken place more than a decade before and had since been condemned at the highest levels, such a vivid depiction of human suffering imposed by the state still seemed too raw to appear as Soviet literature. Tvardovsky let the manuscript sit for more than four months without submitting it.[53]

He did, however, begin to send the story around under the table to those whose opinions he valued, asking established writers to contribute assessments supporting its importance. Some of them simply thought he was wasting his time, because it would never be allowed to see the light of day. Others contributed enthusiastically, comparing Solzhenitsyn to Tolstoy and suggesting "it would be unforgivable to keep this from readers." But the net effect of giving it to a few writers, for even the space of a few hours, was that those writers made and kept their own copies, and then passed them along to their friends. As many as five hundred bootleg copies of *Ivan Denisovich* circulated through unofficial channels; all of Moscow was talking about a novella that did not yet officially exist.[54]

One of those copies ended up in the hands of Nikita Khrushchev's private secretary, who admired the work and was willing to take it directly to his boss. A series of edits was asked for; some caused Solzhenitsyn to balk, declaring that he had waited one decade already, he could wait another.[55] In the end, minor changes were agreed on, and the revised manuscript, accompanied by a cover letter from Tvardovsky, was forwarded to Khrushchev's secretary.

Khrushchev read it and wondered why it had not already been published. The Central Committee, however, was less inclined to move so quickly and demanded copies for all its members. The novel was discussed behind closed doors, where Khrushchev reportedly said, "There's a Stalinist in each of you; there's even some of the Stalinist in me. We must root out this evil."[56]

In the end, *Ivan Denisovich* made its way past the editors, the opinions of the Moscow literati, Nikita Khrushchev, and even the Central Committee. People heard it was coming in the next issue of *Novy Mir*; they waited anxiously for it. Thousands of extra copies were printed, yet in the days after its release, Moscow bookstores ran out of the magazine. *Pravda* and *Izvestia* praised the story; Khrushchev told the plenary session of the Central Committee they should read it. The full run of 95,000 copies of the magazine had sold out entirely.

Within days, Kremlinologists were discussing the novel abroad, heralding a new openness in Soviet literature and wondering about the political implications. Weeks later, English-language translations appeared in the West, to great acclaim. The Soviet information minister felt compelled to ask aspiring Russian writers—so many of whom now seemed keen to address life in Stalin's camps—to keep in mind that there were, in fact, other subjects available to them.[57] In the pages of Western newspapers, comments like these sounded like a joke. In Moscow, they were understood to be a warning.

9

Ivan Denisovich won readers over with his plainspoken decency; *Pale Fire*'s Charles Kinbote, monster that he is, captured them with his outrageous inventions. But for all their differences, the two characters may have something in common.

In tiny asides scattered throughout the novel, Kinbote writes of the ghost toes of amputees and the "frozen mud and horror" in his heart. He compares the story of Zembla that he hoped Shade might tell to a "tale of torture written in the bruised and branded sky." He is suicidal and morbidly fascinated with the spiritual joy that death would bring.[58]

Late in *Pale Fire*, one reason for Kinbote's despair becomes clearer, when a history professor seems to recognize him. The professor has heard a good deal about Kinbote from someone—that he is actually Russian, that his name is not Kinbote but Botkin. Kinbote denies everything, declaring that the professor seems to have mistaken him for someone else. He is, Kinbote insists, "confusing me with some refugee from Nova Zembla." In case readers missed the only appearance of the words *Nova Zembla* in the novel, Kinbote adds a phrase stressing the "Nova" again in brackets in the same line, even as he rejects any link between himself and this other person the professor is thinking of, between his beautiful Zembla and the geography to which the professor would pin him.[59]

In interviews after the book's publication, Nabokov revealed that the history professor is right. Kinbote is not who he says he is; clues in the novel reveal that he *is* a Russian, and his name *is* Botkin.[60] But in the first fifty years after *Pale Fire*'s appearance, no one recalled the stories that had leaked out about Nova Zembla. No one thought it possible for Kinbote to be a refugee not just from the Zembla he had invented, but the historical Nova Zembla as well. It was not understood what such a past would mean—the tragic story that it would imply for Kinbote.

The madman's fantasy carries a grain of truth. Kinbote is no ex-king, but he did escape from Zembla. Like the first king of Nova Zembla, his rule was born in ice and suffering, in a bid to imagine that it might be possible to triumph over death. Nabokov's paranoid, broken narrator hails from a nightmare corner of the Gulag.[61]

In *Pnin*, Timofey Pnin tries to forget the terrible loss of Mira Belochkin in a German camp, because only by pushing it out of his consciousness can he stay sane. Krug, the imprisoned hero of *Bend Sinister*, is touched with madness by the book's narrator to spare him horror and grief in the wake of his son's murder. *Despair*'s Hermann, driven mad in the camps, comes to believe in a resemblance between himself and his victim that does not exist. *The Gift*'s Nikolai Chernyshevsky, "half-crushed by years of penal servitude," becomes an old man "unable to reproach himself for a single carnal thought." Humbert, launched into depravity by the death of his childhood love amid the refugee camps of Corfu, lives with nightmares of women gassed in German camps, and ceases to resist even worse impulses. *Pale Fire*'s author mercifully gives refugee Kinbote the fantasy country of Zembla itself in which to lose his Nova Zemblan past, while he begs to be delivered from "his fondness for faunlets."[62] There is hardly a novel in Nabokov's mature repertoire that does not have a major character shattered by his own imprisonment or haunted by memories of those who perished in the camps.

10

But what of *Pale Fire*'s crown jewels? If Zembla is some transformation of Nova Zembla, Kinbote's attempt to transcend his real history, what kind of crown jewels could be found there? Kinbote, for one, is absolutely sure that the agents hunting on Zembla will never find them. The question dogged readers, though some discounted the jewels as merely a McGuffin intended to render the reader as insane as Kinbote.

History finds echoes here as well. The Soviet quest to gather the Russian crown jewels after the Revolution was widely covered in Western papers; the Bolsheviks' search was reported to have led to torture and murder. The Soviets had even formed a Commission for Excavations to hunt for hidden Imperial treasure on the islands of Solovki.[63] But what treasure would Nabokov have been pointing to on Nova Zembla?

Across time, readers noticed that *Pale Fire*'s index plays all sorts of games, one of which begins with the entry for *Crown Jewels* and leads the reader in a circle. Asked in an interview where the crown jewels were hidden, Nabokov made a reference to the index but also answered directly, explaining that they lay on Zembla "in the ruins, sir, of some old barracks."[64]

The possibility of actual barracks on an actual Zembla—or what kind of treasure might be concealed in their ruins—was not pursued. But a real-world *New York Times* editorial from 1922 had more or less taken up the idea.

The week the world first learned of Russians being exiled to the desolate north, the story reported that the Bolsheviks were simultaneously hunting Imperial gems across the nation, "scrupulously guarding the crown jewels and other priceless treasures." But the paper's editors feared it would all end in tragedy. In their ignorance, Russian leaders were "throwing into the Arctic Sea or over Soviet borders a culture more precious than the wealth of these hoarded jewels." The article warned that if Russia did not stop, all its genius would be in exile, prison, or the grave, and the nation would become one vast, "shut-off Nova Zembla."[65]

The crown jewels in *Pale Fire* will never be found by the Russians hunting them because for Kinbote's author, the real treasure was the creators and inheritors of liberal Russian society, the people lost to the "torture house, the blood-bespattered wall," the "bestial terror that had been sanctioned by Lenin."[66] The real crown jewels of Zembla—of Russia—lay forgotten in the ruins of barracks in not just the distant, mysterious north, but in countless places across the Soviet Union: the dead exiles, the executed prisoners, a beautiful culture, annihilated.

Solzhenitsyn had seen the camps and lived their terrors. Nabokov, however, could not speak to their daily realities with more than borrowed knowledge. How could he tell the story of a place of horror that could barely be imagined? By constructing a fantastic, unbelievable fairy tale on top of unknowable events—the kind of fairy tale Nabokov believed all great novels were at heart, the kind he fashioned to create Zembla, weaving history into his literary vision.

Pale Fire's Charles Kinbote, imaginary king of an Arctic wasteland, stands tribute to the dead exiles and prisoners of the Soviet camps. A fictional escapee who longs to bear witness to what he has seen, he is too insane to tell his tale. Nabokov, like Solzhenitsyn, created a masterpiece memorializing the suffering of his homeland, but he buried the past so deep in madness that the elegy went entirely unnoticed.

CHAPTER THIRTEEN
Speak, Memory

———⋘———

1

In the matter of countries, Nabokov loved most devotedly from a distance. And the longer he lived at the Palace Hotel in Montreux, the easier it was to maintain his support for America without having to navigate the things that troubled him.

He had long realized where his vehement anti-Red stance landed him on the Western political spectrum—in the unwanted company of ultraconservative bigots. And so it was through literal distance that Nabokov could love a country but keep himself separate from the local species of the international fraternity he loathed—"French policemen, the unmentionable German product, the good old church-going Russian or Polish *pogromshchik*, the lean American lyncher," and the latest Soviet equivalent.[1]

As his social circle diminished, his politics became more rigid: a blanket yes to Vietnam and no to student radicals. Living in relative isolation with Véra probably did nothing to soften the stances he had taken—she was even more strident than he was—and headlines about the social upheaval in 1960s America were enough to rattle both Nabokovs.

In such a high-stakes game, Véra had become an advocate of hangings and life sentences, but when it came to the death penalty, Nabokov held fast to his father's position against it.[2] After the Kennedy assassination, Nabokov watched footage of the shooting and the newsreels of the just-captured Lee Harvey Oswald. Not yet twenty-five, a small figure in an old undershirt, Oswald was marched in to meet the press near midnight with a cut on his forehead and swelling over one eye. He seemed confused in his answers and quietly asked for legal assistance. ("How did you hurt your eye?" "A policeman hit me."[3]) Dmitri Nabokov recalled later that his father's sympathy in the moment was all for Oswald, fearing that the police had beaten an innocent man.[4]

Despite his strong personal convictions, Nabokov would not lift a finger in the world of public policy. When the California Committee Against Capital Punishment asked for his help in 1960, he acknowledged that he supported their goal without reservation but would not contribute an article saying so. He had, he told them, already written "a whole book on the subject."[5]

In his eyes his books *were* his political statements, in every sense of the word. Though Nabokov could not help but notice America's vulgarity after seeing it up close, and could not resist threading its book clubs, chewing gum, and prejudice into his stories, this was the treatment he had given almost everything he loved. But he found overt America-bashing distasteful and offensive. When it came to political systems, Nabokov had seen the competition, knew which horse he wanted to win, and was not going to do anything to trip it up.

In the spring of 1964, Nabokov returned to America for a month to promote *Eugene Onegin*. After waiting longer than *Lolita* to see the light of day, the critical edition had finally made it into print through the auspices of a private foundation. While stateside, the Nabokovs headed to Cornell to pull some materials from storage in

Ithaca. Old friends there found Nabokov more imperious than he had been in their fonder recollections, and noted that Véra looked more regal than ever.[6]

Nabokov had visited New York City briefly two years before for the premiere of Kubrick's *Lolita*, but the country to which he returned had changed in his absence. Federal troops had been sent to quell the riots that followed the forced desegregation of the University of Mississippi. Thirty-seven-year-old civil rights leader Medgar Evers had been assassinated by a reactionary the summer before. An African Cornell exchange student had been viciously beaten in Alabama that September, forcing the State Department to make an international apology to Ghana. Two weeks after Nabokov departed Ithaca for the last time, an assistant dean there launched a team-taught seminar on "The Negro Revolt" and what it would mean for America.[7]

Racism against black Americans appalled Nabokov, who had touted Pushkin's interracial background as early as 1942 at Spelman College as an argument against segregation.[8] And in his curious personal mix of conservative and liberal politics, Nabokov found an unlikely kindred spirit in President Lyndon Johnson, whose commitment to war in Vietnam and support for civil rights mixed a perfectly Nabokovian cocktail.

When Johnson had his appendix removed in the fall of 1965 and flashed his scar to reporters (an action entirely outside the possible universe for Véra, who had undergone the same procedure the year before), Nabokov sent the recovering president a telegram wishing him well and praising the "ADMIRABLE WORK YOU ARE ACCOMPLISHING."[9] Johnson had backed the Civil Rights Act the year before and the Voting Rights Act that March, both of which surely pleased Nabokov. And the sustained aerial bombardment of North Vietnam that had begun the same month (and would continue for three years) likely met with equal approval in Montreux, even as it drove tens of thousands of protesters into the streets from Berkeley to New York just days after Nabokov's telegram arrived.

Véra reserved a particular fury for the student demonstrators, wishing their universities would deal more harshly with them, believing that naïve Americans had failed to heed the warnings about Communists who had managed to infiltrate and destroy the U.S. educational system. Nabokov family friend William Buckley, running that month as a dark-horse candidate for mayor of New York City, was also unimpressed. Referring to the protesters as mincing slobs strutting their effeminate resentment, Buckley suggested they were the kind of people who "would have deserted little Anne Frank, if her tormentors had been Communists rather than Nazis."[10]

While Buckley shared the Nabokovs' views on Communism, Vladimir and Véra remained on friendly terms with several people who were less supportive of American foreign policy. Edmund Wilson, it turned out, had not even paid income tax during the 1940s and the first half of the fifties. At the urging of his wife Elena, he had tried to settle up with the IRS in 1955, but the check had bounced. He ended up in court in 1958, and the ruling against him led to liens on his royalties and the small trust fund he had inherited from his mother.[11]

Wilson had his revenge by writing a book about the experience, *The Cold War and the Income Tax: A Protest*, in which he explained that he had not begun his personal tax holiday on principle, but after looking into the IRS and its machinations, he had been deeply disturbed by its labyrinthine nature, and was going to make as little money as possible in the coming years in order to starve the agency and the U.S. imperialism he saw as funded from its coffers.

Wilson nonetheless found himself embraced by the Kennedy administration. When he was personally chosen by Kennedy for the Presidential Medal of Freedom in 1963, the IRS had sent a sixteen-page memo to the White House in protest, noting that he was in the process of writing a diatribe on income tax and the defense budget that denounced both the IRS and U.S. budgetary policy. President Kennedy had refused to retract his choice, answering, "This is not an award for good conduct but for literary merit."[12]

Wilson had not minded Kennedy's affection, but he did not share Vladimir Nabokov's high opinion of Lyndon Johnson. Reluctant to see the U.S. enter even the fight against Hitler, Wilson thought U.S. involvement in Vietnam a disgrace. When he was invited by the Johnsons to a summer arts festival, he responded with a rudeness that shocked staffers and infuriated the president. As the White House festival disintegrated into a public shellacking of the president by assorted esteemed thinkers and artists, Johnson fumed that his intellectual opponents were "sonsofbitches" and "close to traitors." He swore to have nothing else to do with them.[13]

2

In the first months of Johnson's administration, Wilson made his way to Montreux to visit Nabokov. He and Elena stayed three days, having dinner with Véra and Vladimir, and throwing a celebratory lunch for Nabokov on the second day. Wilson's wife Elena, who had come from aristocracy herself, felt Vladimir was living "like a prince of the old regime." The Nabokovs' quarters were modest enough, but Wilson, whose financial troubles had not abated, was put off by the opulence of the Palace Hotel.[14]

The two men had not seen each other for seven years. Wilson complained to a friend in the interim that Nabokov had made "a great grievance" of his dislike for *Lolita*, though his embrace of *Doctor Zhivago* had no doubt added to the strain on the friendship. During their years apart, they had continued to write to each other, but less often. In his growing isolation in Montreux, Nabokov more than once had made overtures to an increasingly silent Wilson, at times sounding plaintive ("You have quite forgotten me").[15]

Perhaps it was this longing for the closeness of their early friendship that led Nabokov to discard the wariness he had developed over the years with regard to Wilson's literary opinions. After dithering, he had hesitantly given permission for prepublication proofs of his *Onegin* to be sent to Wilson in the months before the latter's visit to Montreux—a decision which had surely provoked anxiety on both sides.[16]

But for three days in Montreux, their friendship reverted to its delightful state in the echoing, empty Palace Hotel, largely bereft of visitors in the off-season. The two men took up their "conversational fireworks" and arguments over razors as if Lenin, *Lolita*, *Zhivago*, and the slow death of their twenty-four-year correspondence did not exist.[17]

Among Nabokov's most recent books, Wilson had disliked *Lolita* but admired *Pnin*, calling it "very good." At the time of his arrival in Montreux, the record is not clear on whether he had even read *Pale Fire*, because he never weighed in on it. If he did not, it is a literary tragedy. Nabokov had threaded their shared language and arguments through his mad Zemblan tale as if creating a special dialogue that Wilson alone might understand.

A key discussion of shaving, A. E. Housman, and literary inspiration in *Pale Fire* plays directly off portions of Wilson's *The Triple Thinkers*, which Nabokov had read and critiqued. Wilson had suggested elsewhere that T. S. Eliot's verses stick in one's head; Nabokov replied to Wilson that they did not lodge in *his*—and so *Pale Fire* delivers a girl struggling with Eliot's most obscure words (*grimpen, semipiternal*). The lunatic Kinbote is seen by students in the book as "constantly quoting Housman," whom Nabokov admired but Wilson had criticized as sterile.[18]

John Shade, the very decent poet Nabokov created for *Pale Fire*, is a quintessentially American writer whose work lives in the shadow of Robert Frost. Nabokov, who expressed affection for his invented poet, had himself done readings with Frost, once being in the unenviable position of opening for him in Boston. But Wilson despised Frost, and across his career had accumulated a Nabokov-worthy list of insults against the man, calling him "third-rate," "a dreadful old fraud," and "one of the most relentless self-promoters in the history of American literature."[19]

Pale Fire includes reversed words (*spider, redips*) taken from one of Wilson's poems, "The Pickerel Pond," which also makes a passing reference to Nova Zembla.[20] After reading that poem, Nabokov had sent Wilson several examples of his own in a similar rhyme scheme—including *red wop* and *powder*, *T.S. Eliot* and *toilest*—each of which Nabokov borrowed back and folded, with *spider* and *redips*, into the pages of *Pale Fire*.[21]

Mocked by the uncaring townspeople in the novel, Kinbote is desperately trying to spin the fantasy of the lovely and beautiful Zembla, behind which Nova Zembla lurks. Along with the nods to Kinbote's horrors—which seem to be part and parcel of the early camps under Lenin that Wilson was reluctant to acknowledge—Nabokov had privately folded their literary exchanges into *Pale Fire*, as if baiting Wilson to pay attention, to do the very historical approach favored by him. But Wilson never bit.

He had not, in fact, bitten on the aspects of Nabokov's work he might have best understood for more than twenty years. Returning to Nabokov's 1941 poem "The Refrigerator Awakes," written after a stay at Wilson's house at the beginning of their friendship, it is not hard to peek behind the tale of a dedicated suburban refrigerator and find something darker. The poem, explicitly a desperate attempt to make sure a story will be told, was a first shot across the bow with Wilson, who then, as later, somehow missed or mistook the most important elements of the story at hand: the dead bodies in the ice, a "trembling white heart," the torture house, the mention of Nova Zembla, and the agony of the burden of preserving it all.[22]

3

Instead of *Pale Fire*, Edmund Wilson turned his critical faculties on *Eugene Onegin* for a 1965 essay in the July issue of *The New York Review of Books*. In the first sentence, Wilson declares Nabokov's project "something of a disappointment," and vows not to let his friendship interfere with what he intends to say. The subsequent 6,000-plus words proceed to set off depth charge after depth charge. Nabokov "seeks to torture both the reader and himself." The "lack of common sense" throughout the project led Wilson to interpret Nabokov as trying and failing to integrate his Russian and English selves.

Hating Freud, Nabokov viewed Wilson's psychologizing with equal contempt. But he had been just as biting the year before in an essay on someone else's translation of *Onegin* ("something must be done . . . to defend the helpless dead poet"[23]), and Wilson explicitly used his friend's venom as an excuse to turn Nabokov's method on Nabokov himself. He upped the ante by bringing in personal matters—mentioning Nabokov's limited knowledge of Latin and quoting from their letters.[24]

There was plenty to criticize honestly without resorting to their past correspondence. Nabokov's four-volume set had been out for a year, and other critics had been mixed in their evaluations. Several strongly disapproved of Nabokov's plodding literalism, while others acknowledged the brilliance of his massive commentary. But Wilson also attempted to question his friend's Russian, an unfathomable choice—one he was warned against by friends.[25]

Nabokov defended his *Onegin* tactically, delving even deeper into personal matters once Wilson had struck the first blow. Revealing his years of attempts to correct Wilson's errors during the latter's "long and hopeless infatuation with the Russian language," Nabokov notes how as late as 1957, Wilson had him in hysterics with his complete inability to read *Eugene Onegin* aloud, then proceeds to dismantle some of Wilson's "ghastly blunders."[26] The bulk of both men's arguments lay in dull minutiae that were surely skimmed by most readers, who were riveted only by the spectacle of two living legends skewering each other.

Wilson countered by admitting that he might have made some errors, and had realized in retrospect that his original piece sounded "more damaging than I had meant it to be."[27] Nabokov responded again at length arguing that Wilson had misunderstood the whole motivation for the story, explaining the cause of a deadly duel in *Onegin* lay in Pushkin's stress on the idea that some things, *amour propre* among them, are stronger than friendship.[28]

Having given permission in 1963 for his publisher to send copies of *Onegin* to Wilson, Nabokov believed that his friend had begun plotting his attack before he visited Montreux. Wilson actually began reading the edition much later, but Nabokov did not know the truth, and believed that his friend had played at the charade of their 1964 reunion even as he was preparing to publicly savage their friendship.[29]

And so *Onegin*'s literary duel spurred another in which no lives were lost, but the closest friendship of Nabokov's adult life was permanently broken. Wilson had somehow traveled a path from seeing Nabokov's views as "neither White Russian nor Communist" in the first months of their friendship to adopting a kind of blindness that reduced Nabokov to a stereotype.[30] Yet had Nabokov been less cryptic, or less publicly insistent on his fiction's irrelevance to the real world, and had Wilson read *Pale Fire* with half the attention he had paid to *Eugene Onegin*, the latter might have found new ways to consider so much of what went to the heart of the distance between them.

Nabokov had taken the subjects of many of their conversations and debates and immortalized them. *Pale Fire* did not just bear witness to the imprisoned and the dead of Russia, it was also a chronicle of two decades of repartee between Wilson and Nabokov, an inadvertent elegy for a friendship that would soon be lost.

4

The *Onegin* Wars alternately subsided and staggered on for more than two years, during which Nabokov offered that "Pushkin had almost as much English in the 1830s as Mr. Edmund Wilson has Russian today."[31] As if seeking to rewrite the disintegration of relations between them, Wilson drafted a piece—written under a pseudonym—in which he suggested the whole fight had been orchestrated, with his initial mistakes put in intentionally, and Nabokov's biting response actually penned by him. To his credit, Wilson's letter does not appear to have ever been submitted for publication.[32]

Nabokov did, however, send an interminable, point-by-point refutation of Wilson's piece to *Encounter* magazine for publication in February 1966. And he could not resist strafing other would-be translators with fire on the matter of *Onegin*. Nabokov was published again in *Encounter* that May, when poet Robert Lowell criticized his translation of Pushkin as a "spoof" on readers, and he, in return, asked Lowell to "stop mutilating defenceless dead poets."[33]

For internationally minded Western intellectuals, *Encounter* was a hot forum in publishing well into the 1960s. The brainchild of poet Stephen Spender and Irving Kristol, it regularly published work by notable writers, from E. M. Forster to Sylvia Plath and Jorge Luis Borges. Edmund Wilson had expanded on his early review of *Doctor Zhivago* in its pages; Mary McCarthy had written reviews for it. *Encounter* had even published Solzhenitsyn's follow-up to *Ivan Denisovich*, "Matryona's Home," a story of a beleaguered peasant woman who sacrifices everything she has to an ungrateful and blind village.

By 1963, publication in a forum with some of the most famous names in modern literature was no fluke for Solzhenitsyn. Nearly a million copies of *Ivan Denisovich* had sold in the Soviet Union alone—clearing all the print runs off the shelves. Nevertheless, Solzhenitsyn kept a low media profile, maintaining a control even beyond that exerted by Nabokov. With few exceptions, he simply refused to speak to journalists.[34]

For someone who had grown up in isolation from much of the dynamic literature of his day, Solzhenitsyn was utterly uninterested in seeing what he had missed and was willing to reject more or less everything that he had not read.[35] Whatever literary power Solzhenitsyn had acquired, it was gained in spite of his isolation. By contrast Nabokov had grown up in the embrace of centuries of culture from Russia, Europe, and America, rising to the pinnacle of an international literature that he had studied in depth. They both had read—and admired—Tolstoy and Chekhov. But Solzhenitsyn had less to build on, making it that much more extraordinary that he somehow adopted the emotional power of Tolstoy wholesale and applied it to a different kind of epic history.

After the publication of *Ivan Denisovich*, he began to hear from people who responded to that power, receiving piles of letters from those who had been in camps, who had seen their lives destroyed by the system. He wrote many of them back, asking for more detail on their stories and sending follow-up questions.[36]

His mail included scraps of notes that he recognized as having been smuggled out of the camps, which led him to the realization that despite Khrushchev's promises, the system still existed. Not only did it still exist, but Solzhenitsyn learned that Khrushchev had implemented an even more draconian regime of food restriction.[37]

Solzhenitsyn set up meetings with government officials and experts to discuss these findings and call for mercy in the treatment of the prisoners: more food, permission for family visits, and a day a week free from work. His requests were met with quiet sympathy from like-minded people but also provoked accusations that he wanted to coddle prisoners and that he misunderstood the fundamentally punitive function of the camps.[38]

Even Solzhenitsyn's fans could be critical of him. In a meeting reviewing a new manuscript, one *Novy Mir* editor noted that not only was Solzhenitsyn perpetually stressing the negative aspects of the Soviet state, he seemed to question the value of the Revolution itself. He offered no answer to the question that Chernyshevsky had asked in the nineteenth century and Lenin had addressed again in the twentieth: "What is to be done?"[39] Solzhenitsyn, like Nabokov, found himself rebuked for his focus on the dark side, his spotlight on hypocrisy, and the lack of redeeming elements in his stories.

Novy Mir's editor signed a contract for the excerpt under consideration, but then the board agonized (again) over whether they could actually print it. The publication of *Ivan Denisovich* had become a weapon in the fight over Russia's future. Khrushchev had initially been so excited by Solzhenitsyn's opus that he wanted a personal meeting with the author at his dacha, but by August 1964 he regretted championing the story.[40] Two months later, he had been erased from Party leadership.

It was too late to quash *Ivan Denisovich*, but once Khrushchev had fallen, Solzhenitsyn worried about future publication. He became caught up in a sophisticated game of proxies—his work would be attacked from one quarter, then defended from another, having more to do with disputes over upheaval in the Soviet political system than with any literary issue. *Novy Mir* seemed hesitant to push for publication, given the current atmosphere that re-chilled Khrushchev's thaw. Solzhenitsyn began to circulate some work underground in *samizdat*, and to give travelers copies of his unpublished writings to smuggle to the West.

The winter of Khrushchev's disappearance from public life, Solzhenitsyn retired to the country, where he began work in earnest on his new project documenting the history of the camps through the testimony of those who had been there. For his title, he drew on the account of Dmitri Likhachev, who had spent more than two years on Solovki. Likhachev told Solzhenitsyn that the man responsible for executions there liked to call himself the "Commander of the Forces of the Solovetsky Archipelago." Solzhenitsyn had seized on the image of an archipelago and paired it with *GULAG* to make a rhyme in Russian: *Arkhipelag GULAG*.[41]

Using his own experiences, and the accounts of more than two hundred informants who had provided him with their stories, he conveyed many events that had never been described. He noted that Maxim Gorky, who had paid tribute to the White Sea Canal project, had made a trip to Solovki, too, where a young boy had risked his life to let Gorky know the truth—the stories of mosquito torture, being forced to sit on poles for hours, and the still-living bodies thrown down hundreds of steps from the former chapel on Sekirka Hill.[42] Gorky had nonetheless given his seal of approval to the camp, signing off that even Solovki's punishment cells looked "excellent." The boy, Solzhenitsyn recorded, was shot as soon as Gorky left for the mainland.

Solzhenitsyn, wrote, too, of the nightmare of arrests, of the earliest roots of the camps, the first terrors under Lenin, and the far-flung sites to which people found themselves sent, the first group to each location often arriving with little food and no shelter.

Across the two thousand miles between himself and Nabokov, Solzhenitsyn touched on the same history. From the isolation of rural Solotcha, a village three hours from Moscow, he described how the camps began to expand out from Solovki, carrying its methods and its madness out into the most desolate corners of the nation:

> *There were also camps on Nova Zembla for many years, and the most terrible camps they were—people were confined in them "without right of correspondence." Not a single prisoner ever returned from there. Today we still do not know what those wretched people mined and built, how they lived and how they died.*[43]

Despite the silence from some of the most distant locations, Solzhenitsyn—who was called a pessimist but who saw himself as essentially optimistic—wrote that he hoped against hope one day to hear the story of those who were sent to Nova Zembla.[44]

5

After nearly a year of anxiety over whether de-Stalinization policies would be reversed or continued, it became clear that the news was not good. Liberalization was halted, and a call went out for *Novy Mir* editors to be investigated.[45]

That September, Solzhenitsyn begged for the return of the four copies of his unpublished novel sitting in a safe at the magazine's offices. After a long argument, he prevailed and delivered the copies to friends who were safeguarding his collected writing. Despite his best plans, however, a week later the KGB investigated those friends as the focus of a separate inquiry, and Solzhenitsyn's archive was confiscated.

While Solzhenitsyn agonized over whether and when the KGB would arrest him, another kind of literary intrigue shook the West. In April 1966, editors of the anti-Communist but fairly liberal *Encounter*—in which the work of both Solzhenitsyn and Nabokov had appeared—woke up to find themselves and their longtime funder, the Congress for Cultural Freedom, accused by *The New York Times* of receiving financial support from the CIA.[46]

The suggestion that some of the most liberal thinkers in the West had, wittingly or not, been supported by the CIA as potential pawns in the Cold War created a firestorm in European and American newspapers. Direct support for Nabokov's cousin Nicholas, still Secretary-General of the Congress, came quickly in the form of a letter to the editor cosigned by George Kennan, John Kenneth Galbraith, Robert Oppenheimer, and Arthur Schlesinger. It was followed the next day by an assertion of editorial independence by current and former *Encounter* editors. A week later, Nicholas Nabokov himself wrote to *The New York Times* to say that suggestions "that the Congress has been an instrument of the C.I.A. are deeply unfair to intellectuals around the world who have found in the Congress and its associated activities a chance to write and talk without constraint on the urgent issues and hopes of our age."[47]

But no one quite denied the accusation of CIA funding itself, and so the facts remained uncertain. The following May, former CIA agent Tom Braden wrote a public letter asserting that of course all those organizations had been funded by the CIA through dummy foundations. And not only that, but the CIA had placed agents in an editorial position at *Encounter* and among the staff of the Congress for Cultural Freedom. Why? Because to ignore Communism's cultural assault and cede the entire European political left to the Soviets was foolishness. Those who suggested that all the money should be run through Congress, he argued, were naïve. Socialism was a dirty word on Capitol Hill, he wrote, but it was in fact the anti-Communist left that was deemed most vital to support in the European theater. In his view, the CIA had a vested interest in using money to promote intellectual and cultural alternatives to Communism everywhere it could, including *Encounter*.[48]

Unsettled by the furor and emerging proof that the accusations were true, one of *Encounter*'s editors resigned. The Congress, which had stopped taking CIA funds even before the scheme had been discovered, was effectively blown up and reconstituted. In May of 1967, Nicholas Nabokov delivered the organization's statement of judgment against its executive director (and fellow émigré) Michael Josselson, who had, in fact, been active in American intelligence work in various ways for more than a decade. Nicholas Nabokov had known Josselson since the 1920s, and had worked with him in one way or another for nearly twenty years, but maintained publicly that he had been just as surprised as everyone else to learn about the real funding sources of the Congress.[49]

In the aftermath of the revelations, a former intelligence operative argued in the *National Review* that the truly flawed idea was that there was any value to supporting the non-Communist Left in the first place, as being anti-Communist did not necessarily indicate an affinity with American interests. The point of view was one that President Johnson, who had also had his fill of intellectuals, could sympathize with—as far as he was concerned, when it came to liberals and Communists, "They're all the same."[50]

Though Nabokov had long held up the Socialist Revolutionaries to Edmund Wilson as an example of anti-Bolshevik radicals committed to overthrowing the Tsar, he had likewise become less inclined to make distinctions. After several years of partnership with Harvard linguist Roman Jakobson in the 1950s, Nabokov had withdrawn from the literary project they had been working on.[51] Jakobson had returned to the Soviet Union the year before for a conference, and Nabokov wrote to say that he would not tolerate such "little trips to totalitarian countries." Nabokov was also reported to have begun calling Jakobson "a Bolshevist agent," though he had belonged to the Kadets, the party of Nabokov's father, before the Revolution. The real reason for Nabokov's denunciation may, like Lyndon Johnson's rage, have had more to do with his plans being foiled than anything else—Jakobson had torpedoed Nabokov's chances when his name had been put forward for a post at Harvard.[52]

If Nabokov never wavered on his stand against visiting the Soviet Union himself, he was keen for his novels to make the trip without him. Contacted by Radio Liberty, Nabokov enthusiastically supported a plan to distribute his novels inside Russia, packaged in editions cloaking their origins. Given that his own brother, Kirill, had worked with Radio Liberty in the 1950s, it is not clear whether Nabokov knew that it, too, had been created and funded as part of the culture war brainstormed by George Kennan and executed by the CIA.[53] But he was more than pleased with the goals of the mission, regretting only that *Lolita* would not be its first emissary.

Nabokov allowed others to send his novels out as weapons in the Cold War, but even an appeal from anti-Soviet dissidents could not spur him to direct engagement. In the midst of tumultuous times in Russia, a group of students from Leningrad managed to smuggle a message out to him via a visiting scholar. But Nabokov's policy was straightforward: he did not engage with people inside the Soviet Union under any circumstances, for fear of the danger contact would represent for them.[54] In addition, it was explained in a letter sent back to the intermediary that, while those who wished to contact Nabokov might be genuine in their dissidence, it was not at all clear what their objectives were, and whether they were truly committed to freedom as it was understood in the West. It was a demanding litmus test for a generation born decades after the Revolution.

Véra answered the letter, as she did almost all Nabokov's correspondence, and wrote that "every book by VN is a blow against tyranny."[55] Nabokov knew any number of people in the anti-Communist political realm who might have connected with the young dissidents if he were not prepared to play at Cold War intrigue himself, or if he were worried that the overture was a KGB trick. But in the end, he seems to have meant his books to do that work on his behalf. No one would be arrested, or die, because of anything *he* had done. The enormous political and intellectual talents of Nabokov's father and his allies had ultimately proved insufficient to save his country. By not engaging directly, Nabokov could be certain he would do no harm and could never be history's fool.

Nabokov's name was not on the tip of everyone's tongue in Russia, as was Solzhenitsyn's. But just as he feared, those students who had reached out to him but to whom he did not respond were later rounded up, for other reasons, by the KGB. In subsequent years members of the group were arrested, put in prison, or sent to military service. Others were effectively exiled to desolate places in the Ural Mountains or Kolyma—one of them for possessing the stories of Vladimir Nabokov.[56]

6

After *Pale Fire*, Nabokov returned to his autobiography. He had translated it into Russian years before, and now he worked from that version to revisit the first four decades of his life again. Incorporating photos and additional genealogical history into *Speak, Memory*, he corrected errors he had noticed or that had been pointed out by others. And as if still caught up in the cross-referential mania of *Pale Fire*, he added a foreword and an index, which had its own wide-ranging, cross-linked entry for *Jewels*. He winked again toward *Pale Fire* with the inclusion of both *Nova Zembla* ("of all places," as he notes), and its Russian name, *Novaya Zemlya*, in the index.[57]

Nabokov also spent two paragraphs honoring his youngest brother Kirill, who had died unexpectedly of a heart attack in 1964. Speaking kindly of his brother's writing and his love for Russian poetry, Nabokov acknowledged that they had lived separate lives for most of four decades before being happily reunited in the last years of Kirill's life.[58]

But the most significant change Nabokov made related to his other brother, Sergei. Left more or less unchanged were the thirty-one references made to him in *Conclusive Evidence*. But where Nabokov had tapered off sixteen years before with stories about his brother, he became more expansive. After fleeing St. Petersburg with Vladimir by train in 1917, Sergei appears where he had not earlier, in the Crimea, remaining with his brother for their last months in Russia. A "well-known painter" and a "male ballet artist" have been

THE SECRET HISTORY OF VLADIMIR NABOKOV

added to the Crimean scenes, too, as if to provide Sergei his own companions in Yalta.[59]

Nabokov also inserted two entirely new pages about Sergei. In a passage that begins, "For various reasons, I find it inordinately hard to speak about my other brother," he details the many ways in which the second-born Sergei was relegated to a shadow existence. Less coddled by their parents, Sergei practices piano only to be poked in the ribs by Vladimir, who describes himself as "something of a bully."[60] Nabokov goes on to describe his discovery of Sergei's homosexuality—though that word never appears—through reading his diary. Because he gave the diary to their tutor, he explains, his parents eventually saw the entries, too.

What else did he have to say that he had not in *Conclusive Evidence*? Sergei was left-handed; he played tennis; he had a profound, lifelong stammer. They were in different colleges at Cambridge but shared some friends and graduated with the same degree. They both tutored students in English and Russian—Sergei in Paris, Nabokov in Berlin. The two and a half years before Nabokov fled the country, they saw each other in France on "quite amiable" terms. Nabokov departed for St. Nazaire and America without saying good-bye. During the war, "frank and fearless" Sergei became a translator in Berlin, Nabokov wrote, and criticized the Nazis in front of co-workers, for which he was arrested and sent to a concentration camp in Hamburg, where he died in January 1945.

In Vladimir Nabokov's worlds, characters' lives crescendo in grotesque events—Lolita's mother is killed by a car, *Bend Sinister*'s Mariette is gang-raped by soldiers, Hazel Shade and Kinbote commit suicide, Lolita dies in childbirth. Perhaps it is no wonder, given that Nabokov's real life dead met such bitter ends.

As with so many of the striking events of his life, Nabokov found ways to memorialize the dead in his fiction. In *The Gift*, the beloved larger-than-life father of the writer Fyodor goes missing on an expedition to Central Asia. Fyodor and his mother manage to go on with their lives, but continue, a decade later, to collaborate in preserving their shared memories. And in sleep, he cannot keep away a vivid dream of restoration of all that has been lost and the suffocating joy of his father's embrace.[61] Nabokov, too, dreamed of his lost father.

In *Pale Fire*, the gentle, generous John Shade expresses his faith in the universe only to be shot moments later by a madman who has mistaken him for someone else. Like V. D. Nabokov, another casualty of a botched assassination attempt, he is killed by a bullet that pierces his heart. Biographer Brian Boyd has noted that along with the obvious similarities, John Shade is shot on V. D. Nabokov's birthday, placing "the most grotesquely tragic moment of Nabokov's life" at the heart of the book.[62]

But Vladimir Nabokov's expanded autobiography reveals another chamber of *Pale Fire*'s trembling, strange heart. If Kinbote's crazy Zembla is a fantasy take on the real-world Nova Zembla, then Charles Kinbote is likewise a fantastic distortion of Sergei Nabokov, another left-handed, imprisoned, homosexual, tennis-playing Russian exile who speaks out against tyranny and dies at the age of forty-four.[63]

7

In 1945, Nabokov had asked his cousin Nicholas to find out what he could about Sergei's final months. A decade later, he had the fictional Timofey Pnin travel to Washington, D.C., to see what he could discover about the death of Mira Belochkin. Pnin unearthed some information, as did Nabokov, but there are many things that will never be known.

Here is the little that can be said: Sergei Vladimirovich Nabokov (listed in camp records as Sergej Nabokoff) had been arrested once before, on charges of homosexual activity. But it was his second arrest, for making subversive statements, that made the fatal difference, delivering him to Neuengamme Concentration Camp in the spring of 1944.[64]

By the time Sergei arrived at Neuengamme, track had been laid to allow trains to carry prisoners directly to the camp itself. The move toward efficiency had not been made in the prisoners' interest, but it allowed them to avoid the five-mile march from the next closest station, in the Hamburg suburb of Bergedorf.

Coming off the packed train cars on the grounds of the camp, the arrival ceremony was unchanging. Dogs bayed, the SS cracked whips to roust stragglers, and as prisoners launched themselves out onto the gravel or the ground (there was no actual platform), the officers barked orders in German without attention to whether the prisoners understood.[65] Lined up in rows of five and marched from the southern end of the camp up toward the parade ground, the prisoners had time to survey the barbed wire, the devastated landscape, the thatched roofs of the distant houses like some illustration from the Brothers Grimm, and the rural fields stretching away into nothing.

Prisoners were marched to the center of camp for their first roll call, at which those who had died or been executed en route were accounted for. Herded down into the cellars of one of the large buildings, the newcomers were soon relieved of any personal possessions they had brought with them. Stripped, shaved, and deloused, they were issued clothing cobbled together out of a motley assortment gathered from different nationalities—a Hungarian blouse here, a Soviet hat still sporting its red star there—all finished off with rectangular sections of cloth nicknamed "Russian socks." Wooden-soled clogs rounded out their ensembles; they would be given striped prisoners' uniforms later if they were sent to work offsite.

Unlike Auschwitz or Treblinka, Neuengamme was not one of the death camps, where genocide was the overriding goal and efficient extermination an optimized process. But when the extermination of Jewish prisoners was set forth as policy in 1942, a contingent of Jewish prisoners had been called out with other groups for execution. Not until 1944 did other Jewish prisoners arrive at Neuengamme.

Medical experiments had been conducted on homosexual prisoners elsewhere, but at Neuengamme, the clinical atrocities were limited to an experimental treatment for lice-born typhus and a fatal experiment infecting twenty Jewish children with tuberculosis near the end of the war.[66] There were, however, many other death rituals. Guards shot prisoners after forcing them to try to escape. People committed suicide by throwing themselves on the electric fence. A gallows was part of the camp topography. And behind it all lurked the crematorium.

Prisoners were assigned individual numbers, which were stamped on a small zinc tag and tied with string around their necks.[67] Sergei was prisoner No. 28631.

The duties he was assigned would have made all the difference in the world. For those assigned to tasks nearby, the horrific chore of digging in the clay pits had mostly given way to work in the small-arms factory, and then to offsite projects, working as slave labor in factories, digging anti-tank trenches to block Allied advances, and clearing rubble after bombing raids.[68]

The statelessness that had plagued Nabokov in France may have benefitted Sergei in the camps. With no nationality on record (and thus not noted on his clothing), Sergei was likely spared the harshest work regimes and brutal measures reserved for Russians, more than four hundred of whom had been killed with Zyklon B in a gas chamber at the camp before his arrival.[69] Being arrested a second time for an offense other than homosexual activity may have likewise liberated him from the additional abuse that often resulted from wearing the pink triangle that identified the homosexuals held at Neuengamme.

A typical day would begin at 5:00 A.M. Prisoners had twenty minutes to wash and shave, if they could get to fresh water at all in the overcrowded facilities. But shaving was not optional, as failure to pass inspection could lead to punishment. The resourceful Sergei, who had once taken a bath with a single glass of water, was likely unable to brush his teeth.[70]

Foods that were ghosts of coffee, bread, and marmalade were served in the barracks, and then prisoners lined up in blocks for roll call before being assigned to work parties. Daily work shifts were fourteen hours, with a midday meal to break up the monotony. Every prisoner had to carry his own tin and spoon, but not everyone got full rations, or even food.

At the end of the day roll call was repeated. But with stragglers, some sick and some dying, evening roll call could take as long as three hours, and with it, any free time in the barracks before going to bed. In the earlier days of the camp, before Sergei's arrival, the evening tally had been handled by the SS, who were sloppy and slow in accounting for their ten thousand charges, which meant regular misery for prisoners forced to wait at attention. But by 1944, a former businessman with prior experience accounting for personnel had taken charge and, mindful of the agony of the prisoners at the end of the day, did what he could to wrap up matters quickly.[71]

In that strange calculus of the tiny accommodations made to prisoners, even those held in many Nazi camps were allowed to receive care packages, and Sergei did. After the war, people called the Nabokov cousins in Paris to tell the family that he had distributed clothes and food he received to his fellow prisoners.[72]

Not much more can be known with certainty. At night, in the window that sometimes existed after roll call and before bed, there was one hour in which prisoners could clean their clothes and their equipment. They were not allowed to leave the barracks, but they could talk with some freedom. And as the prisoners had in the internment camps of the First World War, amid the horrors of Solovki, and in the fifty years since the first concentration camps had been built, they gathered and talked about the world that existed outside the camp, the things that were gone and yet could not be taken away. They talked about their favorite foods and exchanged recipes; they shared stories of home and loved ones; they offered up their fantasies and their memories.[73]

More than a hundred thousand inmates were assigned a prisoner number at Neuengamme; only half survived. The average life expectancy of a prisoner on arrival was twelve weeks.[74] Sergei Nabokov may have arrived healthier than most, or, with his multiple fluencies, he may have drawn administrative rather than more brutal general work duties. He lasted an extraordinary ten months. It cannot be said, however, whether those months were a curse or a mercy, because, in the end, they were not long enough. He died on January 10, 1945.[75]

It was three impossible months before the American Army would liberate Buchenwald and Dachau to the south, moving with such speed that the camp staff at those places were not effectively able to ensure the destruction of the records that would so clearly indict them.[76]

Neuengamme, however, was the very last camp to be liberated; the first British advance scouts would not arrive until May 2—which left several additional weeks for records to be destroyed. Much of the administrative minutiae that would have made it possible to pair a life outside the camp to a life inside it were burned in the Neuengamme crematorium.[77]

But the surviving Neuengamme prisoners, who were anxious to tell the stories of what had happened, had known that they would need evidence. So they hid records where they could. Among the items saved were laboratory journals with results of tests on inmates' bodily fluids—the only proof of the presence of thousands of prisoners who had died in the camp—and the *Totenbuch*, the book that recorded the death of Sergei Nabokov.

8

From Hermann to Kinbote, in Nabokov's writing it is often the madman, the murderer, life's losers, or those regarded as freaks who have seen the most. ("Let us bless the freak," Nabokov once told his students.) Attempting to escape history, they tumble into insanity, yet cannot elude their pasts.

Pale Fire's narrator is melodramatic and self-centered, and is often seen as the villain of the book. He is no mirror copy of Sergei, but his presence in the novel becomes a rebuke against readers who judge without divining the full story, as well as a plea for a kind of tolerance that Nabokov struggled and failed to offer to his own brother. Sergei's life, Nabokov writes in *Speak, Memory*, "hopelessly claim[s] a belated something—compassion, understanding, no matter what—which the mere recognition of such a want can neither replace nor redeem."[78]

By revising his autobiography to include details on Sergei's life years after *Pale Fire*'s publication, Nabokov made it possible for yet another understanding of his most innovative book to emerge. In his own lectures, Nabokov had said that all "great novels are great fairy tales." The executioner in *Invitation to a Beheading* announces, "Only in fairy tales do people escape from prison."[79] And so Nabokov created a fairy tale in which a problematic, fictionalized version of his flamboyant dead brother could escape a continent littered with camps. A resurrected sibling could parachute into America to deliver a litany not of his own suffering but the wild fantasies and poetry with which he had consoled himself in a place of horror, as if it were possible (four months too late, twenty years too late) to peek into his diary again and unearth his private imaginings. Part elegy for the victims of the Gulag, *Pale Fire* also shimmers as a memorial to the dead of Nabokov's own life.

CHAPTER FOURTEEN

Waiting for Solzhenitsyn

———∞∞∞———

1

After revising *Speak, Memory*, Nabokov would spend his last decade moving further away from the world, falling deeper into his created universes. His relative isolation in his "portable Winter Palace" at Montreux separated him from many of the mundane settings and human interactions that had provided a compelling present within which he could conceal the past.[1] As a result, the past and the present wrestled for control of his work, and the coherence, often as not, was lost.

He had not yet finished reminding readers of the forgotten past and hypocrisies of the present, but he would do so less and less vibrantly. His last years were split between novels that wandered through decades without the discipline that had focused his best writing and books that addressed death and its aftermath.

Nabokov, like his mother, acknowledged signs and portents, and paid particular attention to his dreams. He had always had nightmares—one from his last years included guillotines set up in his bedroom for Véra and himself. But in the decade after revising *Speak, Memory*, his nights were also full of reveries that crossed unbridgeable gaps. He dreamed of Sergei. He imagined Edmund Wilson coming up behind him and surprising him, triggering a happy reunion. Another night, Nabokov's father came to visit, sitting pale and glum on an imaginary beach.[2]

In between dreams, he completed *Ada, Or Ardor: A Family Chronicle*, a novel sprung out of concepts of time and distance that he had been thinking about for years. Beginning with a reversal of the start of *Anna Karenina*—"All happy families are more or less dissimilar; all unhappy ones are more or less alike"—Nabokov portrayed an inverted take on family life.

Keeping with his penchant for shocking sexual situations, he moved from the mock-incest scenario of stepfather Humbert in *Lolita* to a simpler brother-sister pairing. The sibling lovers of the novel, Van and Ada, are two difficult people living in an alternate reality caught up in an intermittent but lifelong affair, their existences studded with bits of lost and reinvented literature and history.

The book, Nabokov's longest novel, skitters through a maze of puns, wordplay, subplots, and winking references to everything from Chekhov to the book of Genesis. With a loose narrative of the lovers' grievous separation and joyful reunion stringing it all together, *Ada* is by far Nabokov's most rambling work. But as with nearly all Nabokov's mature writing, a sense of a menacing history operates in the background, hinting that Van and Ada have concealed something in their complex reminiscences. Oblique and unconnected nods to blood-filled mosquitoes in a secret location, capital "T" Terror, the grotesque rape of a young boy by Van, and a "first prison term" at a putative school further destabilize the landscape.[3]

Van and Ada's home world, Demonia, is an amalgam of nineteenth- and twentieth-century Earthlike settings. On Demonia, the empire of Tartary rules in the East, and Russians, including Van and Ada's forebears, were transported years before to settle in North America. Legends persist of another, or real, world named

ANDREA PITZER

Terra, but belief in Terra is viewed a form of mental illness, and as a psychiatrist-psychologist, Van studies patients who have such delusions. In his youth, Van writes the book *Letters from Terra* under a pseudonym, recounting these patients' beliefs, but it is read by only a handful of people.

Yet it is the strange world of Demonia—which Van at times navigates upside down, walking on his hands—that may be nothing more than a figment of Van and Ada's imagination. As they begin to detail their family's life on Demonia early in the book, Ada wonders in a parenthetical note if they should describe with such enthusiasm a place which may not have existed outside of the study of dreams. Midway through the novel, Van wonders if he is merely dreaming inside another dream. Elsewhere, Ada says to him excitedly, "You believe, you believe in the existence of Terra?" saying she knows he wants to prove the reality of the other world.[4]

Decades later, a famous director uses old documentary films to turn Van's book about Terra into a wildly popular movie. In the last pages of the book, however, after recounting the craze for stories from Terra that briefly promotes Van to fame, our narrators describe all the letters Van receives from thousands of believers who are convinced that their government has hidden the truth from its people. The ideas of those believers bleed into Van's description of events until it sounds as if it is him talking, and the story that Van and Ada have so carefully constructed across more than five hundred pages unravels: "Our world *was*, in fact, mid-twentieth-century. Terra convalesced after enduring the rack and the stake, the bullies and beasts that Germany inevitably generates when fulfilling her dreams of glory. Russian peasants and poets had not been transported . . . ages ago—they were dying, at this very moment, in the slave camps of Tartary."[5]

Nabokov once again provided, or allowed his characters to construct, a delusion which protects them from reality, even as the epic events of Nabokov's lifetime—the existence of the Holocaust and the Gulag—cannot be excised from the book. Van and Ada seek

THE SECRET HISTORY OF VLADIMIR NABOKOV

refuge in each other and reassemble the last centuries of history in a distorted world in which the apparently mentally ill are the ones most aware of reality, and those who know the truth are subjects for psychiatric study.

The world that Van and Ada spin out of their fantastic imaginings turns inevitably back to the camps—which may have been in the background all along. It seems relevant to note that as Nabokov worked on *Ada*, newspapers and magazines were busy detailing the ways in which psychiatric analysis was used to punish Soviet dissidents. The practice was hardly new—for decades, the noncompliant had been consigned to mental hospitals. But such psychiatric abuses became common knowledge in the 1960s as Russia resorted again to high-profile trials. Russian writer Valery Tarsis was sentenced to a mental hospital for publishing his material abroad, and his case became a *cause célèbre* in the West until he was given permission to emigrate.[6]

Soviet psychiatric "treatment" was ubiquitous enough that it could provide material for comedy. One 1964 editorial on Khrushchev's invisibility in the weeks after his fall from grace suggested that the former leader himself might have been condemned to the involuntary hospitalization inflicted on so many others during his years in power. During Nabokov's final year working on *Ada*, newspapers worldwide reported on a group of Soviet mathematicians who had made a public statement against the institutionalization of their colleague in a psychiatric hospital after he protested the trial of dissident intellectuals.[7]

But upon publication, Nabokov's *Ada* was not viewed as a commentary on modern Russia, and was instead embraced, or loathed, for its fantastic elements, the ways in which it seemed to scramble reality, rather than the ways it echoed bleak current events. A gaggle of studio heads with *Lolita* on their minds made their way to Montreux, where each took his turn with the manuscript and was given a chance to bid on its film rights.[8]

As Nabokov's characters invented an alternate Russia, his sister Elena made plans to visit to see its real-world counterpart.

Beginning in 1969, she started making trips to the Soviet Union nearly every year.[9] Nabokov, who had cut off collaborating with Roman Jakobson over his visit, seems not to have begrudged his sister her travels.

Nabokov did not go to the Soviet Union, but made plans to visit Israel instead. He had been invited late in 1970 and wanted to see butterflies there; however, the Nabokovs' interest was an extension of Nabokov's politics, too. Supporting Israel as an anti-Soviet, democratic state, Vladimir and Véra had cancelled a French vacation in 1967 in protest over the French response to the Six-Day War.[10]

After anti-Israeli attacks, Nabokov tagged her neighbors as Bolshevik stooges and sent money to the Israeli Embassy in Berne noting as much. No fan of religious restrictions, however, he also contributed to the cause of a former Tenishev classmate in Israel, who was promoting greater freedoms for non-Orthodox Jews in Israel. And he continued to send money to the organizations that had directly helped him: the Russian Literary Fund and the Union of Russian Jews.[11]

He had only a single note to sound with friends on the international threat of Communism, but for all his stridency, he sometimes did sit silent. Nabokov told a visitor to Montreux that among their left-leaning acquaintances in Montreux, he "just wouldn't talk about Vietnam." Véra, coaxing old friends to visit, promised not to "discuss Viet Nam or anything political."[12]

But Cold War dynamics lapped at the borders of everything, as politics had for Nabokov's entire life. Just weeks after *Ada*'s publication in the spring of 1969, Nabokov and Solzhenitsyn were both honored by the Academy of Arts and Letters, under the direction of George Kennan, who had been elected president of the Academy.

Nabokov had planned to attend the ceremony, but Véra developed an eye condition, which prohibited travel. Solzhenitsyn was likewise absent, sitting in Moscow, where he had just turned learned that the Writers' Union was toying with the notion of expelling him.

Kennan gave prepared remarks, promoting the value of the arts in a troubled era. "What is essential," he said, "is the will to self-expression with grace and subtlety and power."[13] Though one of the writers he was referencing got credit only for his grace, and the other only for his power, two more self-expressive authors can hardly be imagined.

2

In the wake of *Lolita*, a field of Nabokovians emerged to quiz and take down the words of the master and puzzle over his cryptic phrases. By then deeply committed to a public façade he had created for himself—the genteel, charming cosmopolitan, incapable of being dented or diminished by history—Nabokov lived long enough to monitor the first wave of chroniclers.

Alfred Appel, a former student of Nabokov's from Cornell, had by 1970 assembled an annotated version of *Lolita*, which bracketed the novel with more than 200 pages of literary references, translations of foreign phrases, and attention to recurring themes. Appel had noticed a number of things in the novel that had escaped most readers, and he had the good luck of having a complicit Vladimir Nabokov to point out several more.

Among the fairy-tale history and the Edgar Allan Poe references, Appel identified "the anti-Semitism theme" running through *Lolita*. It was to Appel that Nabokov mentioned Humbert's pity for Lolita's classmate, who was Jewish.[14] Appel also pointed out ideas echoed or amplified in *Lolita* that were bound up with earlier or later works. Trying to explain the novel, he invoked lines from Nabokov's 1923 version of the Wandering Jew story, but Appel assumed that the many people in *Lolita* who believe Humbert is Jewish were mistaken.[15]

Nabokov seemed delighted to have Appel annotating his work—he referred to him with glee in a conversation with a visiting translator as "my pedant. . . . Every writer should have one."[16] Across their relationship, he repaid Appel's diligent work with treasures, in the form of friendship and the interview in which Nabokov identified the location of *Pale Fire*'s crown jewels.

In his hunt for an authorized biographer, Appel would have been a natural choice for Nabokov, but he did not read Russian. And so Nabokov turned to Andrew Field. Field had gotten his master's at Columbia University and then had been part of a Harvard exchange program with Moscow University. During Nabokov's final visit to America in 1964, Field had approached him to give him a book acquired during his stay in the Soviet Union—a collection of essays on criminal law written by Nabokov's father.[17]

A gift of something so rare could only have warmed Nabokov's heart, and he reviewed carefully the draft manuscript of a book Field was preparing on Nabokov's writing. Nabokov invited Field to do a bibliography of his work, and in 1968 Field asked if he might write an actual biography of Nabokov, a question that was answered in the affirmative.[18]

In addition to being a known quantity, Field may have seemed appealing for other reasons as well. He had by then written about pre-Revolutionary Russian literature and Soviet fiction for several years. He also had an understanding of the circumstances of Soviet life that most young and literary Americans did not. Traveling from Moscow with his wife in 1964, Field had gotten into a disagreement with guards on the Soviet-Polish border. An ostensible problem with his visa escalated into confrontation, and he was arrested. The matter turned into an international incident—the State Department had called a press conference about the young American held captive by the Polish authorities. Field spent ten days in jail before being released on bond. Two weeks after his release, he stood trial on charges of assaulting an officer. Field was convicted and given an eight-month sentence, but the sentence was suspended. He had to wait two more weeks before being given permission to depart Poland. The compelling story made for articles day after day in the first weeks of February, totaling more than a half-dozen wire reports from the Associated Press and United Press International on his detention.[19]

In subsequent years, Field's experience gave him a kind of authority in writing about the work of some Soviet authors whose work had been carried to the West. When two dissident writers were put on trial in the Soviet Union in 1966, a trial transcript was smuggled out and published abroad.[20] In statements under interrogation, one of the defendants had quoted Field's statements about his work. Field himself in turn had been invited by *The New York Times* to review the published transcript of the dissidents' trial. For these reasons and others, Nabokov may well have thought that he had found a kindred spirit, a hardworking scholar devoted to his work who understood something of the dangers of Soviet life, not to mention anxiety over identity papers and visas.

Field's visits to Montreux started even before he had taken on the role of authorized biographer. He talked to Nabokov's friends and relations, asking questions in an attempt to address angles that *Speak, Memory* had not. Nabokov in conversation could be playfully revelatory, but at times he remained enigmatic.

On the topic of the Holocaust, it was clear that Nabokov had more to say—despite the encroaching infirmities of age, he informed Field that he was in no way done with writing about what had happened. One day, he declared, he would even *visit* Germany—something he had said he would never do—in order to see for himself the places in which atrocities had been committed: "I will go to those German camps and *look* at those places and write a *terrible* indictment." Field noted that he had never heard Nabokov speak so emotionally about anything.[21]

With regard to Sergei, however, Nabokov did not venture very far from the material included in *Speak, Memory*, except to note how very fastidious his brother had been, and that he had been friends with Jean Cocteau, who had once called Sergei's apartment with a warning that his line was tapped.[22]

Nabokov had defied history, and when writing his own story he emphasized that narrative arc. Recounting his family's shipboard flight from Russia in his autobiography, Nabokov had described the old-world gallantry of playing chess with his father as the Bolsheviks fired on the vessel. Nabokov had not mentioned the Cartier staff calling the police on him in Paris in 1919; he did not discuss the lice or the dog biscuits from the crossing that his sister Elena described to Field.

Nabokov did not mind portraying himself in an occasionally unpleasant light, even as "precious"—but the identity of the victim, the displaced person, the man humiliated by history, was one he utterly rejected. Like his father writing a legal article on the topic of solitary confinement while actually serving a sentence in solitary, Nabokov's persona was built around having triumphed despite history's betrayals. He would never display his wounds publicly. Asked by Field about the details Elena had provided on their flight from Russia after the Revolution, Nabokov acknowledged that they were all probably true but "wince[d] at such obvious refugee clichés."[23]

In his first years of conversation with Field, Nabokov seems to have felt regret for savaging the work of a poet who later died in the Holocaust, and even about the brisk trade in insults that had inspired him decades before to turn the name of critic Georgy Adamovich into *Sodomovich*. Field would later note that Nabokov apparently felt better about it by 1973, when he insulted Adamovich again.[24]

But Nabokov did not want his own style of criticism turned on him. Discussing with Field the deconstruction he had done on the reputation of revolutionary icon Chernyshevsky in *The Gift*, he realized the danger he was in, then paused and pointedly told Field that the biography they were working on "musn't be written this way."[25]

But Field showed every sign of disregarding Nabokov's injunction. He, too, seems to have been interested in looking beyond the legend crafted for history, humanizing the man, and not taking him at his word. The relationship that had developed between Field and the Nabokovs across several years began to cool. Nabokov claimed to Field that he was listening to nonsense from others; Field protested that he had talked, in many cases, to the people to whom Nabokov had sent him. Field occasionally sailed off into strange places—for instance, that V. D. Nabokov "might have been the illegitimate son of Tsar Alexander II." Nabokov began to feel misunderstood by Field, who could also be wobbly on dates.[26]

When Nabokov eventually reviewed Field's manuscript, his disappointment was profound. The biographer he himself had chosen had not written the story he had hoped would be told. He began marking up the manuscript, correcting items, cutting quotes, asking for changes, and denying statements that had been made about him.

As if in response, for his next novel, *Look at the Harlequins!*, Nabokov turned to yet another mad narrator and the conflicting biographies that can exist for one person. Not surprisingly, the narrator Nabokov chose was a man very much like him—Vadim Vadimovich, a Russian exile and writer.

Fragments of the narrator's life are fed back to him in strange form—others seem to know a good deal of information about someone they take him to be but whom he does not recognize as himself. But rather than making the supporting characters completely off-base in their descriptions about the narrator, Nabokov often gives them ammunition from his own life.

Vadim Vadimovich sees himself as distinct from the person that the characters in the book believe him to be, but those characters, with striking consistency, know *our* Nabokov. A bookstore owner recalls that the narrator attended operas with his brother and father, an illustrious member of the First Duma with an Anglophilic manner of speaking. But the mentally ill Vadim Vadimovich is spared the painful memories that Nabokov had about his own father—he maintains that the brother, the father, the opera, the Duma, none of it had anything to do with him. His father, he explains, died six months before his birth.[27]

The novel touches on bits of Nabokov's plots and themes, pointing to a scattershot series of possibilities readers had missed in previous books, and showing that earlier hints he had dropped still preoccupied him decades later. In a nod to *Lolita*, the Russian narrator is accused of betraying his genius and his country to write obscene stories about a little girl raped by a man who, he notes, tucked in among other things, may be "some Austrian Jew."[28] Twenty years on, Nabokov was still directing readers to details in *Lolita* that had not been explored.

On the same page, readers learn from the same character that two other people in the book—a couple living in the Soviet Union—were separated for years when one of them was sentenced to labor camps and psychiatric treatment for his "mystical mania."[29] The lovers, still wildly infatuated with each other, are reunited in the end, when the patient is "cured" and released. No one recognized this brief subplot in a late and minor Nabokov novel as an echo of an earlier storyline and a way to untangle the shattered wonderworld that is *Ada*.

The self-referential madness of the narrator crashes again and again against the rocks of Nabokov's preoccupations from his own life and century. The gentle Jewish-Russian bookseller, with his tender memories of *our* Nabokov's father, later dies trying to escape "in bloodstained underwear from the 'experimental hospital' of a Nazi concentration camp."[30] Near the close of the book, the narrator survives a clandestine re-entry into the Soviet Union, a quest another Nabokov character had embarked on four decades earlier.

If Nabokov meant these roundabout references as clues to the things readers had not yet found in his work, why did he conceal material that was important to him so deeply in the first place? If he was bearing witness to the atrocities of his century, what could be gained from this stealth method?

During his years as a professor, Nabokov himself had spoken on how to approach works of genius:

> Literature, real literature, must not be gulped down like some potion which may be good for the heart or good for the brain—the brain, that stomach of the soul. Literature must be taken and broken to bits, pulled apart,

squashed—then its lovely reek will be smelt in the hollow of the palm, it will be munched and rolled upon the tongue with relish; then, and only then, its rare flavor will be appreciated at its true worth and the broken and crushed parts will again come together in your mind and disclose the beauty of a unity to which you have contributed something of your own blood.[31]

In Nabokov's universe, art which does not challenge, which does not draw blood, is not art. Out of the relics of tragedy, he created literature which calls on readers to examine not just history but also their own assumptions in their own place and time. But only by diving deep into the heart of his books, only by earning their secrets, is it possible to understand the most profound aspects of what he had expressed.

Near the end, perhaps because he did not know if some connections would ever be made, Nabokov let some tricks tumble out of his sleeves. But still he waited for readers to meet him halfway—he did not strip his art entirely of its deceptions. He repudiated the story Field had created from his life, but he did not have long left to fashion whatever he had left to say himself. *Look at the Harlequins!* was the last novel he would finish before his death.

3

An endless authorial loop of reflection and masks is appropriate as a final novel for Nabokov's last years. Field noted later that Nabokov seemed occasionally to get lost in the many versions of himself he had created for his life and his books, to a degree that he may have ended up unsure whether or not any given statement was made in earnest. This was particularly apparent in Nabokov's tendency to describe Edmund Wilson as a very old friend, "in certain ways my closest."[32] He used the same line repeatedly in a stylized bit of theater after which he would eye the recipient of the comment knowingly.

But for all the façade behind which he alternately hid and revealed himself, Nabokov seems to have missed the friendship with Wilson deeply. Years after his dream of a reunion, at a point when both friends had become very old men recording lists of illnesses in their journals, Nabokov wrote to Wilson after hearing he was sick. Saying that he had reread the whole of their long correspondence, Nabokov noted "the warmth of your many kindnesses, the various thrills of our friendship, the constant excitement of art and intellectual discovery." He wanted his friend to know that he did not bear a grudge, and no longer held Wilson's "incomprehensible incomprehension of Pushkin's and Nabokov's *Onegin*" against him.[33]

Wilson responded immediately with a note saying he would correct his own *Onegin* mistakes and point out more of Nabokov's errors in a forthcoming volume on his Russian articles. He related that he had, in fact, had a stroke and now had trouble using his right hand. Warning Nabokov of another volume coming out which would revisit his 1957 trip to the Nabokovs' home in Ithaca, Wilson hoped it would not further crimp relations between them. Despite the warmth of Nabokov's letter and Wilson's polite reply, after mailing his letter back to Nabokov, Wilson shared his feelings about Nabokov in a letter to a friend, writing about how "it always makes [Nabokov] cheerful to think that his friends are in bad shape."[34]

Upstate, Wilson's account of his trip to Ithaca, came out later in 1971. The book provided vivid details with much interpretation by Wilson. Nabokov, he suggested, had triumphed despite "miseries, horrors, and handicaps" that "would have degraded or broken many." He described drinking and exchanging erotic and pornographic literature with Nabokov during his visit. He wrote that Véra seemed to begrudge attention to anyone but her husband, and suggested that Nabokov had suffered humiliation due to some unfathomable combination of not being accepted by the real Russian nobility and because of his father's assassination. Wilson also observed, perhaps more acutely, that Nabokov "has his characters at his mercy and at the same time subjects them to torments and identifies himself with them."[35]

Infuriated by Wilson's description of the visit, Nabokov wrote to the editor of *The New York Times Book Review* suggesting that if he had known Wilson's thoughts at the time, he would have thrown him out of the house. The torments Wilson claimed Nabokov had suffered were "mostly figments of [Wilson's] warped fancy." Wilson had not lived Nabokov's life (true enough) and had never read Nabokov's autobiography (not true). Nabokov explained that *Speak, Memory* had detailed one long happy exile starting almost from birth—an interesting description of a book containing a line about "the things and beings" he loved most being "turned to ashes or shot through the heart." In the interest of compassion, Nabokov noted that he would like to disregard statements made by an ailing "former friend," but Wilson's insults were a matter of "personal honor."[36]

Mutual friends once again took sides. Nabokov had his partisans, but so, too, did Wilson. Katharine White, Nabokov's former editor at *The New Yorker*, wrote to Wilson wondering what had happened to the Nabokov they had once known. Tut-tutting the idea of Nabokov's honor being sullied, she described her sadness at seeing "how an overwhelming ego like his and world-wide success can change a man's personality so shockingly."[37]

The following spring Nabokov wrote again to the editor of the *Book Review* commenting on the feud, but Wilson had fallen into a precipitous decline. Early in May he had another stroke, and made his way back to his childhood home, where the Nabokovs had visited him in 1955. In his last days he sneaked off to a theater to watch *The Godfather*. With an oxygen tank and a phone for emergencies, he stayed focused on his next projects—more of his diaries awaiting publication, planned revised editions, and new writing.[38] Sitting in his pajamas with his back to the corner and a view through the sheer curtains, he worked with his papers and pills laid out on a long table, his wispy hair splayed into a crown of feathers. By mid-June, he was dead.

But Wilson was not through with Nabokov. In *A Window on Russia*, which came out that fall, Wilson took on the writings of Vladimir

Nabokov as a whole for the first time. There is not much to the entry in terms of insight. He finds *Bend Sinister* sadomasochistic and admits his inability to finish *Ada*, but interestingly contrasts "one of Solzhenitsyn's camps from which there can be no escape" with Nabokov allowing a character to escape prison and death.[39]

In another posthumous book, the revised edition of *To the Finland Station* published that August, Wilson finally gave ground on the history that had been the first bone of contention with Nabokov. "I have . . . been charged with having given a much too amiable picture of Lenin," he says in the new introduction, "and I believe that this criticism has been made not without some justification."[40] He makes some excuses as to why the original version of the book had unfolded as it had, but then proceeds to acknowledge in a few pages the much more complicated character of Lenin.

It was not to Nabokov's advantage to spar with Wilson's ghost. A lukewarm survey of Nabokov's writing could not touch him; he had trumped Wilson in the literary pantheon. But two years later, discussing a collaborative plan to publish the Wilson-Nabokov letters, he wrote Elena Wilson saying, "I need not tell you what agony it was rereading the exchanges belonging to the early radiant era of our correspondence."[41]

Despite their many differences, the two men had not always disagreed. Even in their final private exchange, they had come to consensus on the matter of a celebrated author whom both found personally remarkable but uninspiring from a literary standpoint: Alexander Solzhenitsyn. In his last letter addressed to the Montreux Palace, Wilson wrote that perhaps these shortcomings were not surprising: "after all he has nothing to tell but his story of illness and imprisonment."[42]

4

Wilson's indictment is striking, because Solzhenitsyn was wrestling so directly with the intersection between literature and history, and Wilson had committed himself to the creation of a calculus that could describe that region. But his words had little effect; by the time he dismissed Solzhenitsyn, Wilson was no longer a kingmaker in American literary circles, and Stockholm had awarded the novelist of the camps the Nobel Prize for Literature.

It had been a long five years for Solzhenitsyn between the loss of his archive to the KGB and the capture of the Nobel Prize. He had spent months stunned and depressed over what he felt to be this "greatest misfortune" of his life—a more significant blow than even his years in the camps.[43] He chastised himself for losing all the survival skills that had preserved him through so much danger. When he was ready to unleash all the history he had collected all on the world, he reasoned, it would be different, but to be caught *now*, after so many had risked so much to tell him their stories, and then to know that perhaps those stories would never be told, and his countrymen would never be forced to come to terms with "the millions whose last whisper, last moan, had been cut short on some hut floor in some prison camp" was devastating. For a time, he had considered suicide.[44]

In the end, Solzhenitsyn had decided to adopt as public a profile as possible, in the hopes that high visibility would make it more difficult to silence him. At the same time, however, he refused to associate himself with any movement that might jeopardize his historic and literary missions. Like Nabokov, Solzhenitsyn was not a joiner. Even in the case of two dissidents convicted for the statements of their *fictional* characters—writers who had been arrested just as his archive had been seized—Solzhenitsyn would not sign a letter calling for the men's release.[45]

He similarly turned down a request from Jean-Paul Sartre to meet in Russia, on the basis that as a constrained Soviet writer, he would not be able to talk freely or on equal terms (Sartre's companion, author Simone de Beauvoir, believed it was pride and shyness on Solzhenitsyn's part that were to blame).[46]

Though Solzhenitsyn would not sign on to others' causes, in advance of the 1967 Writers' Congress in 1967 he circulated a letter of his own. Condemning oppression, Solzhenitsyn called for the abolition of literary censorship. He wrote with characteristic drama about the high-stakes game in which he was now upping the ante: "I am, of course, confident that I will fulfill my duty as a writer under all circumstances, from the grave even more successfully and unobstructedly than in my lifetime."[47] The letter circulated at the Congress hand-to-hand, creating a buzz that none of the sessions could match. Solzhenitsyn received the written support of nearly a hundred writers. The story made newspapers worldwide.

Meanwhile Solzhenitsyn's unpublished manuscripts spurred debates and denunciations—he was a tool of the West, he was the hope of Russian writers. His own *Novy Mir* editors were still torn about what to do with his work.

He was summoned to assemblies of secretariats and committees, at which he presented himself unapologetically and denounced the KGB (indirectly but clearly) for its plots against him. Summoned for yet another meeting to ensure the publication of the first chapters of a new novel, he was on his way to the train station, headed to Moscow, when he inexplicably turned around and came home.[48] They could debate the matter with among themselves, he said. They could ask questions of his wife, whom he sent in his stead. He would stay alone and as isolated as possible, and *write*.

Solzhenitsyn's public statements guaranteed that no new work would appear from him; but when no new work appeared, it only magnified his prominence. A *Pravda* editor suggested ominously that he was suffering from mental illness; other sources circulated rumors that he had collaborated with the Germans during the war. The situation could not go on indefinitely. He had only one theme to write about; it was the very theme the authorities did not want addressed. (Nabokov, on the other hand, wrote about the same theme with absolute freedom, but did it so cryptically that it was hardly recognizable.)

Solzhenitsyn's celebrity was starting to change him; he began to imagine himself capable not just of recording history but influencing it. He had acquired a stature and power few outside the system could claim. But some friends and acquaintances felt that he had paid a price for his rise—that he had begun to lose his endearing humility, and had somehow had become distant and imperious.[49]

His forty-ninth birthday passed. He finished *The Gulag Archipelago* with Natalia in a frenzy of typing. They prepared microfilms, which were smuggled out by a courier who ran a small but real risk of being caught. Waiting day after day without knowing if his work had been intercepted was agony, but eventually news came that everything had arrived safely, bringing with it profound relief.[50] *Cancer Ward, The First Circle*, and *The Gulag Archipelago* had been safely deposited outside Soviet borders. Whatever role history assigned to him, even if he were killed, Solzhenitsyn's writing would survive. His voice could not be silenced.

But the Soviets could try. In November 1969, the local chapter of the Writers' Union summoned him to an afternoon meeting and voted to expel him on the grounds of "anti-social behavior," truncating his official career as a writer in his homeland.[51] The decision would have real effects, but it is hard to imagine what the Union thought they would accomplish. By then, *Cancer Ward* and *The First Circle* had been published in the West, to monstrous acclaim. He had been hailed as a towering talent, "a major 19th century writer suddenly appearing in the last half of the 20th century."[52] Rumors began to circulate abroad that Solzhenitsyn had something else waiting to come out, something reported in English as "The Archipelago of Gulag."

The following year, Solzhenitsyn won the Nobel Prize. After publicly planning to go to Stockholm, he then reversed his plans for fear he would not be allowed to return to Russia. Though he did not leave the country, the Nobel spurred hope in Solzhenitsyn that his situation might change. It did not, although the prize may have made him almost untouchable. His star had certainly risen high in the West—several biographers were sniffing around. But he issued a public warning to make clear that these people had not talked to him and did not know his life. Their stories were their own.

Not knowing what to do about *The Gulag Archipelago* for the time being, Solzhenitsyn did nothing. Privately, he worked on his own memoir, which careered between judgment and generosity, and would in time shock many friends. He had also started a series of novels, set in the early twentieth century, which aimed to explain what exactly had gone wrong in Russia before the Revolution.

The Writers' Union decision was not the only new stress in his life. He was also caught up in the detritus of his marriage. At fifty-two, he had gotten his mistress pregnant, and his wife was reluctant to be left by a man for whom she had risked so much, a man she still loved.[53]

There were, in fact, many possible reasons behind his hesitation to release *The Gulag Archipelago*, his biggest weapon. Publication might harm the people who had shared their stories with him. He was anxious to finish his novels on the Revolution before he might be arrested or otherwise kept from writing. And, of course, he realized that publishing *The Gulag Archipelago* would change everything.

In the end, the question was taken out of his hands. He was spied on, shadowed, wiretapped, and bugged. An acquaintance retrieving Solzhenitsyn's car for him one afternoon stumbled into the midst of a KGB raid and was brutally beaten.[54]

The police harassment intensified. Solzhenitsyn's typist, Elizaveta Voronyanskaya, was picked up by the KGB, who surely knew (if only from the many articles that had by then appeared in the West) the title and character of the documents they were looking for. Voronyanskaya was taken to Leningrad and interrogated night and day for most of a week, until she revealed the location of Solzhenitsyn's hidden manuscript. Returned to her home under house arrest, she was kept from notifying Solzhenitsyn. Two weeks later, she died in vague circumstances said to involve suicide.[55]

The KGB took its time but eventually picked up the manuscript from its hiding place. And Solzhenitsyn finally tripped the wire, signaling for *The Gulag Archipelago* to be published in Paris.

Six weeks after it appeared, the KGB came for him. He imagined being taken to a dramatic confrontation with Party leaders, but after a brief, unnerving prison stay, the Soviets disposed of the thorn in their side by deporting him to Germany and hoping that would be that.

5

The day Solzhenitsyn left Russia, Vladimir Nabokov sat down to write a note welcoming him to a life of freedom. Apologizing for not answering an earlier letter, Nabokov explained that he had a policy of not writing anyone in the Soviet Union, for fear of endangering his correspondents. "I am, after all, some kind of scaly devil to the Bolshevik authorities—something that not everyone in Russia realizes." He thought it unlikely that Solzhenitsyn had seen his work, but he assured him that "since the vile times of Lenin, I have not ceased to mock the philistinism of Sovietized Russia and to thunder against the very kind of vicious cruelty of which you write."[56]

He explained that he would not make any political statement about the matter—he never made such statements—but privately wanted to extend a warm welcome to the newest Russian exile.[57] If Solzhenitsyn were ever in Switzerland, he would be most welcome to visit. Settling soon after in Zurich, Solzhenitsyn wrote to say that fate had brought him to the same country so that the two men might meet.

Solzhenitsyn got a hero's welcome in Europe, but some commentators questioned whether it would last. William Safire wondered if, "Now that he is out of the Soviet Union . . . his martyrdom shrewdly denied, cracks will appear in the pedestal we have built for him." Seeing his writing judged as literature rather than propaganda, learning more about his religious fervor, "[p]oliticians who praise him now for his opposition to oppression may discover, to their dismay, that their chosen symbol does not share their appreciation for democratic principles."[58]

Safire's words soon hit the mark. Solzhenitsyn quickly startled his supporters by establishing himself as a proponent of a kind of

Russian nationalist religiosity. The West, Solzhenitsyn argued, was in "a state of collapse" due to a moral crisis created by the Renaissance and exacerbated by the Enlightenment. American government was so weak, it could not even protect itself from a rogue reporter, Daniel Ellsberg, who had stolen and published government documents. Britain could not handle her own Irish terrorists. The West did not hold the answers to Russia's problems. Solzhenitsyn would soon predict that the young American men who refused to serve in Vietnam would one day find themselves fighting in a war to defend American territory. Presidential aides began to wonder if he might be mentally unstable after all.[59]

He was damaging his own reputation, but the harm done to the Soviets by *The Gulag Archipelago* was greater. Nabokov, who read the first volume that summer, would have seen the stories of the trial of the Socialist Revolutionaries, the terrors of Solovki, and the details of Lubyanka Prison. He would have read about people whose fates he had mourned, couched in the rhetoric of outrage and offering all the details of their suffering.

He would also have seen that Solzhenitsyn had chronicled the Russian émigré culture of which the Soviet people had known next to nothing. Solzhenitsyn had written about the emergence of "the incredible writer Sirin-Nabokov," as well as the fact that Ivan Bunin had continued to write for decades in exile.[60] Elsewhere, in a less laudatory mention, one of Solzhenitsyn's Gulag witnesses names Nabokov and other émigré authors. After reading their works, he wonders, "What was wrong with them?" How could the brilliant inheritors of Russian culture waste their "unutterably precious freedom" and forget their countrymen?

By the time he read *The Gulag Archipelago*, Nabokov appears to have surrendered his suspicions that Solzhenitsyn was collaborating in any way with KGB schemes. And the changes wrought by Solzhenitsyn's arrival seem to have broken Nabokov's half-century paralysis of public inaction on Soviet matters. Nabokov finally felt that perhaps his speaking out might do more good than harm to those he championed.

Three months after Solzhenitsyn's arrival in Germany, Nabokov took up the cause of Vladimir Bukovsky, a dissident who he noted had been held for years in a psychiatric hospital before recently being sent on to Perm. Bukovsky, who had spent years in medical detention, had most recently been sentenced for turning over case files to the West, offering incontrovertible proof of Soviet psychiatric abuses. Nabokov sent a letter to Britain's *Observer*, urging "all persons and organizations that have more contact with Russia than I have to do whatever can be done to help that courageous and precious man."[61]

In *Bend Sinister* nearly thirty years before, Nabokov had mentioned the camps to which Bukovsky would later be sent, calling them "the ghoul-haunted Province of Perm." But even there his veiled reference to the labor camps had been so oblique that Véra Nabokov had felt the need to make it explicit in a note for the book's translator.[62] Nabokov did not want to recapitulate the miseries of the dying and the dead with the kind of "juicy journalese" used by Solzhenitsyn, but in building something transcendent to memorialize their suffering, the question remains whether he memorialized it or obscured it.[63]

As Solzhenitsyn headed into Montreux on the morning of October 6 to visit Nabokov, it is not clear if he knew that Nabokov had mocked his work in interviews and dismissed him as an inferior author. Neither is it clear if he knew about Nabokov's recent overtures on the behalf of Bukovsky—dozens of luminaries had publicly supported that cause, and Solzhenitsyn was focused on his own mission. Given that Nabokov had written to Solzhenitsyn that he had never stopped thundering against the Soviets, it remains unknown what weight Solzhenitsyn would have given to small overtures on behalf of dissidents nearly sixty years after the Revolution.

Solzhenitsyn, like Nabokov, had been attacked for taking help from others while giving only a cold shoulder in return. But he interpreted what he saw as Nabokov's literary reticence on matters of Russian history as possibly beyond his fellow exile's control, later speculating that perhaps "the circumstances of his life" had kept

Nabokov from being able to serve his country by writing about its destruction.[64]

Rolling up to the driveway of the Palace Hotel on their way to meet the Nabokovs, Alexander Solzhenitsyn and his second wife (also named Natalia) were not clear on whether or not they were welcome. Nabokov had invited them—of that they were sure. And they had sent the date they would stop by, and had made their plans. But they had received no confirmation, and their subsequent phone calls trying to get in touch had not been answered.

For a stemwinding prophet, Solzhenitsyn had an uncharacteristic delicacy in the matter of visits. Years before, he had heard from a former schoolmate who had been threatened with arrest based in part on comments made by Solzhenitsyn. The friend blamed Solzhenitsyn for his close call with prison, but when the latter had risen to fame, the two exchanged letters. Though they realized they had profound differences, they made a plan to meet in person.

Going to his friend's apartment, Solzhenitsyn rang the bell, but there was no answer. After an hour spent waiting in the lobby, he wrote a note and started to slip it through a lidded mail slot in the door. As he did, he glimpsed the slippers on his friend's feet through the slot as the former classmate stood motionless on the other side of the door, unwilling or unable to open it. Solzhenitsyn let down the cover and left.[65] He had chosen a different road for himself, but the pain of addressing the past directly was something that he understood.

As he neared the hotel, Solzhenitsyn did not know that Nabokov was waiting with Véra in the private dining room they had reserved for lunch. Any small harm their mutually critical comments had done was surely irrelevant in comparison to the things that admired about each other. But something made Solzhenitsyn pause.

He acknowledged Nabokov's genius, even as he regretted that his fellow Russian had not used his art to do anything for their homeland. Solzhenitsyn surely wanted to visit. Such a meeting, however, would be complicated. His fondest wish was to move to a rustic cabin somewhere. Did he feel awkward in the face of the luxury setting?

Was he concerned that Nabokov, who was not a young man, was ill or indisposed?

Whatever his worries, Solzhenitsyn did not stop. He did not get out of the car. He did not go with Natalia into the private dining room of the hotel restaurant reserved for them and find the seventy-five-year-old Nabokov, who sat waiting for Solzhenitsyn.

Instead, Solzhenitsyn—with the same sensitivity he had shown to his old friend, or perhaps with the same anxiety over the past that had kept his friend from opening the door—drove away on the Grand Rue of Montreux, heading north just a tenth of a mile to a bend in the road that was Rue du Lac. Another mile to go and they were already out of Montreux.

Nabokov was a thoroughly modern writer, yet somehow he himself had become an anachronism. Embarking on a new existence, Solzhenitsyn was as free to leave his fellow Russian behind as the soldier in Nabokov's first novel had been when he abandoned his childhood love at the train station and sailed into the future on his own terms.

Vladimir and Véra Nabokov sat in the room that they had reserved, where they had hoped to talk with the man whose writing they did not admire but whose bravery they did not dispute, the man who might have understood what Nabokov had done with all those books, if Solzhenitsyn had only known that every one of them was meant to stand against totalitarianism, the man whose exile had somehow persuaded Nabokov to write a public letter during a campaign by Amnesty International in an effort to save a single "precious" life.[66]

The person best equipped to see through Nabokov's elaborate games missed his cue, defying the fate he claimed had brought them together. The Nabokovs waited at the table for more than an hour before rising to go. The two men never met.

6

Having entered the public fray on behalf of those still being subjected to Soviet abuses, Nabokov wrote another missive near the end of the year. At the request of American friends who had built a publishing house specializing in Russian-language literature, he sent a telegram directly to Leningrad calling for the immediate release of dissident short story writer Vladimir Maramzin.[67] Maramzin had been arrested, and his library, containing a copy of *Lolita*, had been burned.

Worried that there had been no response, the Nabokovs attempted to add a little publicity for Maramzin's cause by pointing out that a forthcoming piece in *People* magazine might advantageously make mention of the telegram, which it did.[68]

The rest of the *People* interview from the same year is a mish-mash of truth and deliberate gamesmanship on Nabokov's part. He claimed to loathe student activists and hippies, which was probably true—and he expressed regret that Véra never laughed, which was not. Before the interview, as with nearly every interview he did in Montreux, Nabokov had requested the right to review the story as planned for print and to make corrections.

He made these edits often, even after the fact. In collected interviews published as part of *Strong Opinions* late in Nabokov's life, it is interesting to see what he chose to leave out. He redacted his own comments about the weight he had gained, his chatter about Tolstoy catching a sexually transmitted disease from a Swiss chambermaid, and insults directed at Pasternak and other writers. "I cannot be made to criticize contemporary writers," he wrote in a note to his interviewer, as if he had somehow not already done it or not known he had been speaking to reporters when he did so.[69]

Asked about being a perverse or cruel author in another interview, he had responded, "Is a butcher cruel?" He followed up with an explanation: "If I was cruel, I suppose it was because I saw the world as cruel in those days."

With the back and forth of choreographed answers and revisions, it becomes impossible to trace the thread back to discover which Nabokov is being discussed at any point in time—the public façade of the esteemed writer; the jocular, teasing host; or the magician who buried his past in his art and waited for readers to exhume it.[70] As a result, in his *People* interview it is hard to know if it was the reporter or Nabokov himself who is responsible for a passage in which Nabokov is described as joining "the current of history not by rushing to take part in political actions or appearing in the news but by quietly working for decades, a lifetime, until his voice seems . . . almost as loud as the lies. Deprived of his own land, of his language, he has conquered something greater. . . . He has won."[71]

What had he won? Fame, money, and artistic immortality, without a doubt. But the world consigned Nabokov to the artful prison he had built for himself, and his books, every one of which was meant to fight tyranny, were seen as arch games in a self-referential hall of mirrors.[72]

Nabokov did not live to see the fall of Soviet Russia. But in the autumn of the missed meeting with Solzhenitsyn, other Soviet exiles made their way to Montreux to visit with him. He spent long hours translating *Ada* into French; he entertained a representative from McGraw-Hill, his American publisher. He continued to plan new novels and started on *The Original of Laura*, which would be completed in his mind but never on the page.

He continued to argue over Andrew Field's biography into 1976, by which point relations were fully adversarial. And no wonder Field struggled—the manuscript of the corrections running back and forth between the two parties had transformed into the literary equivalent of Dickens's *Bleak House*. Nabokov was simultaneously doing useful things—clarifying details, making corrections, and editing things that referred to people behind the Iron Curtain— while also cutting out the kind of tidbits that he liked to retract from interviews, now with the intercession of lawyers.

Primed by combat with Field, Nabokov lashed out at critic John Leonard in the last weeks of his life, with just a hint of a threat of legal action over a line describing a legendary forger as "a liar on such an extravagant scale, a Nabokov of Peking."[73] Such matters were hardly worth his time, of which there was not much left. He was caught up in real or imagined slights against his personal honor as if he were still living in pre-Revolutionary Russia, which he nearly was—or at least as close to it as he could get.

He had one eye on eternity, and for all those who dismissed him as a gamesman or chastised him for tormenting his characters, he predicted that another view would prevail in the end: "I believe that one day a reappraiser will come and declare that, far from having been a frivolous firebird, I was a rigid moralist kicking sin, cuffing stupidity, ridiculing the vulgar and cruel—and assigning sovereign power to tenderness, talent, and pride."[74]

The immortality Nabokov had achieved for his writing could not add a single day to his life. He woke one night, thinking he was dying, and screamed for Véra, who did not hear him. That evening was only a dress rehearsal, but it was no secret that death was coming. He had fallen while hiking the year before, and from there slowly began to slide into the world of intermittent illness. It was as if he were returning to his childhood quinsy and pneumonia, but with sleeping-pill–induced hallucinations instead of his own wild imaginings. Fever and urinary tract infection had their way with him. After sentencing characters to die into their stories, leaving the narrative permanently incomplete, he was slowly expiring without any prospect of finishing his last tale.

In the end, there were none of the grotesque details he loved to recount from Gogol's demise—the alternating warm and frigid baths, the invalid's convex belly, the leeches bleeding him, hanging from his nose, slipping into his mouth.[75] Nabokov died the plainest of deaths, with recurrent fever, bronchial congestion, and fluid in his lungs, all of which refused to give ground.[76]

He had planned to go to Israel the May before, but postponed the trip; he had hoped to get to America again. And although he did not believe it would ever happen, he had dreamed of returning to Russia. But Vladimir Vladimirovich Nabokov, who loved small jars of fruit jellies; who resented Pasternak's success as if it could annihilate his own; who was rumored to have wanted to challenge his father's killers to a duel; who had mocked people who ended up dying terrible, unimaginable deaths; who had once referenced the current plotline of the comic strip Rex Morgan, M.D., to an astonished scholar; who stitched more than a century of camps and prisons—real and invented—into his writing, died a distinctly un-Nabokovian death. It was perhaps as good an end as a modern writer can have, short of not dying: before nightfall, with attention to his comfort, in the company of his wife and son, with no question that his works would survive him.

7

Nabokov's life had been surrounded by politics and intrigue from birth, and was bound up in many of the major events of his century, which he preserved through magical flight and escapes that he knew were not the norm but a gift. In retrospect, it seems extraordinary that so many people in his world managed to survive, chief among them his wife and son.

Dmitri Nabokov spent his early adulthood on two things his father had studiously avoided—driving and music. In addition to becoming an opera singer and a race car driver, he was also the pre-ferred Russian-to-English translator of his father's Russian works. He would later become the shepherd of his father's literary estate, defending Nabokov's work and personal reputation fiercely, arguing for a fundamental gentleness and kindness that did not always show up in others' depictions of the man.

Véra Nabokov, who had made herself as invisible as possible to the public during her husband's lifetime, survived more than a decade after his death, carrying on Nabokov's literary legacy, supervising translations, working hand-in-hand with a new biographer to estab-lish a life story for Nabokov that might erase Field's.[77] She kept a grueling schedule but survived to the age of eighty-nine and would eventually earn her own biographer. She died in 1991, living just long enough to witness the beginning of the collapse of the Soviet Union.

8

When the U.S.S.R. imploded, the doors to history opened. Closely guarded records became available, and a broader view of twentieth-century Russian history emerged. If the portrait of 1917 and 1918 became more complicated than Nabokov might have liked, he would have been heartened by documents establishing Lenin's ruthlessness from the beginning.

Open archives also made it possible to match prisoner files to existing oral accounts, and to begin to fill in the landscape sketched by *The Gulag Archipelago* and individual memoirs. The files, of course, were unreliable in their own way—charges were often trumped up; confessions were often not confessions at all. History, it turns out, is complex. But it is not entirely opaque.

Wanting to preserve the enigma of *Pale Fire*, the Nabokovs had made clear to their publisher in 1962 that nobody should know if Zembla really exists. But what of Nova Zembla—the Arctic destination of the Socialist Revolutionaries in 1922? What about the camp from which Solzhenitsyn, too, had dreamed of hearing a story, the place to which Gulag memoirists said a thousand prisoners were sent each year, but none returned?

In addition to the *Times of London* and *New York Times* articles, the mines of Nova Zembla are mentioned in dozens of publications of the 1930s, from Pennsylvania's *Tyrone Daily* to *Popular Science*. An American Federation of Labor Gulag map from 1951 shows two camps on the southern island; a Routledge atlas from 1972 shows just one camp at the top of the northern island. In 1943 a Polish officer named Andrey Stotski recounted his own experiences on Nova Zembla in a memoir excerpted and translated into English under the title "I Dwelt with Death." Classified CIA reports from the 1950s include pictures from Nova Zembla and testimony gathered from POWs after the war, who described in detail the kinds of mining done there, from a copper-pyrite quarry down to the ore-processing plant on the northern island. Robert Conquest references the "virtually unrecorded 'death camps'" of Nova Zembla in his 1990 book *The Great Terror: A Reassessment*.[78]

Yet after years of access to Soviet archives, the human rights organization Memorial began pulling camp records together to create a master listing of Gulag sites. It became clear that the Nova Zemblan accounts from prisoners of war were problematic. Despite the tidal wave of anecdotal evidence that circulated inside and outside Russia in the Soviet era, no wartime files on camps and mines on Nova Zembla have been found. A paper published by Memorial indicates that the details of mining from the prisoner-of-war accounts of the 1940s also do not match up with geological information about Nova Zembla, and suggests that these accounts must be considered with skepticism.[79]

Records do show that in 1925, a Nova Zemblan (*Novozemelskaya*) geological expedition tested ore at a number of places north of the mainland. Five years later, OGPU officers brought in prisoners to begin mining. The expedition landed not on Nova Zembla proper, but on Vaigach Island, the southernmost island of the Nova Zemblan archipelago.

Conditions were miserable, especially during the first winter of 1930-31, when the prisoners had to set up camp on an inlet. Mines were established on the other side of the bay, and altogether almost 1,500 prisoners were ferried over from the mainland. In winter, a series of posts connected with rope ran across the bay from the settlement to the mines, so that prisoners could find their way in poor visibility. In bad conditions, those who lost their way simply died.

The main benefit to the hard work on Vaigach was that every day served on the Nova Zemblan archipelago counted for two days off a prisoner's sentence. Due to the polar bears, prisoners were sometimes given rifles to protect themselves.[80]

One minor rebellion sprang up, but it was put down quickly; there was no question of escape. The climate was brutal, but treatment was often better than prisoners would receive at other camps. In the evenings chess and performances were permitted. A small brass band composed of prisoners once played the "Internationale" for a meeting of the local indigenous Nenets.[81]

In the fourth year of operations, water flooded the mine. By 1936, the Vaigach experiment had come to an end. All the prisoners were pulled away to work more promising deposits or to help build rail lines to new Arctic camps. The Vaigach Expedition may well have been responsible for decades of legends about the severity of Nova Zembla, but it never set foot on Zembla proper.

The 1922 stories about Socialist Revolutionary prisoners sent there are also likely mistaken. Lining up the Nova Zembla camp stories with news accounts turns up another piece of the puzzle. The 1922 stories relayed that because too many prisoners were escaping from the mainland camps around Archangel, the Socialist Revolutionaries would be shipped en masse to Nova Zembla. The announcement of the prisoners' deadly fate was made on the cusp of autumn, but by that point the climate likely made transportation north problematic.[82] Heading north of the mainland would have been ill-advised, so prisoners would likely have been held until spring.

But despite the stories that ran in *The New York Times*, *The Times* of London and the accounts of Berlin's own *Rul*, no camp records unearthed to date indicate that any prisoners were sent to Nova Zembla the following year either. Where did they go?

The question dovetails with a piece of history that is already on the books. In June 1923, just as the seas cleared enough for navigation, Solovki received its first large batch of Socialist Revolutionary prisoners.[83] In retrospect, it seems likely that rumors of a Nova Zemblan destination for the prisoners who had disappeared the previous fall were just that—rumors. The stories were true in spirit—prisoners were, in fact, being sent to a desolate northern island, and it was a place that would soon become a nightmare of horrors—but it was in all probability not Zembla they went to but Solovki.

Later, when stories leaked out in the 1930s and 1940s of people sent to hardship posts in the Arctic to build new mines, confusion reigned again. The name *Vorkuta* circulated, but until the 1931 expedition of prisoners sent to create it, the Arctic city of Vorkuta had not existed. People did not know where it was. Western sources from the *Tribune de Genève* to *The New York Times* accurately relayed that new mines were being worked by tens of thousands of prisoners at a place called Vorkuta. But they mistakenly located Vorkuta on Nova Zembla.[84] And so Nova Zembla—which even before the Revolution had been a setting for expeditions, fairy tales, and starvation—continued in its legendary half-real, half-imagined status.

But what about those who were actually prisoners at Vorkuta, who reported terror at the prospect of being sent further north to Nova Zembla, the site to which as many as a thousand rogue thieves were shipped off each year? While it is possible that they were taken to Nova Zembla and left there, there are no records of functioning mines or prisoner transports sent to them. Those condemned thieves may have been exported to other penal labor sites or simply executed.[85]

But the stories in and outside the camps proliferated. And so Nova Zembla entered the gulag lexicon as the place that allowed prisoners to imagine that no matter how bad things got—and conditions were atrocious at Vorkuta—there was always someplace farther north that was worse.[86]

Revisiting stories of starvation and cannibalism in the fishing villages of Nova Zembla during Nabokov's childhood and the accounts of the apocalyptic Tsar Bomba in his later years, even Nova Zembla's undisputed history has attained mythic stature. No wonder the islands intrigued Nabokov for decades, from his 1941 poem mentioning Nova Zembla to the Nabokov River he references there in *Speak, Memory*, and *Pale Fire*'s very idea of a refugee hailing from its desolate shores.

Nabokov had told his classes that all great stories were fairy tales, but he also knew, as well as anyone, that their horrors were real. How fitting that in the history of the Russian camps, the islands were for a time the false double of two of the system's most notorious and lethal outposts, Solovki and Vorkuta.

9

By the time of Véra Nabokov's death, her husband had been rehabilitated in the Soviet Union, and many of his works had legally entered the country.[87] Dmitri Likhachev, who had reported to Solzhenitsyn about his time on Solovki for *The Gulag Archipelago*, was instrumental in bringing Nabokov's *Eugene Onegin* to Russia.

He likewise brokered discussions about returning the family home on Bolshaya Morskaya to Nabokov's son Dmitri.[88] But in the end the first floor of the house became a museum dedicated to Nabokov's life and writing. Visitors can see first editions of Nabokov novels, his Russian Scrabble game, and his butterfly net. Battered *samizdat* copies of Nabokov works that once circulated underground are kept under glass. A copy of the century-old architectural plans for the house is posted; a seminar room with a film projector shows documentaries, including one in which Solzhenitsyn comments mildly on Nabokov. Solzhenitsyn's remarks are brief, stressing how unexpected Nabokov's work was, coming as it did on the heels of his nineteenth-century Russian predecessors. Solzhenitsyn does not add, as he did elsewhere, that to reach Western readers, Nabokov had broken with the past and lost his Russian roots.[89]

Not long after the aborted meeting with Nabokov, Solzhenitsyn retreated to the hills of Vermont, ranting against the spiritual wasteland of the West and writing about the past, eventually outliving the political regime he despised. In 1994 he returned to Russia in triumph, knowing his writing had changed the course of history. He had engaged the enemy, and he had won.

But engagement had a price. His strident opinions on America, on Western governments, and global history he did not know well permanently dented his international reputation. Compelled by unfolding events to rush translations of his most important works, he was unable to take the time and attention that Nabokov had lavished on his works in other languages. Despite the Nobel Prize that Solzhenitsyn had won—and Nabokov had not—the political aspects of his writing seem destined to overshadow its literary merits.[90]

Westerners who saw Solzhenitsyn as committed to freedom were dismayed to watch him embrace Vladimir Putin, a former KGB official who has held on to nostalgia for aspects of the Soviet past. Solzhenitsyn went on to represent a Russian nationalism that made many squirm. Making a public stand in favor of reinstituting the death penalty in 2001, he pointed out that even Vladimir Nabokov's father, an anti-death–penalty activist, had reversed himself on the issue in 1917 when Russia had been in jeopardy.[91]

Solzhenitsyn died in August 2008. One year later, excerpts from *The Gulag Archipelago* became required reading in Russian high schools, and the Moscow road formerly known as Big Communist Street was named after Russia's most stalwart anti-Communist.[92]

Today in St. Petersburg, a few memorials and museums have found a place in the cityscape. A slab of rock from Solovki sits on a pedestal in front of the House of Political Convicts. A memorial to the founder of the Cheka, that forerunner of Soviet secret police organizations, has become a museum on the history of all the political police in Russia across the centuries. Across the Neva River from Kresty Prison where Nabokov's father was held (where others are held today) sits Mikhail Shemyakin's monument to victims of political repression. A pair of sphinxes face each other, with a stone book and barbed-wire crown between them. Taking just a few steps around to view them from the perspective of Kresty Prison reveals half-skull faces and protruding ribs on the statues' reverse sides.

Germany has created many more memorials for the dead of its camps, though today no train runs from the Hamburg suburb of Bergedorf out to the stop on the grounds of the former concentration camp at Neuengamme, which remained a prison until 2003.

Walking from the rebuilt section of track to the center of the camp, perhaps the most surprising thing is how the acres of the site stretch on and on—a single human being represents a very small presence. Fence posts remain, marking camp boundaries, but the barbed wire and even the fencing are gone. The memorial can be visited twenty-four hours a day. Vandalism happens, but camp staff reports that it is rare.[93]

Taking the train from Germany to Prague in 2011, it is possible to find a car and driver and head into the countryside up and down the hills for hours with a translator who helps to locate a particular retirement home in the far eastern Czech town of Šumperk. On the upper level of the complex lives a man who was once a Gulag prisoner in the Arctic.

A visit to the archives will reveal a copy of his NKVD file that will prove it, and then army records can confirm it, in case doubt lingers.[94] Paperwork shows that the man spent nearly two years at Vorkuta before being released early for the war effort, as so many were, into the relative comfort of crossfire on the eastern front in World War II.

Phoning ahead only leads him to say not to come, that no one wants to talk to such an old person. But pressed, he relents, and seems to like having guests. He introduces his wife as well, who will also soon turn ninety, and she talks about being deported to work in Germany during the war.

Asked about his time in the Gulag, the man offers up stories, including a description of a stint mining ore for blacktop on Nova Zembla, where, he explains, prisoners were sometimes given an extra ration of fish. He stops being at all reluctant. Offering home-made pickles and encouraging guests to stay and listen, he answers every question, sharing what he can about the camps, detailing his war service, spinning his own stories to replace whatever it is he cannot remember or cannot say, talking all about his time on Nova Zembla.

Riding back to Prague with the translator, it is four hours to the heart of the Old Town and Charles University, where Vladimir Petkevič teaches. The great-grandson of V. D. Nabokov and grandson of Nabokov's sister Olga, Petkevič is generous with his time, and talks about his beloved grandmother, whom nature or a privileged childhood had rendered incapable of performing even simple tasks, and his father, who died in despair in communist Czechoslovakia at the age of twenty-nine.

Reminded that Nabokov had once written a scathing letter to Roman Jakobson, the linguist who visited the Soviet Union before its collapse, Petkevič will not defend Jakobson, though he admires the man's work deeply. "I fully agree with Nabokov," Petkevič says, still angry at the Western intelligentsia decades later. "I almost hated them. They didn't understand anything. We did, we who lived here. We knew what it was like."[95]

Flying into Geneva, and taking the train around the lake to Montreux, the station sits just blocks up the hill from the Palace Hotel. It is possible to get a room in October, the time of year that Vladimir Nabokov and Alexander Solzhenitsyn were supposed to meet—though probably not the Nabokov Suite, which is generally booked well in advance by visiting Russians.

One floor above the lobby, the doors stand open on the Salon de Musique, the room where Nabokov waited for Solzhenitsyn. Regulations for the preservation of historic buildings are strict, so not much has changed since Nabokov and Solzhenitsyn's failed meeting. The present recalls the past.

Except for some tables and chairs, and a massive chandelier, the Salon de Musique is empty in the off season. For all the temptation to imagine literary ghosts, no spectral breeze lifts the sheer curtains. Nabokov no longer sits believing that Solzhenitsyn will come, or wonders what they will say to each other, two fiercely independent Russians with incendiary subjects, proud, suspicious, and opposed to Revolution. People book the Nabokov Suite, but no one expects to see Nabokov wander through, and no one thinks that Solzhenitsyn will arrive, young and still feigning humility, or old and hemmed in at the end by as much pride as Nabokov.

Suggesting to Nabokov that Solzhenitsyn had nothing to write about but imprisonment, Edmund Wilson never realized how thoroughly Nabokov had mined the same theme. Solzhenitsyn recorded the suffering of prisoners; Nabokov imagined the ways they had tried to escape.

In the end, both recorded the toll of political oppression on the human spirit. From *The Gift*'s immersion in penal labor under the tsars to *Despair*'s nods to internment camps from World War I, the death camps of *Pnin* and *Lolita*, and, always, "the torture house, the blood-bespattered wall" of the Soviet Gulag, Nabokov had tucked a record of the inhumanity of concentration camps into work after work, chronicling their crushing effects on those savaged by history.

He had used his mother's arts to carry on his father's legacy, indicting anti-Semitism and condemning repression. He had subjected his characters to cruelty and mockery and violent ends, but preserved their dreams and their veiled pasts, which continued to levy a terrible toll in the present. The roots of nearly every Nabokov story lie in "the incalculable amount of tenderness contained in the world," a tenderness that "is either crushed, or wasted, or transformed into madness."[96] Teaching readers a new way of interacting with a story, speaking to them over the heads of the characters, Nabokov ridiculed social novels that aimed to transform whole societies, but he believed it possible to awaken a single reader to the collateral damage of real events—the human lives fractured and forgotten.

Only the long view reveals Nabokov's strategy. As a casualty of history who found a way to escape, magically, again and again, he let his most famous characters find a parallel refuge in insanity. And he, too, hid his own treasures and grief inside his stories, with their created worlds cobbled out of the brittle past: the dead of the camps, the prisoners' wild tales, the tenderness for those he had mocked, the reflections of a world steeped in cruelty, his sorrow at everything that had been lost. Whatever tales Nabokov wished to tell, whatever history he hoped we would remember, must be earned. It is inside his stories that he sits and waits.

Coda

Dmitri Nabokov, who served as his father's literary executor after the death of his mother, had his own larger-than-life experiences and mysteries. In addition to a career as an opera singer and a race car driver, he also acted in an Italian heist film and performed as his father in public readings of the Nabokov-Wilson letters. He survived a car crash in 1980 that resulted in a fractured neck and third-degree burns over almost half his body.

In later years, he spoke to journalists and acquaintances of clandestine work he had done for the United States government, sometimes mentioning being a CIA agent, at other times making vague references to a "noble cause" to which he had been assigned on a "distant shore," but which he had abandoned to be at his father's bedside in the last months of Nabokov's life.

Dmitri Nabokov remained a devoted steward of his father's artistic reputation and legacy for his entire life but does not appear to have wrestled with his father's political doubts. Reminded that Nabokov had once listed torture among the worst things humans can do, Dmitri publicly defended it as a legitimate tool in the face of

suicide bombers willing to level the World Trade Center.[1] He died in
Vevey, Switzerland, just outside Montreux on February 2012.

Véra Nabokov's sister Sonia appears never to have met up with
Carl Junghans again. She worked in New York as a translator at the
United Nations for years, eventually moving to Geneva. Difficult as
they both could be, Sonia and Véra continued to commiserate over
the third, even more difficult Slonim sister, Lena, whose conversion
Véra found so galling.

Carl Junghans, Sonia's paramour on three continents, became a
gardener for Kurt Weill in Hollywood and did minor documentary
work in America.[2] At the end of the war, he became a witness in a
high-profile U.S. trial of a suspected German spy in California. Junghans returned to Berlin years later, where he won the top German
film honor, a Deutschen Filmpreis, for lifetime achievement. He died
in 1984.

Another gifted opportunist, Walter Duranty, whose accounts of
life in the U.S.S.R. shaped so much of the perception of Soviet rule
that Nabokov tried in vain to counter in America, fell into disgrace
as history revealed the degree to which he had tilted his reporting
to favor his hosts, lauding the progress of Gulag projects and denying
the existence of one of the worst famines in history. Two different
Pulitzer committees spent months considering whether his flawed
reporting merited revocation of the Prize he had been awarded in
1932, ultimately leaving it in place but noting how far short he had
fallen of the standards of journalism.

Olga Nabokov, Nabokov's sister in Prague, left the world a year
after he did in May 1978, dying behind the Iron Curtain, receiving
money from her brother's estate each month for as long as she lived.
Olga's ex-husband Boris, for whom the Soviet Army had searched in
vain on its first day in Prague during the war, died in the town of
Halifax in England in 1963, working as an oiler in a textile factory.[3]

Nicholas Nabokov, who seemed to live out an alternative Nabokovian life of political engagement and intrigue, died one year after his
literary cousin. After the Congress for Cultural Freedom's funding

sources had been revealed, Nicholas went on to write the score for the ballet *Don Quixote* and collaborated with W. H. Auden on transforming Shakespeare's *Love's Labour's Lost* into an opera.

Elena Sikorski, Nabokov's youngest sister, outlived her brother by more than two decades. Surviving into the first months of the new century, still promoting her brother's legacy, she was the last link to Nabokov's family life in pre-Revolutionary Russia. Elena died in Geneva at the age of ninety-four.[4]

ACKNOWLEDGMENTS

Authors describe the writing life as one of solitude, but the time I have spent on this book has been spent in the virtual or flesh-and-blood company of many people whose intelligence and insights I have come to treasure. One of the greatest pleasures of finishing the book is having the opportunity to thank them publicly.

The community of Nabokov scholars has been more than generous with feedback, cautionary tales, and encouragement. I would particularly like to thank Tatiana Ponomareva, the Director of the Nabokov Museum in St. Petersburg, for her thoughts on Nabokov and her discussions of Russian history. Steven Belletto, whose focus is Cold War literature, and Matthew Roth, whose particular interest is *Pale Fire*, have been giving advice and assistance to me almost since I began my research. Maxim Shrayer has been thoughtful and forthcoming in conversations on Nabokov and Jewish matters for nearly as long.

Susan Elizabeth Sweeney, who has spent years thinking about the relationship between Vladimir and Sergei Nabokov, was kind enough to include me on a Modern Language Association panel in 2009 and to give me feedback on a paper that resulted from it.

That paper was submitted to a journal, where Zoran Kuzmanovich and anonymous readers improved it immeasurably before it was accepted. Gavriel Shapiro, whom I met briefly at that same MLA, was wonderfully open-minded about new approaches to Nabokov's work. He later saw part of my research and gave me sound advice, as well as generously sharing a key detail from his own forthcoming book about Nabokov's relationship with his father.

Leland de la Durantaye was kind enough to let me sit in on his Nabokov seminar at the beginning of 2008, in the middle of a year I spent at Harvard as an affiliate of the Nieman Foundation for Journalism. Brian Boyd was likewise responsive when I wrote him in my first months of research with a haphazard pile of questions about Nabokov and the Gulag. He put me in touch with Leona Toker, whose expertise in both areas and thoughtful e-mail exchanges over a *Pale Fire* essay I had drafted spurred me to dive deeper into the history in question.

As an academic paper turned into a book for a general audience, Stacy Schiff brought up the perils of declassified materials and generously discussed Véra Nabokov's family with me. Michael Maar understood immediately the story I hoped to tell and made intelligent suggestions on ways to improve this book.

In the world of Gulag and Holocaust experts, Michael Scammell provided a sounding board and kindly answered many questions about his own encounters with Nabokov, Solzhenitsyn, and Soviet-era politics; he later also gave invaluable feedback on part of this manuscript. Reimer Möller, archivist at the Neuengamme Concentration Camp Memorial, spent many hours with me, during which he recreated a typical day in the life of Neuengamme prisoners at the time Sergei Nabokov was a prisoner there.

Anne Applebaum generously let me rifle through her mental store of Gulag history by phone and suggested several invaluable sources for this book. Steven Barnes sat down over lunch to talk about Lenin, Stalin, and recordkeeping in the Gulag. Adam Hochschild offered helpful suggestions on Crimea during the Russian

Civil War. Guillaume de Syon helped me to understand the intricate restrictions faced by Jewish passport holders in France and Germany during World War II.

Vladimir Petkevič, the grandson of Nabokov's sister Olga, talked with me in Prague and proceeded to help with this project from a distance—I am grateful for his time, his patience, and the use of several of his family photos. Lev Grossman kindly shared archival materials with me related to the life of Sergei Nabokov.

Translators played a key role in my research. King among them is Azat Oganesian, my research assistant, who poured through and translated interminable numbers of articles I sent him from *Rul*, the Russian-language newspaper in Berlin, as well as making trips to various libraries on his own to help with this project. Christine Keck and Valia Lestou generously translated German-language articles and correspondence. Ted Whang prepared letters for me in Czech. Adam Hradilek of the Institute for the Study of Totalitarian Regimes led to a connection with a Gulag survivor and translated various Gulag-related Czech records that ended up being extraordinarily useful. A number of people came through with tidbits of timely translation assistance or advice—Maria Balinska (Polish), Anna Badkhen (Russian), David Hertzel (German), and Chris König (German)—for which I am grateful.

Interpreters and guides were indispensible at various points during my travels, particularly Fedor Timofeev in St. Petersburg, and Helena Šípková-Safari in the Czech Republic, who drove far into the countryside on what would surely have been a fool's errand had it not been for her intelligence and enthusiasm.

The librarians and archival staff who helped with this book are legion: Peter Armenti and Travis Westly at the Library of Congress; Isaac Gewirtz, Anne Garner, and Rebecca Filner at the Berg Collection of the New York Public Library; Ann L. Hudak in Special Collections of the Hornbake Library at the University of Maryland; M. Kiel at Berlin's Bundesarchiv-Filmarchiv; Jane A. Callahan at the Wellesley College Archives; Charles Rhéaume of the Directorate of

History and Heritage at Canada's National Defence Headquarters; Demetrius Marshall at U.S. Citizenship & Immigration genealogical research; and various staff members of the Neuengamme Concentration Camp Memorial, the Nabokov Museum in St. Petersburg, Memory of Nations, Vassar College Library, Memorial in Russia, the Hoover Institution, the U.S. National Archives, Harvard's Widener Library, the Ernst Mayr Library of the Museum of Comparative Zoology at Harvard, George Mason University's Fenwick Library, various branches of the Arlington County and Fairfax County libraries in Virginia, and the municipal library of Montreux, Switzerland. I would also like to acknowledge the gracious assistance of the staff of the Montreux Palace Hotel.

In terms of the work of other authors, I am deeply indebted to Stacy Schiff, Brian Boyd, and Andrew Field, the biographers of Véra and Vladimir Nabokov; Maxim Shrayer, who has been investigating the importance of Jewish themes in Nabokov's work for many years; and, again, Michael Scammell, who was Alexander Solzhenitsyn's biographer and the translator of two of Nabokov's Russian-language novels. I would also like to acknowledge Dieter Zimmer's online list of residences and genealogical tables for Nabokov and his family, which saved me a good deal of time when I sat down to create my own chronology of Nabokov's life in the context of world events.

My gratitude for being alive in an era of electronic research is immeasurable. The digital collections of the Russian history and human rights organization Memorial, the central Yad Vashem database of Shoah victims, and *The New York Times* searchable archives provided invaluable information. I accessed electronic databases thousands of times to useful ends. Without digital resources, this book would have taken decades to write.

Research that Mike Adler shared, particularly a series of concentration camp maps, was also very helpful, as were various forms of encouragement, feedback, or assistance from Peter Davis, Justin Kaplan, Anne Bernays, Rose Moss, Thorne Anderson, Marcela Valdes, Alicia Anstead, and Vasil Derd'uk.

This book would be a lesser thing without frank and generous manuscript readers. In addition those already noted above, I would like to thank Brian Snyder, Paul Lombardo, Mark Johnson, Christopher Goffard, Mary Newsom, John Ptak, and Beth Filiano.

I am tremendously grateful to the current and former staff of the Nieman Foundation for Journalism at Harvard, which made it possible for me to take the class that launched this project in 2008. Bob Giles, the curator of the Foundation through 2011, has been a supporter from the beginning.

Adrienne Mayor, who blazed a trail ahead of me as an independent researcher, helped make sure this book would see the light of day by introducing me to my agent, Katherine Boyle of Veritas Literary Agency. Katie has been a tireless champion of this project, a navigator in rough waters, and a source of boundless support.

I am grateful to Claiborne Hancock, Jessica Case, and Maia Larson at Pegasus Books, who have humbled me with their faith in this effort. Jessica, my editor, made many astute suggestions that shaped and refined this book. Maria Fernandez worked her design magic, while Phil Gaskill copy-edited the manuscript into shape.

On a personal level, this project has left a big footprint in my life. Without the support of friends and family, it could not have been written. For various late-night conversations, temporary takeovers of guest rooms, provision of meals, watching of children, and cheerleading, I would like to express my gratitude to Peter and Kathy Vergano, Bob and Patricia Pitzer, Sharon and Frank Mauzey, Rob Pitzer, Cecile Pratt, Gwynn Dujardin, Tom Schumacher, Karen Aldana, Matt Olson, Danielle Tezcan, Gaiutra Bahadur, Lisa Noone, Beth Macy, Kelly King, Kristina Cartwright, and Patricia Ricapa.

And finally, thanks are due to those who have contributed more than anyone else to this effort: my children, David and Kate, and my husband, Dan, who gave up many things, tangible and intangible, so that I could travel the world, research, and write. Across the last five years, Dan in particular has given me a tremendous gift, never wavering in his belief that this story had to be told.

While many institutions and individuals around the world are doing wonderful work, much more needs to be done to preserve the details of the past and consider its role in the present. Twenty percent of the author's proceeds of this book will be donated to relevant charities, split evenly between Nabokov-related organizations and memorial groups focusing on the Holocaust and the Gulag. For more details, or to find out how to donate, please visit *www.nabokovsecrethistory.com*.

ABBREVIATIONS

The Works of Vladimir Nabokov

ADA	*Ada or Ardor: a Family Chronicle*
ANL	*The Annotated Lolita*
BEND	*Bend Sinister*
CE	*Conclusive Evidence*
DEFS	*The Defense*
DESP	*Despair*
EO	*Eugene Onegin* (1990)
GIFT	*The Gift*
ITAB	*Invitation to a Beheading*
KQK	*King, Queen, Knave*
LL	*Lectures on Literature*
LRL	*Lectures on Russian Literature*
LATH	*Look at the Harlequins!*
Mary	*Mary*
NG	*Nikolai Gogol*
PF	*Pale Fire*
PNIN	*Pnin*
RLSK	*The Real Life of Sebastian Knight*
SM	*Speak, Memory*

SO	*Strong Opinions*
SP	*Selected Poems*, edited by Thomas Karshan
STOR	*The Stories of Vladimir Nabokov*
USSR	*The Man from the U.S.S.R. & Other Plays*

Abbreviations for Other Works and Sources

AFLA	*Vladimir Nabokov: His Life in Art*, by Andrew Field (1967)
AFLP	*Vladimir Nabokov: His Life in Part*, by Andrew Field (1978)
BBAY	*Vladimir Nabokov: The American Years*, by Brian Boyd (1991)
BBRY	*Vladimir Nabokov: The Russian Years*, by Brian Boyd (1990)
Berg	Henry W. and Albert A. Berg Collection of English and American Literature The New York Public Library
BFA	Bundesarchiv-Filmarchiv, Berlin
FBI	U.S. Federal Bureau of Investigation
LC	Library of Congress
NYRB	*The New York Review of Books*
NWL	*Dear Bunny, Dear Volodya: The Nabokov-Wilson Letters, 1940-1971*, edited by Simon Karlinsky (2001)
NYT	*The New York Times*
Schiff	*Véra (Mrs. Vladimir Nabokov)*, by Stacy Schiff (2000)
USNA	United States National Archive
TWATD	*The Twelve Who Are To Die: The Trial of the Socialists-Revolutionists*, by the Delegation of the Party of the Socialists-Revolutionists (Berlin, 1922)
USHMM	United States Holocaust Memorial Museum
USCIS	U.S. Citizenship and Immigration Services
VNM	Vladimir Nabokov Museum
Wellesley	Wellesley College Archives
VNSL	*Vladimir Nabokov, Selected Letters 1940-1977*, edited by Dmitri Nabokov and Matthew Bruccoli (1991)

NOTES

INTRODUCTION
1   Chesme Palace's House of Invalids sits next to Chesme Church in the southern part of St. Petersburg.
2   See "A Visit to the Museum" for a story in which a trip to a museum in France transports its narrator to a Russian police state.

CHAPTER ONE: WAITING FOR SOLZHENITSYN
1   Assessments of *Lolita*: "funny," William Styron; "the only convincing love story of our century," *Vanity Fair*; and "the filthiest book I have ever read" by John Gordon, editor of the *Sunday Express*.
2   *John Wayne and Marilyn Monroe*: BBAY, 407-8.
3   *a stable of stories*: See the Lolita-related dissection of period films in Graham Vickers' *Chasing Lolita: How Popular Culture Corrupted Nabokov's Little Girl All Over Again* (2008), 76-83.
4   *cried herself to sleep each night*: Humbert himself notes Lolita's nightly tears (176).
5   Oates, Joyce Carol, "A Personal View of Nabokov," *Saturday Review*, January 6, 1973, 36-7. See Phyllis Roth's *Critical Essays on Vladimir Nabokov* (1984) for the original, as well as a postscript Oates later added to her essay.
6   The Updike quote is from "Van Loves Ada; Ada Loves Van," *The New Yorker*, August 2, 1969, 70; Amis's description comes from "Martin Amis on *Lolita*," an essay published by Random House for the 100th anniversary of Nabokov's birth; *for forty years*: From Karlinsky's "Nabokov and Chekhov: the lesser Russian tradition," *Triquarterly*, Winter 1970, 7-16. This history is also discussed by Leland de la Durantaye in "The Pattern of Cruelty and the

Cruelty of Pattern in Vladimir Nabokov," *The Cambridge Quarterly* (October 2006), 301-326.

7   *Eliot*: NWL, 263; *Dostoyevsky*: LRL, 104; *Faulkner*: NWL, 239; *Pasternak*: SO, 57. The Pasternak reference is to *Doctor Zhivago*, a novel Nabokov abhorred, though he found Pasternak's early poetry remarkable. When it came to women novelists, Nabokov would make an exception for Jane Austen's *Mansfield Park*, and occasionally offered kind words privately about books written by women, such as his praise of some of Mary McCarthy's fiction. In SM (177), Nabokov mentions his dislike of Stendhal, Balzac, and Zola. Malraux and James are dismissed on NWL (19).

8   *the highest human virtues*: "What is the best?" "To be kind, to be proud, to be fearless." (SO, 152); *bloody nose*: BBRY, 267.

9   *"admirable work"*: VNSL, 378; *could not, at any rate, be compared to Stalin's*: SO, 50.

10 Excerpt from Khrushchev's speech as quoted by Alexander Tvardovsky in the foreword to *One Day in the Life of Ivan Denisovich* (2008), vii.

11 *Mikhail Sholokhov on Solzhenitsyn*: See Grose, Peter, "Moscow Unrelenting in Blackout on Solzhenitsyn," NYT, December 12, 1968, 4.

12 *Nabokov receiving only two votes*: Slonim, Marc, "European Notebook," NYT, November 8, 1970, 316.

13 Gwertzman, Bernard, "Solzhenitsyn Shuns Nobel Trip," NYT, November 28, 1970, 1.

14 Lewis, Anthony, "Solzhenitsyn Hailed Despite Absence at Presentation of 1970 Nobel Awards," NYT, December 11, 1970, 3.

15 Solzhenitsyn, Alexander, "Excerpts from Nobel Lecture by Solzhenitsyn," NYT, 25 August 1972, 2.

16 CBS Evening News, "Solzhenitsyn Arrested," Tuesday, February 14, 1974.

17 Scammell, Michael, *Solzhenitsyn* (1984), 857; Shabad, Theodore, "Expulsion by Soviet Highly Unusual Step," NYT, February 14, 1974, 16. It was not lost on readers at the time that expulsion had been only the first tactic used against Trotsky, whose name became synonymous with hysteria over supposed anti-Soviet sabotage and whose life ended with a lurid assassination in Mexico.

18 *Olof Palme*: "Three Nations to Welcome Author," *The New York Times*, February 14, 1974, 1; *Kissinger*: "U.S., Britain and Germany Offer To Welcome Author," NYT, February 14, 1974, 85.

19 *suggesting that he had been an informer*: Scammell, *Solzhenitsyn*, 952.

20 Former prisoner Michael Romanenko had written about GULAG as the acronym for Soviet camp administration in a survey of the Russian penal system publicized in the West as early as 1948, and *The New York Times* mentioned and explained the title of Solzhenitsyn's "The Archipelago of Gulag" as early as November 1969. But it was *The Gulag Archipelago* that gave the word its current meaning of a prison camp system in which forced labor played the lead punitive role for a totalitarian police state.

Kennan: "Speaking Truth To Power," *The Economist*, August 7, 2008; *a public firestorm in French politics*: The Italian CP broke with Moscow, but the French CP attacked Solzhenitsyn, sealing a doom that had (for other reasons) long been approaching. Kritzman, Lawrence et al., *The Columbia History of Twentieth-Century French Thought* (2007), 193; Scott, Michael, et al., *French Intellectuals Against the Left* (2004), 89-94.

21 *a staggering number*: Once records were available, it became possible to assemble a ballpark figure for executions during the Great Purge, though no definitive number exists. In his biography of Stalin, Robert Service estimates that approximately a thousand people a day were shot during the two worst years of Stalin's purges, and another thousand expired on average each week in the camps (356).

every other account: Robert Conquest's *The Great Terror* (1968) had attempted to comprehensively document Stalin's Purges, but had to do so without access to many of the personal accounts that Solzhenitsyn was able to review.

22 *his favorite writers*: A statement made by Nabokov to the *Wellesley College News*, mentioned in BBAY, 122.

23 *not special enough*: Scammell, *Solzhenitsyn*, 25.

24 *lone article in a regional paper*: Scammell, *Solzhenitsyn*, 381.

25 Solzhenitsyn, Alexander, *The Gulag Archipelago: An Experiment in Literary Investigation: 1918-1956* (1974), vol. 1, 163.

26 BBAY, 648.

27 *an interview for The New York Times*: Shenker, "The Old Magician at Home," BR2; "juicy journalese": BBAY, 648; *Véra on Solzhenitsyn*: Schiff, 343 and 428n.

28 *"cackles of laughter" and "manly prose"*: Levy, Alan, "Understanding Vladimir Nabokov: A Red Autumn Leaf Is a Red Autumn Leaf, Not a Deflowered Nymphet," *NYT Magazine*, October 31, 1971, 20; *In a letter*: VNSL, 496.

29 VNSL, 528.

30 Kramer, Hilton, "A Talk with Solzhenitsyn," *NYT Book Review*, May 11, 1980, BR1.

31 See SM, 27.

32 Scammell, *Solzhenitsyn*, 906.

33 Interview for BBC *Bookstand* program, 1962.

CHAPTER TWO: CHILDHOOD

1 *a sensitive woman*: BBRY, 32.

2 Joseph Hessen, one of V. D. Nabokov's closest friends: "For his part, V. D. Nabokov loved to speak about his children, particularly his oldest son whom, I repeat, he literally idolized, and his wife and her parents did this even more so than he . . ." AFLP, 92.

3 *"The Butcher"*: General Valeriano Weyler. See Stuart Creighton Miller's *Benevolent Assimilation: The American Conquest of the Philippines 1898-1903*, 3.

4   *nearly christened Victor*: SM, 21; *Russian Orthodox archpriest*: Father Konstantin Vetvenitski. SM, 21. See "New Light on Nabokov's Russian Years" (*Cycnos*, Volume 10, No. 1) for Boyd's corrections to the baptism story in BBRY.

5   Monas, Silas, "Across the Threshold: *The Idiot* as a Petersburg tale," from *New Essays on Dostoyevsky* (2010), 68.

6   Another prisoner at the Fortress was Alexander Ulyanov, Lenin's older brother who was tried and executed for his bomb-making role in the attempted assassination of Tsar Alexander III.

7   SM, 53.

8   AFLP, 92. During her St. Petersburg days, Olga would become good friends with Alyssa Rosenbaum, who later gained fame in exile under her adopted name, Ayn Rand. For more on Rand and Nabokov, see D. Barton Johnson's "Nabokov, Ayn Rand, and Russian-American Literature or, the Odd Couple," *Cycnos*, vol. 12, no. 2, 1995: 100-108.

9   *boys were permitted*: The girls, by contrast, had to settle for books that were chosen for them. AFLP, 94; *never friends*: "'They were never friends,' says Sikorski. 'There was always an aversion.'" See Lev Grossman's "The Gay Nabokov," *Salon*, May 17, 2001. Much of the rest of the description of Nabokov's childhood relationship with Sergei is taken from SM.

10   *terrorized his son*: SM, 72; BBRY, 30.

11   *nervous, brittle woman*: Nabokov, Nicolas, *Bagazh: Memoirs of a Russian Cosmopolitan* (1975), 108; *letters and numbers in color*: Nabokov would describe the synesthesia he shared with his mother in detail in SM.

12   *moldy and remote little kingdom*: SM, 45.

13   SM, 58-9.

14   While agreeing that measures needed to be taken against what was seen at that time as rising Jewish economic power, Nabokov's grandfather resisted the *ad hoc* implementation of the May Laws, new anti-Semitic measures. See Klier, John, *Russians, Jews, and the Pogroms of 1881-82* (2011), 216.

15   *choosing to stay with his fellow detainees*: BBRY, 27.

16   *more attention than his wife's*: AFLP, 87.

17   *"massacre these vile Jews"*: *The Bessarabetz*, whose translated article appears in James Harvey Robinson and Charles Beard's *Readings in Modern European History*, vol. 2 (1909), 371-372.

18   Facing a rising tide of intolerance and seeing their legal status worsen year after year, more than two million Jews left Russia between 1881 (the year Alexander II was assassinated) and 1914. Obolensky-Ossinski's work from 1928 is quoted from *Demography: Analysis and Synthesis* (426).

19   SM, 188.

20   "Chinese for Jews: Benefits for Kishineff Sufferers in Doyers Street Theater," NYT, May 12, 1903, 3.

21   *the same publisher*: Pavel Krushevan later also represented Kishinev in the Second Duma; *complete forgeries*: purporting to be an account of a meeting of rabbis that occurred once a century to plot world domination, *The Protocols of the Elders of Zion* were a Russian stew cooked out of existing European novels and stories. The original tales had nothing to do with Jews, rising instead out of rants against Freemasons, political condemnations of Napoleon III, and the fictional melodramas of French writer Eugene Sue, author of *The Wandering Jew*, whose literary sins were many in the eyes of Vladimir Nabokov and included undue influence on Fyodor Dostoyevsky.

22   *off the low bridges*: "Russian Tells Story of Sunday's Massacre," NYT, January 25, 1905, 1; *breaking windows and taking fruit*: "Civil War Threatened," NYT, January 23, 1905, 1; *were picked off by soldiers*: SM, 184. Nabokov was not in St. Petersburg at the time. BBRY, 54.

23   *Peter and Paul Fortress*: Revolutionary writer Maxim Gorky was also arrested and imprisoned at this time. See Simon Oscar Pollock's *The Russian Bastille* (1908), 12.

      fighting Japanese sailors: "Russian Tells Story of Sunday's Massacre," NYT, January 25, 1905, 1.

24   *stripped of his court title*: BBRY, 57; *"dark forces"*: SM, 155.

25   *unanimous passage*: BBRY, 34; *preparation of a petition*: Pipes, Richard, *A Concise History of The Russian Revolution* (1996), 47; *"lounging . . . and openly smirking"*: Morrison, John, "The State Duma: A Political Experiment," from *Russia Under the Last Tsar*, Anna Geifman, ed. (1999), 146.

26   Stockdale, Melissa, *Paul Miliukov and the Quest for a Liberal Russia* (1996), 162.

27   *a leading Kadet*: Mikhail Gertsenshtein—see Hoffman, Stefani and Ezra Mendelsohn, *The Revolution of 1905 and Russia's Jews* (2008), 63; *friends convinced him of the wisdom*: BBRY, 67.

28   *Holdups and burglaries*: The S.R.s officially repudiated their extremist members and cousins, but on a local level they often accommodated the violent deeds, resorting to theft and extortion themselves. As parts of Russia fell into gangster anarchy, the economic terrorism provided cover for the Tsar to further restrict liberties and establish martial law. See Geifman, Anna, *Thou Shalt Kill* (1995), 75-77.

      Lenin: While it may not be possible to pinpoint the first time V. D. Nabokov first heard of Lenin as *Lenin*, a strong guess can be made as to when he first encountered the family name of Ulyanov. Lenin's older brother Alexander had come to the capital in 1883 to study at St. Petersburg University, where he joined the terrorist wing of a revolutionary group. When two would-be bombers were arrested on Nevsky Prospect in an assassination attempt on the life of the Tsar, the trail led back to Alexander. He confessed, claiming responsibility for the plot, for building the bomb, for everything— far more responsibility, in all likelihood, than he actually had. But he refused to express remorse and was executed by hanging on May 8, 1887.

Since the name Lenin was not even a whisper in history's mind at that point, it is possible to feel a profound sympathy for the sixteen-year-old Vladimir Ulyanov, sitting in his progressive home at Simbirsk in southern Russia in the last days of studying with his sister Olga for his gymnasium (roughly the equivalent of high school) exams. News of their brother's death arrived in the first days of the month-long testing. In a testament to their education, intelligence, or resoluteness, both Vladimir and Olga received the highest marks available in all ten subjects. His teacher, headmaster Fyodor Kerensky, would write with pity to recommend the young Vladimir for university study, explaining his brilliance and preemptively defending his moral development, while acknowledging that he was highly antisocial. See Robert Service's *Lenin: A Biography* (2002), 59-62.

29 Lenin, Vladimir, "When You Hear the Judgement of a Fool," pamphlet dated January 1907.

30 They were tried under article 129, which set penalties for "inciting rebellion, 'sowing hostilities between classes or specific groups of the population,' or advocating the overthrow of the existing civil structure of the state." Lennoe, Matthew Edward, *The Kirov Murder and Soviet History* (2010).

31 SM, 29; BBRY, 76.

32 *a treasured catch from his own childhood*: SM, 75: *Vladimir sent a butterfly*: BBRY, 76.

33 *V. D. Nabokov's mother had forbidden*: BBRY, 77.

34 SM, 68.

35 SM, 188; BBRY, 98.

36 *even from those who liked him*: SM, 74.

37 SM, 160. The Jewish Zelenski's family had at some point converted to Lutheranism—a path taken, as Maxim D. Shrayer notes, by many Russian Jews to avoid restrictions and quotas established in the 1880s. See his article "Jewish questions in Nabokov's art and life" in *Nabokov and His Fiction: New Perspectives* (1999).

38 SM, 185.

39 AFLP, 123.

40 *Nabokov helped edit*: BBRY, 118.

41 *passages that clarified Sergei's homosexuality*: SM, 257-8; *several distressing romances*: BBRY, 106.

42 *his schoolmaster described him*: Boyd, "New Light on Nabokov's Russian Years."

43 *begging on his knees*: SM, 188.

44 Geifman, Anna, ed., *Russia Under the Last Tsar* (1999).

45 Geifman, *Russia Under the Last Tsar*, 161-3.

46 "Russians Anxious over Beiliss Jury," NYT, November 2, 1913, C4.

47 Samuel, Maurice. *Blood Accusation: The Strange History of the Beiliss Case* (1996), 230.

48   *enough Christians to go around*: Samuel, 213; *no Jews left to save*: Samuel, 27.
49   *One trial chronicler*: Maurice Samuel; *groups clearly supporting Beilis's prosecution*: one French newspaperman helpfully put together a book of accounts of Jewish ritual murder from the last eight centuries; *might be committing ritual murder*: Samuel, 239.
50   *could not be kept aloft*: The priest who had written on the dark rituals of the Talmud was found, upon cross-examination, to not know much about the Talmud at all. The police officer who had investigated the murder refused to participate in the sham trial and, after being fired from his job, went on to publicly identify the boy's real killers. Hundreds of telegrams arrived to congratulate Beilis; telephone switchboard operators in Russia announced the word "Acquitted!" before they even asked callers which number to dial. No pogroms erupted in protest, but Beilis had to be taken back to his cell until the crowds dispersed. He left the following year for Palestine. Samuel, 249-254.
51   Samuel, 26 (taken from Alexander Tager's *Decay of Tsarism*).

CHAPTER THREE: WAR

1   *composing verse for years*: BBRY, 108.
2   SM, 232.
3   *V. D. Nabokov was mobilized*: BBRY, 111; *could not bridge the deep-rooted subservience*: SM, 47.
4   Stibbe, Matthew, "The Internment of Civilians by Belligerent States during the First World War," *Journal of Contemporary History*, vol. 41, no. 1, January 2006.
5   *exonerations did not take place as planned*: In addition, civilian prisoners were often housed alongside soldiers or sailors captured in battle. Since the civilians were not actually prisoners of war (even when they were held in the same camps with them), civilian internees generally had fewer rights than the captured soldiers.
      languished near starvation for years: Tiepolo, Tiepolo, Serena, ed., *"Reports of the delegates of the Embassy of the United States of America in St. Petersburg on the situation of the German prisoners of war and civil person in Russia,"* (1916) gathered as extracts in *DEP*, no. 4 (2006), 2-3. The toll of civilian internment eventually got a political label when "barbed-wire syndrome" entered the diplomatic lexicon during the war (see Stibbe). From the first years of its existence, it was understood as a hysterical psychosis followed by depression, a disease with literary antecedents drawn from the real world: Napoleon's incarceration at St. Helena, Dostoyevsky's stories of Siberian convicts, and the diaries kept by polar explorers. See "Military Medicine" entry in *Medical Record*, November 30, 1918, 944. The stress of ongoing imprisonment for civilian and military prisoners alike led to a new kind of conflict casualty that was recognized during the war by both Britain and Germany as grounds for transfer to a neutral country. Yet the Red Cross

---

and other brokers had great difficulty carrying out these transfers on the massive level that was required.

6 The hereditary nobility often escaped such measures, but as rhetoric escalated, there were dramatic detentions of high-ranking civilians in camps (Stibbe, 10).

7 *tools of Imperial justice for centuries*: Stalin, Trotsky, and Lenin had all been sentenced to exile—though Trotsky and Stalin had escaped. See Robert Service's *Stalin: a biography* (68) and *Trotsky: a biography* (67-69). See also Chapter 15 of Trotsky's autobiography *My Life* (1930).

8 *savaged in the minor press*: SM, 238; *Hessen expressed his dismay*: BBRY, 118; *under no circumstances*: SM, 238.

9 SM, 199-200.

10 *made him a millionaire*: SM, 71; *less than pleased*: BBRY, 121.

11 SM, 240.

12 Service, *Lenin*, 253.

13 *a red flag was hung*: "Revolution in Russia; Czar Abdicates," NYT, March 16, 1917, 1; *the first corpse he had seen*: SM, 89.

14 Realizing he would likely be forced into exile, Nicholas was reluctant to leave his adolescent, hemophiliac son at the helm of their collapsing nation.

15 Montefiore, Simon Sebag, *Young Stalin* (2008), 309.

16 Service, *Lenin*, 256.

17 Medlin, Virgin and Steven Parsons, *V. D. Nabokov and the Russian Provisional Government* (2006), 119.

18 For Trotsky's account of his time in a concentration camp, see Chapter 23 of his autobiography.

19 Buchanan, George, *My Mission to Russia* (1923), 120-1.

20 Anne Applebaum notes that "*kontslager* first appeared in Russian as a translation from the English, probably through Trotsky's familiarity with the history of the Boer War" (*Gulag*, xxxiv). His first-hand experience of a British camp further underlines the British connection Applebaum mentions and offers an even more direct route.

21 Medlin and Parsons, *V. D. Nabokov*, 149.

22 *supporting the imposition of the death penalty*: Gavriel Shapiro mentions this incident in his forthcoming book *The Tender Friendship and the Charm of Perfect Accord: Nabokov and His Father*. His source is Ariadna Tyrkova, "V. D. Nabokov i pervaia duma," *Russkaia mysl'* 6–7 (1922): 272-83.
   buttons . . . should be banned: Medlin and Parsons, 134.

23 *sophisticated older Jewish girl*: Eva Lubrzynska. BBRY, 123.

24 *machine-gun fire in the streets*: BBRY, 133; *armed street fighters*: SM, 181-2.

25 *taking his exams weeks early*: BBRY, 133; AFLP, 137. Nabokov's marks would fall just shy of Lenin's perfect exam record from two decades earlier.

26 SM, 243.

27 *staying . . . would merely return him to prison*: Medlin and Parsons, *V. D. Nabokov*, 173-77.

28 *the Bolsheviks demanded to be recognized as the majority*: Their argument was that a November split in the Socialist Revolutionary Party invalidated the election results. They claimed that the S.R. faction that now allied itself with the Bolsheviks made the Bolshevik Party the majority.

29 "Bolsheviki Drowned Victims in Masses," NYT, June 4, 1918, 5.

30 *an estate that Tolstoy had visited years before*: They stayed at the home of Countess Sofia Panin (BBRY, 136). Panin was detained in Petrograd at the time, in prison. After decades of work establishing and funding workers' facilities, Panin would find herself the first person tried by the Bolshevik Revolutionary tribunals. "Farcical Trial of Countess Panin," NYT, December 26, 1917, 2.

31 *when Kaiser Wilhelm's divers swept the harbor*: Brian Boyd first noted Count Obolensky's memoir and the poem, "Yalta Pier," that Nabokov composed that summer (BBRY, 148). Additional reports appear in German and even American newspapers of bodies washing up on the shore en masse in the months after the executions.

32 BBRY, 157.

33 *"Strike at the Jews"*: Fishman, Lala and Steve Weingartner, *Lala's Story: a memoir of the Holocaust* (1998), 28; *hundreds of pogroms*: Pipes, *A Concise History*, 262.

34 Gilbert, *Churchill and the Jews* (2008), 32. Regrettably, the Protocols that had fanned the flames of prejudice made their way back from the war, in English translations passed to European and American officials who believed them, and tucked into the rucksacks of doughboys who had served in several theaters of war.

Churchill himself, however, was caught up in the same framework for discussing Jewry that so often hampered useful discussions, citing an openly anti-Semitic historian in 1920 to support the idea of a "sinister confederacy" of "International Jews" that had threatened the world for more than a century and calling on Jews to stand against it. ("Zionism versus Bolshevism," *Illustrated Sunday Herald*, February 8, 1920, 5.)

35 *tens of thousands of Jews were massacred*: The degree to which Petliura himself advocated, permitted, or discouraged these murders is, a century later, still a matter of widespread and heated debate. Petliura's forces fought both the Bolsheviks and the White Army in the drive for Ukrainian independence.

more than a hundred pogroms: For more on the atrocities, read Isaac Babel's *Red Cavalry*. Babel witnessed the violence of the region firsthand in 1920, as a traveling journalist embedded with a cavalry unit.

fifty to one hundred thousand Jews: Pipes, *A Concise History*, 264. Just as White Army forces had associates like V. D. Nabokov, who were horrified by the targeting of Jews and the attacks on civilians, a segment of actors on all sides urged restraint. In some regions, activists of different religions and cultural identities tried to band together to organize democratic rule locally. The independent Ukrainian state even created a Ministry of Jewish Affairs. Their efforts, however, met the same fate as V. D. Nabokov's idealism. In addition, Jewish civil defense leagues united and occasionally fought off marauding forces, but their successes were overshadowed by the militant anti-Semitism arrayed against them. For more detailed attention to the complexity of the region, see Henry Abramson's *A Prayer for the Government, Ukrainians and Jews in Revolutionary Times, 1917-1920* (1999).

36 *"Jewish-looking young men"*: Medlin and Parsons, 43; *could "have been called the Sanhedrin"*: Medlin and Parsons, 151. The latter is a strange aside for a formal political account—and Nabokov's father quickly notes that the Jewish Council Member sitting next to him pointed it out first.

   "servile": Medlin and Parsons, 128; *"impudent Jewish face" and belonging to "the repulsive figure"*: Medlin and Parsons, 177. The face belongs to Moisei Uritskii.

37 Virgil Medlin and Stephen Parsons, the translators of V. D. Nabokov's memoir, found "the apparent evidences of anti-Semitism" troublesome and asked Vladimir Nabokov directly about them. Nabokov replied that his father had believed himself so beyond accusations of anti-Semitism that he "used to make it a point—and go out of his way to make it—of being as plainspoken about Jew and Gentile as were his Jewish colleagues . . ." (10).

38 *"burning hatred of the English"*: Zeman, Zbyněk A. B., *Germany and the Revolution in Russia: documents from the archives of the German Foreign Ministry* (1958), 82. Trotsky had immortalized his Nova Scotian detour in one of the earliest documents in the widely circulated Red Army traveling library collection. Trotsky's pamphlet on his incarceration appeared before Karl Marx's *Communist Manifesto* on the list of documents prioritized for inclusion in front-line traveling libraries.

   a concentration camp: Applebaum, *Gulag*, 8.

39 the sort of people: Some POWs and enemy aliens had been released after the Treaty of Brest-Litovsk which ended Russia's participation in the war, but many in the south sheltered in place amid the turbulent back-and-forth of the Civil War, lacking money, food, or a safe path to try to get home.

   Trotsky wrote a memo: Applebaum, *Gulag*, 8.

   "sweeping floors," etc.: Trotsky, Leon, "A Prisoner of the English," a Red Army pamphlet dated May 17, 1917.

40 Applebaum, *Gulag*, 8.

41 Ibid.

42 Nabokov himself would make this distinction later in *Bend Sinister*: "While the system of holding people in hostage is as old as the oldest war, a fresher

note is introduced when a tyrannic state is at war with its own subjects and may hold any citizen in hostage with no law to restrain it" (xiii).

43 *"regime of bloodshed, concentration camps, and hostages"*: CE, 176.

44 Nabokov must have been persuasive enough—Boyd notes that the soldiers ended up bringing butterflies to him soon after (BBRY, 142).

45 *make his stage debut*: AFLP, 131.

46 *godforsaken*: AFLP, 131; Medlin and Parsons, 35; *make use of the libraries*: BBRY, 149-150.

47 The nineteen-year-old Vladimir would remember that V. D. Nabokov referred to his title as minister "of minimal justice," and in truth, with the regional government dependent upon the Volunteer Army for protection, justice was ill-served in the south. V. D. Nabokov found himself badly positioned to prosecute military abuses, and was distrusted as part of a government led by both Jewish and Tatar elements. He managed to transform the local judiciary but could not do much more (BBRY, 155 and 158; SM, 177). Dana Dragunoiu writes of a case in which known Bolsheviks had killed Army officers. Army officers demanded the death penalty, but the regional government had outlawed it. The proceedings were moved to another location that was more stable, and on the way, the soldiers responsible for transporting them shot the defendants. *Vladimir Nabokov and the Poetics of Liberalism* (2011), 123.

48 SM, 200; AFLP, 134; BBRY, 158.

49 *westward to Sebastopol in a car* and *misappropriated government funds*: BBRY, 159.

Chapter Four: Exile

1 *lice-ridden quarters*: AFLP, 135. Lice were more than unpleasant—they were a vehicle for the transmission of typhus, which killed more people in the Russian Civil War than died in combat. See Evan Mawdsley's *The Russian Civil War* (2007), 287.

   a single glass of water: AFLP, 135.

2 BBRY, 163.

3 Ibid., 164.

4 Nabokov, V. D. "A Distressing Problem," February 7, 1920, from *Struggling Russia, Volume 2*, Arkady Joseph Sack, ed., 737. My thanks to Matthew Roth for passing along this piece.

5 *New Russia: Rul* eulogies of V. D. Nabokov, March and April 1922, LC; *jewels were sold*: BBRY, 165.

6 *transcript of Samuil Rosov*: Nabokov was apparently showing it to them to explain that he and Rosov had received nearly identical marks, but college admissions staff members seem to have thought it was Nabokov's own. AFLP, 137.

   changed to literature: BBRY, 170.

7 Lucie Leon's reminiscences, *Triquarterly*, Winter 1970, 212.

8 AFLP, 139-40; BBRY, 168. The count, Robert de Calry, had a Russian mother but had not grown up in Russia.

9 *threatened with fines*: BBRY, 167; *got into fistfights*: BBRY, 181; *smeared food, etc.*: BBRY, 175.

10 *did not see eye to eye*: SM, 261; *whom V. D. Nabokov had hosted*: SO, 104; *praised Bolshevik ideals*: Wells did make a point of finding some Bolshevik methods problematic but regrettably necessary—which given his general support, was a finer point that would not likely have impressed either V. D. Nabokov or his son. "H. G. Wells Lost in the Russian Shadow," NYT, December 5, 1920, 102.
    "Kill the Yids!": BBRY, 179.

11 *amusing and regrettable*: BBRY, 179; AFLP, 139.
    Protocols of the Elders of Zion: Those *Protocols* had made their way west in the luggage or pockets of more than one Russian exile, and had become instantly popular abroad. They would in short order be translated, printed, and distributed across five continents. But they received what may have been their biggest boost a year after Nabokov's arrival in England, when American inventor Henry Ford incorporated them into a series of articles for *The Dearborn Independent*, which had a vast circulation. The same year, Ford also published *The International Jew: The World's Foremost Problem*, a book drawn from the first installments of the series. It purported to make a clear link between Bolshevism and a Jewish plot for world hegemony. The book alone was translated into more than a dozen languages, and soon made its way back to Russia (see USHMM Web site, http://www.ushmm.org/wlc/en/article.php?ModuleId=10007244).
    By 1921 the *Protocols* had been definitively debunked as a hoax in the *Times of London*, which outed the original stories and novels from which they had been cribbed (originally denunciations not of Jews, but of Napoleon and freemasons). They would nonetheless continue to proliferate world-wide.

12 *"Jewish revolution"*: Belloc, Hilaire, *The Jews* (1922), 182; *"provoked and promoted by Jewish interests"*: Belloc, 50; *"a monopoly of Jewish international news agents"*: Belloc, 48; *proportional representation*: Belloc, 48.

13 *longing letters*: BBRY, 177; *"composing verse"*: 167; SM, 268.

14 BBRY, 180; STOR, 4-5.

15 BBRY, 189.

16 *Herbert Hoover's American Relief Administration*: Once Hoover had signed on, the Soviets disbanded their own domestic relief committee and arrested several of its members. Yedlin, Tova, *Maxim Gorky: A Political Biography* (1999), 135-6.
    five million people: Lynch, Allen, *How Russia Is Not Ruled: Reflections on Russian Political Development* (2005), 67.

17 SM, 179.

18 Lutz, Ralph Haswell, *The German Revolution*, vol. 1 (1922), 129.

19 *Frank Foley*: "Address given at the unveiling of a plaque commemorating Foley's service," British Foreign and Commonwealth Office, February 11, 2011; *Willi Lehmann*: Siddiqi, Asif, *The Rockets' Red Glare* (2010), 171; *"central office for espionage abroad"*: Lukes, Igor, *Czechoslovakia between Stalin and Hitler: the diplomacy of Edvard Beneš in the 1930s* (1996), 20.

20 Milyukov continued to see the Socialist Revolutionaries as the vital link, but V. D. Nabokov resisted the notion of playing to class concerns or joining an international revolutionary front. As unlikely as V. D. Nabokov's interventionist strategies were, Milyukov's current approach represented equally wishful thinking. By the end of 1921, the Socialist Revolutionaries certainly had no interest in a Kadet alliance. They were undercut from the Left by Lenin's New Economic Policy, which allowed farmers to retain control over much of their crops, wiping out a source of farmer and peasant affection for the S.R.s. After months of Milyukov's efforts to build bridges, the Russian S.R. leadership openly rejected his courting, repeating descriptions of him as "a pittiful [sic] fragment of the Kadet party" and saying that he "represented nobody." The S.R.s were not playing hard to get—they had had enough of the Bolsheviks trying to link them to monarchists and anti-revolutionary forces, and they were not about to help their opponents make the case.

21 BBRY, 189.

22 Ibid., 180-1.

23 Ibid., 192.

24 "Czarist Officers Shot at Milukov," NYT, March 30, 1922, 3.

25 Ibid.

26 "The Death of V. D. Nabokov," *Rul*, March 30, 1922, LC.

27 "Anti-Milukov Plot Under Munich Inquiry," NYT, March 31, 1922, 3.

28 Shabelski-Bork also held Milyukov responsible for the hardships suffered by the Russian émigré community, and claimed to have written repeatedly to demand the return of letters belonging to the Tsarina which Milyukov had in his possession. Taboritski, who at first claimed not to be involved in the plot, later confessed to a part in the conspiracy but claimed he had not shot anyone. "Czarist Officers Shot at Milukov," NYT, March 30, 1922, 3.

29 The police, however, made clear that they could not guarantee the monarchists' safety and demanded the cancellation of the conference. Trains heading south from the city were monitored for any collaborators who might have been planning to flee. "Czarist Officers Shot at Milukov," NYT, March 30, 1922, 3.

30 "Anti-Milukov Plot Under Munich Inquiry," NYT, March 31, 1922, 3; *Rul*, March 29, 1922, LC.

31 BBRY, 198.

32 Milyukov's tribute to V. D. Nabokov in the pages of *Rul*, March 30, 1922, LC.

33 Taken from a March 19, 1922 letter from Lenin to Molotov on the Black Hundreds' anti-clerical campaign. The Bolsheviks had already revoked the amnesty extended years earlier to the S.R.s who had opposed them in the Civil War. When new waves of arrests unfolded in early 1922, the number of targeted groups expanded to include additional S.R. leaders, priests, academics, and intellectuals.

34 *Nabokov would reference decades later*: EO, Commentary, Part 2, 121-2; *above the table hung a red banner*: Early film footage exists from the trial and the public holiday/pro-death penalty events occurring surrounding it.

35 Chief among the foreign attorneys was Belgian Emile Vandervelde, former chair of the Second Internationale, a collective of socialist and labor organizations to which Lenin and Trotsky had previously belonged for nearly a decade.

36 The defendants were divided into three groups: those who had committed lesser offenses, those who had become witnesses for the prosecution, and twelve prisoners who pleaded not guilty. The group of twelve represented the heart of the Socialist Revolutionary Party in Russia. "Thirty-four Persons on Trial," NYT, June 10, 1922, 5.

37 *foreign attorneys announced*: Shub, David, "The Trial of the SRs," *Russian Review*, Vol. 23, No. 4 (Oct 1964), 366. News reports appeared suggesting that Vandervelde had been assassinated, but in truth, the attorneys had only been detained. They were refused exit visas and had to go on a hunger strike before they were permitted to leave Russia.

38 TWATD, 22; Yedlin, *Maxim Gorky: A Political Biography*, 162.

39 Duranty, Walter, "Soviet Chiefs Stage Anti-Treason Show," NYT, June 22, 1922, 3.

40 TWATD, 84.

41 *waited ten hours*: TWATD, 86.

42 Nabokov liked Blok's poetry in general but loathed "The Twelve," which he described as having a "pink cardboard Jesus" stuck onto its end (Gold, Herbert, "The Art of Fiction, No. 40, Vladimir Nabokov," interview from *The Paris Review*, Summer-Fall 1967). In TWATD, Karl Kautsky, a German Marxist who had fallen out with Lenin and Trotsky, writes: "There is no material difference between the rule of a 'legal' Czar and a clique that accidentally established itself in power. There is no difference between a tyrant who lives in a palace and a despot who misused the revolution of the workers and peasants to ascend into the Kremlin."

43 *"a slow torturous death"*: Rul, August 15, 1922, LC; *sent to concentration camps*: Rul, August 25, 1922, LC.

CHAPTER FIVE: AFTERMATH

1 BBRY, 194.

2 SP, 7.

3 BBRY, 194.

4   *the acquisition of a steady job*: BBRY, 196; *as good as the women*: "Hives of Russian Refugees," NYT, Jan 8, 1922, 84.

5   De Bogory, Nathalie, "The New Russian Exile and the Old," NYT, April 24, 1921, BRM4.

6   *down to one meal a day*: "The New Russian Exile and the Old," NYT, April 24, 1921, BRM4; "Princesses Work as Riga Typists," NYT, May 3, 1921, 8; *fever for hidden jewels*: Stories of men and women being tortured to death in the hunt for concealed treasure leaked out from Russia in the first years after the Revolution. See, for example, "Streams of Jewels Out of Russia," NYT, June 11, 1922, 91.

7   "Dying Refugees Crawl into Brest-Litovsk," NYT, August 9, 1921, 3.

8   *stagnant quarters*: "Constantinople's Russians," NYT, April 23, 1922, 105; *dying with a slow grace*: "Hives of Russian Refugees," 84.

9   AFLP, 147.

10 *Alice in Wonderland*, whose heroine Nabokov transformed into Anna, became *Anya v Stranye Chudes* in Russian.

11 Nabokov worked in the orchards of Solomon Krym, who had headed up the Crimean regional government in which Nabokov's father had been Minister of Justice.

12 *"awaited one"*: BBRY, 207; *lost permission to practice*: As Maxim D. Shrayer notes in "Jewish Questions in Nabokov's Art and Life," Véra's father had refused to solve the problem, by converting to Christianity, as so many others had (75). See also AFLP, 177.

13 Nabokov had grown up with tales of explorers and adventures from childhood, and the rough outline of events and language he chose hew surprisingly close to those of the real Scott's journal. But Nabokov also bent his story to his own needs. He renames the last surviving expedition members, and more strangely, as the characters are freezing to death miles from the *South* Pole with no prospect for rescue or return, his invented Scott records seeing the northern lights (USSR, 280). The real Scott had mentioned the lights generically in his diary, but Nabokov transformed the plain *aurora* into their northern variety. The move further dislocates the story and recalls others then facing starvation in a desolate, snowbound landscape—the Russian exiles of the far north.

14 Jewish wandering was diagnosed as "a racial, pathological disorder" at Jean-Martin Charcot's Paris hospital in the 1890s. See Henry Meige's "*The Wandering Jew* in the Clinic: a Study in Neurotic Pathology," in *Nouvelle Iconographie de la Salpêtrière, Hasan-Rokemand Dundes*, 190-194. The account was also published in the U.S. in *Popular Science*, vol. 44 (February 1894). Nabokov was familiar with some of Charcot's work and mocked it in passing in his book on Gogol.

15 *The Wandering Jew* debuted in Manchester in August 1920 and London a month later, moving on to the Knickerbocker Theater in New York the following year.

16 *"staged symphony"*: USSR, 28—only *Agasfer*'s prologue survives; *Jean-Paul Marat*: Marat had coined the phrase "enemy of the people," a phrase that gained a new life in post-Revolutionary Russia. By 1922, Marat was so lauded by the Soviets that they had named multiple ships after him.

17 AFLP, 163.

18 Schiff, 8.

19 Ibid., 30.

20 *considered herself a socialist*: AFLP, 177; *anti-Bolshevik assassination plot*: Schiff, 55.

21 BBRY, 220; SM, 48.

22 *unaware that he intended*: Schiff, 10; *"I shall have you come here"*: AFLP, 174.

23 AFLP, 87.

24 "Shun Russian Mail in Fear of Typhus," NYT, March 18, 1922, 2.

25 Lucie Leon in *Triquarterly*, Winter 1970, 214.

26 BBRY, 234.

27 Ibid., 233.

28 Ibid., 239.

29 SM, 249; BBRY, 146.

30 BBRY, 271.

31 *fairly talented*: Nabokov would in the next sentence describe Pasternak's verse as "convex, goitrous, and goggle-eyed" but remained a fan of him as a poet, if not as a novelist. Barnes, Christopher and Boris Leonidovich Pasternak, *Boris Pasternak: 1928-1960, A Literary Biography* (1989), 308.

32 Klein, Sandy, "Nabokov's Inspiration for *The Defense*," note on NABOKV-L, the Nabokov Listserv, May 28, 2011. The German chess master was Count Curt von Bardeleben. See Daniel Johnson's *White King and Red Queen: How the Cold War Was Fought on the Chessboard* (2008), 68.

33 *"snatched a gun"*: BBRY, 343, quoting Lev Lyubimov in the March 1957 *Novy Mir; redeem their very existence*: Berberova, Nina, *The Italics Are Mine* (1999), 315.

34 BBRY, 355.

35 Nabokov specifically noted later that he had made Martin (*Martyn* in the original Russian) singularly untalented. For more on why, see Leona Toker's *Nabokov: The Mystery of Literary Structures* (1989).

36 Nabokov had real-life examples of such exploits (the original Russian title of the book, *Podvig*, translates as Deed or Exploit). As Maxim D. Shrayer has noted, *Glory* recalls Boris Savinkov, who was part of the Socialist Revolutionary Party's political assassination wing with Abram Gotz and Ilya Fondaminsky before the Revolution, and an anti-Bolshevik provocateur after it, sneaking over the border to meet with conspirators in the Soviet Union. He was lured inside the Soviet Union in 1924, captured and put on trial, dying in captivity soon afterward. See Shrayer's "The

Perfect *Glory* of Nabokov's Exploit," *Russian Studies in Literature*, vol. 35, no. 4, 29-41.

37 The beautiful castle complex built across the centuries came to play an intermittent role in Russian history. The monks of Solovki ran their distant outpost in quasi-independence from Moscow in its first three hundred years, then were more closely monitored from St. Petersburg in the next two centuries. As early as the sixteenth century, a first lone religious prisoner was sent there by the Tsar. For a full history of the islands, see Roy Robson's *Solovki* (2004).

38 Applebaum, *Gulag*, 20.

39 *shorthand for Bolshevik cruelty*: CE, 202; NWL, 222; *suicides and executions*: "Emma Goldman Denounces *Rule* of Soviets," NYT, April 5, 1925, XX4; "Russian Arrests Drop," NYT, February 17, 1924, 56; *most feared prison*: Emery, Steuart, "Soviet Sends Exiles to Jail by Airplane," NYT, March 21, 1926, XX24.

40 "Soviet Will Start Prisoners' Air Service To Take Exiles to Lonely Solovetsky Island," NYT, January 24, 1926, E1.

41 The first reference I found to the mosquito torture in the Western press came from Emma Goldman in 1925. She discussed the terrors of Solovki but mentioned the mosquito torture in connection with other camps. Soon after, the two would be linked. Goldman, Emma, "Emma Goldman Denounces *Rule* of Soviet," NYT, April 5, 1925, XX4.

42 *beaten by guards*: "British Tory Fights Reds' Forced Labor," NYT, February 8, 1931, 15; *chopping off their own hands, feet, or fingers*: "House Committee To Press Embargo on Soviet Products," NYT, February 1, 1931, 1; *international boycott*: Toker, Leona, *Return from the Archipelago* (2000), 16.

43 Gregory, Paul and Valerii Lazarev, *The Economics of Forced Labor*, Hoover Press (2003), 45.

44 Nabokov's story "A Matter of Chance" has a protagonist who is a cocaine user; as does a Russian novel *Cocaine Romance* (or *Novel with Cocaine*), written by an anonymous émigré, whom some believed to be Nabokov, though this was later disproven.

45 BBRY, 353.

46 Ibid., 376; AFLP, 160.

47 *two years training at a Berlin drama school*: Sonia Slonim studied at the city's celebrated Hoeflich-Gruening School (see Slonim's application for work with the U.S. Army in her FBI file); *once found himself chosen as an extra*: AFLP, 159.

48 "*The cinema must reflect social reality*": Clara Zetkin, quoted in *Film und revolutionäre Arbeiterbewegung 1918-1932*, vol. 2, (1975), 55; *responded to Zetkin's appeal*: Zetkin, meanwhile, proved herself a master of political theater of another kind by serving on the prosecuting team at the trial of the Socialist Revolutionaries.

49 In later years, Nabokov liked to mangle Eisenstein's name and refer to him as Eisenstadt—and believed that his experiments with montage had given the false impression that the arts were flourishing in the Soviet Union. Nabokov mentions him repeatedly in his letters to Edmund Wilson. NWL, 222.

50 A friend of Junghans and Sonia Slonim in touch with both of them later recalled first meeting Slonim as Junghans's girlfriend in Berlin in 1930. Carl Junghans's internment file, USNA.

51 Sonia Slonim worked at Houbigant Cheramy Perfume. Nabokov would reference Houbigant in his play "The Man from the U.S.S.R.," *USSR*, 70.

52 BBRY, 395.

53 Schiff, 99.

54 Yet he could recite poetry flawlessly in four languages. See Grossman's "The Gay Nabokov."

55 *he wanted to address the distance*: BBRY, 396; *handsome and charismatic*: Grossman, "The Gay Nabokov."

56 BBRY, 396.

57 The Soviets had invited him to collaborate on a film about American racism with Langston Hughes. See Arnold Rampersad's *The Life of Langston Hughes*, vol. 1 (2002), 247-9.

58 *Anna Feigin*: Feigin was Véra's cousin but had moved in with Véra's father (who was not a blood relation to Feigin) after Véra's parents had separated. Schiff, 42-3.

   turn the story over to his delusional narrator: Nabokov had already been practicing with disturbing first-person narration, having finished "The Eye," a novella with a dislocated Russian émigré as narrator who dies at the beginning of the novel.

59 *German films of the nineteen-twenties*: People have long seen resemblances between Nabokov's work and *Dr. Caligari*—see Norman Page's *Vladimir Nabokov* (1982), 21.

   fascination with doubles: The references to Dostoyevsky would be underlined when the book was translated into English. See Dolinin, Alexander, "The Caning of Modernist Profaners: Parody in *Despair*," originally in *Cycnos*, vol. 12, no. 2, 1995, 43-54, expanded and posted online at http://www.libraries.psu.edu/nabokov/doli1.htm.

60 When *Despair* was published in English, Nabokov would underline the Astrakhan setting for readers by including a reference to the Caspian Sea as Hermann has a flashback to his internment.

61 Tiepolo, *"Reports of the delegates of the Embassy of the United States of America in St. Petersburg on the situation of the German prisoners of war and civil person in Russia,"* 3.

62 The historic murders echo through *Despair*. "Dead water" and its reflections abound. In an interior story in the novel, evidence is tied to a stone and sunk

in water (144). After the murder, a bag and a gun are submerged in the Rhine (174). And Hermann himself wanders by his own lakeside murder scene with "stone-heavy shoes" (172). For an account of the executions at Astrakhan, see Thomas Remington's *Building Socialism in Socialist Russia* (1984), 109.

63   When *Despair* was translated into English, Nabokov had Hermann express his "belief in the impending sameness of us all" as rationale for his faith in Communism, more explicitly linking his politics with his own murder plot. DESP, 20.

Nabokov worked not just the early camps but a whole tapestry of Russian history into *Despair*. At the height of Stalin's drive toward collective farms, with its mass executions and the founding of the Gulag, Hermann's wife declares that Russian peasants have become extinct (23). We learn that his wife's cousin, Innocent, was executed by a firing squad just after Hermann and his bride escaped Russia (47). And her other cousin, Ardalion, bears a huge scar from his time with the White Army (39).

64   Nabokov later suggested in the intro to the English translation that the book had less appeal to White Russians than his previous novels.

CHAPTER SIX: DESCENT

1   See Michael Morukov's piece from Gregory and Lazarev, *The Economics of Forced Labor*, Hoover Press (2003), 160.

2   Figes, Orlando, *The Whisperers: Private Life in Stalin's Russia* (2008), 114-115.

3   *longer than the Panama and Suez Canals*: Duranty, Walter, "Soviet Hopes High as Industry Gains," NYT, July 3, 1933, 3; "merciful as well as merciless": Duranty, Walter, "Soviet Releases 12,484 in Record Amnesty," NYT, August 5, 1933, 1.

4   In advance of FDR's first campaign for the White House, Roosevelt publicly consulted with Duranty about Russia. After Roosevelt won, he sent representatives to Moscow to open discussions on normalizing relations. That November, Walter Duranty traveled with Soviet Foreign Minister Maxim Litvinov to the U.S., where formal diplomatic relations were established between the two countries. At the banquet given in Litvinov's honor at New York's Waldorf Astoria, Duranty received a standing ovation. He would come to refer to Litvinov's visit as the "ten days that steadied the world." See S. J. Taylor's *Stalin's Apologist: Walter Duranty, The New York Times' Man in Moscow* (1990), 190-91.

5   Taylor, 208.

6   *celebrated in the Nabokov family apartment in Berlin*: BBRY, 117; *the release of his brother*: Figes, *The Whisperers*, 194.

7   Scammell, *Solzhenitsyn*, 81-2.

8   *a novel called Chocolate: Despair*, the next novel Nabokov wrote after meeting Tarasov-Rodionov, would be narrated by a man who makes chocolate but has utterly lost his moral compass; *grew alarmed*: BBRY, 375.

9   Kessler, Harry and Charles Kessler, *Berlin in Lights: The Diaries of Count Harry Kessler, 1918–1937* (2001), 428.

10 *"who endanger state security"*: "Ein Konzentrationslager für politische Gefangene in der Nähe von Dachau" *Münchner Neueste Nachrichten* (from The Holocaust History Project), March 21, 1933: "The Munich Chief of Police, Himmler, has issued the following press announcement: On Wednesday the first concentration camp is to be opened in Dachau with an accommodation for 5000 persons. 'All Communists and—where necessary—Reichsbanner and Social Democratic functionaries who endanger state security are to be concentrated here, as in the long run it is not possible to keep individual functionaries in the state prisons without overburdening these prisons, and on the other hand these people cannot be released because attempts have shown that they persist in their efforts to agitate and organise as soon as they are released.'"

    haunting stories and lullabies: "Party Foes Held by Nazis Decline," NYT, April 15, 1934, E2. In addition, Morris Janowitz notes that a traditional prayer wishing to be good had been transformed into one that translates (rather awkwardly) as: "Dear God, make me dumb/so I will not to Dachau come." "German Reactions to Nazi Atrocities," *The American Journal of Sociology*, vol. 52, no. 2 (September 1946), 141–146.

11 *"'Siberias' of the German revolution"*: "Party Foes Held by Nazis Decline," NYT, April 15, 1934, E2; *"preventive custody"*: "Anti-Nazi Feeling Grows in Bavaria," NYT, Nov. 11, 1933, 8.

12 "German Fugitives Tell of Atrocities at Hands of Nazis," NYT, March 20, 1933, 1.

13 Maar, Michael, *Speak, Nabokov* (2010), 24-5.

14 Schiff, 67; Tim, Annette, *The Politics of Fertility in Twentieth-Century Berlin* (2010), 88.

15 AFLP, 199.

16 *was in Berlin for the festivities*: Johnston, Robert Harold, *New Mecca, New Babylon: Paris and the Russian Exiles 1920-45* (1988), 110; *should not speak*: Schiff, 68; BBRY, 403.

17 *"Educated among monkeys"*: BBRY, 400; *"completely Jewified"*: Shrayer, Maxim D., "Jewish questions in Nabokov's art and life," *Nabokov and His Fiction: New Perspectives*, 90n7.

18 BBRY, 400; *unpleasant prospect*: on his way back to France, Bunin had been strip-searched by the Gestapo, made to swallow castor oil, and detained until the laxative had done its work, just to prove that he was not smuggling hidden jewels. AFLP, 195.

19 "Nazi Violence," editorial in NYT, March 12, 1933, E4.

20 Lenin had borrowed Chernyshevsky's title *What Is To Be Done?* for a key political treatise. And the Paris Socialist Revolutionaries had named their

journal *Contemporary Annals* in part as a tribute to Chernyshevsky's own *Contemporary.*

21 GIFT, 275.

22 *"half-crushed by years of penal servitude"*: GIFT, 228; *who slept on a bed of nails*: Chernyshevsky, Nikolai, and Michael Katz, *What Is To Be Done?* (1989), 288; *"sometimes weeps and sobs"*: GIFT, 288.

23 BBRY, 405.

24 Ibid., 403.

25 Ibid., 407.

26 Schiff, 69; BBRY, 407.

27 *served as a translator*: AFLP, 199; *a hidden cache of weapons*: "Nazis Hunt Arms in Einstein Home," NYT, March 21, 1933, 10; *idiocies of "liberalistic" university education*: "In the liberalistic era, the professor who became important and famous was the one whose theories were least comprehensible, Herr Frank asserted. Only this, he added, could account for the cult like [sic] that reared around Dr. Albert Einstein." "Reich Professors Warned by Nazis," NYT, Oct. 6, 1934, 4.

28 ITAB, 114.

29 *transcribing the speeches*: AFLP, 199-200; *they claimed to be surprised*: Schiff, 67.

30 SM, 286-7; BBAY, 423.

31 AFLP, 195.

32 Michael Maar notes the spare power of Victor Klemperer's diary of life under the Nazis in 1942, in which Klemperer lists thirty-one prohibitions—among them buying cigars, possessing fishing licenses, owning typewriters, and using lending libraries. Klemperer notes that they are all nothing compared to "home invasion, abuse, prison, concentration camps and violent death," but the meanness of the restrictions amplified their power and sometimes seemed as significant as the violence. See Maar's "Tagebücher: warum schreibt man sie, warum liest man sie?," *Schriftenreihe der Vontobel Stiftung*, 2012.

33 Marvin, Carolyn, "Avery Brundage and American participation in the 1936 Olympic Games," *The Journal of American Studies* vol. 16 (1982), 82-3. Brundage would later host Leni Riefenstahl when she came to America to try to market her film of Hitler's Olympics.

34 The earlier effort by Junghans to collaborate with Langston Hughes and the Soviet film company Meschrabpom had ended in international disaster. The group of educated, sophisticated African Americans who came with Hughes from America to help make a film about capitalist racism did not at all fit the Soviets' expectations of what oppressed black American workers should look like—they were too young, too fair-skinned, and too intellectual. And as Junghans realized to his shock during screen tests for *Black and White*, most of them were completely unable to sing Negro spirituals.

Junghans tried to revise the script that he had been handed, but even with his revisions, Hughes dismissed the idea of the proletariat (or in other drafts, the Red Army) coming to the rescue of black steelworkers in Alabama as "not even plausible fantasy." Everyone involved with the film meant well, Hughes believed, but they had no workable conception of racism in America. See Rampersad's *The Life of Langston Hughes* as well as Meredith Roman's "Forging Freedom: Speaking Soviet Anti-Racism," *Critique*, vol. 39, no. 3 (August 2011).

After the Olympic project, Junghans collaborated on pro-Fascist movies about the Spanish Civil War and *Die Grosse Zeit*, a tribute to the "Great Age" begun under Hitler.

35 "Reich Reclaiming Huge Moor Region," NYT, Dec 25, 1936, 1.

36 Ibid.

37 For more on the labor camps of Southwest Africa—and for a wide-ranging history of the evolution of concentration camps across the twentieth century—see Kotek et al., *Le Siècle des Camps: Détention, concentration, extermination—cent ans de mal radical* (2000).

38 Mindful of the suffering of the poor, a group of American writers, including novelist John Dos Passos and New York critic Edmund Wilson, had signed a letter in 1932 supporting the Communist Party in the United States. Taylor, *Stalin's Apologist*, 156-157.

39 Duranty's name, apartment, and words are mentioned several times in Wilson's diary *The Thirties*.

40 Reef, Catherine, *E. E. Cummings: A Poet's Life* (Houghton Mifflin Harcourt, 2006), 79.

41 *Red Army banquet and theater performances*: Dabney, Lewis, *Edmund Wilson: A Life in Literature* (2005), 209.

42 *felt like a prison*: Dabney, 211; *"moral top of the world"*: Taylor, 217.

43 *Night of the Long Knives*: Don Levine, Isaac, "Soviet 'Purge' Condemned," NYT letter to the editor, December 12, 1934, 22; *might fade over time*: Dabney, 201-2.

44 *"can't make an omelette"*: Taylor, 185; *"Judas Trotsky": History of the Communist Party of the Soviet Union (Bolsheviks), Short Course* (1948), 324; *"no one left to purge"*: The speaker is Vice Chairman of the Soviet State Planning Commission Valery Obolensky-Ossinsky, from "66 Are Executed by Soviet, Accused of Terrorist Plots," NYT, Dec. 6, 1934, 1.

45 *flying to Oslo*: Conquest, *The Great Terror: A Reassessment*, 152; *twenty minutes*: Conquest, 421.

46 *coveted paycheck vanished*: Schiff, 74; *chance windfall*: BBRY, 429; Schiff, 75.

47 Schiff, 77.

CHAPTER SEVEN: PURGATORY

1 *every day*: Schiff, 78.

2 *a reputation*: Schiff, 87; *Nabokov stopped in*: Schiff, 86; *became lovers*: BBRY, 433.

3   *money . . . they did not have*: BBRY, 434.
4   Psoriasis entry from PubMedHealth at the U.S. National Library of Medicine: http://www.ncbi.nlm.nih.gov/pubmedhealth/PMH0001470/
5   BBRY, 434.
6   *to raise money for the trip*: BBRY, 435; *alienated members*: Schiff, 83.
7   AFLP, 228; Schiff, 83.
8   *bad checks*: "Ex-Prince Declares He Can Beat Roulette," NYT, July 23, 1926, 13; *would soon leave him*: Schiff, 100; *she was living in a hotel*: Schiff, 83 and 100.
9   Schiff, 85 and 90. Véra told Nabokov's first biographer the former, and the latter is drawn from Nabokov's letters at the time.
10 Nicholas' life played out the alternate scenario of Vladimir's 1937 drama: after his wife divorced him for his infidelity, he remarried, to a former student of his. The marriage lasted seven years, more or less, until his second wife filed for divorce on the grounds of desertion. He would have five wives in all. Nicholas Nabokov's FBI file.
11 Schiff, 85.
12 The same month, Nabokov wrote to Samuil Rosov, a Tenishev classmate who had tracked him down. In response to a letter with reminiscences of their friendship and Nabokov's kindness to him as a boy, Nabokov sent a warm three-page missive recalling the class bully, a teacher driven to weeping by their classmates, a yogurt treat they used to eat with aluminum spoons, and the ride down Nevsky Prospect during which he first understood that sex was sometimes for sale. Nabokov suggested that there were two kinds of people in the world, those who remember and those who do not. AFLP, 125-6.
13 *a colleague of Fondaminsky's*: Vadim Rudnev.
14 BBRY, 441-43.
15 Ibid., 443.
16 *the press bureau itself*: Denny, Harold, "Soviet 'Cleansing' Sweeps through All Strata of Life," NYT, September 13, 1937, 1; *had to settle for cooks and nurses*: Denny, 1; *sausage stuffed with strychnine*: "Thirty-one Are Executed," NYT, October 5, 1937, 10.
17 Scammell, Michael, *Koestler: The Literary and Political Odyssey of a Twentieth-Century Skeptic* (2009), 158-9.
18 "Coughlin In Error, Kerensky Asserts," NYT, November 29, 1938, 20. Kerensky pointed out that not a single Jew had been present in the first Provisional Government. Coughlin had millions of weekly listeners at the time and was in the process of republishing the *Protocols of the Elders of Zion* in serial form in his own newspaper, *Social Justice* (USHMM: http://www.ushmm.org/wlc/en/article.php?ModuleId=10007244).
19 One article compared the chaos to G. K. Chesterton's *The Man Who Was Thursday*, a nightmare novel in which the police are anarchists and anarchists

are police. "Purge of Red Army Hinted in Removal of Four Generals," NYT, June 10, 1937, 1.

20 *knew enough to see through the show trials*: Scammell, 94-95. Ironically, in his last year of university studies at Rostov State University, Solzhenitsyn transformed the student newspapers, jolting them into relevance, and received a prestigious Stalin scholarship.

21 *"Better Hitler Than Blum"*: Haas, Mark, *The Ideological Origins of Great Power Politics* (2007), 130; *"a subtle Talmudist"*: Judt, Tony, *The Burden of Responsibility* (2007), 76; *the Kerensky of France*: Trotsky, Leon, "Whither France? The Decisive Stage," June 5, 1936.

22 *Blum had resigned*: Blum, who had been inspired to enter politics by the anti-Semitism of the Dreyfus trial, had maintained an uneasy alliance with the Soviet government despite the news of purges coming out of Russia, but took umbrage when a Soviet finance minister was assassinated in Paris just days before he was to make public revelations about the show trials. Faced with fiscal challenges and attacks from the far right and his own party, Blum was urged to launch a socialist revolution in France, but surrendered power according to the rules and conditions under which he had been given it. See "Foreign News: Stalin, Navachine and Blum," *Time* magazine, February 8, 1937.

André Gide detailed Soviet human rights abuses: Gide's reversal would not change Nabokov's impression of his writing; he later labeled Gide one of his three most-detested writers (reported in the *Wellesley College News*, mentioned in BBAY, 122).

a group of writers: Together they formed the American Committee for the Defense of Leon Trotsky. Holding on to the shreds of their earlier revolutionary idealism, the inquiry spawned by the Committee was dedicated to proving Trotsky's innocence in the Soviet plots attributed to him. Committee members met in Mexico with Trotsky himself. Despite its tendency to caress the exiled revolutionary, the commission managed to gather definitive proof that central pieces of evidence against Soviet party leaders facing execution had been fabricated. A hotel where a key conspiracy was said to have had been hatched turned out to have been torn down years before the supposed rendezvous. A clandestine airplane trip to Norway to meet with Trotsky had landed at an airfield that had been out of service for months at the time of the flight. A report hundreds of pages in length debunked the evidence in the show trials as fraudulent.

23 SM, 272.

24 BBRY, 480.

25 "Nazis to Answer 'Eternal Road,'" NYT, February 14, 1937, 35.

26 *a book: Der Ewige Jude*, Munich: Zentralverlag der NSDAP, Franz Eher Nachfolger GmbH, 1937; *exhibition was condemned*: "Boycott of Jews Reviving in Reich," NYT, December 29, 1937, 6.

27 Shrayer, Maxim D. "Jewish Questions," *Nabokov and His Fiction: New Perspectives*, 86.

28 Sachsenhausen would soon hold Martin Niemöller, a Lutheran pastor who defended Jews and publicly denounced Nazi rule.

29 "Hitler Is Pleased to Get Rid of Foes," NYT, March 27, 1938, 25.

30 McCormick, Anne O'Hare, "Europe," NYT, July 4, 1938, 12.

31 Newton, Verne, *FDR and the Holocaust* (1996), 131-4.

32 *"assimilable immigrants"*: "Reich Again Urged To Assist Emigres," NYT, July 30, 1938, 5; *fleeing Austrian Jews*: "Cold Pogrom in Vienna," NYT, July 9, 1938, 12.

33 After the conference that fall, Switzerland and Germany worked out a border arrangement whereby all Jews in German territories would have a red "J" stamped on their passport. Any bearer of a J-stamped passport would be denied access to the Swiss border, while Germans considered Aryans could travel freely back and forth without any special visa (see the "J Stamp" entry from *Antisemitism: A Historical Encyclopedia of Prejudice and Persecution*, 363).

34 *shot German Embassy staffer Ernst vom Rath*: A little over a week earlier, Grynszpan's father, a Polish Jew, had been directed to report to a local police station in Hanover, Germany. From there, he had been held overnight and forcibly deported to Poland with thousands of other men. See Nicholson Baker's *Human Smoke* (2008), 94; *Jews would be punished*: "Reich Embassy Aide in Paris Shot To Avenge Expulsions by the Nazis," NYT, November 8, 1938, 1.

35 USHMM: http://www.ushmm.org/wlc/en/article.php?ModuleId=10005201

36 Schiff, 100.

37 USHMM: http://www.ushmm.org/wlc/en/article.php?ModuleId=10005539

38 *essential awkwardness . . . had never vanished*: Elena Nabokov, in Grossman's "The Gay Nabokov"; *marriage to her had damaged Vladimir*: Schiff quotes Sergei writing to Nabokov's ex-fiancée that if she had married Vladimir, "He would never have turned out so badly" (99); *would have been in dire straits*: Schiff, 99.

39 A prize-winning novel called *Silbermann* by Jacques de la Cretelle published in 1922 plumbed French anti-Semitism. A problematic presentation of the issue, it was nonetheless lauded for its humanity at the time and went on to be named one of the best novels of the first half of the twentieth century in 1950 by *Le Figaro*. The Silbermann of the story, savaged by French anti-Semitism and a trial against his father, goes to America to work for his uncle's business.

40 *60 percent of Americans were opposed*: Newton, Verne, *FDR and the Holocaust*, (1996), 57; *without ever receiving a full vote*: Introduced in February 1939, the Wagner-Rogers refugee aid bill was sponsored in the United States Senate by Senator Robert F. Wagner (D-N.Y.). Anti-Semitism on the part of State Department officials also appears to have been part of the reason for the "failure to admit more refugees" under existing quotas (http://www.ushmm.org/outreach/en/article.php?ModuleId=10007698).

41 BBRY, 506.

42 Shrayer, "Jewish Questions," 76.

43 Grossman, "The Gay Nabokov."

44 Paragraph 175 was the section of the German code that dealt with homosexual behavior. V. D. Nabokov had supported Hirschfeld's battle against this part of the code more than a decade before (Dragunoiu, 177).

45 Few stories of homosexual prisoners have been preserved, because they continued to be prosecuted under Paragraph 175 (the law the Nazis had strengthened) even after the war. Karl Gorath was arrested in 1939 and sent to Neuengamme and later to Auschwitz, and survived: http://www.ushmm.org/wlc/en/idcard.php?ModuleId=10006529.

    heightened the risk: USHMM, http://www.ushmm.org/wlc/en/article.php?ModuleId=10005261.

46 *The Hour of Decision* and *The Great Age.*

47 *three British movies from recent years*: The three movies were *The Rothschilds, Jew Süss,* and *The Wandering Jew.* Friedlander, Saul, *The Years of Extermination: Nazi Germany and the Jews 1939-1944,* 20-23. All three targeted films were features, and in two of them the anti-Nazi German film star Conrad Veidt played the lead.

    After fleeing Germany with his Jewish wife in the early 1930s, Veidt had immediately set about attacking anti-Semitism in film. Interestingly, the "Eternal Road" exhibition that had spurred the original Nazi Eternal Jew exhibition in 1937 had been put on by Max Reinhardt, the other German superstar who had abandoned his country to speak out against Nazi policies. The Nazis were apparently sensitive to the power of movie stars to generate bad press.

    In one of the last scenes of *The Wandering Jew*, Veidt delivers a haunting monologue rebuking his monstrous Inquisitors. Acknowledging his own sin against Christ, he declares that their hatred and ignorance have nonetheless rendered them unfit to judge him.

48 Friedlander, 21-2.

49 Erich Stoll, Hans Winterfeld, and Heinz Kluth worked for Junghans on *Youth of the World* in addition to being cinematographers for *The Eternal Jew.*

50 He was also contributing to the right-wing nationalist newspaper *Aux Ecoutes,* and worked in a minor capacity in the French film industry. He appears to have extended a helping hand to the FBI through the French government, giving them notice that a Nazi agent and friend of Hermann Goering would be heading to New York. (Carl Junghans internment file, USNA.)

51 *One from Bunin*: VNSL, 30; Gaiton-Marullo, Thomas, *Ivan Bunin: the twilight of émigré Russia* (2002), 69 and 203; *circus clown*: For an in-depth look at Bunin and Nabokov, see Maxim D. Shrayer's "Vladimir Nabokov and Ivan Bunin: A Reconstruction," 339-411; *willing to help*: By now, Bunin's name was firmly

associated with sympathy for Jews. Parisian anti-Semites from the paper *Renaissance* called him the "kike father." Gaiton-Marullo, 210.

52 *Véra Nabokov's skills as a domestic*: Schiff, 103; *route for Jews to enter the country*: This was understood to be true in both the U.S. and England, though the historical analysis has been laid out more clearly in the case of England (see, for example *Whitehall and the Jews* by Louise London, in which London writes that "demand for women to undertake such work appeared inexhaustible").

53 BBRY, 486-9.

54 Schiff, 104.

55 SM, 192.

56 *Vasily Shishkov*: Shishkov was the maiden name of Nabokov's great-grand-mother; *"a great poet"*: STOR, 667.

57 BBRY, 511.

58 For more on "Vasily Shishkov," see Shrayer's chapter devoted to it in *The World of Nabokov's Stories* (1999).

59 STOR, 497.

60 *the mention of his rival's name*: Berberova, Nina, *The Italics Are Mine* (1999), 258.

61 BBRY, 515.

62 Ibid., 521-2.

63 *"France has been invaded a hundred times and never beaten"*: Diamond, Hanna, *Fleeing Hitler: France 1940* (2007), 8.

CHAPTER EIGHT: AMERICA

1 *fired its guns at a whale*: BBAY, 11; *sailing into New York Harbor*: "French Liner *Champlain* Here," NYT, May 27, 1940, 25; ship's records from the 1940 voyages of the S.S. *Champlain*.

2 *a note in New York's Russian-language daily newspaper*: BBAY, 13; *Jewish passengers' home cities*: USCIS files and ship's records from the S.S. *Champlain*. Nabokov's USCIS file: C-6556567; Véra's: C-6556566 and Véra visa file: 3027265.

3 Though the U.S. was not yet in the war, the country had already begun jailing members of the Socialist Workers' Party, a Trotskyite group that had publicly taken an anti-war stance and made speeches against democracy. Baker, *Human Smoke*, 351.

4 AFLP, 231; BBAY, 12

5 They would arrive there two years before the movie *Casablanca* itself was made. Not only would the film tell the story of a reunion of another pair of star-crossed lovers, one of them married, it would also include a scene with Ilka Gruening, a head instructor from Sonia Slonim's Berlin drama school.

6 Reston, James B., "Arrests in Britain," NYT, May 12, 1940, 1.

7 Leysmith, W. F., "Britons in Dispute over Enemy Aliens," NYT, April 7, 1940, 33.

8 "Alien Arrests Net Women in Britain," NYT, May 28, 1940, 7.

9 Koch, Eric, *Deemed Suspect: A Wartime Blunder* (1980), 17.

10 *ill-matched cargo*: Auger, 23; *their long-term fate*: Auger, 52-3. Many prisoners went to Canada, but some were shipped to Australia and other remote locations.

11 BBAY, 12.

12 Schiff, 108.

13 SO, 290.

14 AFLP, 234.

15 Ibid., 235; BBAY, 22.

16 Schiff, 110.

17 *124 pounds*: Vladimir Nabokov USCIS, C-File; *commissions*: NWL, 12.

18 *these first pieces*: on a biography of Ballets Russes founder Sergei Diaghilev and an author named John Masefield BBAY, 18; *delivery boy for Scribner's*: AFLP, 234; *heavily accented Russian*: AFLP, 247; BBAY, 44.

19 BBAY, 18.

20 *doing a somersault*: Meyers, Jeffrey, *Edmund Wilson: A Biography* (2003), 73; *physical decline*: Dabney, *Edmund Wilson: A Life in Literature*, 4 and 141.

21 *"not had to save his soul"*: Dabney, *Edmund Wilson*, 174.

22 While the NAACP hesitated to come to the aid of the Scottsboro defendants, the Communist Party was more than happy to provide counsel and champion their cause. For More on Wilson's reporting, see "Edmund Wilson: Letters to John Dos Passos," NYRB, and Dabney, *Edmund Wilson*, 177.

23 For a look at the similar pro-Soviet sympathies in England, see *Koba the Dread*, Martin Amis' consideration of the fifteen-year devotion of his father, novelist Kingsley Amis, to the Communist Party.

24 Wilson, *To the Finland Station*, 386.

25 BBAY, 20.

26 Wilson biographer Jeffrey Meyers would later suggest that it would have been more honest to end the story with the annexation (223).

27 Wilson, *To the Finland Station*, 379.

28 *wrote his first real articles on Lepidoptera*: BBAY, 24; *his earlier story*: Boyd called the original story Nabokov's "first attack" on Nazi Germany. Over time and in translation, "Cloud, Castle, Lake" evolved to be even more specifically anti-Nazi. As Maxim D. Shrayer notes in *The World of Nabokov's Stories*, during the translation process preparing it for publication, Nabokov shifted the song lyrics from disturbing forced camaraderie to overt calls for murder and destruction (136).

    eager to see more works: BBAY, 26.

29 *a secretarial position*: Schiff, 111; *denouncing Vichy policies*: Cull, Nicholas John, *Selling War: the British Propaganda Campaign against American "Neutrality" in World War II* (1996), 131; *promoting U.S. entry into the war*: White, Dorothy Shipley, *Seeds of Discord: De Gaulle, Free France and the Allies* (1964), 119-122; *a job she loved*: Schiff, 111.

30 Sonia Slonim, FBI file No. 121-HQ-10141: "Telegram dated 27 January 1941 from Fort de France to the Secretary of State: 'Suggest that Sofia Slonim, Russian, arriving New York aboard French vessel Guadeloupe about January 29 be observed due to unofficial report here that she may be a German spy.'" See also Department of the Army file on Sonia Sophia Slonim.

31 Carl Junghans's USCIS A-file 7595300 and ship records of the S.S. *Carvalho Araujho*.

32 Ship records of the S.S. *Carvalho Araujho*.

33 Carl Junghans's internment file, USNA.

34 Ibid.

35 Ibid.

36 *enjoyed immensely*: BBAY, 28; *little houses*: Schiff, 116.

37 VNSL, 25 August 1940, 33.

38 Rutkowski, Adam, "Le Campe de Royallieu à Compiègne, 1941-44," *Le Monde Juif* 101 (81), 124.

39 CE, 205-6.

40 Poznanski, Renée, *Jews in France during World War II* (2001), 202-3.

41 Poznanski, 208.

42 BBAY, 29.

43 NWL, 53.

44 *catching butterflies*: BBAY, 33; *tragic farce*: NWL, 53.

45 Abraham, Richard, *Alexander Kerensky* (1990), 371.

46 Abraham, *Alexander Kerensky*, 371. Kerensky had become a historical relic dreaming of a dead world, and, in the words of Nina Berberova, had himself died in 1917, but had somehow built up his armor—his beak, claws, and tusks—and continued to exist. See *The Italics Are Mine*, 301.

47 Scammell, *Solzhenitsyn*, 109.

48 Ibid., 112-3.

49 Solzhenitsyn's battery was scattered along listening posts strung together by telephone wire. The phone network required around-the-clock monitoring at each station. Securing a small collection of books from a library, Solzhenitsyn arranged for the operators to read stories and poems over the phone lines to help keep the artillerymen awake—Tolstoy, of course, and even contemporary Soviet poetry. Scammell, *Solzhenitsyn*, 124-5.

50 Meyers, 36-7 and 244.

51 *continue to get work*: NWL, 42; *less reverence*: Nabokov admired Tolstoy tremendously, but noted in a letter to Wilson how painful it was to watch the writer struggle to reunite Bolkonsky and Natasha in the novel *War and Peace*. NWL, 54.

52 NWL, 54.

53 Ibid., 56 and 34.

54 Ibid., 56.

55   BBAY, 47.

56   *months spent in a military hospital*: Meyers, 39; *"to save their own people"*: Meyers, 247. Noting that on nearly every other topic Wilson resisted anti-Semitism, biographer Jeffrey Meyers characterizes Wilson's later argument that American entry into the war was propelled by American Jews—and was in vain, because mass exterminations were already under way by the time of U.S. entry into the war—as "certainly the most foolish sentence [Wilson] ever wrote."

57   *his mother had exposed him to*: Dabney, 176; *foreigners and Jews*: Gordon, "America First: the Anti-War Movement, Charles Lindbergh, and the Second World War, 1940-1941," presented at a joint meeting of the Historical Society and The New York Military Affairs Symposium on September 26, 2003.

58   NWL, 53.

59   Ibid., 57.

60   BBAY, 37-38, 47.

61   Letter to Roman Grynberg, December 1944, quoted by BBAY, 48.

62   *longed to write a book in Russian*: AFLP, 250; *submitted "Ultima Thule"*: BBAY, 39.

63   Nabokov, Vladimir, "Softest of Tongues," SP, 158.

64   NWL, 38.

65   Ibid., 40.

66   Ibid., 41.

67   Ibid., 3.

68   Nabokov, Vladimir, "The Refrigerator Awakes," *The New Yorker*, June 6, 1942, 20.

69   NWL, 59.

70   "Textual Excerpts from the War Speech of Reichsfuehrer in the Reichstag," NYT, December 12, 1941, 4.

71   A small percentage were actually suspected as spies, but the vast majority were entirely innocent of any wrongdoing and had no interest in aiding America's military foes.

72   "Two Austrian Skiers at Sun Valley Are Seized," NYT, January 8, 1942, 19; "Short-Wave Sets of Aliens Curbed," NYT, December 21, 1941, 4.

73   "Brief Overview of the World War II Enemy Alien Control Program," USNA Web site: http://www.archives.gov/research/immigration/enemy-aliens-overview.html.

74   *Japanese as animals*: Dabney, 304; *registered for the draft*: BBAY, 43; *started a new novel*: BBAY, 40.

75   Nicholas Nabokov FBI file No. 77-2199.

76   But after 1941, the war effort took precedence over the more intimate and subtle kinds of films that Ophüls hoped to make. It would be years before he would have the opportunity to direct a studio film in America. See Lutz Bacher's *Max Ophüls in the Hollywood Studios* (1996), 29.

77   He had looked up William Dieterle, an Oscar-winning director who had been sending him money in New York. Junghans also reestablished ties with Jan

Lustig, a screenwriter who had just finished a project for rising star Rita Hayworth. Junghans's internment file, USNA.

78 *"a thorough-going Nazi"*: Hans Kafka covered film and the exile community in Hollywood for the New York newspaper *Aufbau*. Copies of his articles of December 19, 1941 and January 9, 1942 and his testimony appear in Junghans' USCIS A-file No: 7595300.

 Anti-Defamation League: Letter dated May 12, 1941. Carl Junghans's USCIS file.

 FBI case file: Junghans admitted that he had visited Russia in the early 1930s to make a film for the Soviet government. Acquaintances interviewed by Bureau agents reported that Junghans was completely unreliable and liked to brag about his work for the French secret police and his connections to Hitler, as well as claiming that he was working for the U.S. government. His file reveals that he had lagged Sonia Slonim in departing New York City by several weeks because his New York landlord managed to hold his bus ticket to keep him from skipping out on his unpaid rent. He was, in the words of one acquaintance, "a real four-flusher."

 Under questioning, Junghans denied ever being a Communist or a Nazi, and stressed his service to France Forever, his work with the French secret police in Paris, and intelligence he said he had turned over to U.S. agencies when he was in Europe, as well as contacts he had with the FBI since his arrival in America. In his statements, Junghans clearly misrepresented his Communist and Nazi connections.

 His stories of work for French intelligence seem to have been exaggerated, too. He did make propaganda for the government, but at least two acquaintances believed that in terms of intelligence, he was nothing more than a low-level informant, helping the French round up people for internment in concentration camps. Junghans's internment file, USNA.

79 Junghans claimed these agents were trained in the dialects of Odessa and Warsaw, and had even been placed in German concentration camps to provide better cover before they were into the West with their passports stamped "J" to do Hitler's bidding.

80 *200,000 paying visitors*: Poznanski, Renée, *Jews in France during World War II*, 211; *"the Communist, a Jewish product"*: Poznanski, 211-2.

81 Poznanski, 209 and 212.

82 Ship's passenger records.

83 Transit records. Frumkin is listed as their U.S. contact—the person who will vouch for them in America.

84 Plant, Richard, *The Pink Triangle: the Nazi war against homosexuals* (1988), 149.

85 NWL, 174; Grossman, "The Gay Nabokov"; November 2011 interview with Reimer Möller, archivist of the Neuengamme Concentration Camp Memorial.

86 "Nazis Blame Jews for Big Bombings," (via United Press) NYT, June 13, 1942, 7.

87 *"national health and hygiene"*: Poznanski, 255-6; *for being sympathetic to the Jews*:"Anti-Jewish Move Is Harming Laval," NYT, September 6, 1942, 14.

88 Poznanski, 265.

89 USHMM Web site: http://www.ushmm.org/wlc/en/article. php?ModuleId=10005215.

90 "French Jews Sent to a Nazi Oblivion," NYT, April 1, 1943, 2.

91 Yad Vashem central database of Shoah victims; Klarsfeld, Beate et Serge. *Le Memorial de la deportation des juifs de France*, Paris 1978.

92 Rashke, Richard, *Escape from Sobibor* (1995), 79-80; Patenaude, Bertrand. *A Wealth of Ideas: revelations from the Hoover Institution Archive* (2006), 156.

93 *aided the French Resistance*: Schakovskoy Family Papers, Amherst College Center for Russian Culture; *working with the Jesuits in Berlin*: Schiff, 265; *despite having an infant son*: Schiff, 100. Lena had left her husband before the start of the war.

94 Bunin, Ivan. *The Liberation of Tolstoy: a tale of two writers* (2001), 21 and related note on 160.

95 Interview with Vladimir Petkevič, grandson of Olga Nabokov, Prague, November 2011.

96 November 2011 interview with Vladimir Petkevič; see also earlier interview in Russian of Petkevič by Ivan Tolstoy, "110th anniversary of Vladimir Nabokov's Birth," *Myths and Reputations*, Radio Svoboda, April 2009.

97 BBAY, 48; Belletto, Steven, *No Accident, Comrade: Chance and Design in Cold War American Narratives* (2011), 4.

98 BBAY, 69.

99 Ibid., 68.

100 *taking her turn at France Forever* and *only to be turned away*: Sonia Slonim's FBI file.

101 Interview with Petkevič, Prague, November 2011; also, Tolstoy, 2009.

102 Brigham, Daniel, "Inquiries Confirm Nazi Death Camps," NYT, July 3, 1944, 3.

103 Koestler, Arthur, "The Nightmare That Is a Reality," NYT, January 9, 1944, SM5.

104 Karski, Jan, *The Story of a Secret State* (1944), 322.

105 VNSL, 47-8.

106 AFLP, 235.

107 STOR, 593.

108 Currivan, Gene, "Nazi Death Factory Shocks Germans on a Forced Tour," April 16, 1944, 1.

109 AFLP, 29. Shrayer, Maxim D., "Saving Jewish-Russian Émigrés," International Nabokov Conference in Kyoto, Japan, March 2010: http://fmwww.bc.edu/ SL-V/ShrayerSavingJRE.pdf.

110 Shrayer, Maxim D., *An Anthology of Jewish-Russian Literature* (2007), 462-3.

CHAPTER NINE: AFTER THE WAR

1   BBAY, 88.
2   VNSL, 63.
3   Ibid., 60–64; the poet he mentioned was Alexei Apukhtin.
4   NWL, 173.
5   *"human life"*: NWL, 175; *"destroying whole Japanese towns"*: Dabney, 304.
6   NWL, 173.
7   Ibid., 174. As Dabney notes, even Mary McCarthy returned to friendly terms with Wilson later (296); BBAY, 78.
8   NWL, 175.
9   VNSL, 63.
10 *a terrible price*: In "Conversation Piece" (originally "Double Talk"), Nabokov has a very unsympathetic Russian insist that when the Red Army came into Germany, no one was harmed. The group discusses its anxieties over the Soviets sending "intellectuals and civilians—to work like convicts in the vast area of the East," STOR, 594.

    to strip bare the countries they occupy: McCormick, Anne O'Hare, "Abroad: When the Policemen Want to Go Home," NYT, January 14, 1946, 18; Hill, Gladwin, "Flow of Displaced Tangled in Europe," NYT, May 30, 1945, 12. The Russian émigré community in New York, many of them now American citizens, protested the agreement at Yalta that forced Soviet citizens to return to Russia. See "Russian Exiles in U.S. Censure the Soviet," NYT, August 1, 1945, 9.

    rather than heading home: Clark, Delbert, "Soviet Deserters Said To Be Hiding to Avoid Forced Return To Russia," NYT, March 26, 1947, 12.
11 Scammell, *Solzhenitsyn*, 140.
12 Ibid., 132.
13 It is a request Nabokov likely never made of Véra. While Natalia was there, Solzhenitsyn taught her to shoot a pistol (Scammell, *Solzhenitsyn*, 130), a skill Véra had acquired decades before (Schiff, 55).
14 Scammell, *Solzhenitsyn*, 136.
15 Ibid., 142.
16 Schiff, 137.
17 NWL, 173; VNSL, 66-7.
18 "Mr. Churchill's Address Calling for United Effort for World Peace," NYT, March 6, 1946, 4.
19 BBAY, 126.
20 NWL, 144.
21 Ibid., 97-8.
22 Ibid., 171.
23 BBAY, 107; Schiff, 134; ANL, 436.
24 Information from Sonia Slonim's U.S. Army Military Intelligence file.

25 Information from Sonia Slonim's FBI file.

26 VNSL, 72-3. In what seems to be an argument for either the ineffectiveness of the program or Nicholas Nabokov himself, a composition student of Nicholas Nabokov's would later recall his claim about the post that his "most significant contribution was unmasking the radio theme song for 'The FBI in Peace and War' as the work of a Communist." See Argento, Dominick, *Catalogue raisonné as memoir* (2004), 2-3.

    but Nicholas had: Nicholas Nabokov's references are listed in his FBI file.

27 All material on Nicholas Nabokov here is taken from his FBI file (No. 77-2199), including a summary of a 1948 interview of George Kennan by the FBI.

28 Nicholas Nabokov FBI file.

29 Stonor Saunders, Frances, *The Cultural Cold War: The CIA and the World of Arts and Letters* (2000), 43.

30 Schiff, 332.

31 Schakovskoy Family Papers, Amherst College Center for Russian Culture.

32 *"we must build an organization for war"*: Stonor Saunders, 93; *"no artist . . . can be neutral"*: "Atomic Physicist Scraps Defense of Reds at Cultural Talk as Result of Korea Attack," NYT, June 28, 1950, 9.

33 Stonor Saunders, *The Cultural Cold War*, 93.

34 *other moral failings*: Krug is on the verge of molesting "a very young girl" a third his age when he and his son are arrested (137 and 197); *for five years*: Krug related that as a child, he had tripped the Toad and sat on his face every day (50-1).

35 BEND, 233.

36 Albeit with an American twist—as Boyd notes, the last sentence, "The child is bold" is a line from Nabokov's own 1945 citizenship test. BBAY, 87.

37 BEND, xiii.

38 The narrator references "the ghoul-haunted Province of Perm," a notorious Gulag site (BEND, 38); *BEND*, 108-9.

39 Krug is willing to cave, however (as Nabokov once noted he himself would cave), confronted with a choice between maintaining his principles and saving his child.

40 Watts, Richard, "Comic Strip Dictator," *The New Republic*, July 7, 1947.

41 *Darkness at Noon* would be published in England by a British publishing house as Koestler sat interned in Pentonville Prison in north London. Scammell, *Koestler*, 196.

42 He noted as much in a letter to Colonel Joseph Greene in a letter dated January 14, 1948. VNSL, 80.

43 Letter from Nabokov to Edmund Wilson dated February 1945. Quoted here from BBAY, 85.

44 Slonim testified before the Jenner Committee on March 20, 1953. "Sarah Lawrence Under Fire: The Attacks on Academic Freedom During the McCarthy

Era," 14. See Sarah Lawrence's online exhibit at http://archives.slc.edu/exhibits/mccarthyism/14.php.

refused to fire him: Nash, Margo, "ART REVIEW: Telling Its Story; The College That Roared," NYT, August 21, 2005, WE7.

45 NWL, 187.

46 Frustrated by his situation near the end of the war, Nabokov had written a Hollywood agent mentioning his interest in becoming a screenwriter. BBAY, 77.

47 BBAY, 123; Diment, Galya, *Pniniad* (1997), 31.

48 Though Nabokov did spend a summer picking fruit in the south of France during the summer of 1923, he himself noted how his employer—a friend of his father's—allowed him the occasional escape to chase butterflies. AFLP, 202.

49 "Red Cornell," Glenn Altschuler and Isaak Kramnic, *Cornell Alumni Magazine*, July 8, 2010.

50 See Schiff, 192, and Belmonte, Laura, *Selling the American Way: U.S. Propaganda and the Cold War* (2008), 25-26. Warning that making such a selection would result in damage costing the American taxpayer as much as thirty-one million dollars, the congressman was apparently ignorant of the fact that the book had been removed from the list of selections before the hearings had even begun.

51 *declared obscene*: Dabney, *Edmund Wilson*, 340-1.

52 Véra called McCarthy an "insignificant figure" (Schiff, 193). Later, when he started declaring open season on cultural figures, even those who had clearly repudiated Stalin, the American branch of the Nicholas Nabokov-led Congress for Cultural Freedom got mired in the issue. The U.S. branch engaged in a bitter argument over the mission of the Congress. If it was truly about cultural freedom, then many anti-Stalinist leftists argued that McCarthy was more of a threat to America than Communism. The more right-wing members of the Congress tried to block any broad-brush criticism of McCarthy's anti-Red crusades. Nabokov was peripherally connected to this debate through his cousin (who ran the organization), his best friend in America (who had been attacked by McCarthy), and his best friend's ex-wife (who was defending Wilson).

53 See the series of FBI files titled "Communist Infiltration into Education—Yale University," April 1953, and similar titles, all of which look at colleges and universities.

befriended Ithaca's resident G-man: AFLP, 235; BBAY, 311.

54 Newman, Robert, *Owen Lattimore and the "Loss" of China* (1992), 215; Schiff, 191-2.

55 Vladimir Petrov's *Soviet Gold* was published in 1949, and Elinor Lipper's *Eleven Years in Soviet Prison Camps* appeared in 1951. After realizing that he had been duped, Vice President Wallace later apologized to Petrov. See Adam

Hochschild's *The Unquiet Ghost: Russians Remember Stalin* (2003) for more on Wallace and Lattimore's trip.

    could not understand: Hochschild, *The Unquiet Ghost*, 269.

56   Schiff, 198.

57   NWL, 188.

58   Wilson and Nabokov, the early years: "His point of view is neither White Russian nor Communist. The family were landowning liberals, and intellectually the top of their class" (Meyers, 260).

59   NWL, 208; BBRY, 179.

60   NWL, 210.

61   Ibid., 222-3.

CHAPTER TEN: LOLITA

1   Alfred Appel's "Remembering Nabokov" from *Vladimir Nabokov: His Life, His Work, His World*, Quennell, Peter, ed. (1980), 18. Appel appears to be describing an improvisation witnessed by others from the semester before he studied with Nabokov. See also, BBAY, 172.

2   LL, 5; BBAY, 115.

3   *the real clash*: A statement he later amended to "between the author and the reader." SO, 183; CE, 220; *linked forever*: LL, 2.

4   LL, 385, 259-60.

5   NWL, 268.

6   *Keep it down*: NWL, 237. In his letter, Nabokov used the Russian term for ideological content.

      superficial: NWL, 245.

7   Dabney, *Edmund Wilson*, 287.

8   NWL, 271.

9   *a Russian narrator*: "That in Aleppo Once," STOR, 563; *first fictional representation of Holocaust denial*: Author interview with Maxim D. Shrayer, February 2012.

      In addition, the story "Time and Ebb" introduced a Jewish scientist who flees France and the Holocaust as a child, surviving well into the twenty-first century. His continued existence is a triumph, but the past—Hitler and the "indescribable tortures . . . inflicted by a degenerate nation upon the race to which I belong"—remains the unchangeable past (583).

10 *the same jars of jelly*: BBAY, 115; *lush, unforgettable images*: To his students, Nabokov explained that art can "improve and enlighten the reader" but only "in its own special way," when "its own single purpose remains to be good, excellent art" (BBAY, 111).

11 NWL, 238.

12 *chastised Alexandra Tolstoy*: Shrayer, Maxim D., "Jewish Questions," *Nabokov and His Fiction: New Perspectives*, 90, n11; *"Bloom's Jewishness too full of clichés"*: BBAY, 170.

13 SO, 228; NWL, 173. Sartre, who had written a dismissive review of *Despair* a decade earlier framing Nabokov as a second-rate Dostoyevsky, had been repaid in kind. In the review itself, Nabokov pointed out, with some disdain, that the songwriter of that particular (real-world) song was not Jewish but Canadian. The "Negress" whom the main character believes sings the song, Nabokov notes, was actually Sophie Tucker, a Jewish-Russian émigré. Nabokov highlights these apparent errors in the core of his savage review, but in fact, Sartre seems to have known this song well, having referenced it a decade before in the context of anti-Semitism the very year *Nausea* had been published in French. Nabokov may well have made the same mistake he abhorred in his own reviewers: confusing the character's unpleasant attributes with the author's. See Judaken, Jonathan, *Jean-Paul Sartre and the Jewish Question* (2007), 44.

14 *Christian propaganda*: EO, Commentary, 354-7; *no reason to drag in*: EO, Commentary, 354; *blintzes*: EO, Commentary, Index, 43.

15 SM, 9.

16 In *Contingency, Irony and Solidarity*, Richard Rorty suggests that in contrast to novelists such as Dickens, Nabokov's writing "gives us the details about what sorts of cruelty we ourselves are capable of, and thereby lets us redescribe ourselves" (xvi). Leona Toker refined some of Rorty's arguments and added her own in "Liberal Ironists and the 'Gaudily Painted Savage,'" from *Nabokov Studies*, vol. 1, 1994, 195-206.

17 CE, 78.

18 Ibid., 26.

19 CE, 177.

20 Ibid., 10. Interestingly, Nabokov was mistaken in his belief that Zhernosekov had been executed. He later corrected this in *Speak, Memory*.

21 NWL, 287.

22 Shrayer, Maxim D., "Vladimir Nabokov and Ivan Bunin: A Reconstruction," *Russian Literature XLIII* (1998), 392.

23 Scammell, *Solzhenitsyn*, 144-48; Solzhenitsyn, *The Gulag Archipelago*, Volume 1, 15-17.

24 Scammell, *Solzhenitsyn*, 156.

25 Solzhenitsyn, Alexander, *The Gulag Archipelago*, Volume 1, 220.

26 Solzhenitsyn, *The Gulag Archipelago*, 136.

27 Scammell, *Solzhenitsyn*, 257, 377, and 305.

28 Ibid., 325.

29 Under the heading of Nabokov's books addressing Russian subjects, *Lolita* would merit the briefest of mentions, with only a White Russian named Maximovich—a taxi-driving colonel and former advisor to the Tsar who cuckolds Humbert, urinates noisily in his toilet, and then steals his Polish wife.

30 VNSL, 128.

31 *Ukrainian man*: NWL, 229-30; *young girls kidnapped*: Nabokov refers to the kidnapping of Sally Horner in *Lolita*, a real-life event covered in newspapers as he worked on the novel. See Dolinin, Alexander, "What Happened to Sally Horner?" *The Times Literary Supplement*, September 9, 2005, 27-8.

     one of his colleagues at Stanford: BBAY, 33; *literary acquisition of various limbs*: BBAY, 211.

32 *likely to interpret the narrator*: VNSL, Véra Nabokov to Katharine White, 142; *the English-language novels he had already written*: One of which has a narrator named V., the other of which has a narrator who is a moth-collecting writer.

33 *"acute nervous exhaustion"*: NWL, 194; *before Véra intervened*: Schiff, 166; *no precedent in literature*: VNSL, 140.

34 BBAY, 73.

35 Scammell, *Solzhenitsyn*, 253. Natalia had divorced Solzhenitsyn because the lab where she worked had been declared classified, and if she had revealed on a new staff questionnaire that she was married to a prisoner convicted as a counter-revolutionary, she would have lost her job. She explained the reason for her actions, but news of the decision fell very hard on Solzhenitsyn.

36 Solzhenitsyn, *The Gulag Archipelago*, vol. 3, 420.

37 Cornell itself may have provided Nabokov a literary inspiration for *Pnin* in the form of Professor Marc Szeftel, a Jewish-Russian émigré who was a lesser light in the firmament of the university faculty. Szeftel, who helped arrange Nabokov's schedule with him prior to his first classes at Cornell, and who worked with him on a project related to *The Lay of Igor's Campaign*, bore a startling resemblance to the portrait of Pnin Nabokov outlined for the book's cover. Szeftel had lost his mother in a German camp, and never seemed to navigate America or academia with anything approaching Nabokov's confidence. It is not hard to see an echo of Szeftel's grief and displacement in Pnin, who is also an object of ridicule by his co-workers, shown up by the arrogant countryman who ultimately outshines him. While Nabokov's arrival did not force Szeftel out, he cast his fellow Russian further into shadow. See Galya Diment's thorough treatment of the Szeftel-Pnin parallels in her *Pniniad*.

38 PNIN, 135.

39 Ibid., 136 and 168.

40 BBAY, 270.

41 VNSL, 178.

42 BBAY, 288.

43 VNSL, 143-4 and 153.

44 Rape that happened three times a day, as Nabokov underlines in the Russian translation he himself later did of the book (BBAY, 490). For all that the idea

of a willing, seductive *Lolita* has entered the lexicon as a slightly naughty underage delight, Nabokov seems to have intended to cast his girl-child as a victim of brutality.

45 ANL, 284.
46 LL, 2; BBAY, 175.
47 *under his own name*: BBAY, 264; *look for one in Europe*: NWL, 321.
48 BBAY, 267.
49 Ibid.
50 VNSL, Vladimir Nabokov to Girodias, July 18, 1955, 175.
51 Donleavy would eventually have his revenge, and then some. After twenty years of litigation with Girodias over the rights to sell the novel in England, he would shut out Girodias altogether when he bought the Olympia Press name at a bankruptcy hearing. See James Campbell's "The spice of life," *The Guardian*, June 25, 2004.
52 BBAY, 293.
53 *more than one Olympia Press title: Histoire d'O* and Jean Genet's *Notre-Dame-des-Fleurs*; NWL, 320.
54 *"is a highly moral affair"*: NWL, 331; *"no moral in tow"*: ANL, 314
55 *vain and cruel wretch*: SO, 94.
56 *"broke her spell"*: The words are Humbert's own: "... until at last, twenty-four years later, I broke her spell by incarnating her in another." ANL, 15.

rooted in a tragedy the world had forgotten: Nabokov knew this history because he had lived it. He had spent the same summer, the summer of 1923, only before the bombing, picking apples in southern France, only miles from the Riviera coastline where Humbert and Annabel Leigh met that fictional summer. The refugee crisis had poured out across the sea that year, with thousands of Armenian refugees also housed in hotels and held in camps in Marseille and along the French coastline.

CHAPTER ELEVEN: FAME

1 BBAY, 295.
2 VNSL, April 4, 1957, 215.
3 John Hollander's Autumn 1957 *Partisan Review* critique of *Lolita*, taken from Page's *Vladimir Nabokov* (83).
4 Popking, Henry, "The Famous and Infamous Wares of Monsieur Girodias," NYT, April 17, 1960, BR4.
5 "published by some shady firm": NWL, 322; *pulled the books from the shelves*: BBAY, 300.
6 Nabokov makes clear that Humbert is an anarchist in the afterword that he added before *Lolita* was published in America (315).
7 There were in fact many expeditions (and wartime battles) over meteorological stations in the Arctic, the vague outlines of which had been covered

in the news of the day, but Junghans seems to have invented the details and names that he gave the FBI on this topic.

8   "cold labor": ANL, 34; "menial work": 33: who were anarchists: Nabokov well knew the fate of anarchists in wartime America, and would underline it in his next book, where Pnin is detained as a result of a incorrect belief that he is an anarchist.

9   DHH 90/237, at the Directorate of History and Heritage, Canadian National Defence Headquarters.

10   "British move assailed: 'Congress Is Told Jewish Relief Worker Is Interned,' " NYT, March 3, 1945, 8. Civilian internees arriving in Camp Q reported being robbed of their possessions on arrival at the camp, after which they had to sleep on wet ground in makeshift tents that had been thrown up when it was clear there was not enough space in the barracks. Sleeping in tents, however, was nothing compared to the futility of trying to explain that some of them were not military prisoners at all. They were called traitors by one camp commander, who told them he would rather deal with full-fledged Nazis than refugees. See Koch, Deemed Suspect, 92.

Newspaper coverage tilted heavily toward escape attempts. Civilians occasionally made the effort, and there were spectacular attempts by groups of Nazi officers, including one gang of twenty-eight which was initially successful. Only one person, however, managed to get to still-neutral America and avoid deportation. Some were shot for their trouble. (See, for example, "28 Nazi Fliers Tunnel to Liberty in Canada," NYT, April 20, 1941, 1; "2 Nazi Airmen Slain in Canadian Break," NYT, April 22, 1941, 3; "German Flier Escapes in Canada," NYT, January 9, 1943, 4; etc.)

11   "Putzi's Progress," The New Yorker, November 1, 1941, 12. A half-dozen articles on Hanfstaengl's unusual situation also ran in the NYT, though none of them mentioned Camp Q by name.

12   BBAY, 301 and 357.

13   Putnam's publisher was Walter Minton; the showgirl was Rosemary Ridgewell (Schiff, 237n). It is not clear whether Ridgewell got the promised finder's fee.

14   VNSL, 226. When Dmitri walked through the door in uniform for the first time, Nabokov recalled his cousin Yuri, whose coffin he had helped to carry in the Crimea almost forty years before.

15   Girodias knew that he was losing a fortune in potential sales, and in November 1958 sued the French government for more than 32 million francs (then about $75,000). He was not about to let the nymphet go without extracting his portion of the proceeds, potential or real.

16   BBAY, 362.

17   at liberty to appeal: "British Seize 'Lolita,'" NYT, May 5, 1959, 36; game of cricket: Middleton, Drew, "Blue-Law Reform Sought in Britain," NYT, January 12, 1959, 12.

18   *"dull, dull, dull" and "repulsive"*: Prescott, Orville, "Books of the Times," NYT, August 18, 1958, 17; *"nothing more than plain pornography"*: quoted in Lewis Nichols's "In and Out of Books," NYT, August 31, 1958, BR8.

19   *followed suit*: "'*Lolita*' Shunned in Newark," NYT, October 8, 1958, 19; *roiled the staff*: "Library Bans '*Lolita*,'" NYT, September 19, 1958, 23.

20   Berkman, Sylvia, "Smothered Voices: Nabokov's Dozen," NYT, September 21, 1958, BR5.

21   ANL, 32, 262, and 254.

22   *thirty-two-year stretch*: If you take the most conservative tack and include "The Enchanter," which is actually a novella. "The Enchanter" was finished in 1939, and *Transparent Things* in 1972.

   for which that statement is true: It is also true that in two stories written during the same period, Nabokov created characters who appear to be Jewish but are not labeled as such directly. In "Time and Ebb," the narrator mentions the "indescribable tortures being inflicted by a degenerate nation on the race to which I belong." In "Signs and Symbols," the family's Aunt Rosa is put to death by the Germans; it is her story and their earlier roots in Minsk, and other names in the story—Isaac, Rebecca—that serve as clues and make the identity of the family apparent.

   in an attempt to hide it: In *Femininity* (1985), Susan Brownmiller mentions that Jewish immigrants in Brooklyn particularly made use of elocution lessons for their daughters when they could, in an effort to improve their prospects (108).

   When Nabokov wrote *Lolita*, Brooklynese was a clear social marker, and one that could be used to discriminate. In *Underground to Palestine* (1946), I. F. Stone noted the "thick Brooklynese" of the American Jews when he sailed on an American-manned boat which set out to deliver displaced European Jews to Israel as part of an illegal convoy (116). C. K. Thomas of Cornell University, writing in *American Speech* on Jewish dialect in 1932, noted that his Jewish students' "speech is distinctly inferior, and this inferiority raised the question whether there might be a clearly defined dialect which is characteristic of New York Jews." He further noted the number of these students who had been sent to elocution schools that had become "popular among the higher class Jewish families of New York." "Jewish Dialect and New York Dialect," *American Speech*, vol. 7, no. 5, June 1932, 321.

23   *"trained servant maid"*: ANL, 82; *service as a maid*: Schiff, 103.

24   ANL, 261.

25   *stamped on its stationery*: ANL, 261; *typically shorthand*: Kendal, Diana Elizabeth, *Members Only: Elite Clubs and the Process of Exclusion* (2008), 59.

26   Alfred Appel would be the first Nabokov reader to publicly note the hidden meaning of "near churches" in the novel.

27 *official complaint in the State of New York*: "State Ban Asked against Ad 'Bias,'"
    NYT, December 21, 1952, 52; *if they happen to be Jewish*: "Discrimination by
    Hotels Seen," NYT, March 17, 1953, 28.

28 *"a certain strange strain"*: ANL, 75. *Lolita's* progressive schoolmistress also
    inquires about Humbert's religion, only to be told to mind her own business
    (194); *refused admission to a store*: ANL, 268; *"a Gentile's house"*: ANL, 297. In
    another wink from Nabokov, Quilty seems to think Humbert is German or
    "Australian" (297), likely a fumbling attempt on Quilty's part to refer to him
    as Austrian. This slip becomes relevant again later, when Nabokov writes *Look
    at the Harlequins!* (see Chapter 14, section 2, of this book).

29 *the only Jew*: ANL 363 (note 3 from page 53 of the novel); *the word "kikes"*:
    Shrayer, Maxim D., "Evreiskie voprosy v zhizni i tvorchestve Nabokova,"
    Weiner Slawistischer Almanach 43 (1999), 112.

30 *a half-dozen people*: Two hotel clerks (years apart) at The Enchanted Hunters,
    Clare Quilty, Jean Farlow, the headmistress of *Lolita's* school, and Charlotte Haze.

31 BBAY, 363.

32 Schiff, 26.

33 "How did they ever make a movie of *Lolita*?" was the tag line for the film's
    posters and the theme of the movie's trailer.

34 *sold for $100,000*: Schiff, 237; *television skits*: BBAY, 373; Schiff, 233; *"for six
    years, till she's eighteen"*: BBAY, 376; *bestselling novels of 1959*: Prescott, Orville,
    "A Critic's Holiday Toast," November 29, 1959, NYT, BR3. The other was Leon
    Uris's *Exodus*, also published the year before.

35 *"new variety of sexual sensationalism"*: Prescott, Orville, "Books of the Times,"
    October 23, 1959, 27; *"rotten mackerel in the moonlight"*: Adams, J. Donald,
    "Speaking of Books," NYT, October 26, 1958, BR2. "Yet [Nabokov] writes, in
    Lolita, of nothing of consequence, save as leprosy, let us say, is of consequence.
    Here is admirable art expended on human trivia. Mr. Nabokov rightly insists
    that his book is not pornographic. I found it revolting, nevertheless, and was
    reminded of John Randolph's excoriation of Edward Livingston: 'He is a man
    of splendid abilities, but utterly corrupt. He shines and stinks like rotten
    mackerel by moonlight.'"

36 Nabokov was not an admirer of such reverse emigration. Though he was not
    immune to the longing to return home, he could not imagine the existence
    of a true artist in the Soviet Union. Somehow, however, Pasternak skirted
    dictates and expectations, and the authorities tolerated a style and indepen-
    dence from him that doomed other writers during the purges. In an effort to
    find a middle ground, he had pared his poetry down and written patriotic
    poems during the war, moving on to the relative safety of translation when
    his original work met with too much disapproval. It was rumored again and
    again that Stalin exempted him from the savagery of camps and trials. Barnes,
    Boris Pasternak, vol. 1, 304-13.

37 When someone proposed Nabokov as a candidate to translate the *Zhivago* poems, Pasternak objected. Barnes, vol. 2, 432n.

38 Schiff, 244.

39 Ibid., 243.

40 Shrayer, Maxim D., *An Anthology of Jewish-Russian Literature*, 593.

41 Schiff, 243, n2.

42 "Olga Ivinskaya, 83: Pasternak Muse for '*Zhivago*,'" NYT obituary, September 13, 1995.

43 Schiff, 233.

44 Wilson, Edmund, "Doctor Life and His Guardian Angel," *New Yorker*, November 15, 1958, 216 and 238.

45 BBAY, 386.

46 NWL, 320.

47 *wine, jewels, and silk*: ANL, 9; All were not just professions permitted for centuries to European Jewry but fields where they were concentrated.

48 Humbert at one point seeks to lose "a Protestant's drab atheism" (his mother was the granddaughter of two English parsons) and turn to the Roman Catholic Church (282).

49 See Nabokov's foreword to the English-language translation of *Despair*. He explained that Humbert would be allowed out one evening a year to walk a green lane in Paradise—a parallel escape to that offered to Judas after his death, who was allowed to return to earth and wander in the polar regions as relief from Hell each Christmas Eve because he had once given his cloak to a leper. See Matthew Arnold's poem "Saint Brandan."

50 ANL, 265.

51 Olga Skonechnaya has looked at Nabokov's use of the Wandering Jew in his Russian and French work, linking *Agasfer*, *The Gift*, and his essay "Pouchkine ou le vrai et le vraisemblable," all of which retell or refract the Wandering Jew story in ways large or small.

    In addition to the representative Silbermann character in *The Real Life of Sebastian Knight*, the Wandering Jew is more explicitly mentioned as a stock character in a book read by the protagonist in *Invitation to a Beheading*. In *King, Queen, Knave*, the inventor of automannequins is newly arrived in Germany, a "nondescript stranger with a cosmopolitan name," and the narrator mentions that he might be Czech, Jewish, Bavarian, or Irish.

    There are, of course, classic narrative reasons to use roving protagonists who act out taboo and forbidden behaviors. And a wandering, anguished figure clearly evokes a kind of distorted, winking self-portrait of Nabokov himself. But he is also explicitly looking at the meaning of the Wandering Jew figure across the length of his career, simultaneously attending to Jewish culture and suffering as he does so. Nabokov was not the only person to try to invert the traditional Wandering Jew character.

Jewish-Russian exile Marc Chagall adopted the same character and strove to reclaim it through art, as have other later artists, including R. B. Kitaj. Nabokov did not care for Chagall's later work, though he expressed admiration for his early "Jew in Green," a portrait of a battered Wandering Jew-type character painted before the Revolution. See SO, 170 and Richard Cohen's *"The Wandering Jew*: from Medieval Legend to Modern Metaphor" in *The Art of Being Jewish in Modern Times* (2008).

52 In *Lectures on Russian Literature*, Nabokov claimed Dostoyevsky mistakenly thought that "physical suffering and humiliation improve the moral man" (115). In Nabokov's description, Dostoyevsky had refused to believe that prison in Siberia had damaged him, insisting that that nothing had been lost, and he had survived as "a better man."

53 If Humbert is Jewish, it is no accident that he is Swiss. During the war, the Swiss government deliberately and publicly revoked any responsibility to protect its own Jewish citizens in France. By 1942, stories of Swiss Jews interned in France circulated, and newspaper articles noted how the Swiss had ceded any demands that their Jewish citizens be afforded any special treatment distinguishing them from other foreign Jews. A Jewish Humbert still in France could have faced the same fate as Raisa Blokh—whom Nabokov had mocked so cruelly and who was turned back at the border—and ended up in Drancy or Gurs.

54 ANL, 316. From Nabokov's afterword to the novel "On a Book Entitled *Lolita*."

55 *Juanita Dark*: ANL, 312.

56 Nabokov once told Alfred Appel that "Humbert identifies with the persecuted." ANL, 363.

57 *Pnin*, 174. Michael Maar discusses the speck of coal dust in terms of Hans Christian Andersen's "The Snow Queen" in *Speak, Nabokov* (19).

58 AFLP, 250.

59 Nabokov's heart, Stephens suggested, was with the Russian people, not just the "liberal gentry" that had nourished him. Letter from Isabel Stephens to Barbara Breasted, February 25, 1971, 3, Faculty files, Wellesley.

60 On closer inspection, given Nabokov's sensitivity to Jewish historical persecution, it might seem more surprising if he had *not* found sections of *Zhivago* disappointing. Pasternak, part Jewish by birth, wholly identified as a Russian and with the Russian Orthodox Church. In his most celebrated novel, he put words in the mouth of a Jewish character criticizing Jewish intellectual leaders' thinking as "facile," seeming to fall prey to the automatic conflation of the Revolution and Jews that dominated worldwide. Pasternak mentions the suffering of the Jews multiple times, but permits a character an extended monologue to argue that for all the tragedies and persecution Jews have faced across the millennia, they had refused the miracle that Christ had delivered in their midst. They had not assimilated;

they had not converted; they had *chosen* their martyrdom. For all his own efforts to draw a hard line between the protagonist and the author of *Lolita*, it is hard to imagine Nabokov swallowing this passage without choking. Yet Pasternak was himself vilified—part of the campaign against him after *Zhivago* came out was framed in frankly anti-Semitic terms. For more on this issue with Pasternak, and a comparison with Solzhenitsyn and Dostoyevsky, see John Bayley's introduction to the Everyman's Library hardcover of *Doctor Zhivago* and Maxim D. Shrayer's *Anthology of Jewish-Russian literature.*

61   *telegraphed his acceptance*: Barnes, *Boris Pasternak: 1928-1960, A Literary Biography*, vol. 2, 342; *declining to attend*: Barnes, vol. 2, 346.

CHAPTER TWELVE: *PALE FIRE*

1   VNSL, 302. On this count, Nabokov was not mistaken. Louis Aragon was then a member of the central committee of the French Communist Party and, despite occasional public contravention of the Party line, would remain so for decades.

2   "Le triomphe de *Lolita*," an excerpt from Maurice Couturier's *Nabokov ou la tentation française* (2011). See NABOKV-L, January 2011, for this excerpt. The first quotation is from Madeleine Chapsal in the May 8, 1959 issue of *l'Express*, the second from Jean Mistler in *L'Aurore*, on May 12.

3   *a celebration in Nabokov's honor*: BBAY, 294; Couturier, *Nabokov ou la tentation française*. These recollections are from then-newly-minted *Figaro* literary critic Bernard Pivot, who would do a legendary interview with Nabokov much later in his career.
      a marvelous ball: Schiff, 254.

4   Nor had things improved with Olympia Press publisher Maurice Girodias, whose Olympia contract Nabokov had been declaring void for more than two years. Girodias appeared at the reception, and later claimed to have been snubbed by Nabokov, who declared that he had not seen Girodias at all, let alone talked with him. Given Girodias's conduct, Nabokov's propensity to snub, and his equal tendency to be completely unaware of others in social settings, it can only be said with confidence that 1) both men were in the room that night, and 2) they did not leave as friends. (See Boyd's, Schiff's, and Girodias's account.)

5   *slow to forgive such slights*: BBAY, 396; *"nightmare and deceit"* and *"friends of his darkest days"*: BBAY, 396.

6   Schiff, 265.

7   *he would be dead*: Nabokov's nephew Rostislav, for whom he had written an affidavit in the hopes of getting him into the West (BBAY, 126), would die in 1960 behind the Iron Curtain at the age of 29, from what his son would later describe as a combination of several factors bound up with profound despair.
      had collaborated with the Nazis: November 2011 Interview with Vladimir Petkevič.

8   BBAY, 394.

9   Ibid., 171.

10 *a crab, a kitten*: STOR, 616. For more on Nabokov and Sergei in "Scenes from the Life of a Double Monster," see Susan Elizabeth Sweeney's essay "The Small Furious Devil" in *A Small Alpine Form* (1993). Sweeney suggests that in his Siamese twin tragedy, Nabokov was working with something so troubling that it resulted in one of his few failures to transform his own emotional struggles into "transcendent fiction" (198).

11 BBAY, 185.

12 Ibid., 415.

13 VNSL, 212. *President Kennedy*: Oddly enough, President Kennedy had yet to be elected when Nabokov composed the letter.

14 VNSL, 297.

15 *halfway done with the book*: BBAY, 421.

16 *Duck Soup*. See SO, 165.

17 *longs to be delivered*: Watching a child fly a model plane, Kinbote begs, "Dear Jesus, do something" (PF, 93); *absolution from the horror*: PF, 258; *end his life with a handgun*: PF, 220; *alive long enough*: Dolbier, Maurice, "Nabokov's Plums," interview with Vladimir Nabokov, *New York Herald Tribune*, June 17, 1962, B2; also mentioned in Nabokov's diary—see BBAY, 709 n6.

18 BBAY, 463–4.

19 *group of islands*: McCarthy, Mary, "A Bolt from the Blue," *The New Republic*, June 4, 1962, 21; *Zembla had been used centuries before*: In "An Essay on Man," Alexander Pope drew on Nova Zembla's northern location as an analogy for corruption and vice that always seems relative to those engaged in it, and always apparently more extreme in some location farther along:

> Ask where's the north?—at York 'tis on the Tweed;
> In Scotland at the Orcades; and there
> At Greenland, Zembla, or the Lord knows where.

See Chapter 14, note 128 for a longer excerpt from Pope's verse.

20 *had known about for decades*: In his poem "The Refrigerator Awakes," written in 1941, Nabokov makes several polar references to real and imagined explorers, and includes a nod to Nova Zembla, "with that B in her bonnet." That B, William Barents, spent the winter of 1596-7 trapped on the northern tip of Nova Zembla. The legendary story of the expedition's survival was printed by the Hakluyt Society, whose accounts of voyages Nabokov and Véra had both read and admired.

21 This account of Barents's voyage is taken from Gerrit de Veer's *The Three Voyages of William Barents to the Arctic Regions (1594, 1595, and 1596)*.

22 *saw three suns*: Interestingly, on the very first page of *Pale Fire*, narrator Charles Kinbote talks of *parhelia*, known as sun dogs or mock suns.

23 Khalturin, Vitaly et al., "A Review of Nuclear Testing by the Soviet Union at Novaya Zemlya 1955-1990," *Science and Global Security*: 13 (2005),1-42; "Parameters of 340 UNTs Carried Out at the Semipalatinsk Test Site," Lamont-Doherty Earth Observatory web site, Columbia University: http://www.ldeo.columbia.edu/~richards/340STS.html.

24 Day, Duane. "Of myths and missiles: the Truth about John F. Kennedy and the Missile Gap," *The Space Review*, January 3, 2006.

25 The U.S. would face similar attention in the wake of injuries and increased rates of cancers and deformities after its test blasts in the Pacific at Bikini and Rongelap Atolls. (See 2009 Newsday project *Fallout*).

26 Meaning Bertrand Russell, noted philosopher of logic and peace activist whose leftist politics Nabokov disliked. See Herbert Gold's interview "The Art of Fiction, No. 40, Vladimir Nabokov," in *The Paris Review*, Summer-Fall 1967.

27 Gruson, Sidney. "U.S. and Russians Pull Back Tanks from Berlin Line," NYT, October 29, 1961, 1.

28 *"bits of straw and fluff"*: SO, 31 as first noted in BBAY, 306; *a new testing ground*: "Arctic Called Soviet Test Site," NYT, March 9, 1958, 41.

29 From a March 1959 letter cited in BBRY, 17.

30 *"Fall-outs . . . by US-made bombs,"* PF, 266; *"antiatomic chat"*: PF, 49.
      "any jackass can rig up the stuff": PF, 270. The uncertainty with regard to who is speaking is deliberate. The poem has sections of discarded lines—variants—that Kinbote includes in his commentary. Several have clearly been tampered with (Kinbote goes so far as to claim some of his contributions), and the authorship for the rest must remain in doubt, with Kinbote as the most likely suspect.
      "Mars glowed": PF, 58.

31 *50-megaton hydrogen bomb*: Topping, Seymour, "Policies Outlined," a summary of Khrushchev's speech to the Twenty-Second Party Congress, NYT, October 18, 1961, 1; *resolution imploring the Soviets*: Telsch, Kathleen, "U.N., 87-11, Appeals To Soviet on Test," NYT, October 28, 1961, 1.

32 DeGroot, Gerard, *The Bomb: A Life* (2005), 254.

33 *five hundred miles away*: Khalturin et al., 18; *all the explosives used in World War II*: DeGroot, 254; *an effort to stave off birth defects*: Sullivan, Walter, "Bomb's Fall-Out Moving To Urals," NYT, October 31, 1961, 14; *trace levels of radiation*: Khalturin et al., 19.

34 Steven Belletto would be the first to point out the strength of *Pale Fire*'s Cold War references and note that Nova Zembla (Novaya Zemlya in Russian), was a key nuclear test site at the time of the book's composition. See "The Zemblan Who Came in from the Cold," *ELH*, vol. 73, no. 3, 755-80.

35 Scammell, *Solzhenitsyn*, 407.

36 Ivan Bunin, too, had been rehabilitated, but just a little too late to see his work return to the Soviet Union—he died in 1953 (Scammell, *Solzhenitsyn*, 401).

37 Scammell, *Solzhenitsyn*, 378.

38 Ibid., 390.

39 Ibid., 400. Apparently, Solzhenitsyn's arsenal eclipsed the French and the British atomic capabilities.

40 *an unknown writer*: It is unlikely his lone, irritable article about the Soviet postal system had brought him to anyone's attention.
      one page at a time: Scammell, *Solzhenitsyn*, 377 and 385.

41 *a vast account*: Scammell, *Solzhenitsyn*, 379; *the camp theme was already percolating*: Scammell, 410-1.

42 *Mary McCarthy*: "A Bolt from the Blue"; *Macdonald, Dwight*: review of *Pale Fire*, *Partisan Review*, vol. 39, no. 3 (summer 1962), 437-42.

43 Dolbier, Maurice, "Nabokov's Plums," *New York Herald Tribune*, June 17, 1962, B2.

44 There are many Cold War references, from a mention of Soviet generals arriving in Zembla, and passing mention of BIC (215), which was used in contemporary politics to indicate a country or region Behind the Iron Curtain which separated the Soviet sphere of influence from the West.

45 *an international youth exchange*: The actual article is "30 Children Join Picnic of Nations," NYT, July 20, 1959, 12; *Khrushchev canceling a visit*: "Khrushchev Calls Off Plan for Visit to Scandinavia," NYT, July 21, 1959, 1.

46 Noble managed to get word of his fate to Germany via a postcard smuggled out by a barber, and was freed after President Eisenhower made public calls for his release. See Adam Bernstein's obituary "John H. Noble Survived, Denounced Soviet Captivity," from *The Washington Post*, November 17, 2007.

47 *they could be worse*: Joseph Scholmer and Edward Buca also wrote memoirs of their time in Vorkuta. See Buca's *Vorkuta* (1976) and Scholmer's *Vorkuta* (1954).
      "from which there is no return": Noble, John, "Varied Groups Found in Vorkuta, Arctic Slave Camp of the Soviet," NYT, April 5, 1955, 12. For nearly mirror descriptions of Nova Zembla, see Buca (325-6) and Scholmer (82).

48 *a mass grave in Katyn Forest*: The missing Polish officers had disappeared from prisoner of war camps. A year later, many of the bodies would be unearthed in a mass grave at Katyn Forest in Russia, along with several other similar sites. The discovery by the German Army led to the fracture of the short-lived Soviet-Polish alliance. In 1990, the Russian government would finally acknowledge Soviet responsibility for the massacre.
      "the barren and desolate island of Nova Zembla": Post, Robert. "Nazi Spring Drive in Russia Expected," NYT, January 10, 1942, 6.

49 *plans to build an Arctic resort*: "An Arctic Resort for the Russians," NYT, April, 22, 1934, XX12; *sightings of mysterious airplanes*: "Plane Shown Clearly in Arctic Photograph," NYT, August 22, 1931, 5.

50 "Exiled Russians To Leave This Week," NYT, August 28, 1922, 10.

51 Scammell, *Solzhenitsyn*, 411-4.
52 Ibid., 416 and 418.
53 Ibid., 422.
54 *it would be unforgiveable*: Scammell, *Solzhenitsyn*, 425. The opinion quoted is that of Samuil Marshak, poet and celebrated children's author.
   As many as five hundred bootleg copies: Scammell, *Solzhenitsyn*, 428.
55 Solzhenitsyn, Alexander, *The Oak and the Calf* (1980), 38.
56 Scammell, *Solzhenitsyn*, 435.
57 Salisbury, Harrison, "Books of the Times: Changes Perception Surviving Is a Triumph," NYT, January 22, 1963, 7. The tide was already turning against Khrushchev, and by extension, Solzhenitsyn (Scammell, *Solzhenitsyn*, 468-470).
58 *"frozen mud and horror"*: PF, 258; *"tale of torture"*: PF, 289; and when he writes of the temptation to die, Kinbote recounts the story of a young boy who is told his family "is about to migrate to a distant colony where his father has been assigned to a lifetime post." The trusting boy believes that the new land where his family will live forever will be even better than his current home (219).
59 *not Kinbote but Botkin*: Nabokov would play many games in *Pale Fire*, several of which take place in the index of the novel, with its inclusion of things that have little or no presence in the rest of the book. *Botkin*, of course, is a scrambling of *Kinbote*, and one *Botkin, V.* shows up in the Index as a scholar of Russian descent. Botkin is mentioned in the body of the novel in absentia as a professor teaching in another department.
   a phrase stressing the "Nova" again: PF, 267.
60 Dolbier, "Nabokov's Plums."
61 Richard Rorty hypothesizes that after a reader becomes attentive to the suffering he previously failed to note in Nabokov's novels, he is "suddenly revealed to himself as, if not hypocritical, at least cruelly incurious," and recognizes "his *semblable*, his brother, in Humbert and Kinbote" (*Contingency, Irony and Solidarity*, 163). The interpretation of *Pale Fire* I am suggesting reconfigures that reading by adding another level to it. If we recognize Kinbote's incuriosity in ourselves, we can apply a newfound attentiveness not only to events like the death of the poet Shade's daughter (which Rorty specifically addresses), but also to Kinbote himself. Instead of settling for the stock character of a "monstrous parasite" (PF, 172), a lunatic, a homosexual, or a pedophile, persistent curiosity will be rewarded with a richer story.
62 *"unable to reproach himself"*: GIFT, 228; *ceases to resist even worse impulses*: Humbert mentions at one point that his mind fought his body in the matter of nymphets (not always successfully, apparently) through his twenties and into his early thirties (ANL, 18). Again, after *Lolita* escapes from him, he seeks help from a Catholic priest.
   his fondness for faunlets: Nabokov clarified in SO that this was what the "Dear Jesus" line in *Pale Fire* meant (290).

63   Robson, *Solovki*, 229. And even as a concentration camp, the Solovki monastery complex was well known for many of the elements Nabokov used to construct Kinbote's escape—a castle prison, hidden tunnels, and a theater company.

64   *all sorts of games*: The Crown Jewels entry leads to *Hiding Place*; *Hiding place* leads to *potaynik*; *Potaynik* links to *taynik*; *Taynik* has a definition of "Russ., secret place," and then directs readers back to the *Crown Jewels* entry. *Potaynik* is merely an old form of *taynik*. See Brian Boyd's *Nabokov's Pale Fire: The Magic of Artistic Discovery* (1999), 124.

       in the ruins, sir, of some old barracks: SO, 92. Nabokov further mentioned that the ruins of the barracks were near Kobaltana. Kobaltana, which makes no appearance at all in the body of the book, is listed in the index as a mountain resort in a remote and desolate place that is still familiar to military families. It may have been a bid to clue readers in to the link between the imaginary Zembla and its real-world counterpart, Nova Zembla, which, like Kobaltana, had planned a resort, was remote and desolate, and did have a military presence, as well as barracks.

65   "Russian Academic Freedom," NYT, September 1, 1922, 9.

66   SM, 262.

Chapter Thirteen: *Speak, Memory*

1   SM, 264.

2   Schiff notes that Véra "was all for civil rights, but 'hooligans' should be put away—for good" (336). Unlike her husband, Véra favored the death penalty. See Alan Levy's "Understanding Vladimir Nabokov."

3   CBS News, "Oswald Midnight Press Conference," recorded November 22/23, 1963.

4   Dmitri Nabokov later reported his father watching the newsreel and saying, "If they have worked over this poor little guy needlessly. . . ." (BBRY, 22).

5   Presumably *Invitation to a Beheading*. BBRY, 35.

6   AFLP, 278-9.

7   *international apology to Ghana*: Smith, Hedrick, "U.S. Apologizes to Ghana," NYT, September 11, 1963, 33; *"The Negro Revolt"*: "News Notes: Classroom and Campus," NYT, April 19, 1964, E7.

8   BBAY, 50.

9   VNSL, 378.

10   *who had managed to infiltrate and destroy*: Schiff, 336; *would have deserted little Anne Frank*: Buckley called the protesters "young slobs" and condemned their "mincing ranks" as well as their "epicene resentment." Burks, Edward, "Buckley Assails Vietnam Protest," NYT, October 22, 1965, 1.

11   Dabney, *Edmund Wilson: A Life in Literature*, 453-4.

12   Meyers, *Edmund Wilson: A Biography*, 417.

13   *U.S. involvement in Vietnam a disgrace*: Dabney, 486; *infuriated the president*. Another invitee to the Festival, poet Robert Lowell, had his refusal printed

in full on the front page of *The New York Times*, expressing his support for Johnson's civil rights policies but offering only "dismay and distrust" over current U.S. foreign policy (See "Robert Lowell Rebuffs Johnson As Protest Over Foreign Policy," NYT, June 3, 1965, 1).

"close to traitors": Goldman, Eric, *The Tragedy of Lyndon Johnson* (1974), 529.

14 Dabney, *Edmund Wilson: A Life in Literature*, 404.

15 *"a great grievance"*: Dabney, 401. Wilson mentioned this to their mutual friend Roman Grynberg; *"You have quite forgotten me"*: NWL, 366.

16 BBAY, 496.

17 Schiff, 330; From a letter from Rowohlt to Véra Nabokov, BBAY, 480.

18 *did not lodge in his*: NWL, 360; *most obscure words*: PF, 46; *"constantly quoting Housman"*: PF, 25. Wilson's Housman essay was also in *The Triple Thinkers*. There are many more such points of common interest, such as Proust, whose place among American readers had been secured by Wilson's landmark work on modernism, *Axel's Castle*. In *Pale Fire*, Kinbote says that he had not originally believed that Proust's masterpiece had any connection to its time and place, or to real people, but that he had since realized that he was wrong. For more on Nabokov/Wilson/Housman, see Rorty, *Contingency*, 149, n10.

19 *shadow of Robert Frost*: PF, 48; *Nabokov's admiration of Shade*: SO, 119. See also Socher's "Shades of Frost: a Hidden Source for Nabokov's *Pale Fire*," *Times Literary Supplement*, July 1, 2005. Boyd further notes that Nabokov had also rented Frost's house through a third party in Cambridge in 1952. BBAY, 222.

"third-rate": Meyers, *Edmund Wilson*, 464; *"fraud"* and *"self-promoter"*: These latter two are from a Wilson letter to Lionel Trilling, referenced in Colm Tóibín's "Edmund Wilson: American Critic," NYT, September 4, 2005, F1.

20 Wilson, Edmund, *Night Thoughts* (1961), 233-45. Matthew Roth found Wilson's poem "The Pickerel Pond: A Double Pastoral" paired with the letters between the two men, and linked it to the language in *Pale Fire*.

21 PF, 45 and 193.

22 "The White Heart" is a sentimental story about the excesses of the First World War and Revolutionary period, and the true heart of a Russian grandmother who passes on her piety and strength in the face of suffering to those she meets. It was written by Alexey Remizov, whom James Joyce had admired but whom Nabokov disliked intensely. A translation had appeared in 1921 in *The Dial*, a publication for which Edmund Wilson had written his landmark essay on T. S. Eliot. Though it's hard to believe Nabokov would have admired any of the story's literary technique, it demonstrates the existence of a widely recognized symbolism of the "white heart" of Nabokov's poem, not unlike the later reference in the poem to "edelweiss" (which translates as "noble white").

23 Nabokov, Vladimir, "On Translating Pushkin Pounding the Clavichord," NYRB, April 30, 1964.

24 Wilson writes that "his speaking of the eclogues of 'the overrated Virgil' as 'stale imitations of the idyls of Theocritus' would seem to demonstrate that he cannot have had any very close acquaintance with this poet in the original"; and later "which the author, in a letter, once described to me...." From "Letters: The Strange Case of Pushkin and Nabokov," NYRB, July 15, 1965.

25 Dabney, *Edmund Wilson: A Life in Literature*, 406.

26 Nabokov, Vladimir, "Letters: The Strange Case of Nabokov and Wilson," NYRB Letters, August 26, 1965.

27 Both Nabokov's and Wilson's responses are from the August 26, 1965 issue of NYRB.

28 *Amour propre*: self-love, one's self-esteem. SO, 264.

29 BBAY, 496.

30 Meyers, *Edmund Wilson: A Biography*, 259-60. Wilson wrote this description of Nabokov in a November 1940 letter to his mentor at Princeton, Christian Gauss.

31 VNSL, 424.

32 Barabtarlo, Gennady. "Nabokov in the Wilson Archive," *Cycnos*, Volume 10 n°1, posted online June 13, 2008.

33 Nabokov, Vladimir, *Encounter*, Letters to the editor, May 1966, 91.

34 Nabokov, *Encounter*, May 1966, 458.

35 Ibid., 477.

36 Ibid., 511.

37 Ibid., 486.

38 Ibid.

39 Solzhenitsyn, *The Oak and the Calf*, 83-4.

40 *a personal meeting*: Taubman, William, *Khrushchev: The Man and His Era* (2004), 527; *regretted championing*: Solzhenitsyn, *The Oak and the Calf*, 86.

41 Scammell, Michael, "Circles of Hell," NYRB, April 28, 2011.

42 Solzhenitsyn, *The Gulag Archipelago*, vol. 2 (1997), 62.

43 An excerpt from Solzhenitsyn's *Архипелаг ГУЛАГ, 1918-1956: опыт художественного исследования*, Volume 2 (*Советский писатель*, 1989), 68; English translation of the passage has been adapted from page 343 of Vladimir Abarinov's *The Murderers of Katyn* (1993).

44 This passage would not make the editing cut for the version that appeared in Paris and was translated into English and became the definitive document. It would find publication only in some later Russian-language versions and collected writings of Solzhenitsyn.

45 Scammell, *Solzhenitsyn*, 524.

46 "Electronic Prying Grows: CIA Is Spying from 100 Miles Up," NYT, April 27, 1966, 1.

47 *a letter to the editor*: "Record of Congress for Cultural Freedom," NYT letters to the editor, May 9, 1966, 38; *current and former Encounter editors*: "Freedom

of Encounter Magazine," NYT letters to the editor, May 10, 1966, 44; *Nicholas Nabokov himself wrote*: "Group Denies C.I.A. Influence," NYT letters to the editor, May 16, 1966, 46.

48 Braden, Thomas, "Speaking Out: I'm Glad the CIA Is 'Immoral'," *The Saturday Evening Post*, May 20, 1967, 10-14.

49 *active in American intelligence work*: Josselson himself described his history and clearances in a draft memoir (Stonor Saunders, *The Cultural Cold War*, 42).

Strangely enough, the declassified portions of Nicholas Nabokov's very thick FBI file do not include any pages from 1948, when he ostensibly left government employment, up until April 1967, two weeks' before the effective dissolution of the Congress.

50 *a former intelligence operative argued*: Stonor Saunders, Frances. *The Cultural Cold War: The CIA and the World of Arts and Letters* (1999), 402; *"They're all the same"*: Stonor Saunders, 401.

51 The critical volume they were preparing was about another classic of Russian literature, *The Song of Igor's Campaign*. Nabokov and Jakobson had been working with a third person, Marc Szeftel. For a fuller account of the Nabokov/Jakobson/Szeftel collaboration, see Diment's *Pniniad*.

52 *"little trips"*: VNSL, 216; *"Bolshevist agent"*: Diment, 40; *had belonged to the Kadets*: Meyer, Priscilla, "Nabokov's Critics: A Review Article," *Modern Philology* 91.3 (1994), 336; *Jakobson had torpedoed Nabokov's chances*: Diment, 40 and 167.

53 "A Look Back . . . ," U.S. Central Intelligence Agency Web site: https://www.cia.gov/news-information/featured-story-archive/2007-featured-story-archive/a-look-back.html.

54 VNSL, 431-2. Letter from Véra Nabokov to Lauren Leighton.

55 VNSL, 431.

56 Slavic scholar Lauren Leighton sent a postscript to NABOKV-L, the Nabokov Listserv, detailing what had happened to the young Leningrad writers after he had exchanged letters with Véra Nabokov (Leighton, Lauren, note to NABOKV-L, the Nabokov Listserv, July 14, 1995: https://listserv.ucsb.edu/lsv-cgi-bin/wa?A2=nabokv-l;54cd537.950y). Mikhail Meylakh was the writer arrested in 1983 for having a copy of *Speak, Memory*.

57 *a foreword and an index*: For those inclined to go down the ubiquitous rabbit holes in the field of Nabokovian interpretation, it may be worth noting that Nabokov closed his foreword with a mention of the index: "through the window of that index climbs a rose" (SM, 16). In addition to the English and Russian versions of Nova Zembla that are listed in the index, Nova Zembla is in fact a rose variety—a hardy strain, widely cultivated, and more than a century old.

"of all places": SM, 52.

58 SM, 256.

59 Ibid., 248.

60 Ibid., 257.

61 GIFT, 355.

62 BBAY, 456.

63 These *Pale Fire* parallels bring a certain tragic note to the repeated appearances of the word "Hamburg" in *Lolita*, which ostensibly occur in the book as a play on Humbert's name (see pages 109, 261, and 262) but also echo Sergei's fate. If Humbert is recalling forgotten world history, he may also be carrying water for his author. For more on Sergei in *Pale Fire*, see Maar, *Speak, Nabokov*, 40-41.

64 Neuengamme Camp archives.

65 "Le céremonial est toujours le même . . ." *Neuengamme, Camp de Concentration Nazi* (2010), 185.

66 *an experimental treatment for lice-born typhus*: Neuengamme entry, USHMM Web site, http://www.ushmm.org/wlc/en/article.php?ModuleId=10005539; *a fatal experiment*: 20 Jewish children were chosen by Dr. Heissmeyer to have tubercular infection blown into their lungs through rubber tubes inserted in their noses. When the Allies were advancing, the children were taken offsite, injected with morphine, and hanged. Their remains were destroyed for fear of anyone learning about the experiment. The doctor conducting the experiment remained in practice in East Germany (which was desperate for trained medical professionals) for twenty years after the war, when he crossed paths with a local Party Official and was put on trial, after which we was sent to prison for the rest of his life.

67 *Neuengamme, Camp de Concentration Nazi*, 197-8.

68 November 2011 interview with Reimer Möller.

69 Russians formed the largest contingent of the camp population during Sergei's months at Neuengamme. Other significant population groups of prisoners included Poles, French, and Norwegians, in that order, though there were many other countries represented. "Death, Neuengamme Concentration Camp." Neuengamme Web site: http://www.kz-gedenkstaette-neuengamme. de/index.php?id=990

70 November 2011 interview with Reimer Möller.

71 Ibid.

72 Grossman, "The Gay Nabokov," Salon.

73 November 2011 interview with Reimer Möller.

74 Ibid.

75 The Neuengamme book of the dead and hospital records seem to be at odds on whether Sergei died January 9 or 10; but the camp archivist Reimer Möller determined January 10th as the correct date.

76 November 2011 interview with Reimer Möller.

77 Ibid.

78   SM, 258.
79   *fairy tales*: LL, 2; *escape from prison*: ITAB, 114.

CHAPTER FOURTEEN: WAITING FOR SOLZHENITSYN

1   *portable Winter Palace*: a reference to Nabokov later made by John Leonard in his piece on Isaac Babel, "The Jewish Cossack" in *The Nation*, November 26, 2001.

2   *always had nightmares*: SM, 108-9; Boyd's "New Light on Nabokov's Russian Years"; *guillotines set up*: Schiff, 347; *dreamed of Sergei*: Vladimir Nabokov diary, 1967, Berg; *a happy reunion*: BBAY, 499; *father came to visit*: Vladimir Nabokov diary, 1973, Berg Collection.

3   *blood-filled mosquitoes*: Literary mosquito tropes appear throughout *Ada* (this one on 108), but the reference to sated insects in a secret habitat carries echoes of one of the most notorious tortures of Solovki and other camps, which was written about in American and European newspapers as early as 1925. Prisoners were sent or tied naked outside to be tortured by mosquitoes. Robson, *Solovki*, 238.

      first prison term: ADA, 81; *rape of a young boy*: ADA, 355.

4   *outside the study of dreams*: ADA, 15; *the existence of Terra*: ADA, 264.

5   ADA, 582.

6   *high-profile trials*: Stories of Yuli Daniel's and Alexander Esenin-Volpin's involuntary institutionalizations became widespread during the 1960s, in the wake of Daniel's public trial and Esenin-Volpin's re-institutionalization by the state. No public stance was taken on the issue by the World Psychiatric Association until records of actual case histories were smuggled into the West in 1971. Even then, it took six years for the Association to officially condemn the Soviet practice. "Soviets finally condemned for psychiatric malpractice," *New Scientist*, September 8, 1977, 571.

      sentenced to a mental hospital: Shabad, Theodore, "Soviet Said to Jail Writer Suspected of Criticism Abroad," NYT, October 19, 1965, 1.

7   *former leader himself might have been condemned*: Sulzberger, C. L. "Foreign Affairs," NYT, October 28, 1964, 44.; *a group of Soviet mathematicians*: It was not even the first time the state had institutionalized mathematician Alexander Esenin-Volpin. For information on his 1968 institutionalization, see "Action on Dissident Protested in Soviet," NYT, March 13, 1968, 6.

8   Schiff, 330.

9   BBAY, 569.

10 *wanted to see butterflies there*: For a full discussion of the plans of the trip to Israel, which was never made, see Yuri Leving's "Phantom in Jerusalem," *The Nabokovian*, Fall 1996, 30-44; *French response to the Six-Day War*: BBAY, 526.

11 BBAY, 582.

12 *just wouldn't talk about Vietnam*: AFLP, 216; *coaxing old friends to visit*: Schiff, 343.

13 Fosburg, Lacey, "Art and Literary people urged to look inward," NYT, May 22, 1969, 52.

14 In his *"Lolita* class list," Gavriel Shapiro notes that when he translated *Lolita* into Russian, Nabokov changed Irving Flashman's name to Moisei Fleishman, emphasizing his Jewishness. With the addition of the first part of the word "kike" to a slur earlier in the novel, it is another sign that given a chance to revisit the anti-Semitic theme for another audience, Nabokov emphasized it in more than one location. *Cahiers du Monde Russe*, XXXVII 3, July–September 1996, 317-335.

15 ANL, liii.; In *Vladimir Nabokov: His Life in Art*, Andrew Field also observed that Nabokov's mature books had grown from seeds apparent in his works from the 1920s. Like Appel after him, he directly linked Nabokov's *Agasfer* and its Wandering Jew roots to its future transformation into *Lolita* (79).

16 Levy, Alan, "Understanding Vladimir Nabokov: A Red Autumn Leaf Is a Red Autumn Leaf, Not a Deflowered Nymphet," *NYT Magazine*, October 31, 1971, 20.

17 BBAY, 483.

18 AFLP, 8.

19 *an international incident*: "U.S. Student Held by Poland On Issue of Border Transit," NYT, February 1, 1964, 3; *ten days in jail*: Field, Andrew. "Prime Exhibits," NYT, September 18, 1966, 419; *he stood trial*: "Poles Free U.S. Student after Prison Sentencing," NYT, February 16, 1964, 16; *had to wait two more weeks*: "Poland Allowing Field To Go," NYT, March 3, 1964, 5. In fact, he waited around even longer in the hopes of getting back the $3,000 bond his parents had posted, but finally left empty-handed. The bond money, minus court fees, was later returned to Field's family after his conviction was thrown out that April.

20 Yuli Daniel and Andrei Sinyavsky, whose work had found widespread publication in the West.

21 AFLP, 201.

22 Ibid., 208.

23 Ibid., 135.

24 Ibid., 30. Nabokov noted that Adamovich's only passions in life had been "Russian poetry and French sailors."

25 AFLP, 30.

26 *illegitimate son of Tsar Alexander II*: AFLP, 13; *wobbly on dates*: BBAY, 619-20.

27 LATH, 95.

28 Ibid., 218.

29 Ibid.

30 LATH, 95.

31 LRL, 105.

32 AFLP, 25.

33 NWL, 372.
34 *crimp relations between them*: NWL, 373; *his friends are in bad shape*: Letter written days later to Helen Muchnic, quoted here from Meyers, 445.
35 Wilson, Edmund, *Upstate: Records and Recollections of Northern New York* (1971), 162.
36 Wilson, *Upstate*, 219; SO, 218-9.
37 Dabney, Lewis, *Edmund Wilson: A Life in Literature*, 510, from a December 22, 1971 letter to Edmund Wilson from Katharine White.
38 Dabney, 512.
39 Wilson took the position that Cincinnatus in *Invitation to a Beheading* is not executed, but "simply gets up and walks away." Wilson, Edmund, *A Window on Russia* (1972), 233.
40 Wilson, Edmund, *To The Finland Station* (2003), xxiii.
41 NWL, 2.
42 Ibid., 373.
43 Solzhenitsyn, Alexander, *The Oak and the Calf*, 103.
44 Ibid., 104.
45 Solzhenitsyn, paradoxically, was critical of the two men for sending their works to the West, suggesting that they had "sought fame abroad." Solzhenitsyn, *The Oak and the Calf*, 557.
46 Ibid., 558.
47 Kunitz, Stanley, "The Other Country Inside Russia," *NYT Sunday Magazine*, August 20, 1967, 24.
48 Scammell, *Solzhenitsyn*, 606.
49 Ibid., 574 and 558-9.
50 Ibid., 629.
51 Ibid., 675.
52 Salisbury, Harrison, "The World as a Prison," NYT, September 15, 1968, BR1.
53 Scammell, *Solzhenitsyn*, 726.
54 Ibid., 740. The acquaintance was Alexander Gorlov. A year after Solzhenitsyn had been expelled, he emigrated to the United States.
55 An additional tragedy, as Michael Scammell notes, is that the copy whose location Voronyanskaya revealed was one Solzhenitsyn had repeatedly asked her to burn, but she had been worried that the other copies might be confiscated, and so she had preserved it. Scammell, *Solzhenitsyn*, 816.
56 VNSL, 528.
57 Two weeks later, Nabokov was invited by *The New York Times Magazine* to write an open letter to Solzhenitsyn, an offer he predictably refused. VNSL, 529.
58 Safire, William. "Solzhenitsyn without Tears," NYT, February 18, 1974, 25.
59 *American men who refused to serve in Vietnam*: Solzhenitsyn, Alexander, "The Big Losers in the Third World War," NYT, Jun 22, 1975, 193; *if he might be mentally unstable*: Scammell, *Solzhenitsyn*, 917.

60 Solzhenitsyn, Alexander, *The Gulag Archipelago*, vol. 1, 263.
61 VNSL, 531.
62 BBRY, 316.
63 Kelly Oliver has explored the concept of the impossibility of witnessing in relation to atrocity, arguing that the effort to do so is nonetheless what gives rise to our very agency and humanity. She paraphrases Shoshana Felman's arguments in a way that finds echoes in Kinbote's dissociation:

> What would it mean to bear witness to the Holocaust? asks Felman. To witness from the inside, from the experience of the victims? She argues that it would first mean bearing witness from inside the desire *not* to be inside. Also, it would mean testifying from inside the very binding of the secret that made victims feel as though they were part of a secret world. It would mean testifying from the inside of a radical deception by which one was separated from the truth of history even as one was living it. Moreover, it would mean testifying from inside otherness, bearing "witness from inside the living pathos of a tongue which nonetheless is bound to be heard as noise" (from *Witnessing: Beyond Recognition*, 2001, 90).

It is true that the Gulag is not the Holocaust, and that psychoanalyzing a fictional character can be a futile exercise. But it is possible to look at Nabokov's fiction as embracing a similar notion of art serving as a way to acknowledge and explore what is beyond our ability to understand or express directly, no matter what recorded history we bring to bear.

64 Solzhenitsyn, *The Gulag Archipelago*, vol. 1, 220; Scammell, *Solzhenitsyn*, 906.
65 Scammell, *Solzhenitsyn*, 593-4.
66 In his letter, Nabokov referenced an appeal made by Viktor Fainberg. Fainberg, a dissident who had been released, had worked out of Amnesty International's offices, helping to free Bukovsky. See William Burridge's "How Amnesty Is Fulfilling Pope's Holy Year Appeal," *Catholic Herald*, March 7, 1975.
67 *at the request of American friends*: The friends, Carl and Ellendea Proffer, had named their publishing house Ardis, which is the name of the family estate in Nabokov's *Ada*. The Proffers were responsible for a tremendous amount of Russian and Soviet literature getting into print (or staying there) in the United States, and became friends with the Nabokovs.
  he sent a telegram: VNSL, 540.
68 The cable may well have helped, but the publicity for it came too late. The March 17 *People* profile ran after Maramzin had already been released. "Soviet Writer Gets Suspended Sentence," NYT, February 22, 1975, 2.
69 VNSL, 359.

70   Michael Wood has most thoroughly considered the different façades Nabokov offered the world—and their effects on his art—in *The Magician's Doubts: Nabokov and the Risks of Fiction* (1997).

71   Salter, James, *People* profile of Vladimir Nabokov, March 17, 1975.

72   *Ada* had ridden in on the tails of Nabokov's most stellar works and been treated with mercy. Coming on the heels of *Ada*, Nabokov's next novel, *Look at the Harlequins!*, had been treated much more roughly by critics.

73   VNSL, 564.

74   SO, 193.

75   NG, 2-3.

76   BBAY, 663.

77   Brian Boyd would have his challenges, too. Véra would reject the use of statements she had made to him herself, and even of things she had written. Trying to discuss Nabokov's affair with Irina Guadanini with Véra, Boyd would find that Véra maintained it had never happened right up until he mentioned that their letters still existed. Schiff, 344.

78   *Pennsylvania's Tyrone Daily*: "Gold in Arctic," from the Tyrone (Pa.) *Daily Herald*, February 4, 1933; *Popular Science*: Armagnac, Armand, "New Cities in the Arctic," *Popular Science*, May 1937, 25-6 (text and map); *American Federation of Labor Gulag map*: Mike Adler, author of *Dreaded Island: A History of Novaya Zemlya* (2011) unearthed this map and also pointed out to me the existence of Andrey Stotski's memoir in Polish and English.

      a Routledge atlas: Gilbert, Martin, *The Routledge Atlas of Russian History, Fourth Edition* (2007), 111-2. First published 1972; *his own experiences on Nova Zembla*: The English-language version of Stotski's story ran in the *Plain Talk* anthology, Don Levine, Isaac, ed. (1976), and was originally published in the magazine of the same name from May to August 1947.

      "virtually unrecorded 'death camps'": Conquest, Robert, *The Great Terror: A Reassessment* (2007), 330.

79   Larkov, S and F. Romanenko. "The Northernmost Island of *The Gulag Archipelago*," from the Memorial Web site: http://www.memorial.krsk.ru/Articles/2007Larkov2.htm.

80   Kizny, Tomasz. *Gulag: Life and Death inside the Soviet Concentration Camps* (2004), 186. See also Applebaum's *Gulag*, 82.

81   *rebellion sprang up*: Figes, *The Whisperers*, 212; *small brass band*: Kizny, 186.

82   Even today with warmer temperatures and a reduced ice pack, most routine trips to Solovki end in September.

83   Applebaum, Anne, *Gulag: A History* (2003), 21.

84   "Russians Said to Get Coal from New Arctic Mines," February 14, 1947, 3.

85   *who reported terror*: ". . . we heard a terrifying rumour that the camp was to be closed down and we were to be sent to Novaya Zemlya on the Polar Sea—a place from which there would be no return." Buca, 325-6; *were shipped off*

each year: See Noble's *I Was a Slave In Russia* (1960) and Joseph Scholmer's *Vorkuta; no records of functioning mines*: Mineshafts were dug on Nova Zembla later, when it became a nuclear testing ground. But there is no record of prisoner transports used as manpower for them. (There are, however, records of non-prisoner military personnel, engineers, and miners brought to the island to do the work of constructing test site facilities and mineshafts for underground explosions.)

Which leaves Polish Gulag prisoner Andrey Stotski's account of having worked mines on Nova Zembla. To its credit, Stotski's story was written just after his release to fight in the war, rendering it more reliable than hearsay accounts recorded decades later. It is also incredibly detailed. But the vast network of mines and sophisticated equipment like pneumatic drills that Stotski describes would demand organizational planning and transportation sufficient to administer a true mining enterprise, which would also require the kind of massive resources that would show up in multiple records. It is possible that these mines existed, and all paperwork related to them was destroyed before it could be collected by Gulag archivists. It may be more likely that Stotski was somehow misled that he was on Nova Zembla, or that his story, as with those of many former prisoners, somehow encapsulated the terror of Nova Zembla, which was felt so deeply that it became bound up with Gulag experiences, even for those who were never sent there.

86   This fusion of the extremes of horror and geography echoes Alexander Pope's *Essay on Man*, part of which Kinbote quotes in *Pale Fire*, and another part of which also makes reference to Zembla:

> Vice is a monster of so frightful mien,
> As to be hated needs but to be seen;
> Yet seen too oft, familiar with her face,
> We first endure, then pity, then embrace.
> But where th'extreme of Vice was ne'er agreed:
> Ask where's the north?—at York 'tis on the Tweed;
> In Scotland at the Orcades; and there
> At Greenland, Zembla, or the Lord knows where.
> No creature owns it in the first degree,
> But thinks his neighbour farther gone than he;
> E'vn those who dwell beneath its very zone,
> Or never feel the rage or never own;
> What happier natures shrink at with affright,
> The hard inhabitant contends is right.

87   BBAY, 662.

88 NABOKV-L, the Nabokov Listserv, Archives from October 2, 1999: https://listserv.ucsb.edu/lsv-cgi-bin/wa?A2=ind9910&L=nabokv-l&F=&S=&P=1464. The discussions reportedly fell apart when the mayor lost his reelection bid.

89 Kramer, Hilton, "A Talk with Solzhenitsyn," *NYT Book Review*, May 11, 1980, BR1.

90 Solzhenitsyn biographer Michael Scammell suggests that some of the criticism that has been leveled against Solzhenitsyn's skill as a writer is a result of translations that fail to fully deliver on the richness of the original text (author interview with Scammell, February 2012).

91 He neglected to point out that the extraordinary measures had been futile, and that V. D. Nabokov had returned to his original stance shortly afterward.

92 Not everyone was happy with the renaming. See Harding, Luke, "Signs of dispute on Moscow's Solzhenitsyn Street," *The Guardian*, December 12, 2008.

93 Interview with Reimer Möller, November 2011.

94 NKVD and Soviet Army Records obtained with the assistance of Adam Hradilek, head of the Oral History Group of the Study of Totalitarian Regimes, Prague, the Czech Republic.

95 Interview with Vladimir Petkevič, November 2011.

96 A line from "Signs and Symbols" explaining the world view taken on by the Jewish-Russian refugee mother of the boy who has gone mad (STOR, 601).

CODA

1 Stringer-Hye, Suellen, "*Laura* Is Not Even the Original's Name," an interview with Dmitri Nabokov, *The Goalkeeper* (2010), 177.

2 Pflaum, H. G., "Film Director Carl Junghans at 75," *Süddeutsche Zeitung München*, October 9, 1972.

3 Boris Petkevič death certificate, County Borough of Halifax, General Registry Office, England, August 29, 1963.

4 Dieter Zimmer's Nabokov Family Web: http://dezimmer.net/NabokovFamilyWeb/nfw01/nfw01_042.htm

INDEX